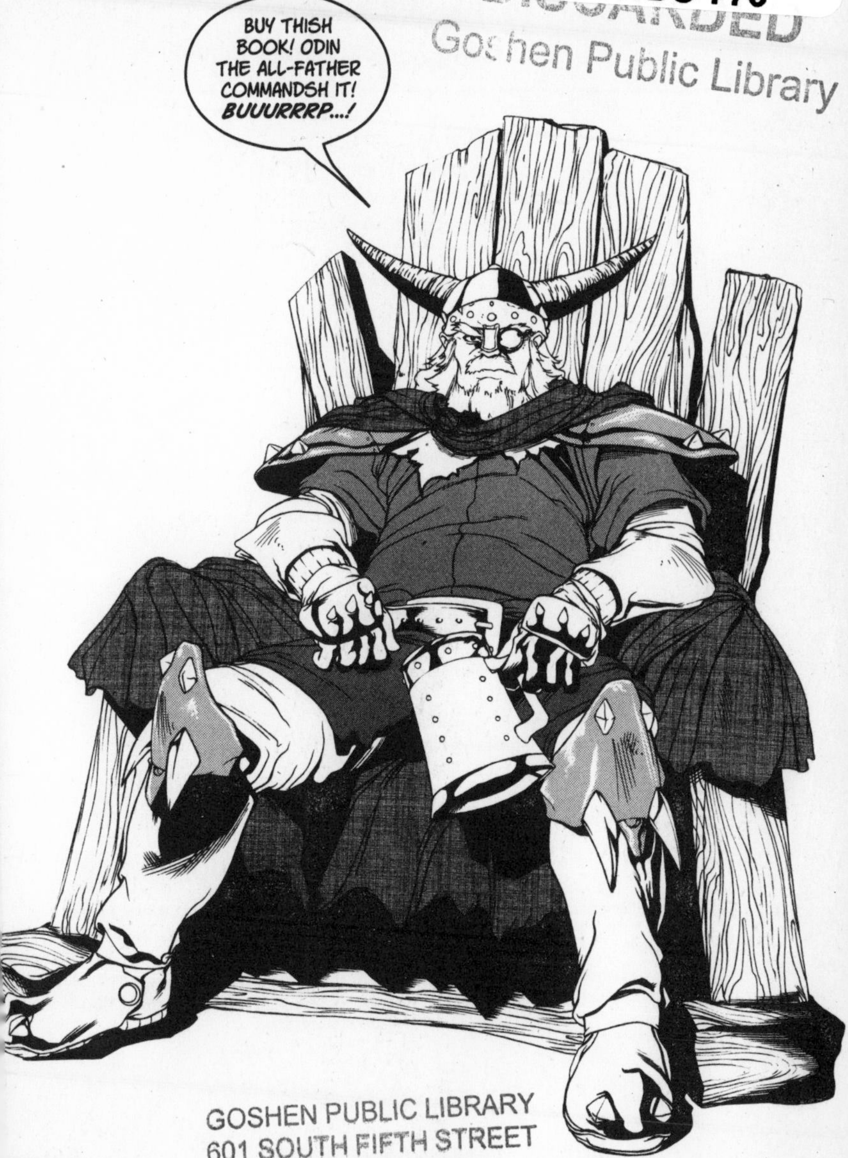
BUY THISH BOOK! ODIN THE ALL-FATHER COMMANDSH IT! *BUUURRRP...!*

Pantheon High Vol. 2
Created by Paul Benjamin and Steven Cummings

Lettering - Janice Chiang
Copy Editor - Shannon Watters
Production Artist - Lucas Rivera
Cover Design - Colin Graham

Editor - Paul Morrissey
Digital Imaging Manager - Chris Buford
Pre-Production Supervisor - Erika Terriquez
Production Manager - Elisabeth Brizzi
Managing Editor - Vy Nguyen
Creative Director - Anne Marie Horne
Editor-in-Chief - Rob Tokar
Publisher - Mike Kiley
President and C.O.O. - John Parker
C.E.O. and Chief Creative Officer - Stuart Levy

A  Manga

TOKYOPOP and  are trademarks or registered trademarks of TOKYOPOP Inc.

TOKYOPOP Inc.
5900 Wilshire Blvd. Suite 2000
Los Angeles, CA 90036

E-mail: info@TOKYOPOP.com
Come visit us online at www.TOKYOPOP.com

ISBN: 978-1-59816-735-1

First TOKYOPOP printing: February 2008
10 9 8 7 6 5 4 3 2 1
Printed in the USA

PANTHEON HIGH

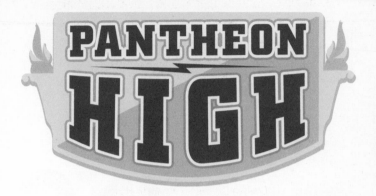

VOL. 2

WRITTEN BY
PAUL BENJAMIN

ART BY
STEVEN & MEGUMI CUMMINGS

TOKYOPOP®

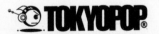

HAMBURG // LONDON // LOS ANGELES // TOKYO

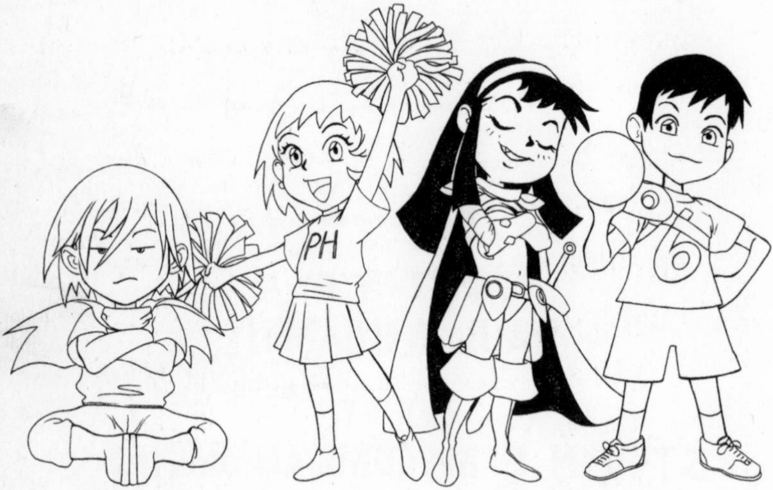
PH
6

CONTENTS

ROLL CALL

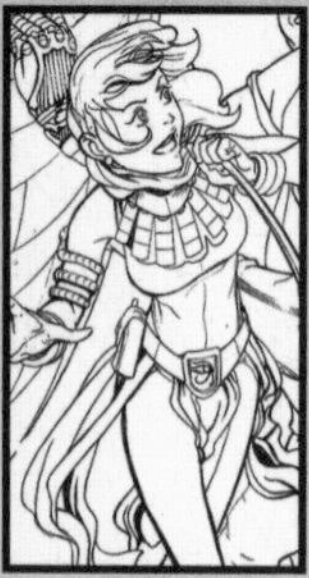

AZIZA EL RA: Daughter of Ra, Egyptian god of the sun. Literally the hottest girl in school.

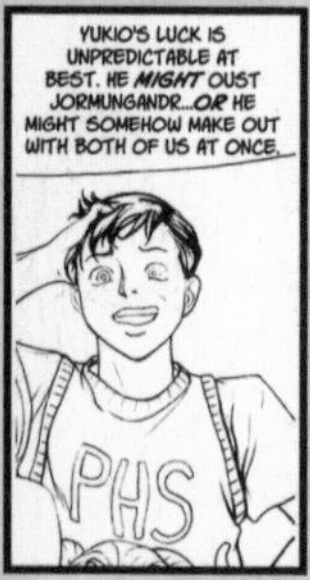
YUKIO'S LUCK IS UNPREDICTABLE AT BEST. HE *MIGHT* OUST JORMUNGANDR...*OR* HE MIGHT SOMEHOW MAKE OUT WITH BOTH OF US AT ONCE.
PHS

YUKIO TAKAHASHI: Son of the Japanese luck goddess, Benten. His unpredictable good luck is based on a high-school boy's priorities.

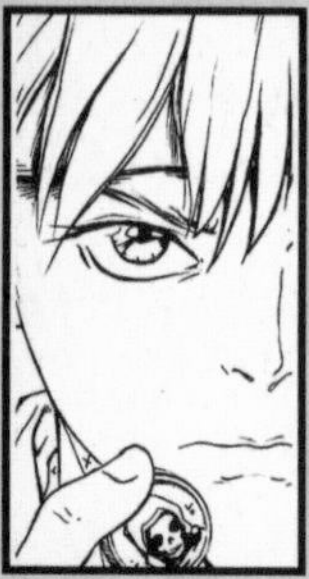

GRIFFIN PIERCE: Son of Hades, Greek god of death. He can inflict poetic justice upon others for brief moments, much like the fates those in his father's realm suffer.

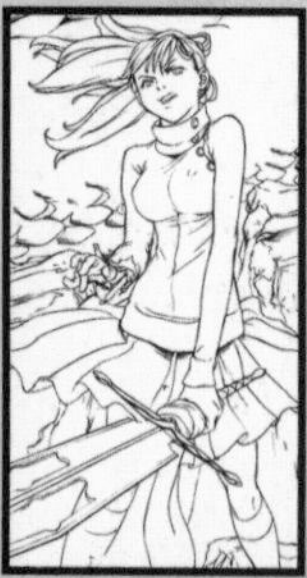

GRACE MORGENSTERN: Brilliant daughter of Tyr, Norse god of war. She is a master of combat and strategy, but would rather be studying for midterms.

ROLL CALL

KATYA EL BASTET & SCARAB: Daughter of the Egyptian cat goddess, Bastet. She can change into a feral form for combat and has a psychic link to her familiar, Scarab.

JOANNA EL ISIS: Daughter of Isis, Egyptian goddess of magic. The powers of Egyptian sorcery are hers to command.

TODD TEMPLETON: Son of Boreas, the North Wind in Greek myths. He can create cloud formations as strong as steel.

TIERCE: The Pantheon High school mascot. He's a fire-breathing chimera from Greek mythology.

PREVIOUSLY IN

Four demigods with little in common found themselves unlikely allies when the children of evil gods used a sleeping potion on the rest of the school. The evil students planned to siphon off their classmates' powers so that they could become full-fledged gods themselves. Grace, Yukio, Aziza and Griffin managed to stop the villainous students, but in the course of their battle, Griffin was killed. A few times... But that was no big--until Jormungandr, the Midgard Serpent, ate him. The giant snake followed up by chomping Grace's hand into a useless mess. Grace finally faced her fate and dove down Jormungandr's throat with her sword going snicker-snack, sending the beast fleeing so that the gods could come to the students' aid.

PROFESSOR PAUL SAYS...

You'll notice throughout the book that many pages have a thunderbolt symbol with a page number. That's an indicator that there's more information in the back of the book regarding some mythological reference on that page. Enjoy!

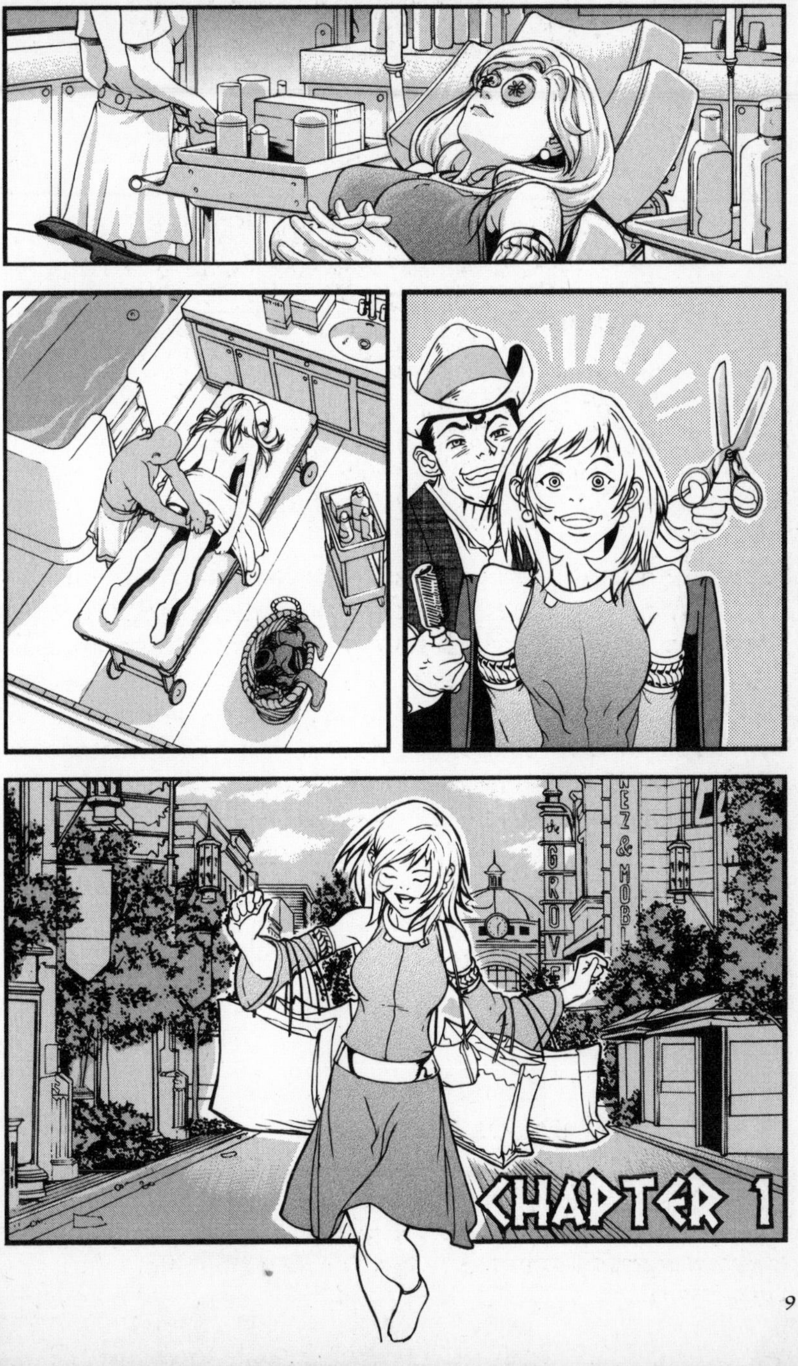
the GROVE
CHAPTER 1

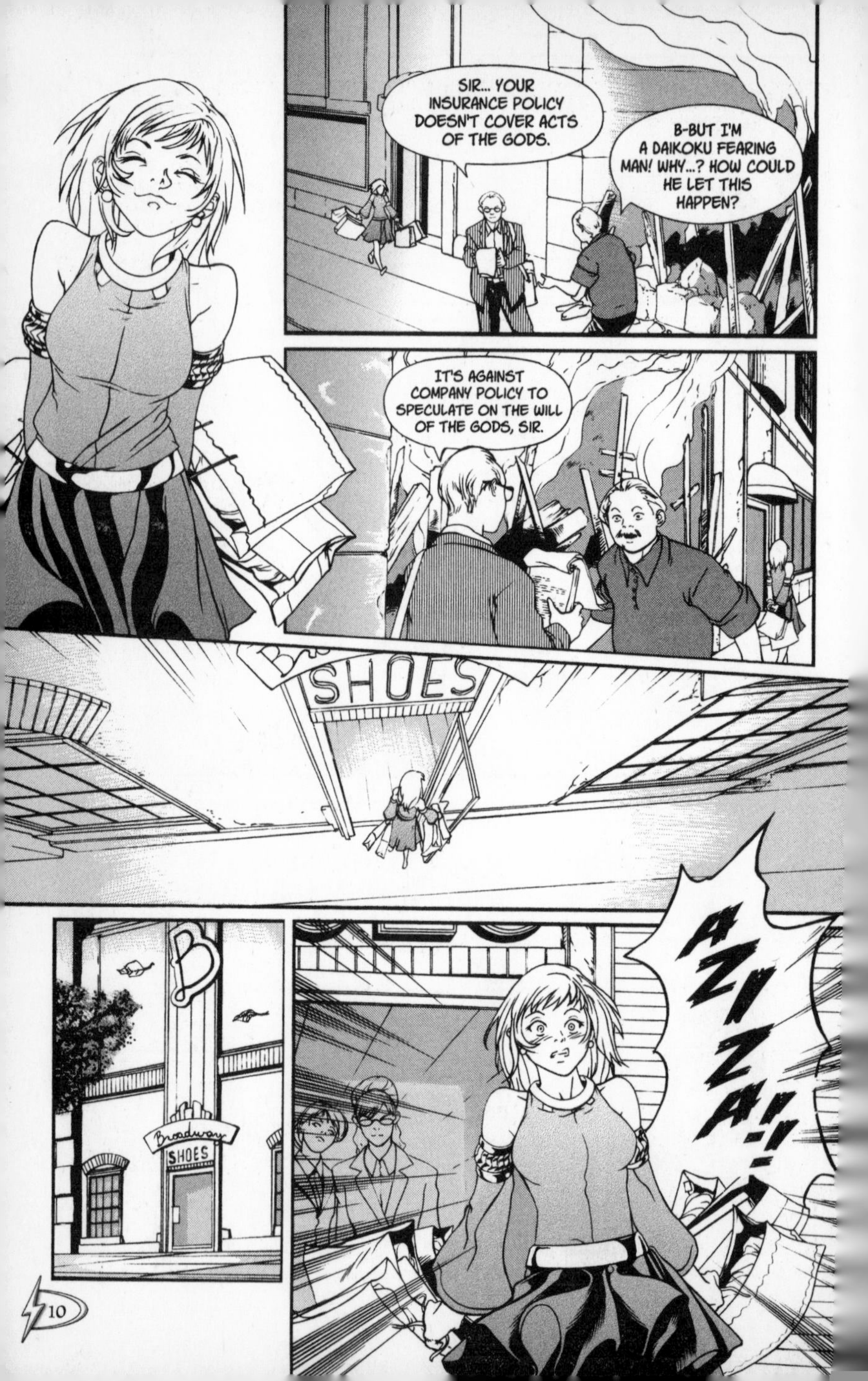
SIR... YOUR INSURANCE POLICY DOESN'T COVER ACTS OF THE GODS.
B-BUT I'M A DAIKOKU FEARING MAN! WHY...? HOW COULD HE LET THIS HAPPEN?
IT'S AGAINST COMPANY POLICY TO SPECULATE ON THE WILL OF THE GODS, SIR.
SHOES
Broadway
SHOES
AZIZA!!

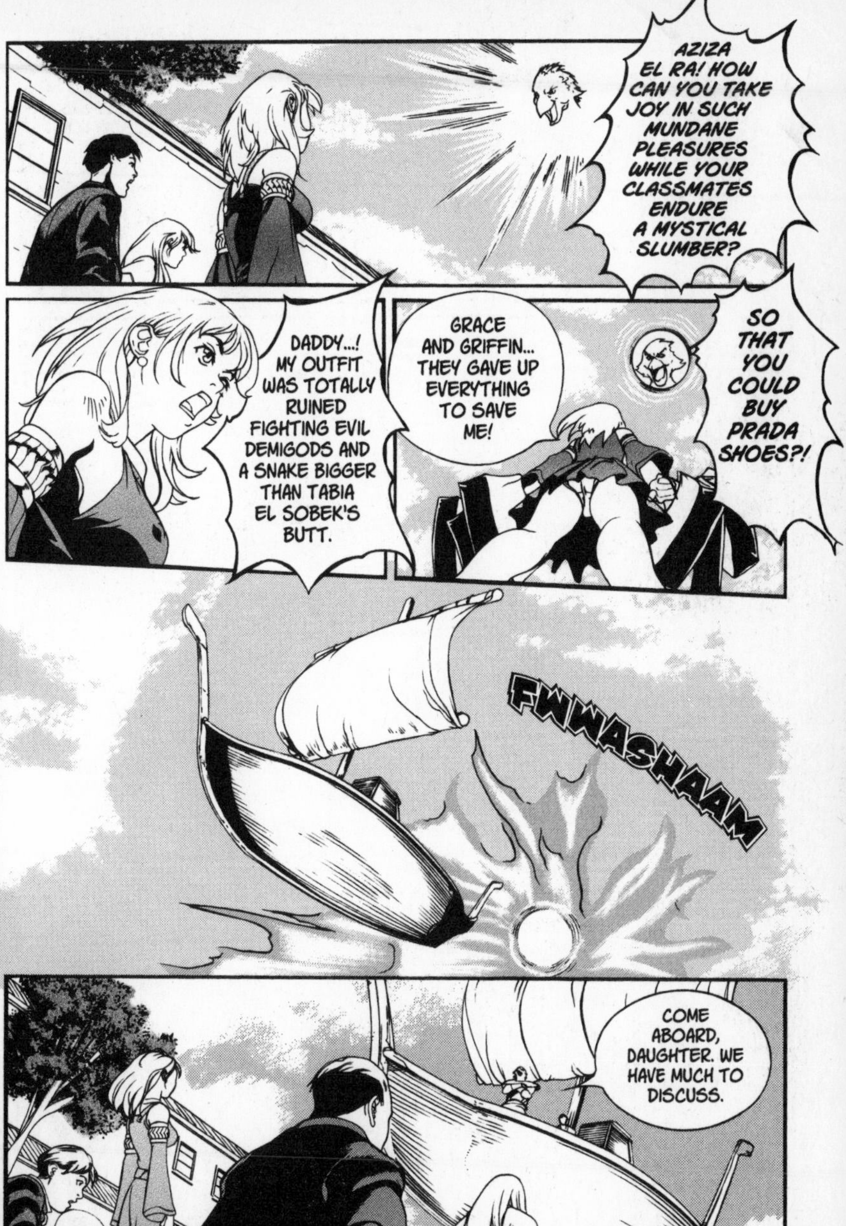
AZIZA EL RA! HOW CAN YOU TAKE JOY IN SUCH MUNDANE PLEASURES WHILE YOUR CLASSMATES ENDURE A MYSTICAL SLUMBER?
DADDY...! MY OUTFIT WAS TOTALLY RUINED FIGHTING EVIL DEMIGODS AND A SNAKE BIGGER THAN TABIA EL SOBEK'S BUTT.
GRACE AND GRIFFIN... THEY GAVE UP EVERYTHING TO SAVE ME!
SO THAT YOU COULD BUY PRADA SHOES?!
FWWASHAAM
COME ABOARD, DAUGHTER. WE HAVE MUCH TO DISCUSS.

YUKIO? WHAT'RE YOU--

HEY, 'ZIZ. WE... THERE'S BAD NEWS....

THOUGH IMHOTEP AND HIS PHYSICIANS HAVE SAVED YOUR SCHOOL-MATES' LIVES--

--THEY CANNOT WAKE THEM. YOU AND YUKIO MUST CONTINUE YOUR EDUCATION UNTIL THE GODS REVERSE THE SLEEP SPELL.

BUT, DADDY... WE SAVED THE WHOLE SCHOOL! CAN'T WE JUST... TAKE A BREAK?

SHE... HAS A POINT, SIR. IMHOTEP'LL PROBABLY HAVE AN ANTIDOTE IN A FEW DAYS.

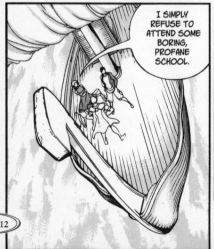

I SIMPLY REFUSE TO ATTEND SOME BORING, PROFANE SCHOOL.

OF *COURSE*. THAT IS WHY YOU WILL ATTEND *GILGAMESH HIGH!*

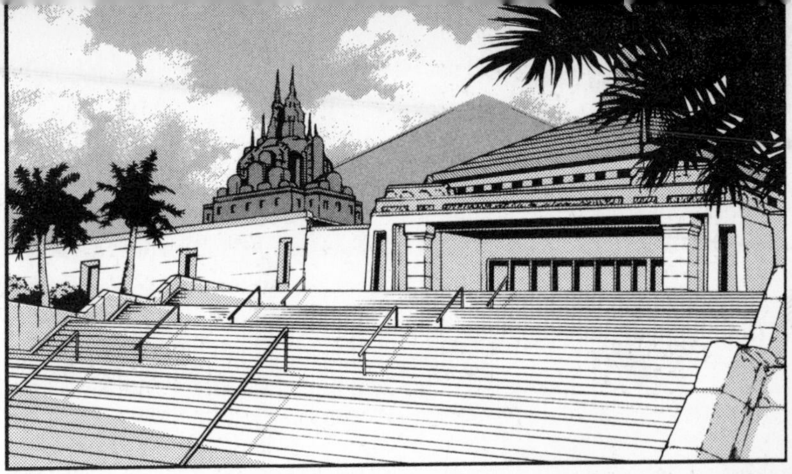

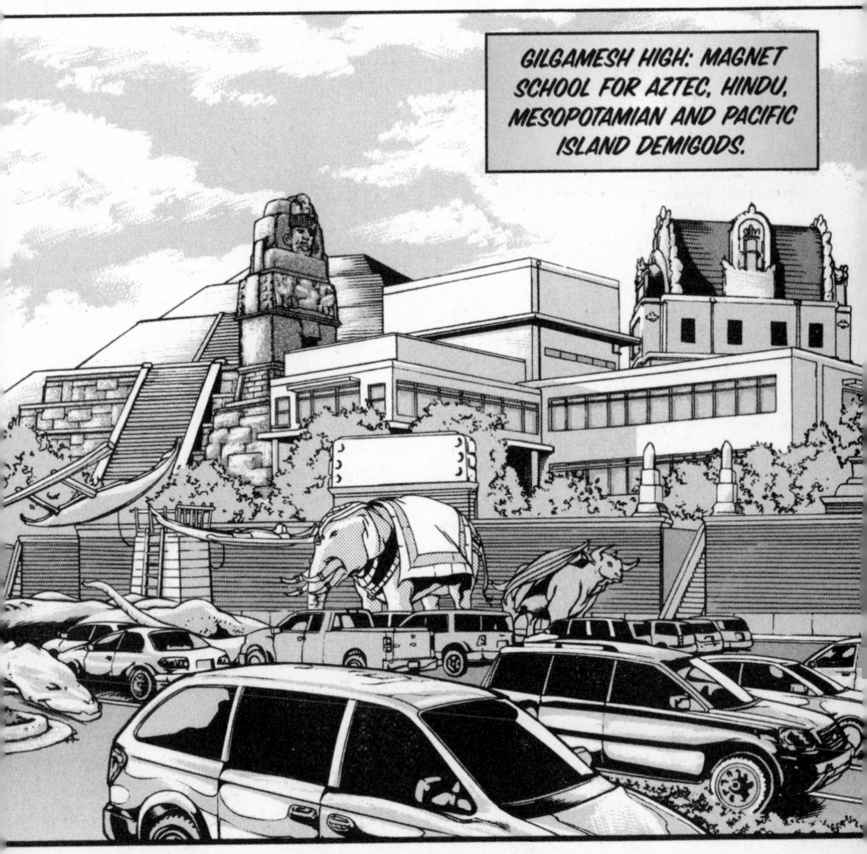
GILGAMESH HIGH: MAGNET SCHOOL FOR AZTEC, HINDU, MESOPOTAMIAN AND PACIFIC ISLAND DEMIGODS.

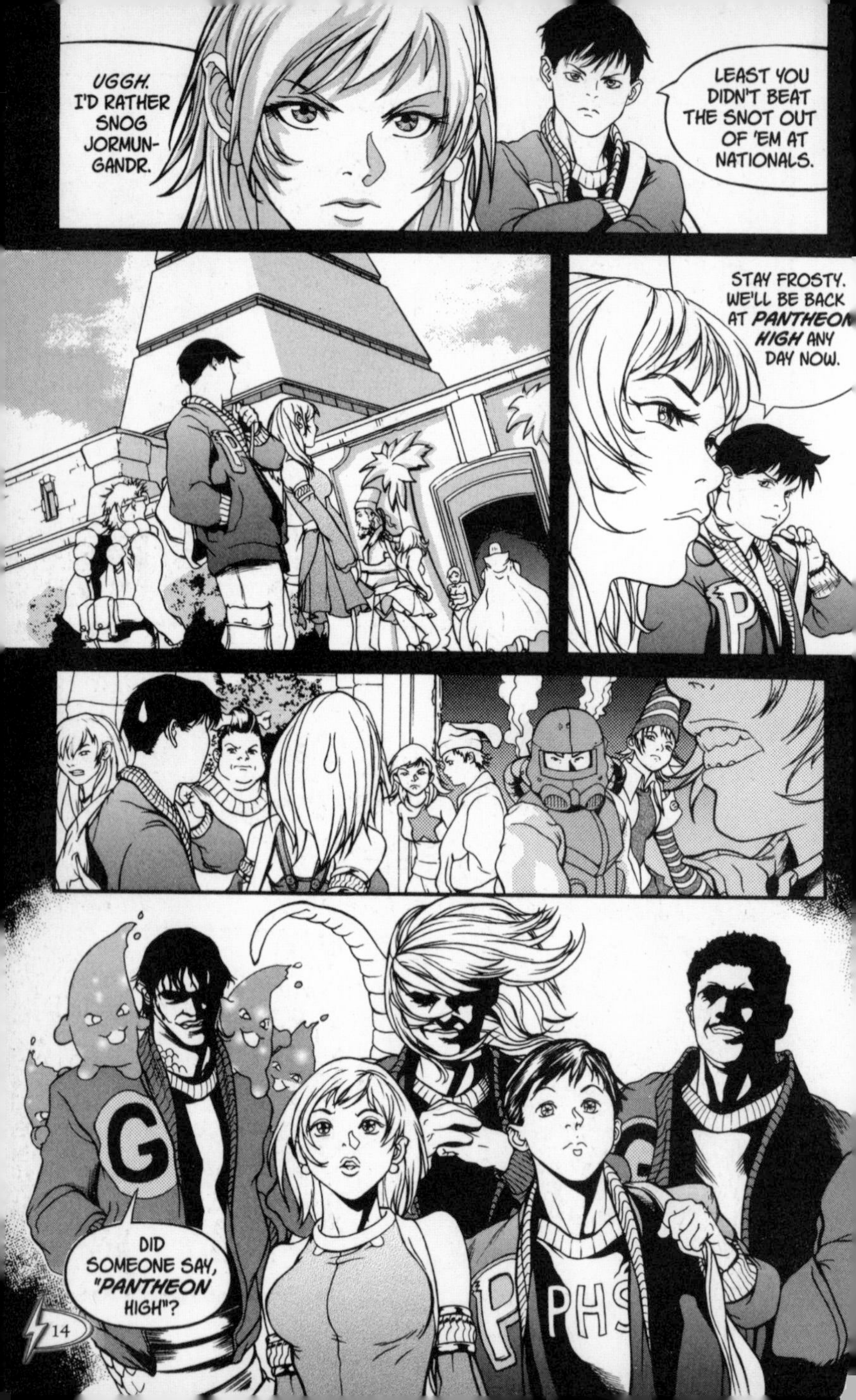
UGGH. I'D RATHER SNOG JORMUN-GANDR.
LEAST YOU DIDN'T BEAT THE SNOT OUT OF 'EM AT NATIONALS.
STAY FROSTY. WE'LL BE BACK AT *PANTHEON HIGH* ANY DAY NOW.
DID SOMEONE SAY, *"PANTHEON HIGH"*?
PHS

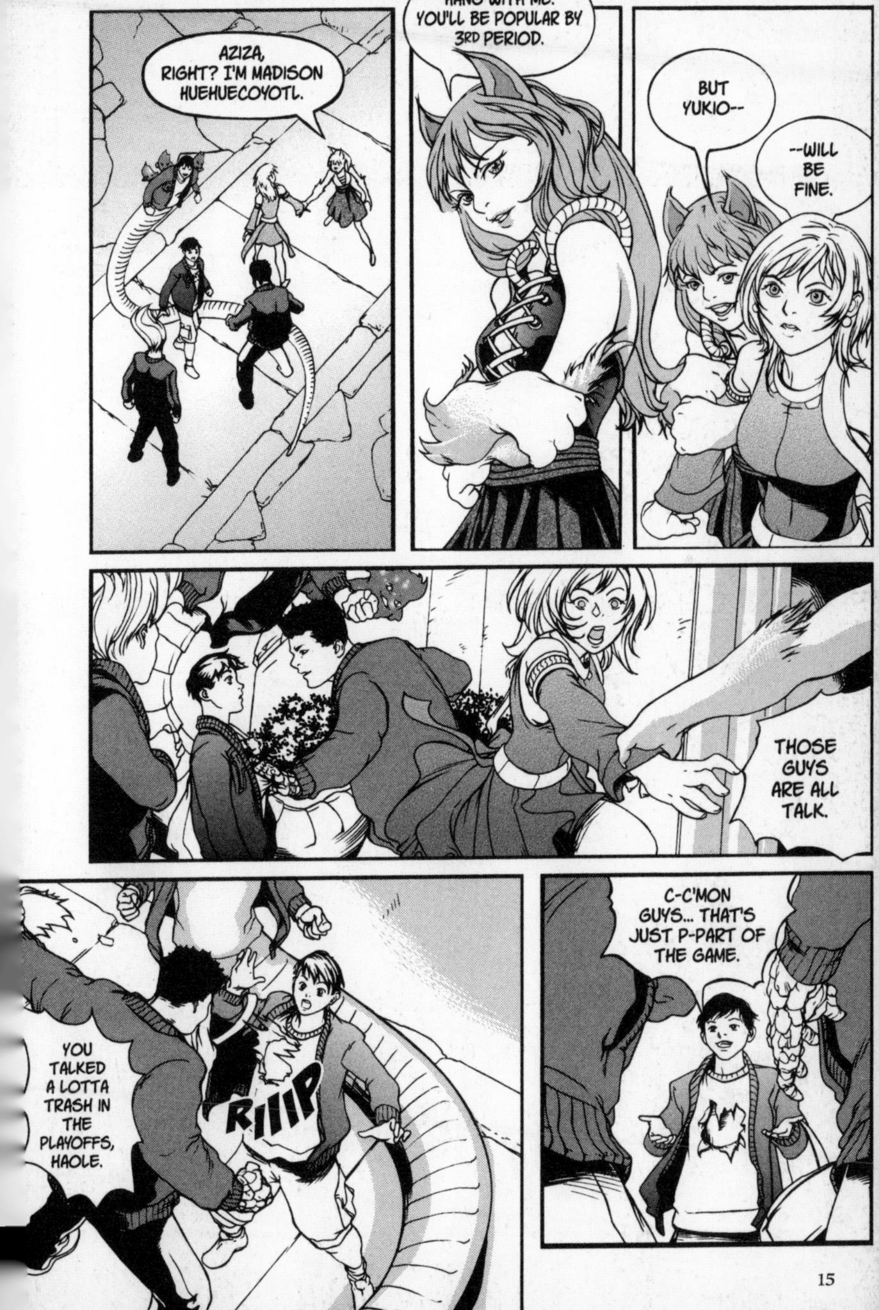
AZIZA, RIGHT? I'M MADISON HUEHUECOYOTL.
HANG WITH ME. YOU'LL BE POPULAR BY 3RD PERIOD.
BUT YUKIO--
--WILL BE FINE.
THOSE GUYS ARE ALL TALK.
YOU TALKED A LOTTA TRASH IN THE PLAYOFFS, HAOLE.
RIIIP
C-C'MON GUYS... THAT'S JUST P-PART OF THE GAME.

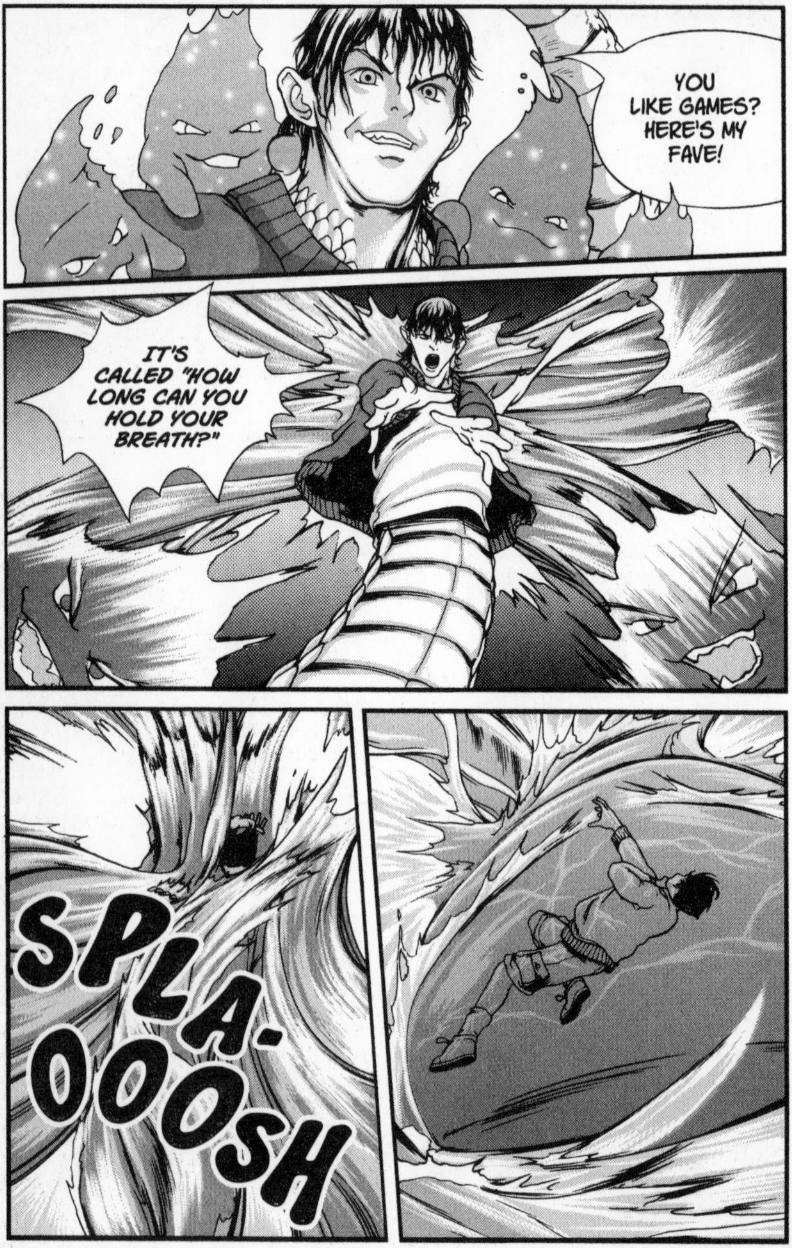
YOU LIKE GAMES? HERE'S MY FAVE!
IT'S CALLED "HOW LONG CAN YOU HOLD YOUR BREATH?"
SPLA-OOOSH

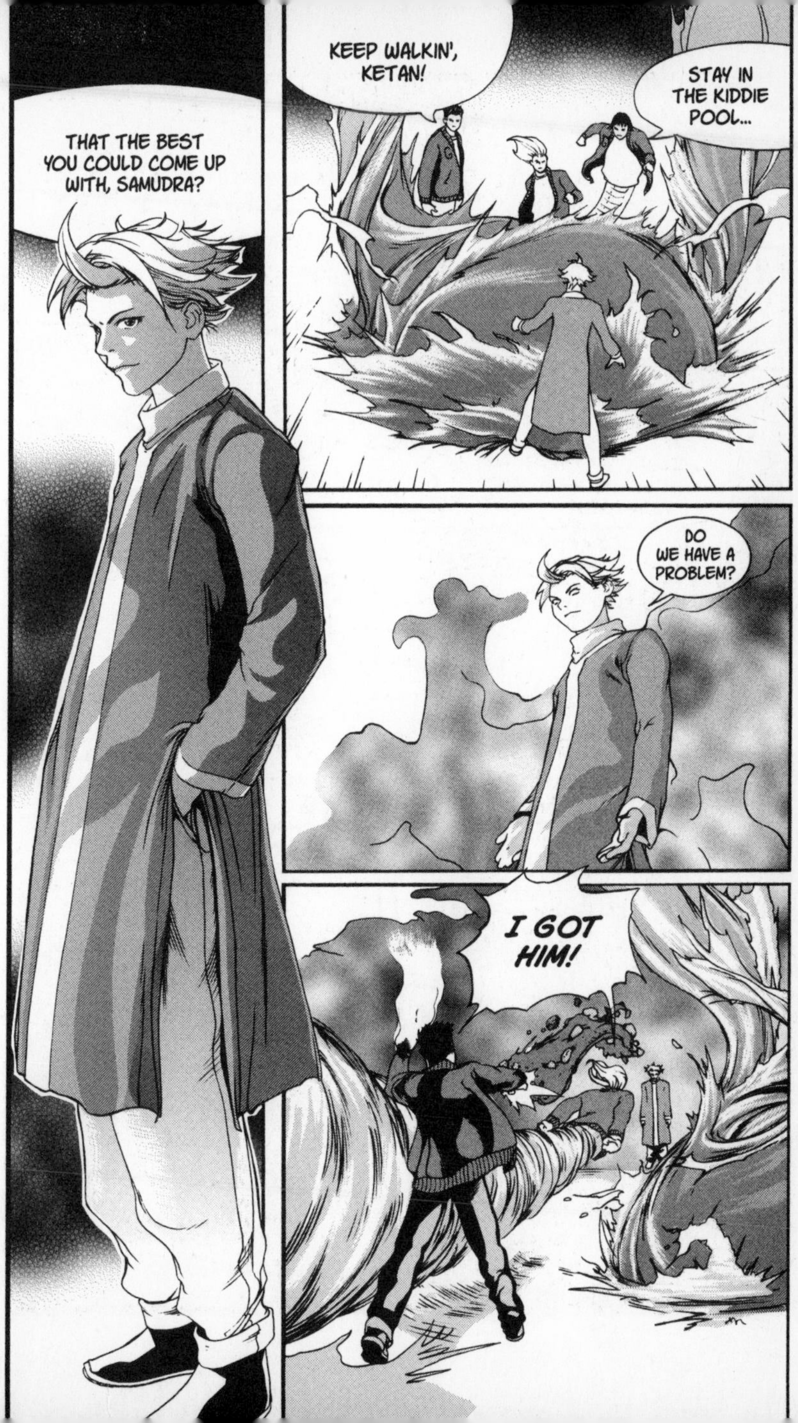
THAT THE BEST YOU COULD COME UP WITH, SAMUDRA?
KEEP WALKIN', KETAN!
STAY IN THE KIDDIE POOL...
DO WE HAVE A PROBLEM?
I GOT HIM!

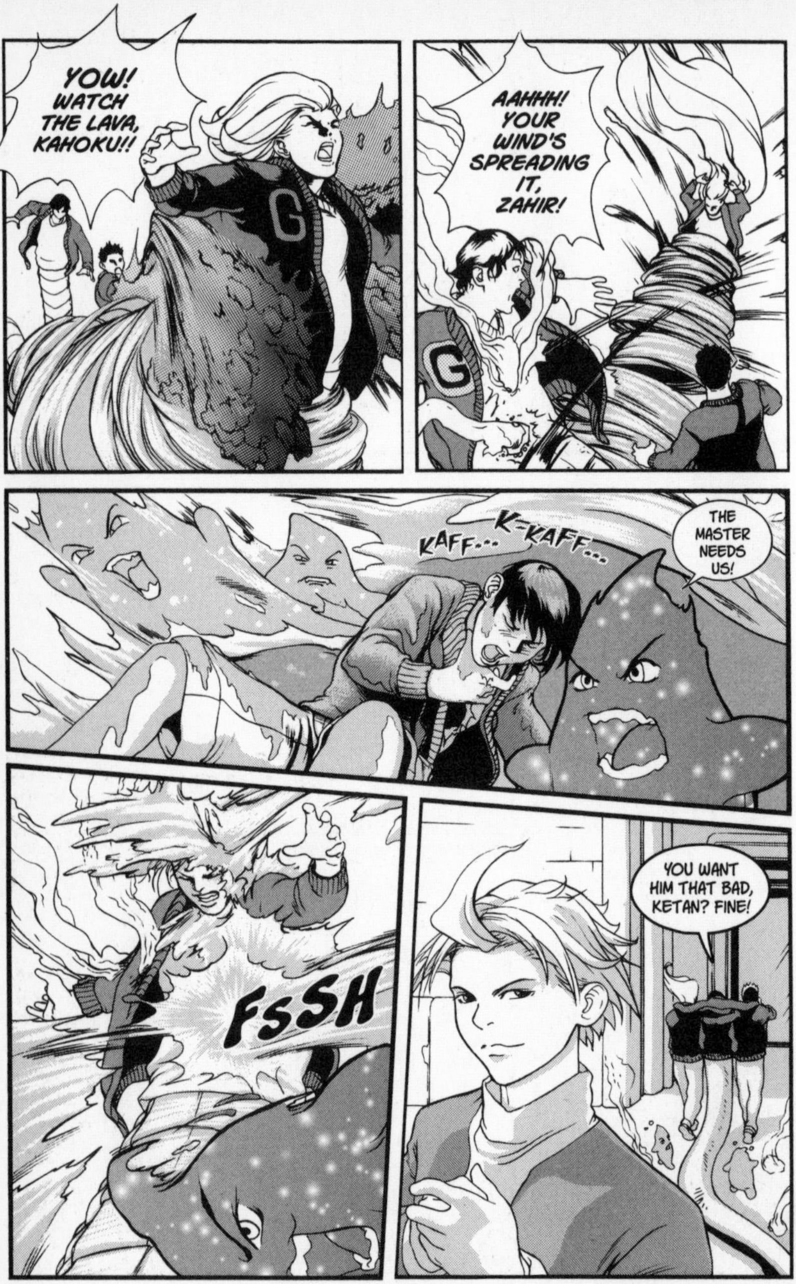
YOW! WATCH THE LAVA, KAHOKU!!
AAHHH! YOUR WIND'S SPREADING IT, ZAHIR!
KAFF... K-KAFF...
THE MASTER NEEDS US!
FSSH
YOU WANT HIM THAT BAD, KETAN? FINE!

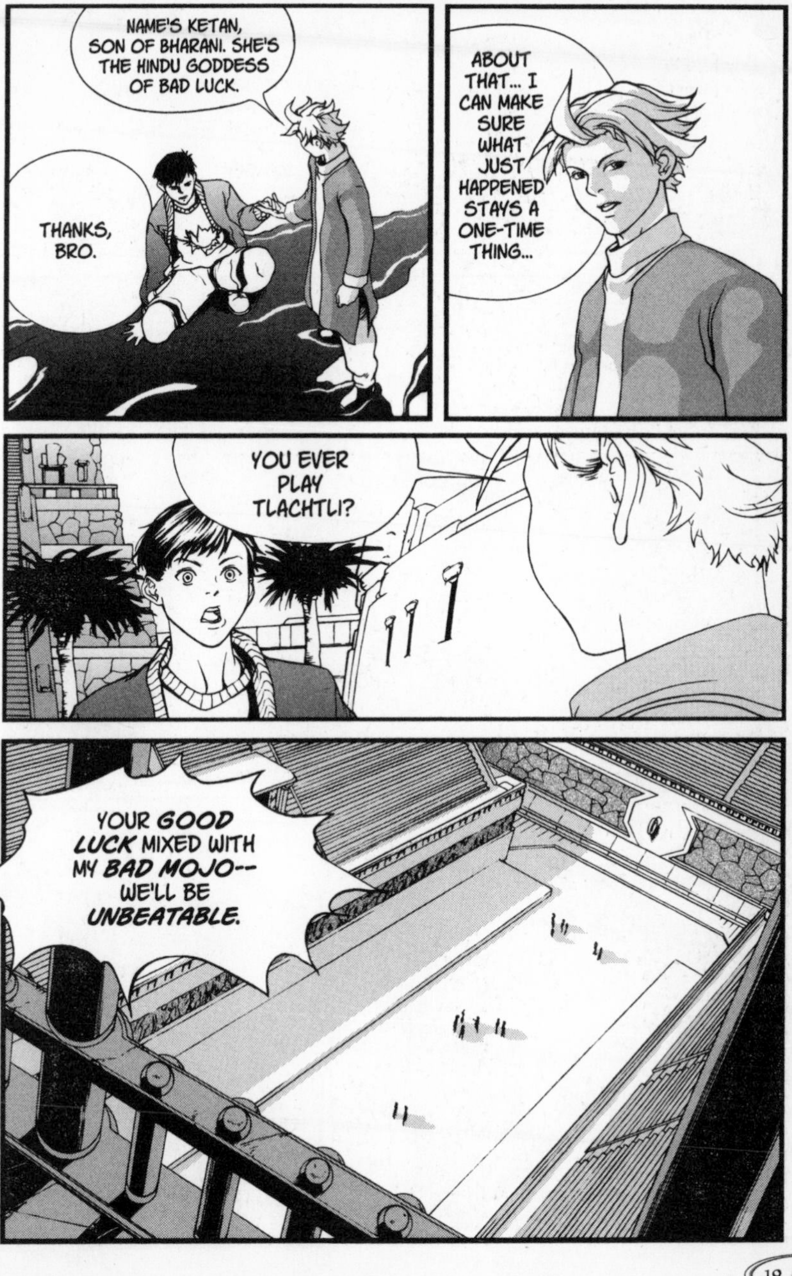
NAME'S KETAN, SON OF BHARANI. SHE'S THE HINDU GODDESS OF BAD LUCK.
THANKS, BRO.
ABOUT THAT... I CAN MAKE SURE WHAT JUST HAPPENED STAYS A ONE-TIME THING...
YOU EVER PLAY TLACHTLI?
YOUR GOOD LUCK MIXED WITH MY BAD MOJO-- WE'LL BE UNBEATABLE.

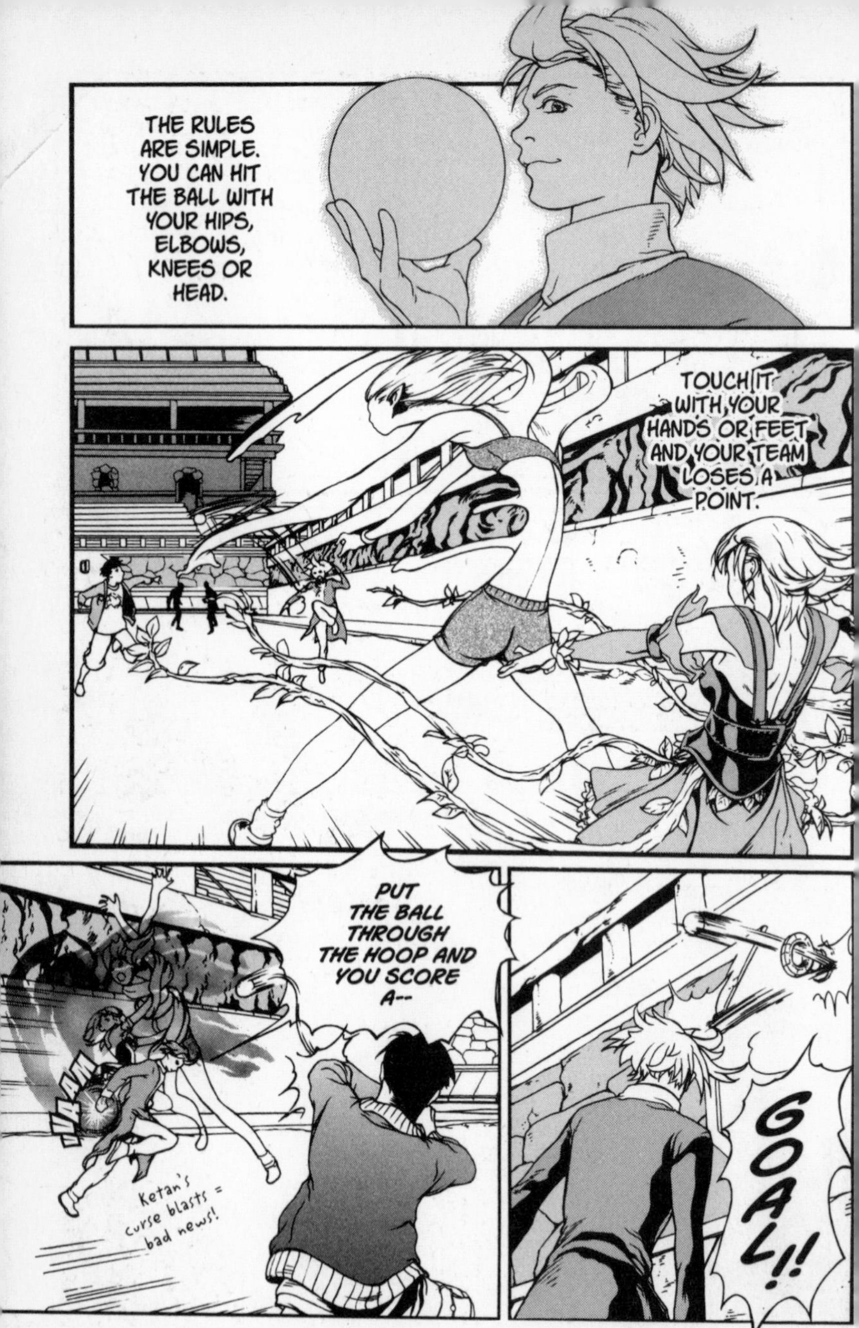
THE RULES ARE SIMPLE. YOU CAN HIT THE BALL WITH YOUR HIPS, ELBOWS, KNEES OR HEAD.
TOUCH IT WITH YOUR HANDS OR FEET AND YOUR TEAM LOSES A POINT.
PUT THE BALL THROUGH THE HOOP AND YOU SCORE A--
Ketan's curse blasts = bad news!
GOAL!!

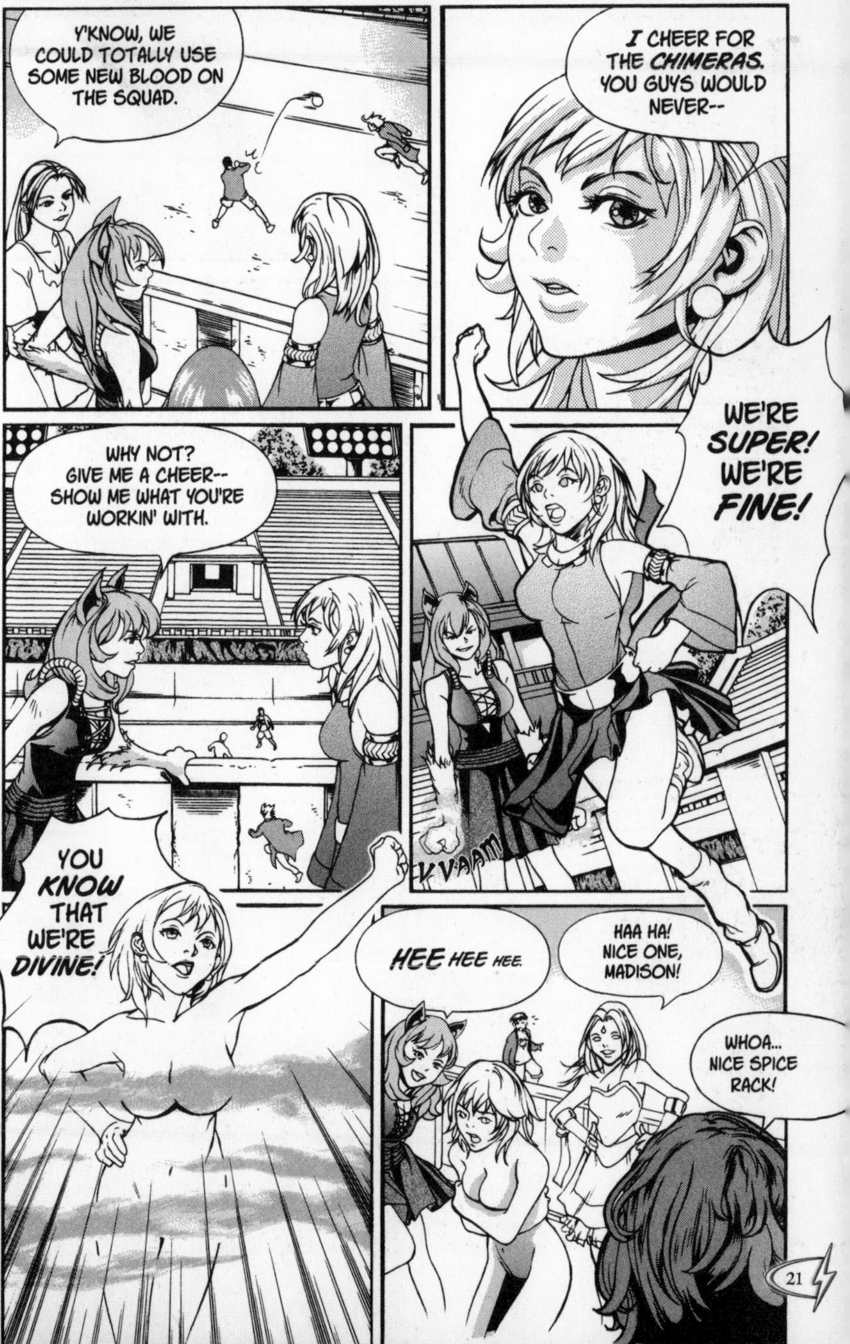
Y'KNOW, WE COULD TOTALLY USE SOME NEW BLOOD ON THE SQUAD.
I CHEER FOR THE CHIMERAS. YOU GUYS WOULD NEVER--
WHY NOT? GIVE ME A CHEER-- SHOW ME WHAT YOU'RE WORKIN' WITH.
WE'RE SUPER! WE'RE FINE!
VVAAM!
YOU KNOW THAT WE'RE DIVINE!
HEE HEE HEE.
HAA HA! NICE ONE, MADISON!
WHOA... NICE SPICE RACK!

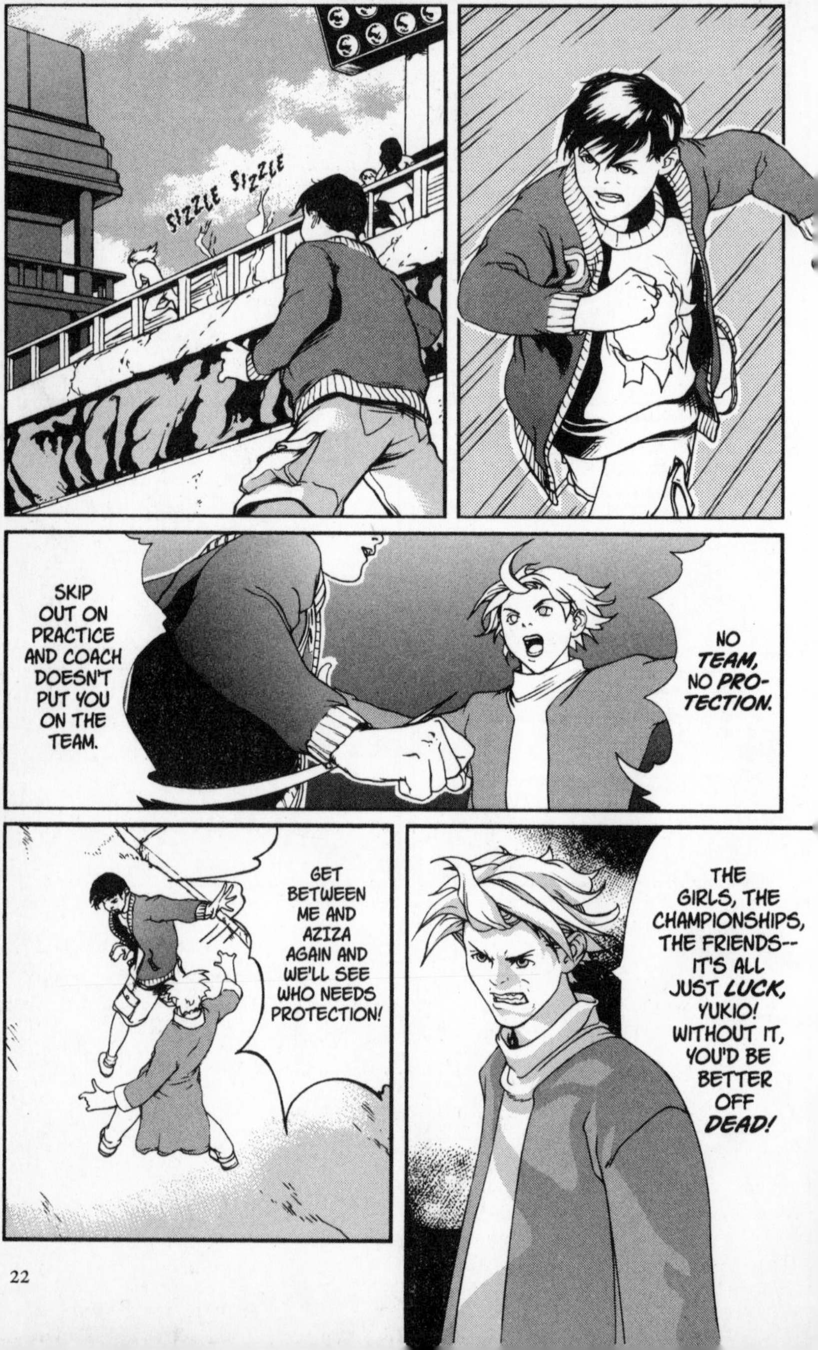
SIZZLE SIZZLE
SKIP OUT ON PRACTICE AND COACH DOESN'T PUT YOU ON THE TEAM.
NO *TEAM,* NO *PRO-TECTION.*
GET BETWEEN ME AND AZIZA AGAIN AND WE'LL SEE WHO NEEDS PROTECTION!
THE GIRLS, THE CHAMPIONSHIPS, THE FRIENDS-- IT'S ALL JUST *LUCK,* YUKIO! WITHOUT IT, YOU'D BE BETTER OFF *DEAD!*

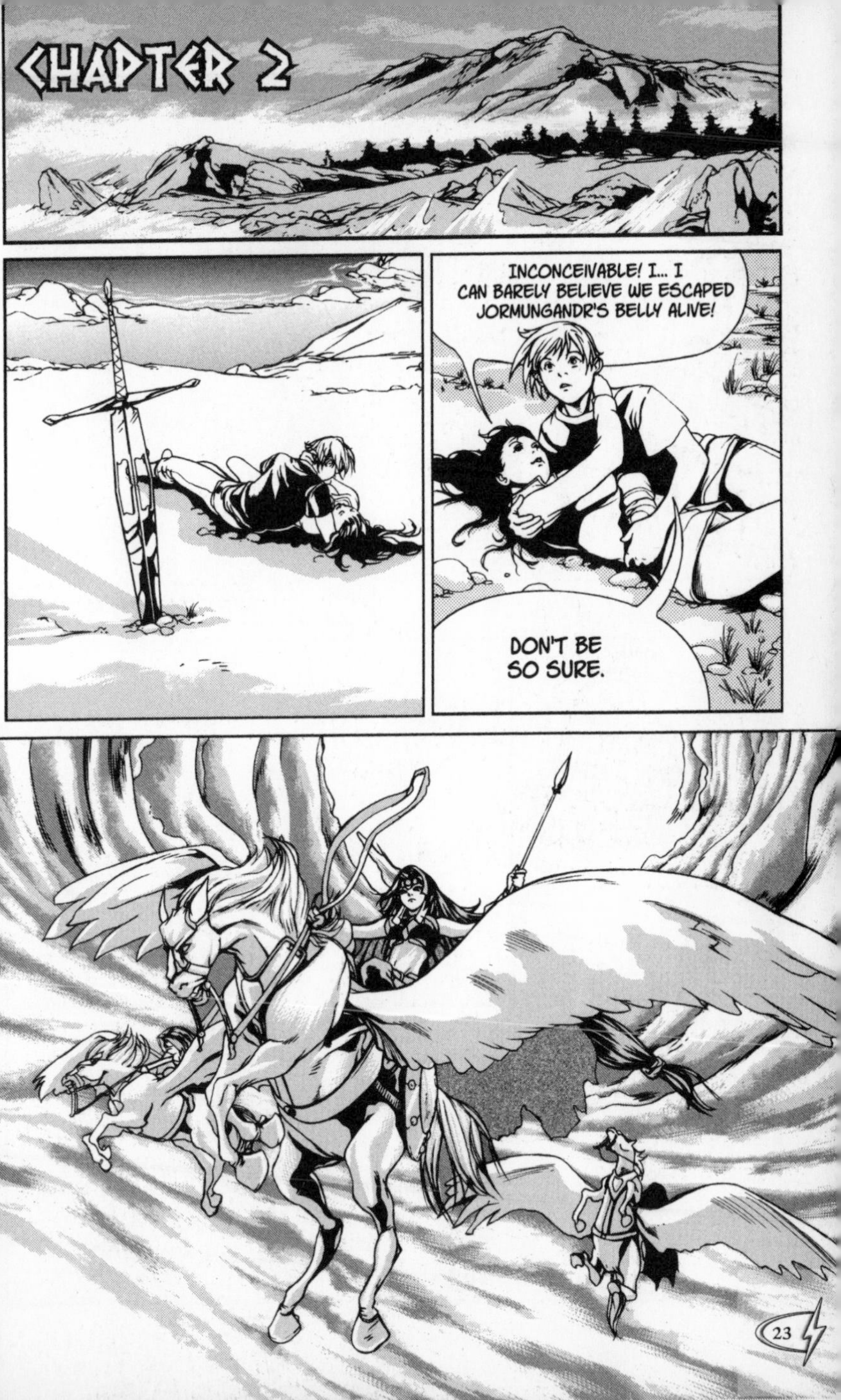
CHAPTER 2
INCONCEIVABLE! I... I CAN BARELY BELIEVE WE ESCAPED JORMUNGANDR'S BELLY ALIVE!
DON'T BE SO SURE.

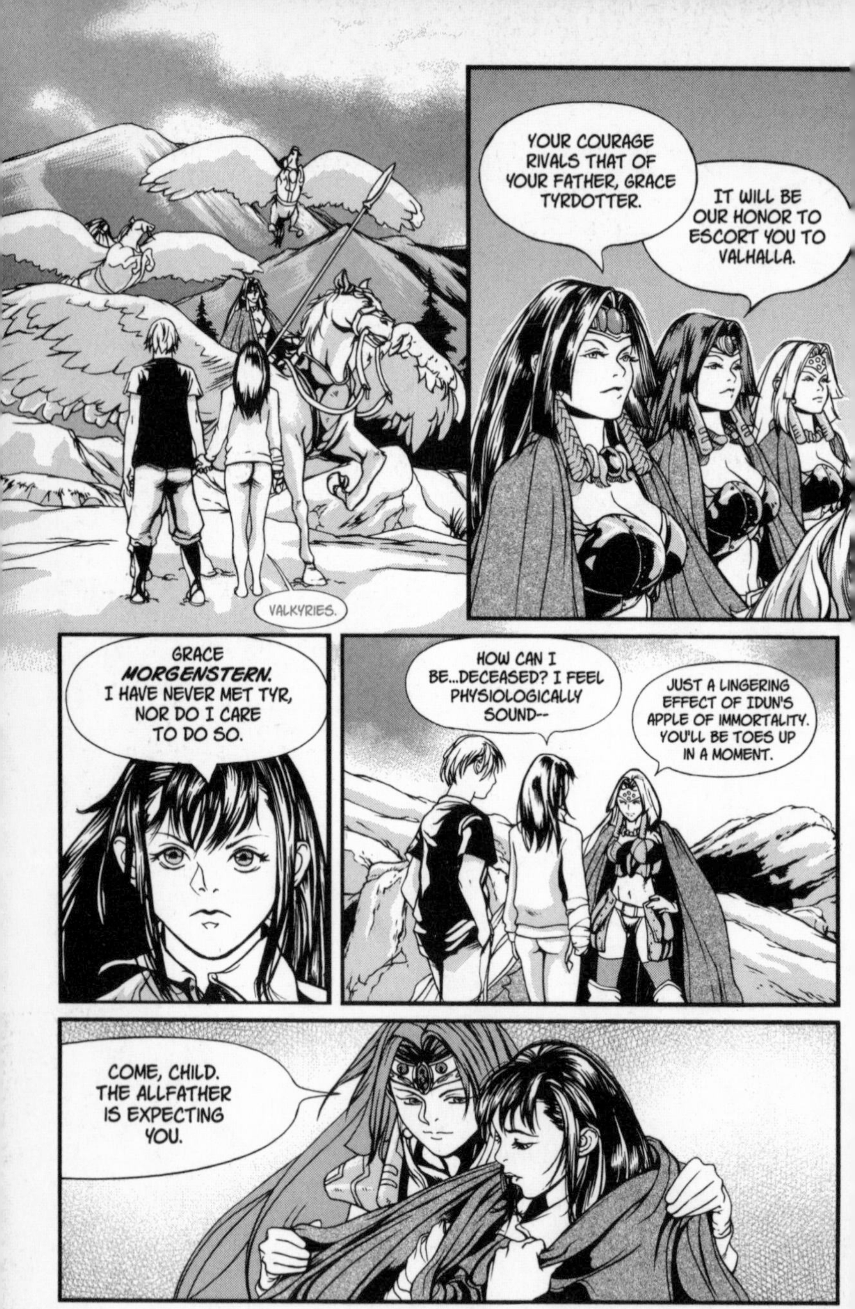
VALKYRIES.
YOUR COURAGE RIVALS THAT OF YOUR FATHER, GRACE TYRDOTTER.
IT WILL BE OUR HONOR TO ESCORT YOU TO VALHALLA.
GRACE *MORGENSTERN.* I HAVE NEVER MET TYR, NOR DO I CARE TO DO SO.
HOW CAN I BE...DECEASED? I FEEL PHYSIOLOGICALLY SOUND--
JUST A LINGERING EFFECT OF IDUN'S APPLE OF IMMORTALITY. YOU'LL BE TOES UP IN A MOMENT.
COME, CHILD. THE ALLFATHER IS EXPECTING YOU.

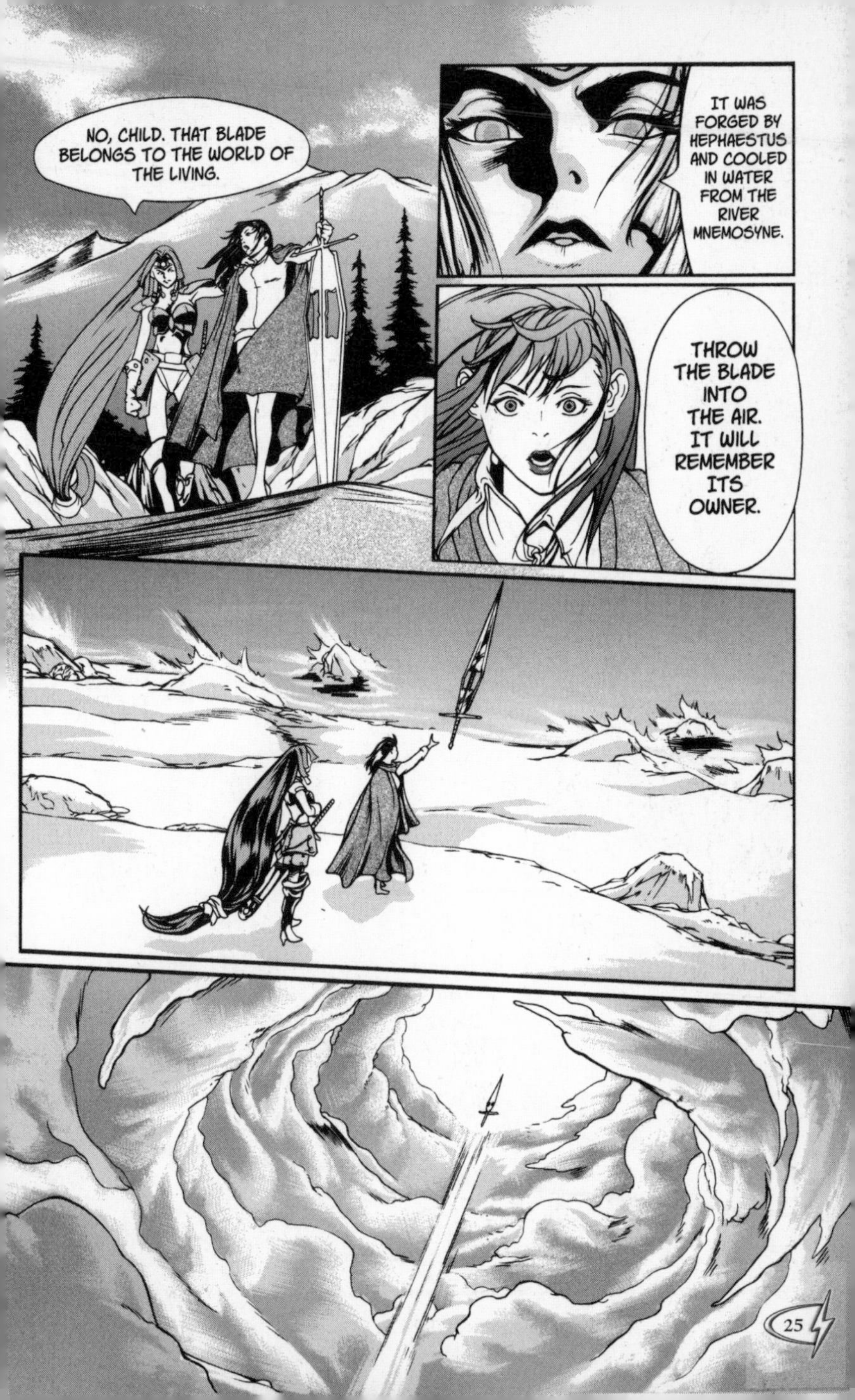
NO, CHILD. THAT BLADE BELONGS TO THE WORLD OF THE LIVING.
IT WAS FORGED BY HEPHAESTUS AND COOLED IN WATER FROM THE RIVER MNEMOSYNE.
THROW THE BLADE INTO THE AIR. IT WILL REMEMBER ITS OWNER.

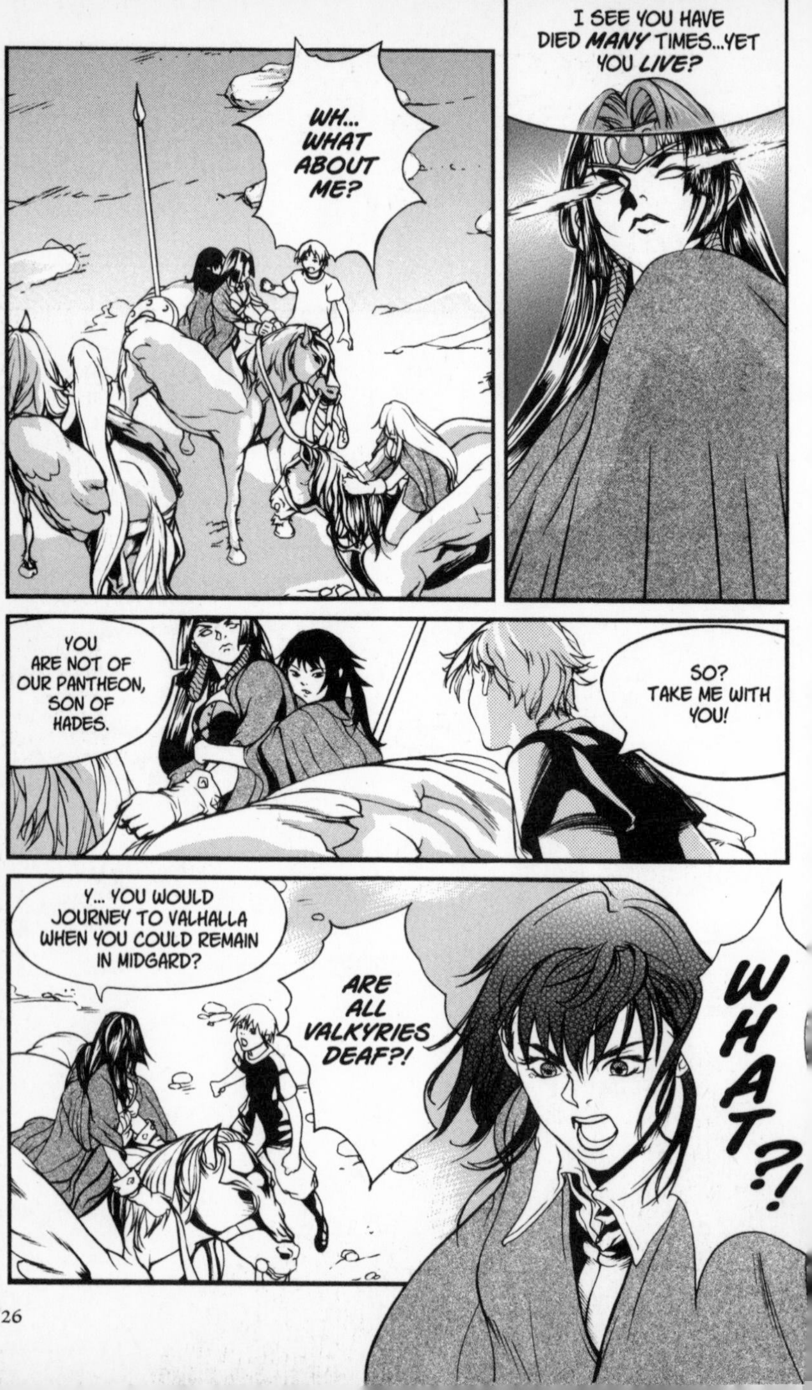
WH... WHAT ABOUT ME?
I SEE YOU HAVE DIED *MANY* TIMES...YET YOU *LIVE?*
YOU ARE NOT OF OUR PANTHEON, SON OF HADES.
SO? TAKE ME WITH YOU!
Y... YOU WOULD JOURNEY TO VALHALLA WHEN YOU COULD REMAIN IN MIDGARD?
ARE ALL VALKYRIES DEAF?!
WHAT?!

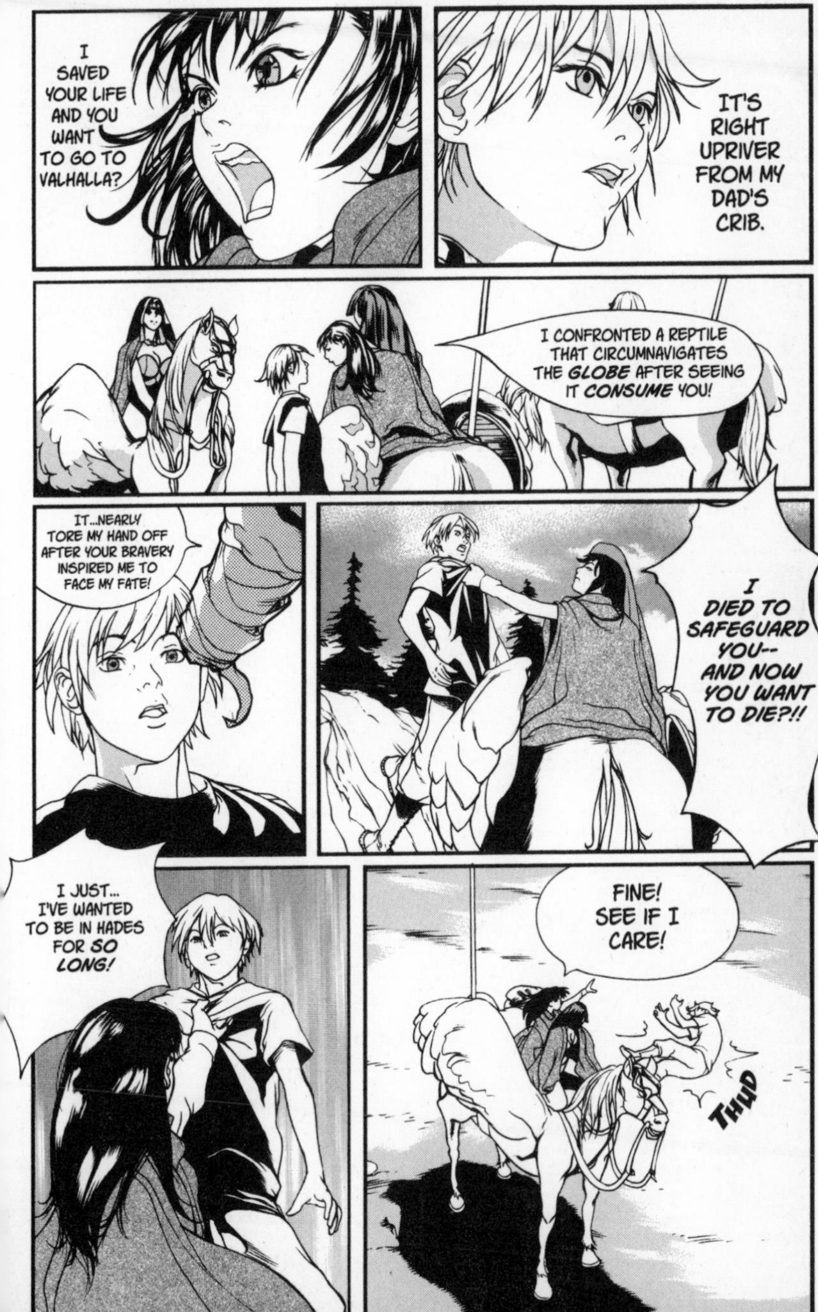
I SAVED YOUR LIFE AND YOU WANT TO GO TO VALHALLA?
IT'S RIGHT UPRIVER FROM MY DAD'S CRIB.
I CONFRONTED A REPTILE THAT CIRCUMNAVIGATES THE *GLOBE* AFTER SEEING IT *CONSUME* YOU!
IT...NEARLY TORE MY HAND OFF AFTER YOUR BRAVERY INSPIRED ME TO FACE MY FATE!
I DIED TO SAFEGUARD YOU-- AND NOW YOU WANT TO DIE?!!
I JUST... I'VE WANTED TO BE IN HADES FOR *SO LONG!*
FINE! SEE IF I CARE!
THUD

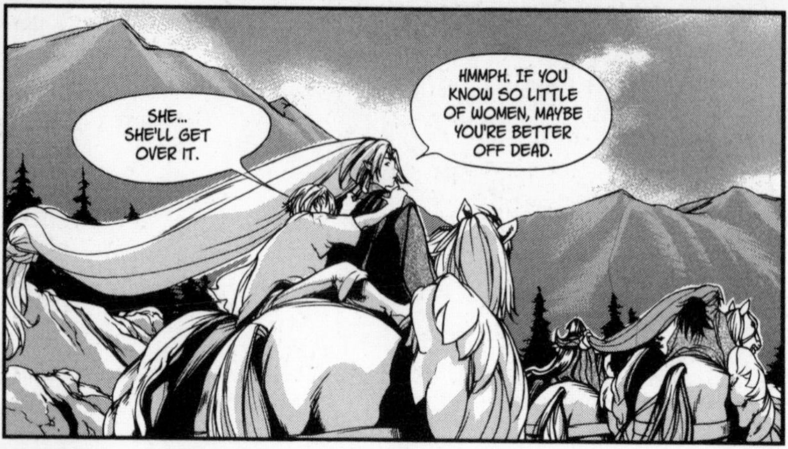
SHE... SHE'LL GET OVER IT.
HMMPH. IF YOU KNOW SO LITTLE OF WOMEN, MAYBE YOU'RE BETTER OFF DEAD.
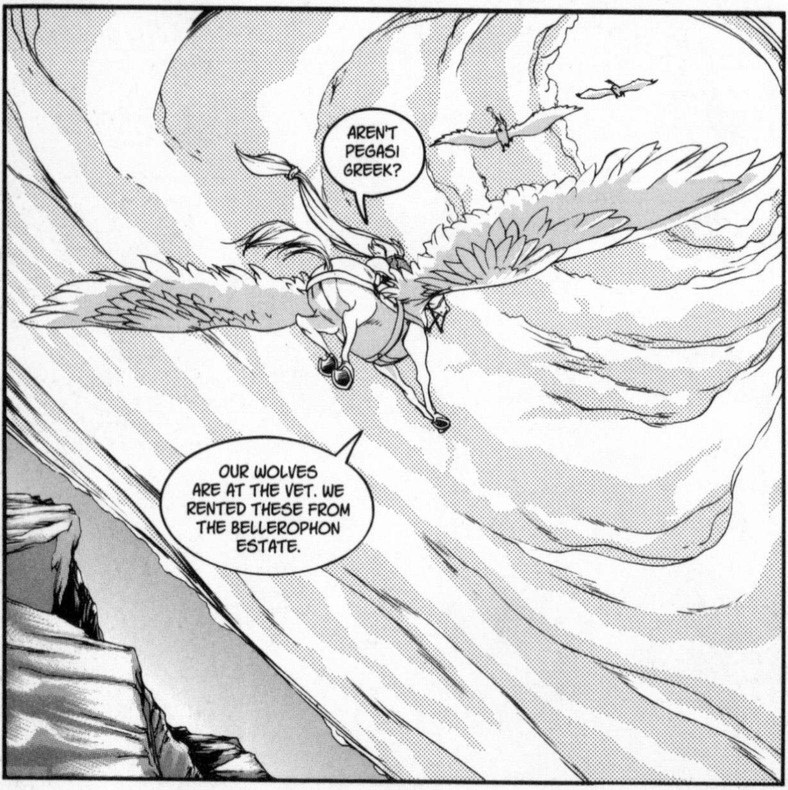
AREN'T PEGASI GREEK?
OUR WOLVES ARE AT THE VET. WE RENTED THESE FROM THE BELLEROPHON ESTATE.

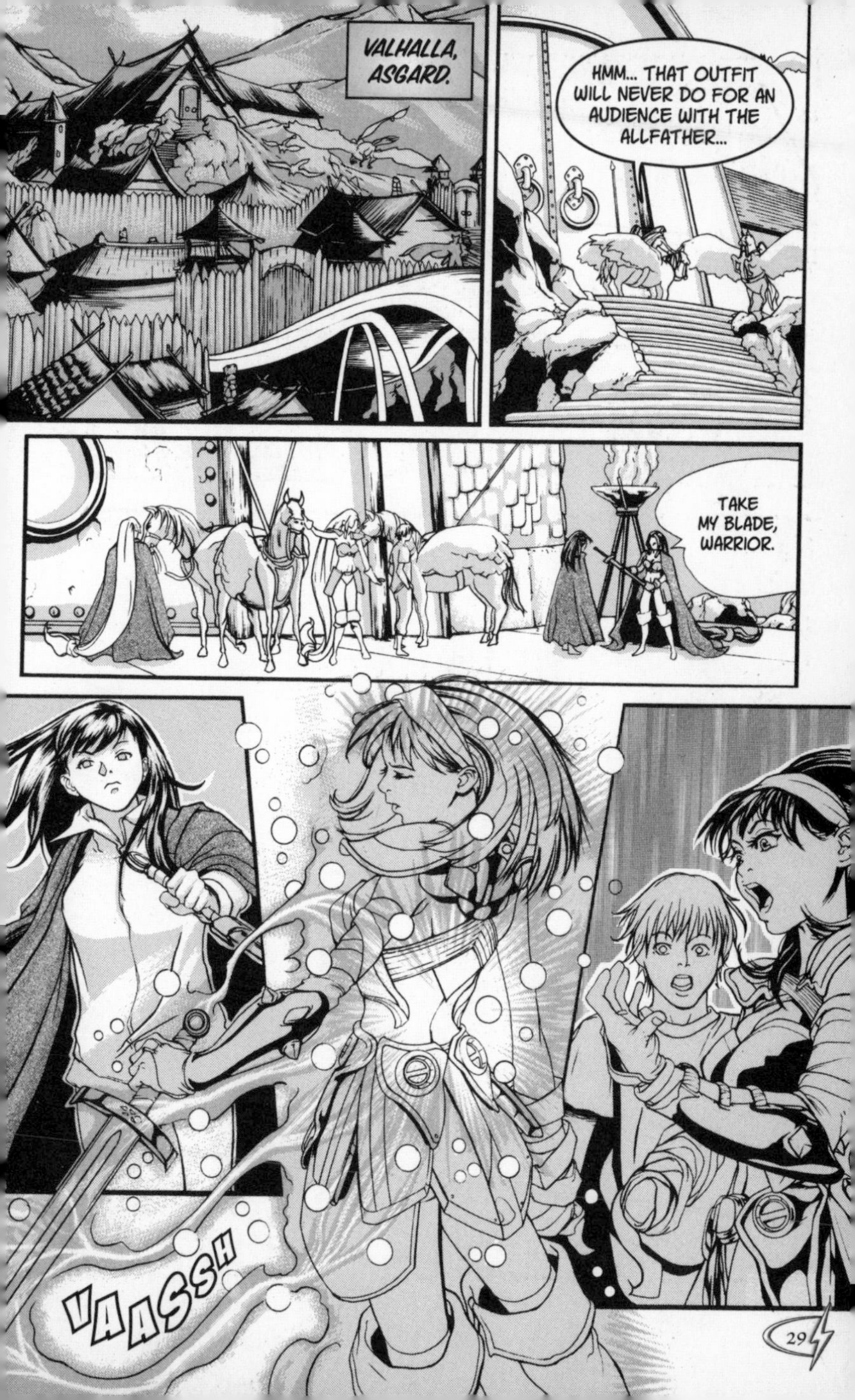
VALHALLA, ASGARD.
HMM... THAT OUTFIT WILL NEVER DO FOR AN AUDIENCE WITH THE ALLFATHER...
TAKE MY BLADE, WARRIOR.
VAASSH

HUGIN

MUNIN

MY LORD, ALLFATHER. MAY I PRESENT GRACE TYRDOTT-- MORGENSTERN.

YOU FOUGHT JARMON... JORMUD... THE MIDGARD SSSERPENT SHINGL- HANDED. IMPRESSHIVV.

IS HE INEBRIATED?

AHEM...

COME, EINHERIAR. IT'SSH TIME TO SSHTART THE DAY OF BATTLE!

SAVED BY THE BELL.

EXCUSE US, MY LORD ODIN. WE HAVE A PICK UP.

"Ride of the Valkyries" ringtone

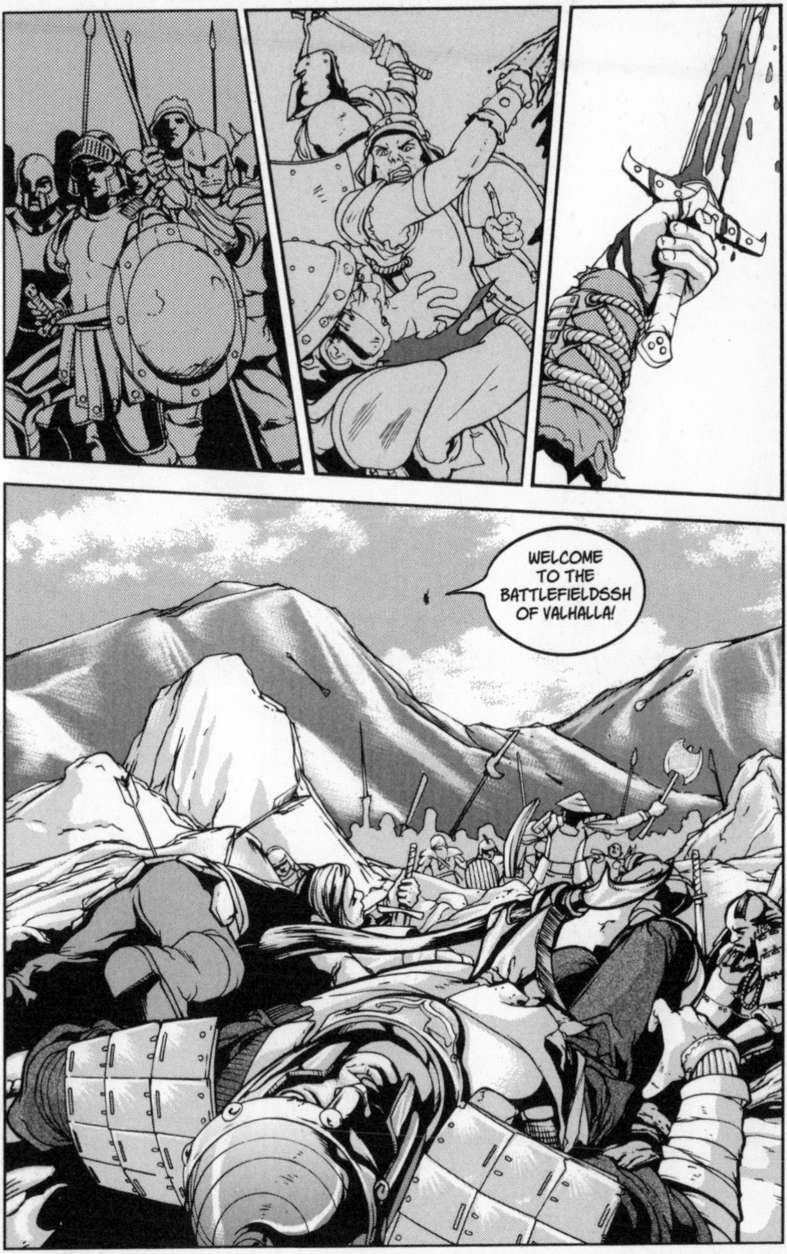
WELCOME TO THE BATTLEFIELDSSH OF VALHALLA!

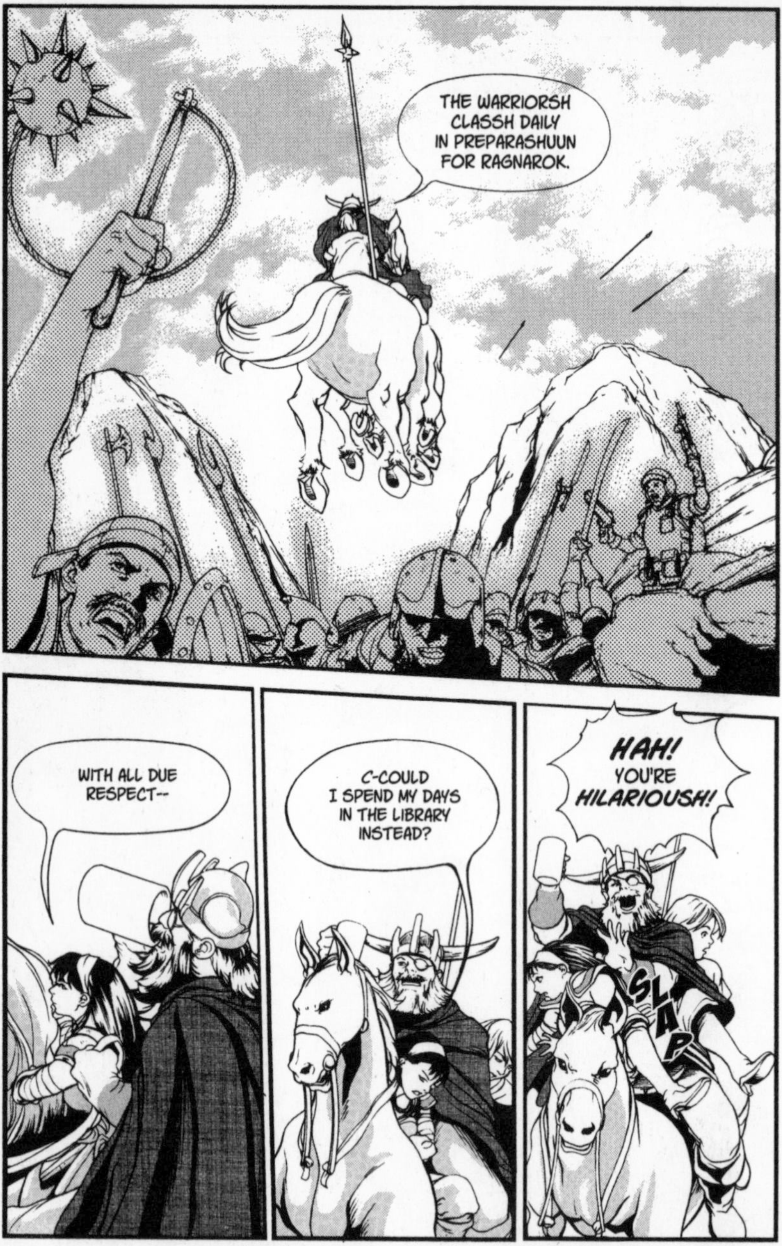
THE WARRIORSH CLASSH DAILY IN PREPARASHUUN FOR RAGNAROK.
WITH ALL DUE RESPECT--
C-COULD I SPEND MY DAYS IN THE LIBRARY INSTEAD?
HAH! YOU'RE HILARIOUSH!
SLAP

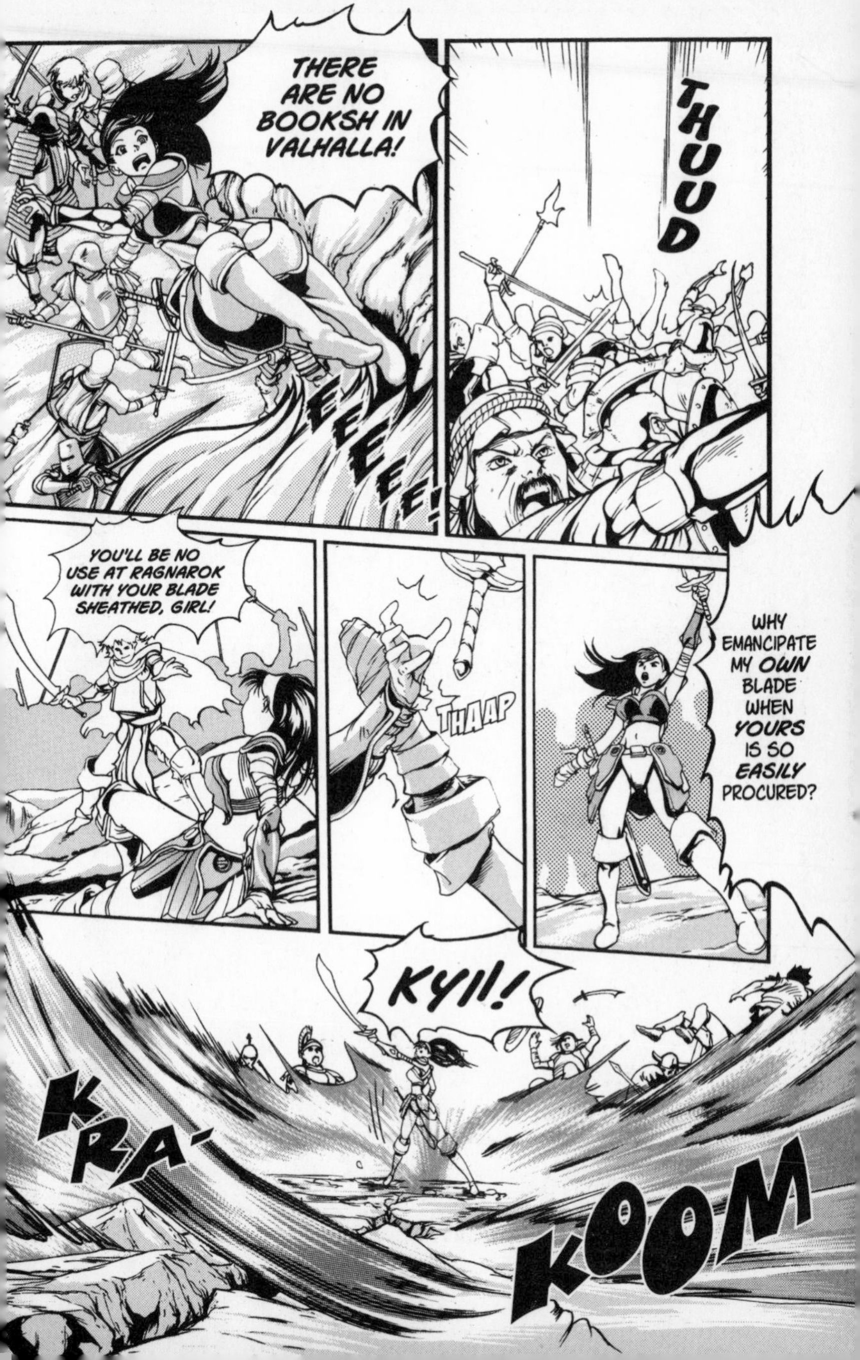
THERE ARE NO BOOKSH IN VALHALLA!
EEEEE!
THUUD
YOU'LL BE NO USE AT RAGNAROK WITH YOUR BLADE SHEATHED, GIRL!
THAAP
WHY EMANCIPATE MY OWN BLADE WHEN YOURS IS SO EASILY PROCURED?
KYII!
KRA-
KOOM

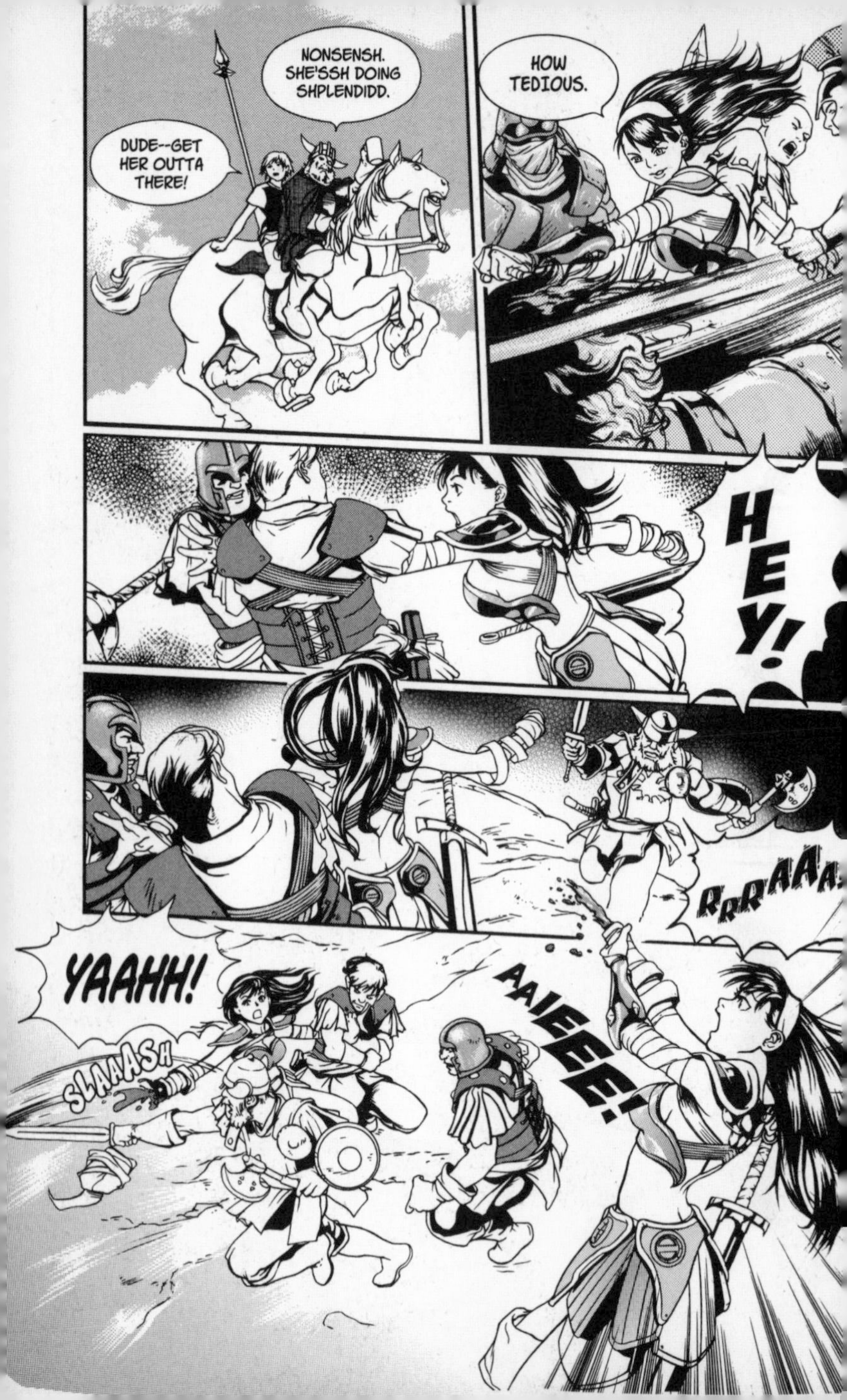
DUDE--GET HER OUTTA THERE!
NONSENSH. SHE'SSH DOING SHPLENDIDD.
HOW TEDIOUS.
HEY!
RRRAAAA
YAAHH!
SLAAASH
AAIEEEE!

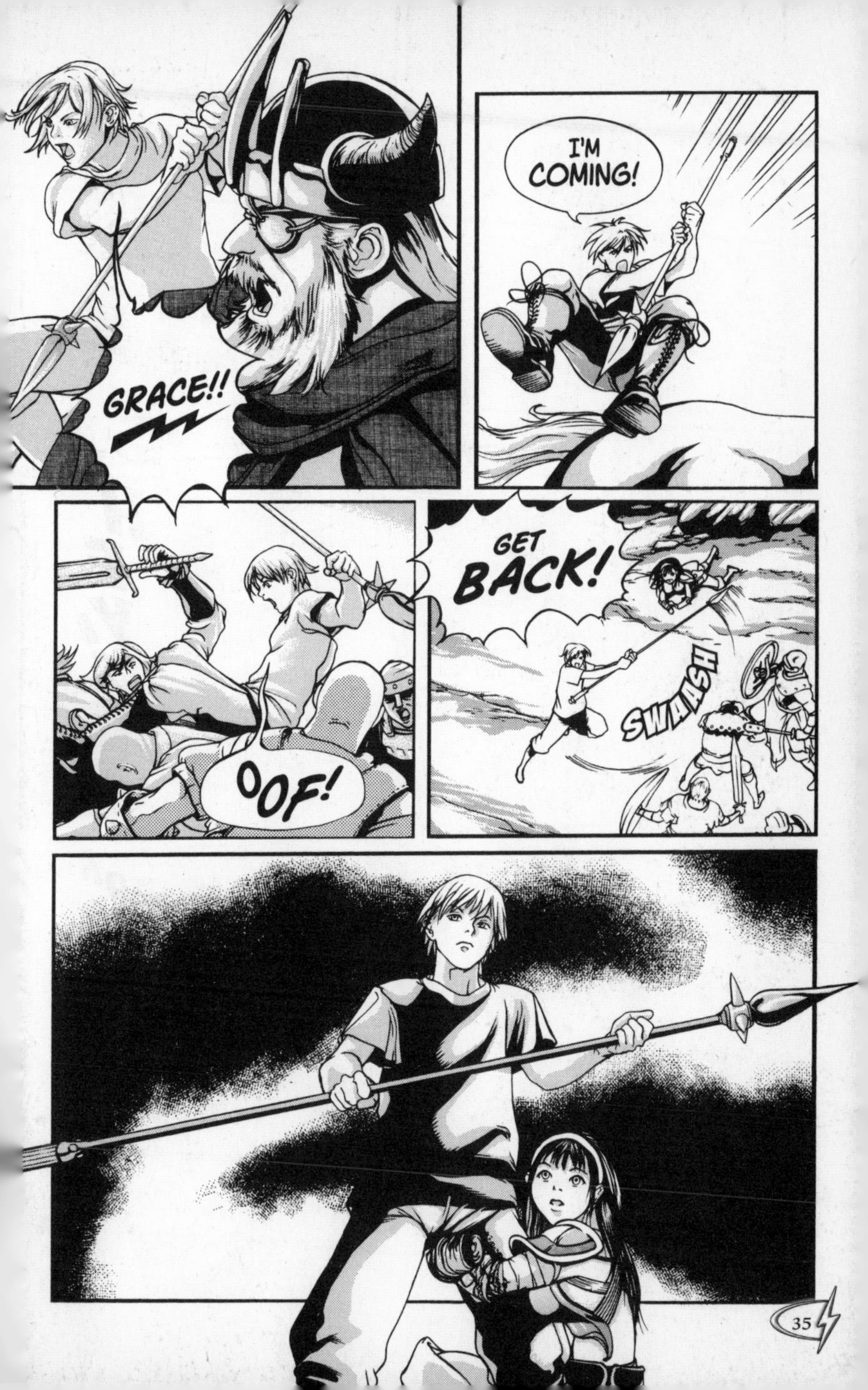
GRACE!!
I'M COMING!
OOF!
GET BACK!
SWAASH

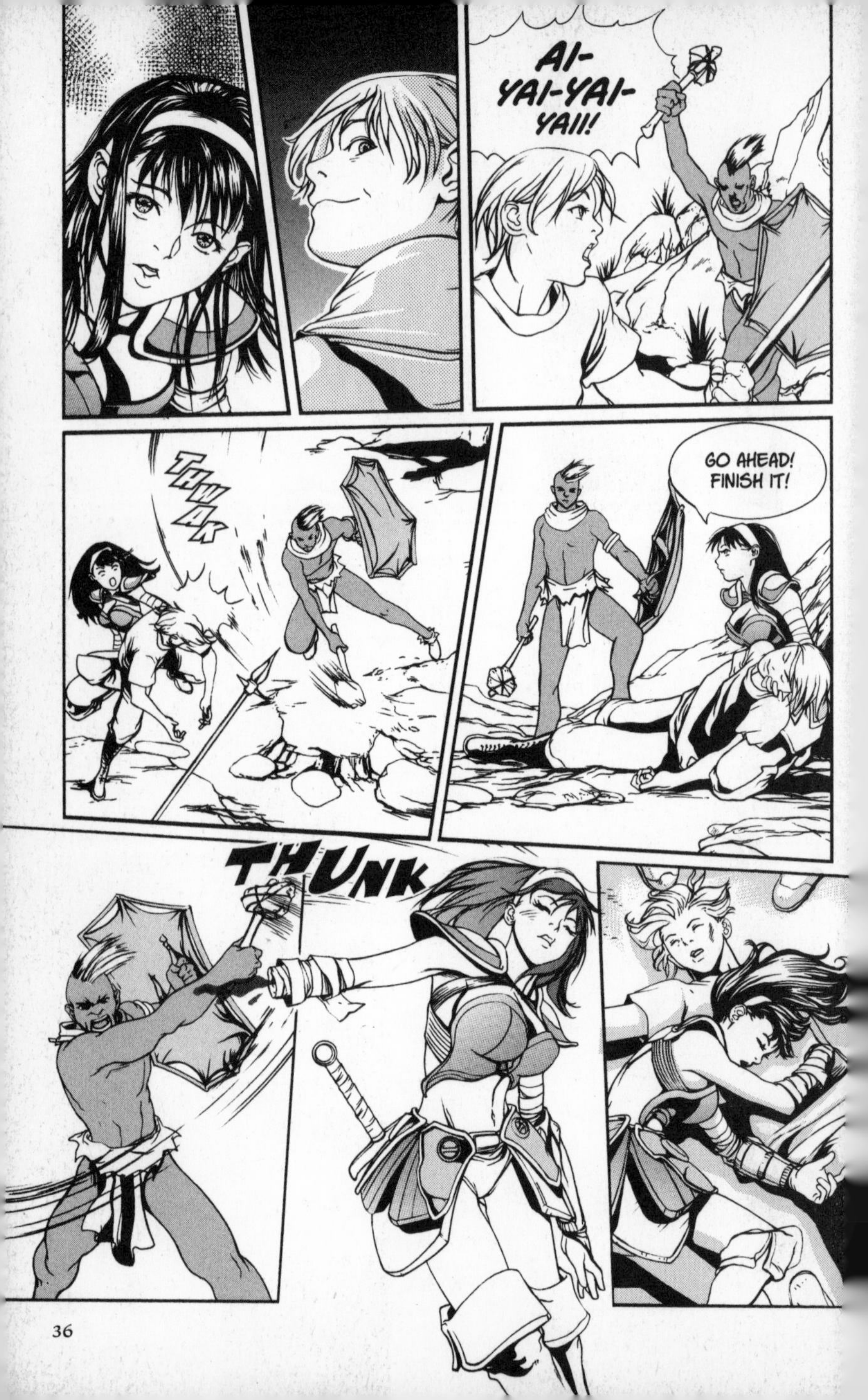
AI-YAI-YAI-YAII!
THWAK
GO AHEAD! FINISH IT!
THUNK

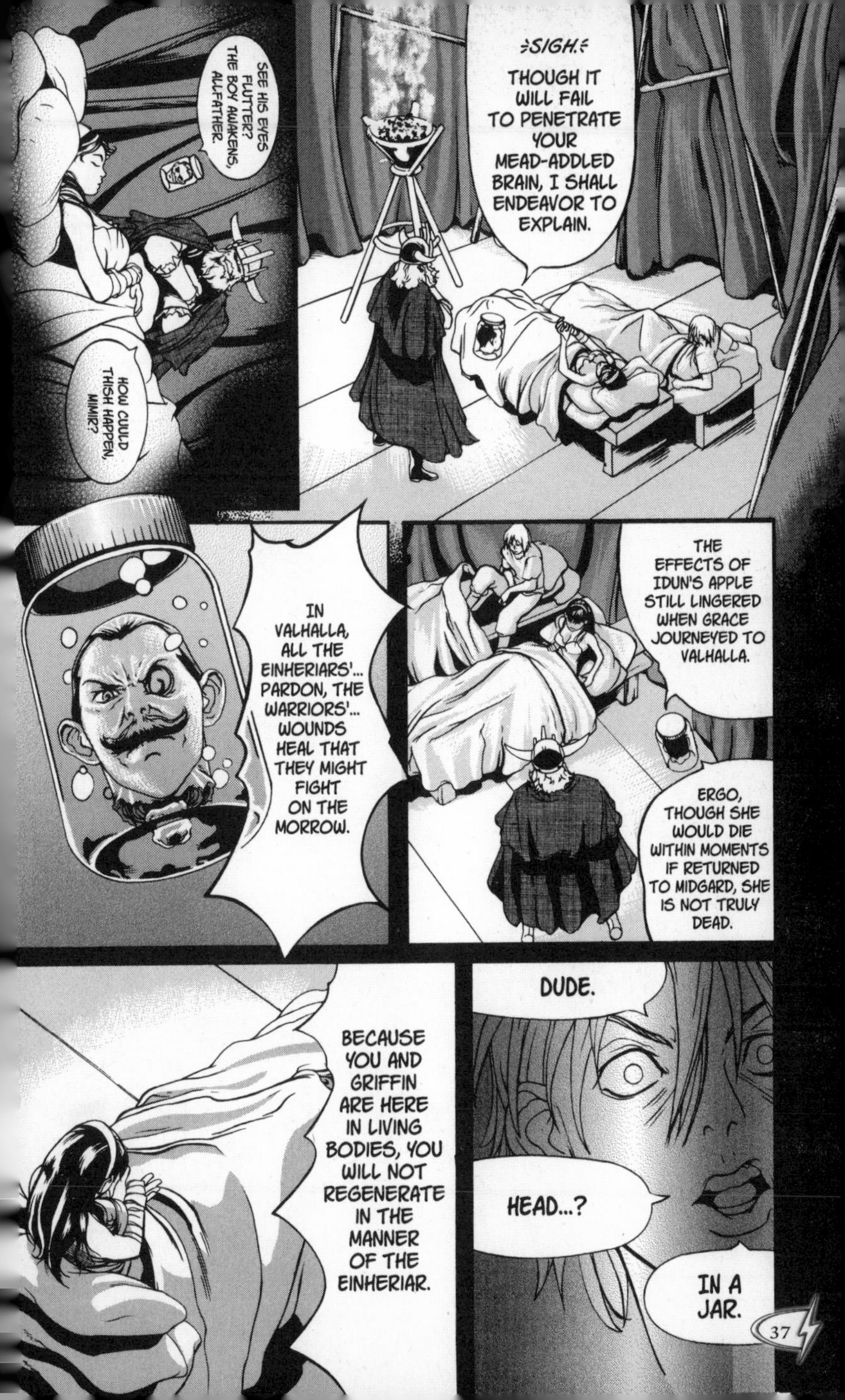
SEE HIS EYES FLUTTER? THE BOY AWAKENS, ALLFATHER.
HOW CUULD THISH HAPPEN, MIMIR?
SIGH.
THOUGH IT WILL FAIL TO PENETRATE YOUR MEAD-ADDLED BRAIN, I SHALL ENDEAVOR TO EXPLAIN.
IN VALHALLA, ALL THE EINHERIARS'... PARDON, THE WARRIORS'... WOUNDS HEAL THAT THEY MIGHT FIGHT ON THE MORROW.
THE EFFECTS OF IDUN'S APPLE STILL LINGERED WHEN GRACE JOURNEYED TO VALHALLA.
ERGO, THOUGH SHE WOULD DIE WITHIN MOMENTS IF RETURNED TO MIDGARD, SHE IS NOT TRULY DEAD.
BECAUSE YOU AND GRIFFIN ARE HERE IN LIVING BODIES, YOU WILL NOT REGENERATE IN THE MANNER OF THE EINHERIAR.
DUDE.
HEAD...?
IN A JAR.

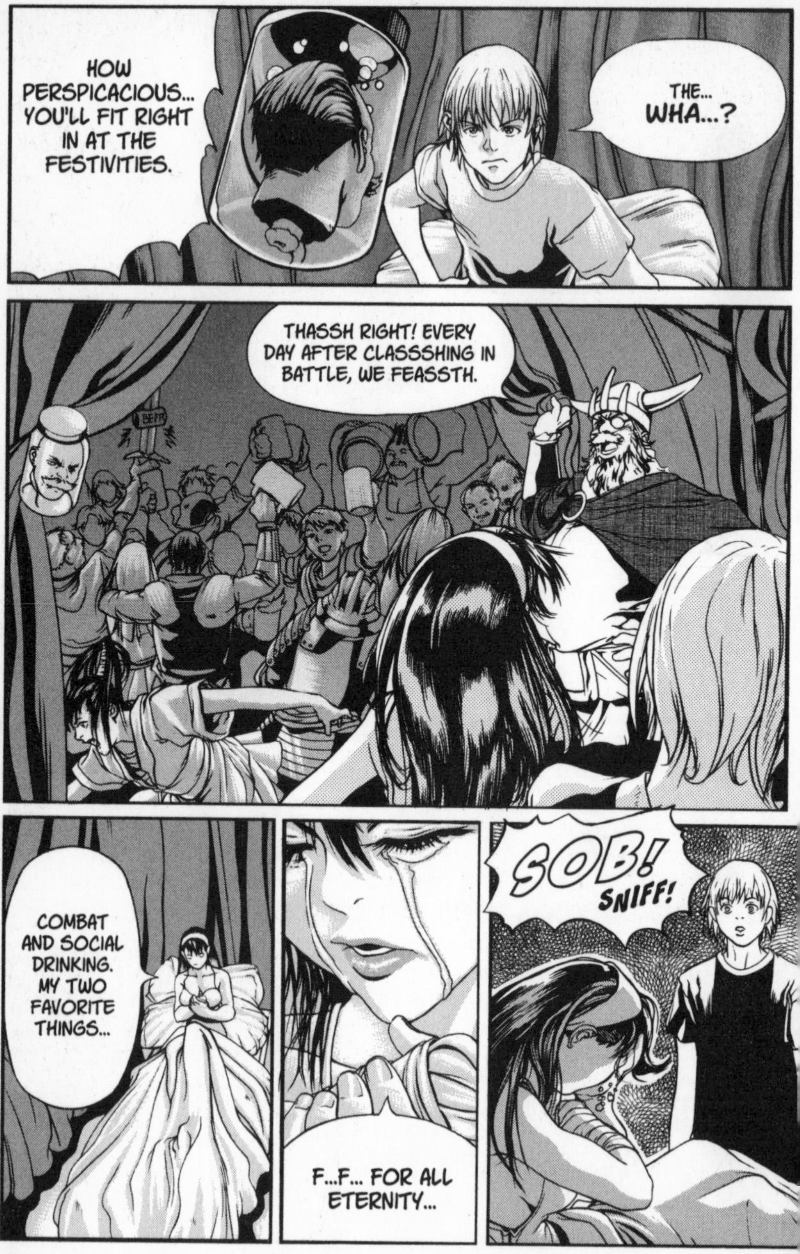
HOW PERSPICACIOUS... YOU'LL FIT RIGHT IN AT THE FESTIVITIES.
THE... WHA...?
THASSH RIGHT! EVERY DAY AFTER CLASSSHING IN BATTLE, WE FEASSTH.
COMBAT AND SOCIAL DRINKING. MY TWO FAVORITE THINGS...
F...F... FOR ALL ETERNITY...
SOB!
SNIFF!

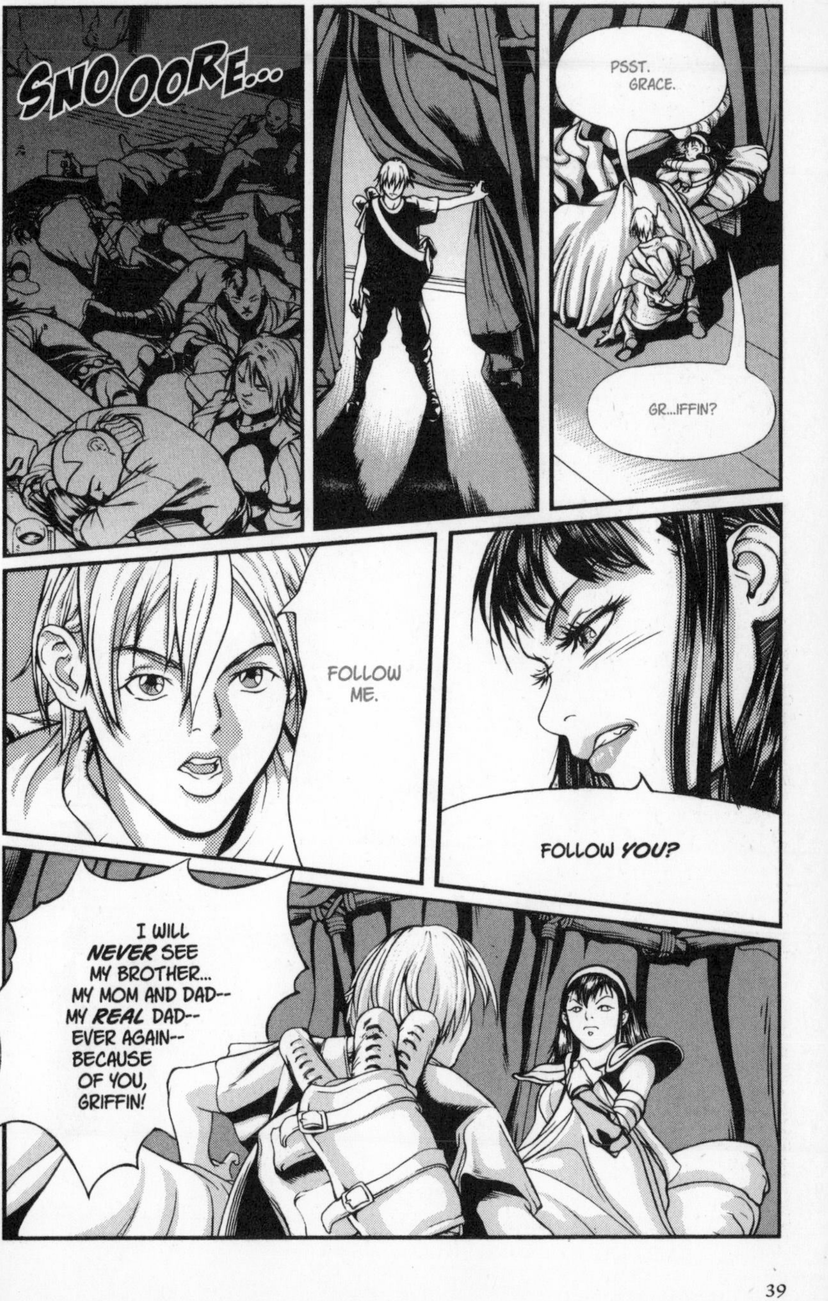
SNOOORE...
PSST. GRACE.
GR...IFFIN?
FOLLOW ME.
FOLLOW *YOU?*
I WILL *NEVER* SEE MY BROTHER... MY MOM AND DAD-- MY *REAL* DAD-- EVER AGAIN-- BECAUSE OF YOU, GRIFFIN!

PUH...PLEASE? LET ME MAKE IT UP TO YOU!

WE CAN TRAVEL DOWNRIVER TO HADES.

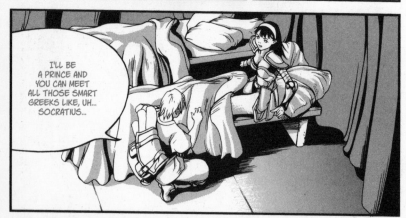

I'LL BE A PRINCE AND YOU CAN MEET ALL THOSE SMART GREEKS LIKE, UH... SOCRATIUS...

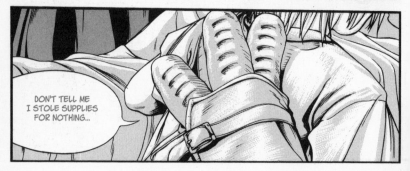

DON'T TELL ME I STOLE SUPPLIES FOR NOTHING...

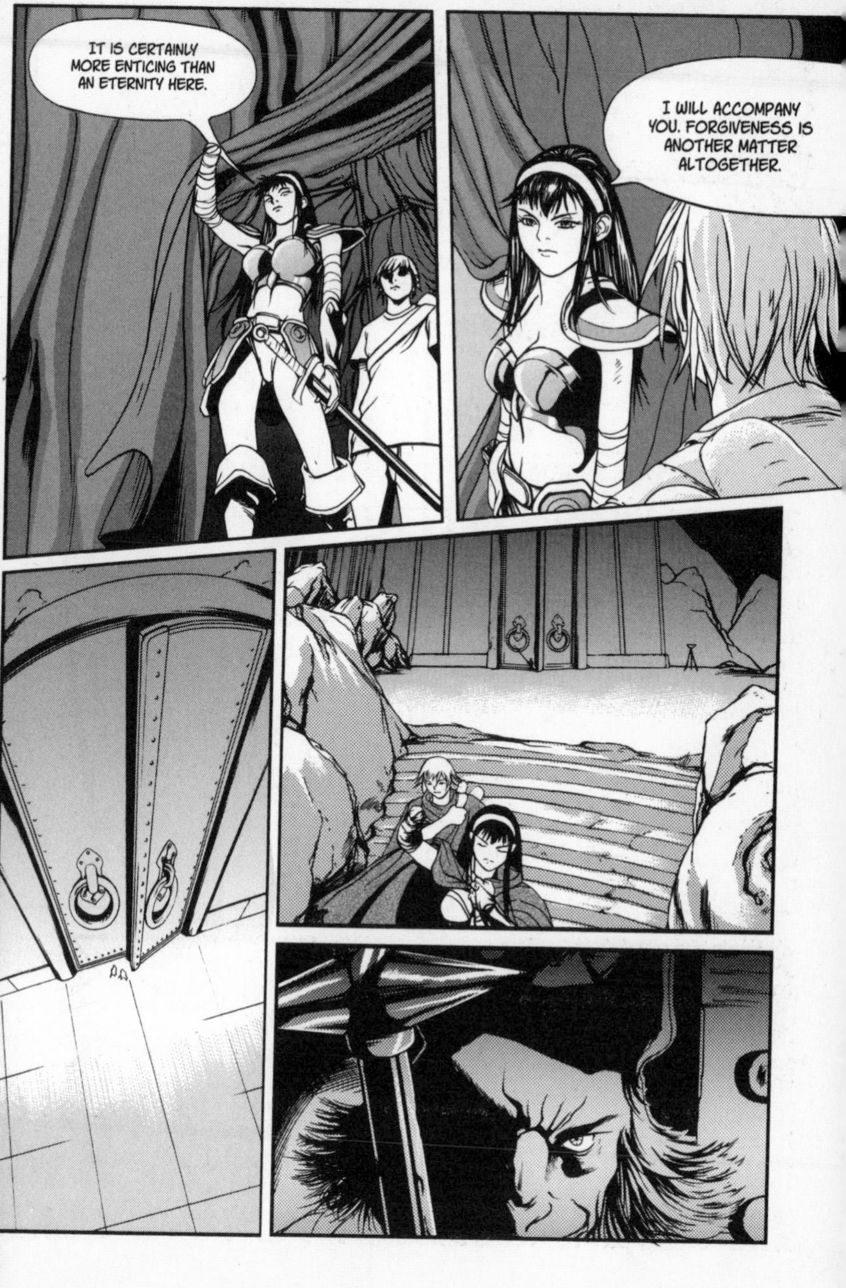
IT IS CERTAINLY MORE ENTICING THAN AN ETERNITY HERE.
I WILL ACCOMPANY YOU. FORGIVENESS IS ANOTHER MATTER ALTOGETHER.

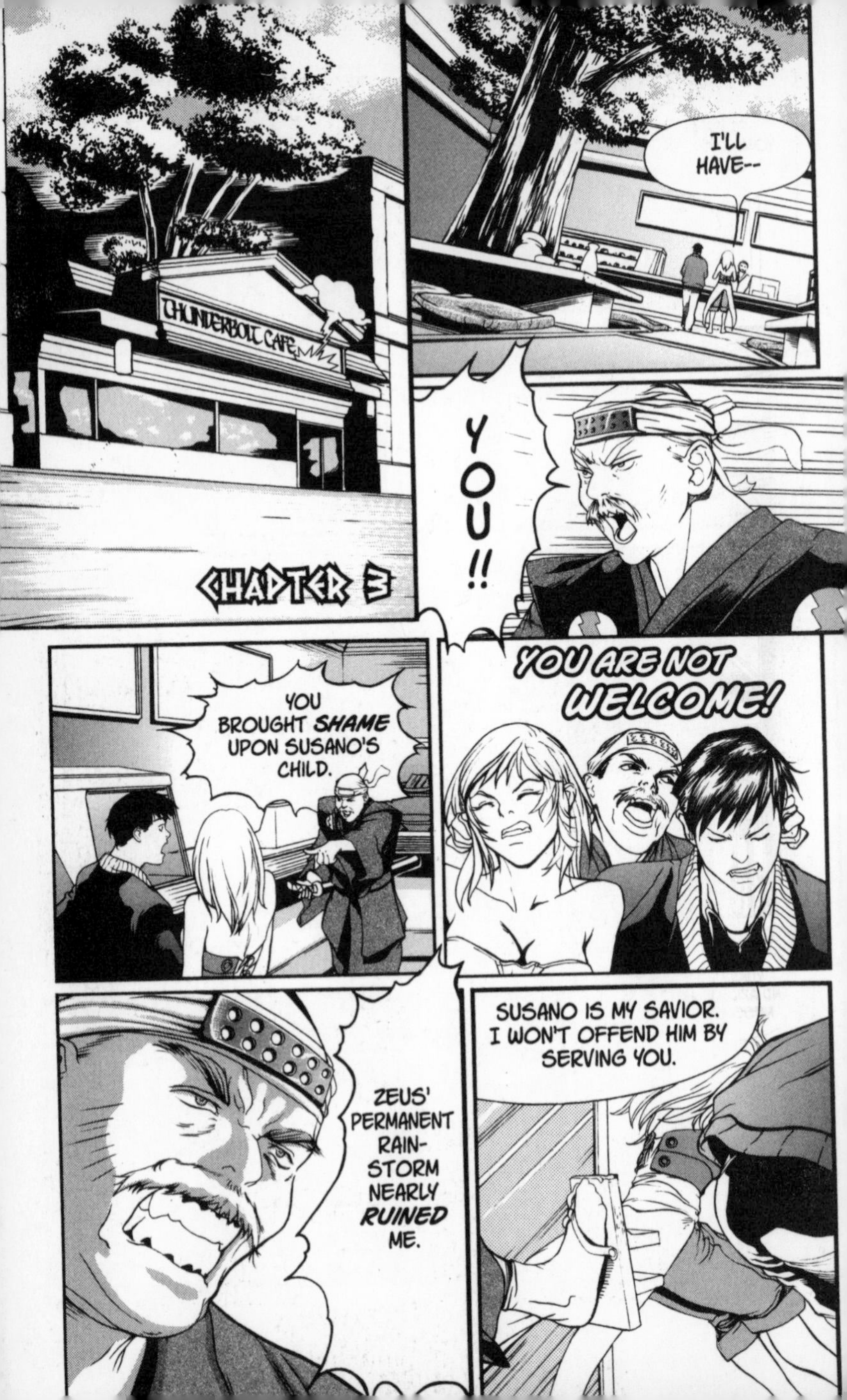

THUNDERBOLT CAFE
CHAPTER 3
I'LL HAVE--
YOU!!
YOU BROUGHT SHAME UPON SUSANO'S CHILD.
YOU ARE NOT WELCOME!
ZEUS' PERMANENT RAIN-STORM NEARLY RUINED ME.
SUSANO IS MY SAVIOR. I WON'T OFFEND HIM BY SERVING YOU.

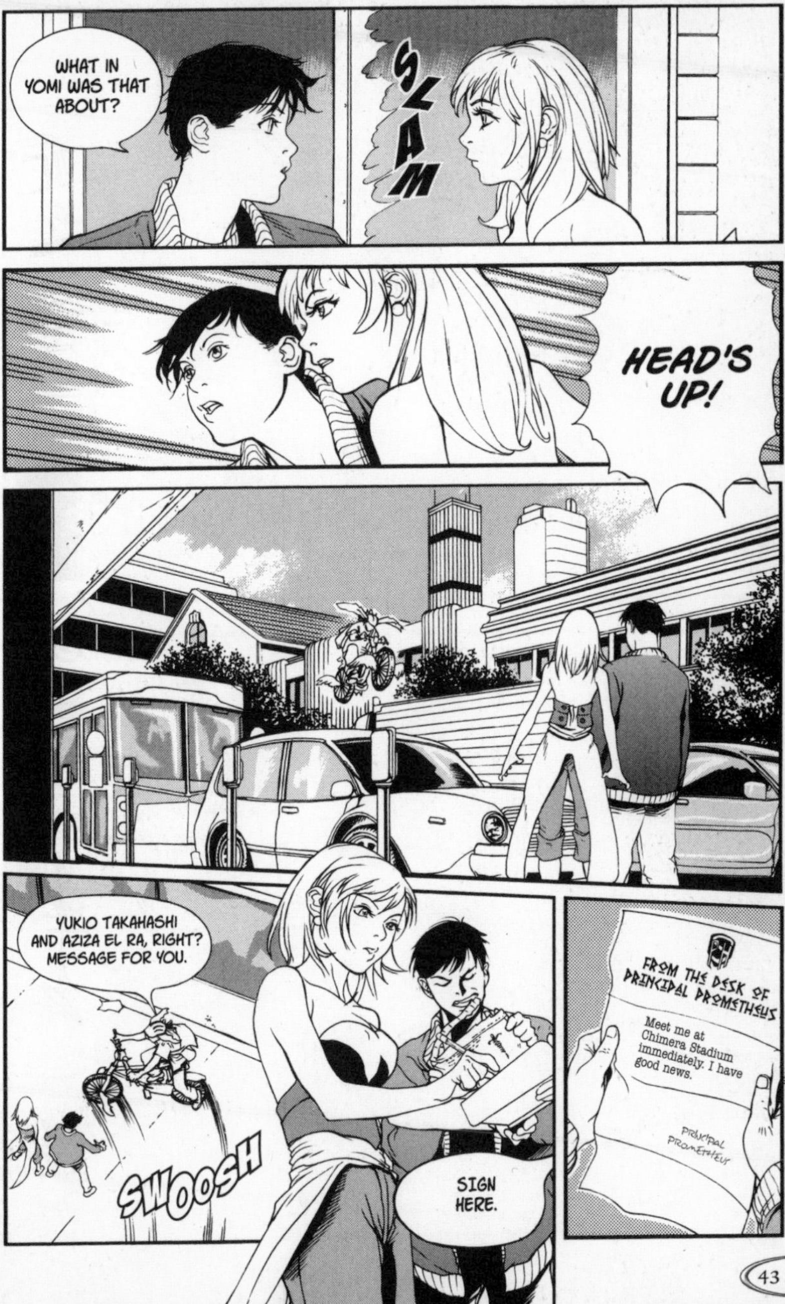
WHAT IN YOMI WAS THAT ABOUT?
SLAM
HEAD'S UP!
YUKIO TAKAHASHI AND AZIZA EL RA, RIGHT? MESSAGE FOR YOU.
SWOOSH
SIGN HERE.
FROM THE DESK OF PRINCIPAL PROMETHEUS
Meet me at Chimera Stadium immediately. I have good news.
PRINCIPAL PROMETHEUS

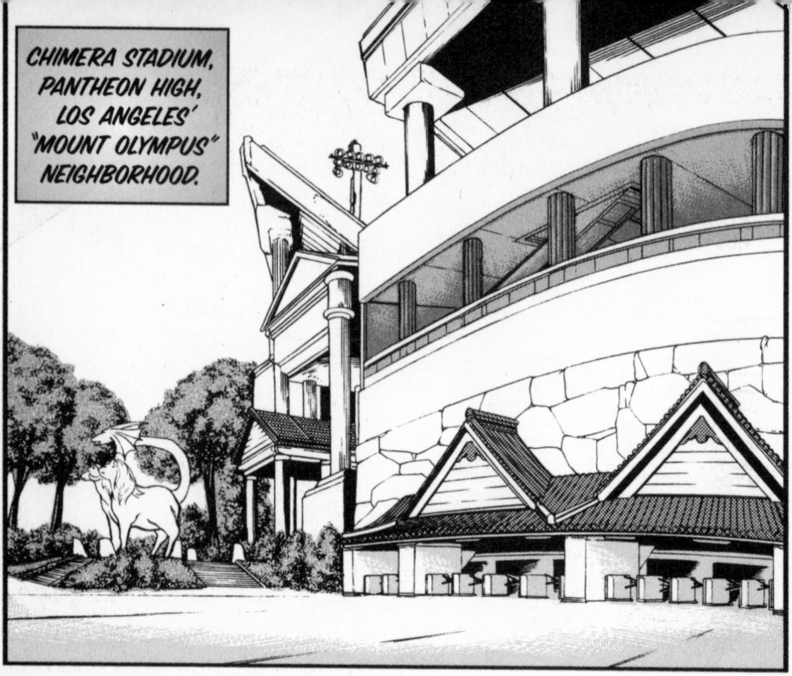
CHIMERA STADIUM, PANTHEON HIGH, LOS ANGELES' "MOUNT OLYMPUS" NEIGHBORHOOD.

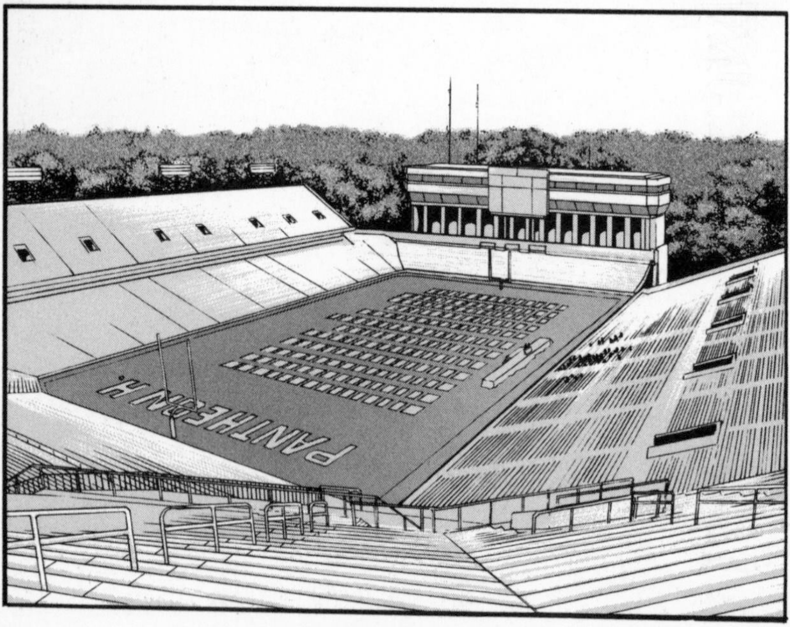
PANTHEON H.

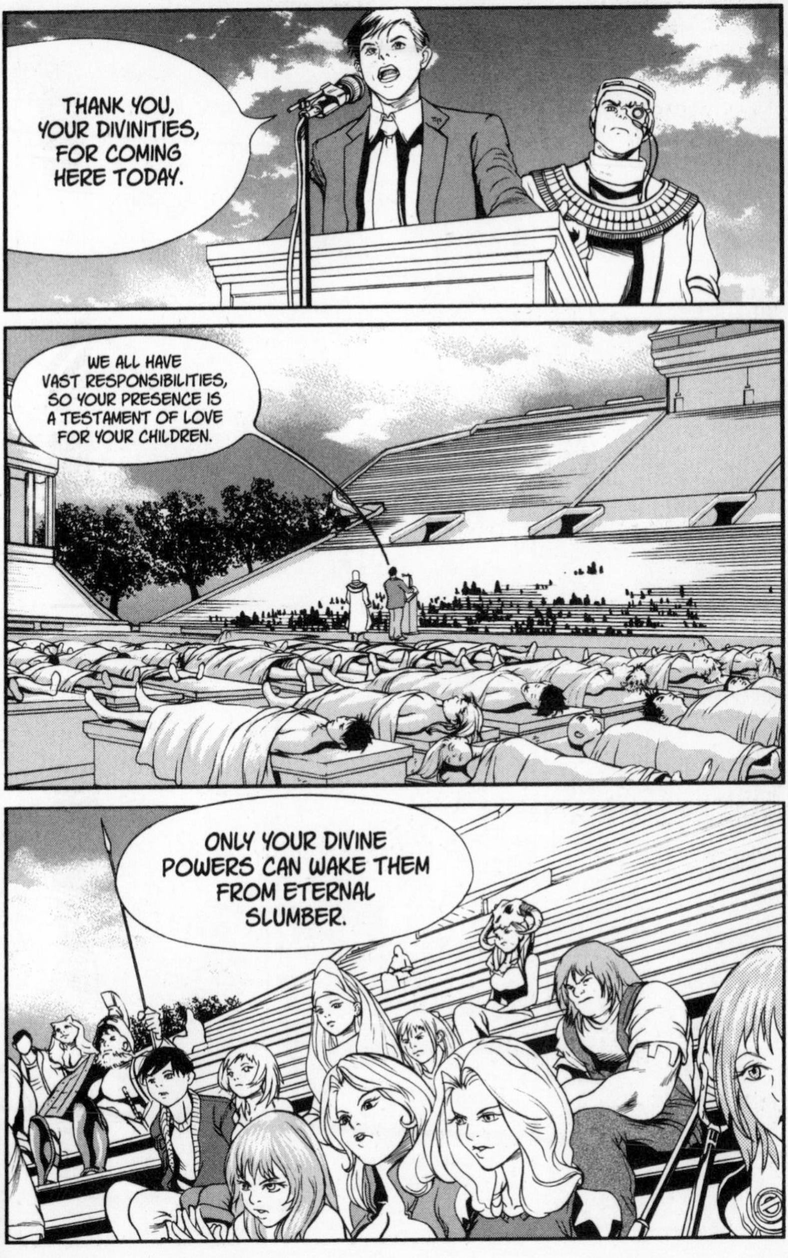
THANK YOU, YOUR DIVINITIES, FOR COMING HERE TODAY.
WE ALL HAVE VAST RESPONSIBILITIES, SO YOUR PRESENCE IS A TESTAMENT OF LOVE FOR YOUR CHILDREN.
ONLY YOUR DIVINE POWERS CAN WAKE THEM FROM ETERNAL SLUMBER.

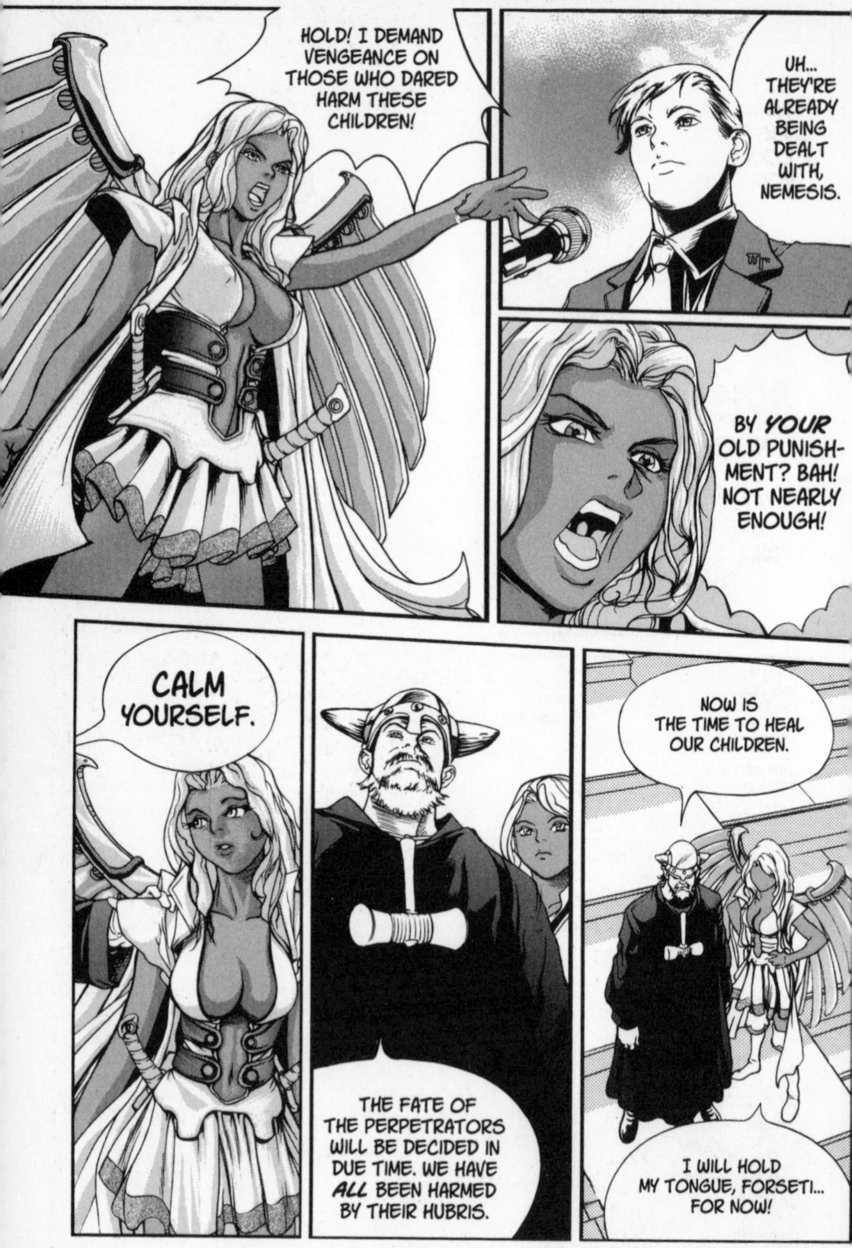
HOLD! I DEMAND VENGEANCE ON THOSE WHO DARED HARM THESE CHILDREN!
UH... THEY'RE ALREADY BEING DEALT WITH, NEMESIS.
BY *YOUR* OLD PUNISHMENT? BAH! NOT NEARLY ENOUGH!
CALM YOURSELF.
THE FATE OF THE PERPETRATORS WILL BE DECIDED IN DUE TIME. WE HAVE *ALL* BEEN HARMED BY THEIR HUBRIS.
NOW IS THE TIME TO HEAL OUR CHILDREN.
I WILL HOLD MY TONGUE, FORSETI... FOR NOW!

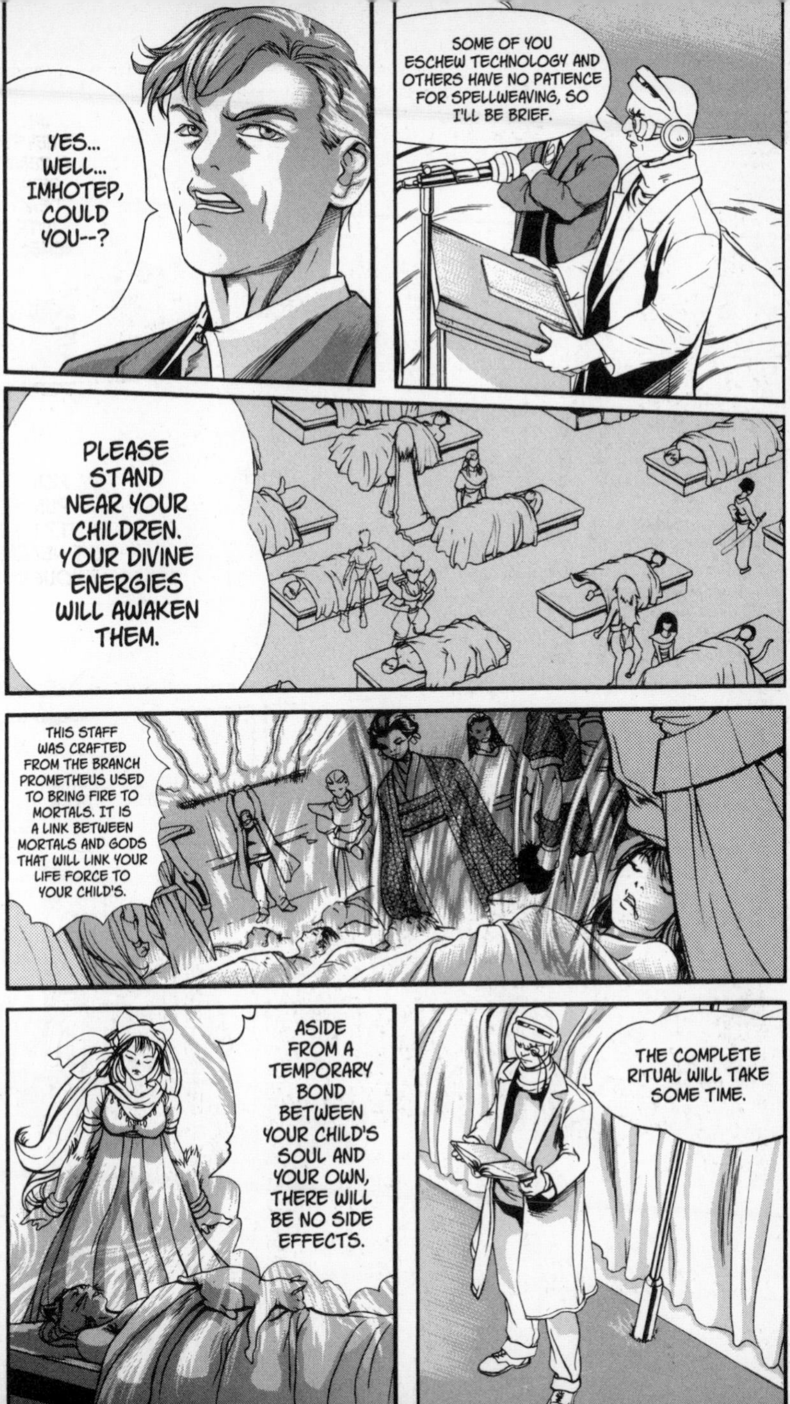
YES... WELL... IMHOTEP, COULD YOU--?
SOME OF YOU ESCHEW TECHNOLOGY AND OTHERS HAVE NO PATIENCE FOR SPELLWEAVING, SO I'LL BE BRIEF.
PLEASE STAND NEAR YOUR CHILDREN. YOUR DIVINE ENERGIES WILL AWAKEN THEM.
THIS STAFF WAS CRAFTED FROM THE BRANCH PROMETHEUS USED TO BRING FIRE TO MORTALS. IT IS A LINK BETWEEN MORTALS AND GODS THAT WILL LINK YOUR LIFE FORCE TO YOUR CHILD'S.
ASIDE FROM A TEMPORARY BOND BETWEEN YOUR CHILD'S SOUL AND YOUR OWN, THERE WILL BE NO SIDE EFFECTS.
THE COMPLETE RITUAL WILL TAKE SOME TIME.

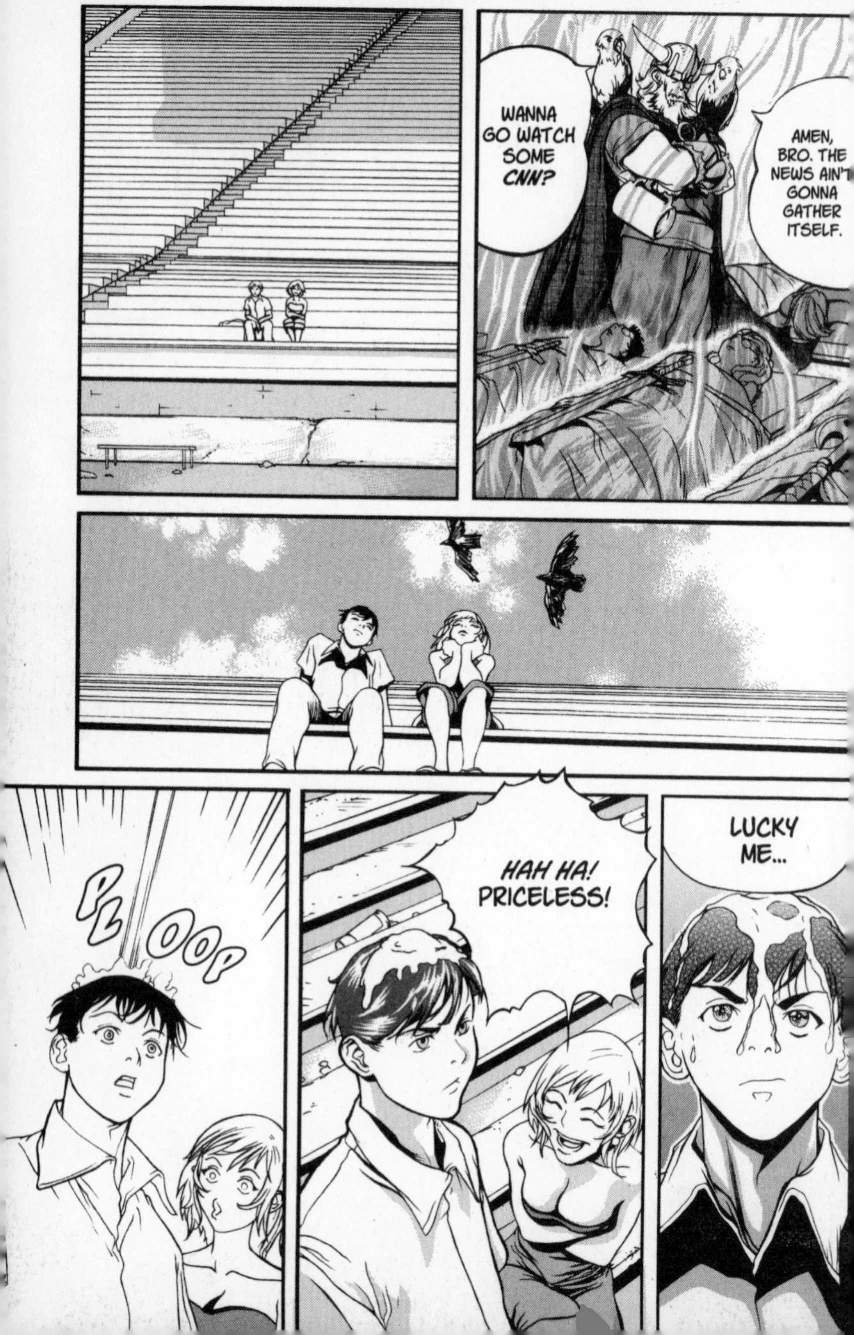
WANNA GO WATCH SOME CNN?
AMEN, BRO. THE NEWS AIN'T GONNA GATHER ITSELF.
PLOOP
HAH HA! PRICELESS!
LUCKY ME...

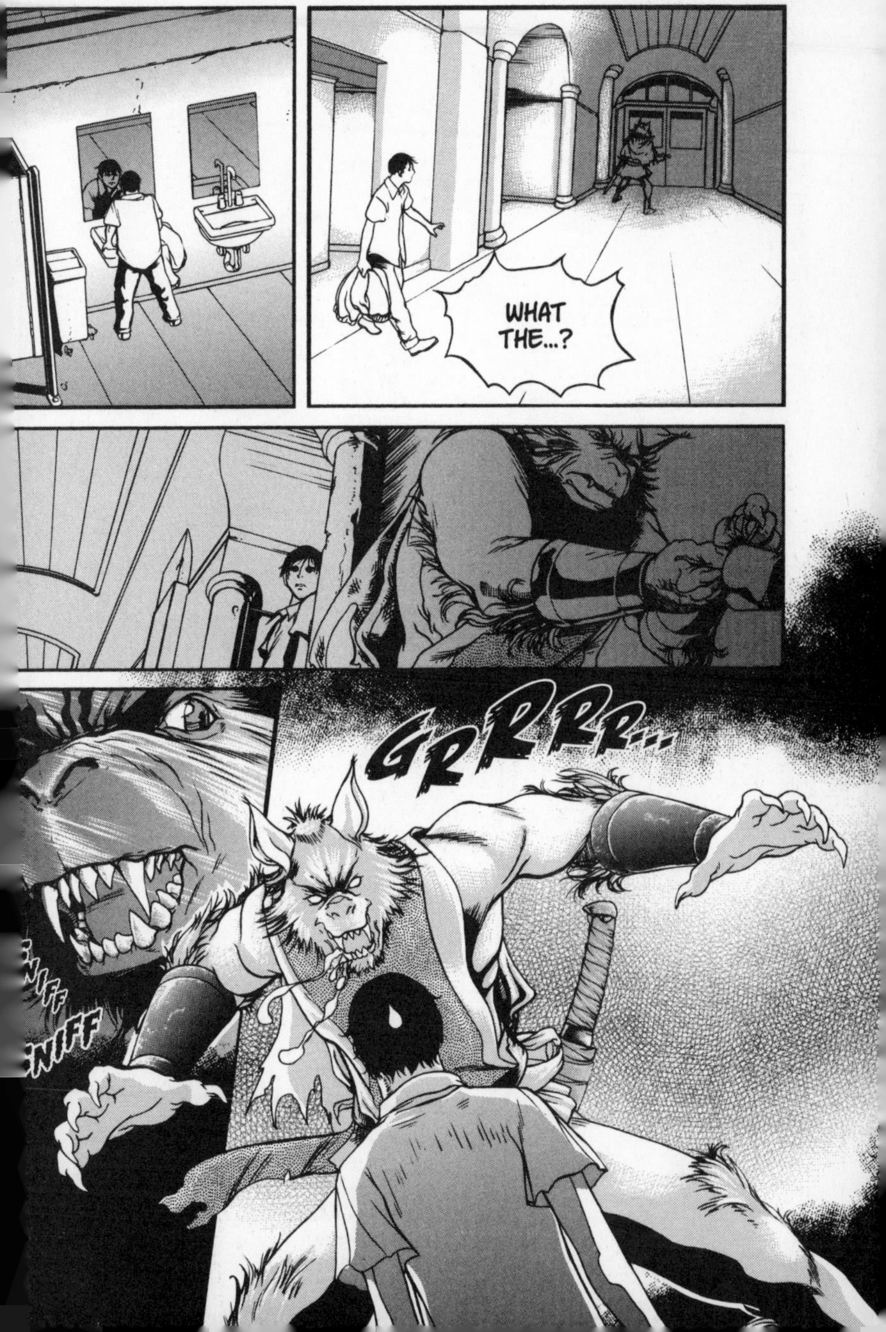
WHAT THE...?
GRRRR...
SNIFF
SNIFF

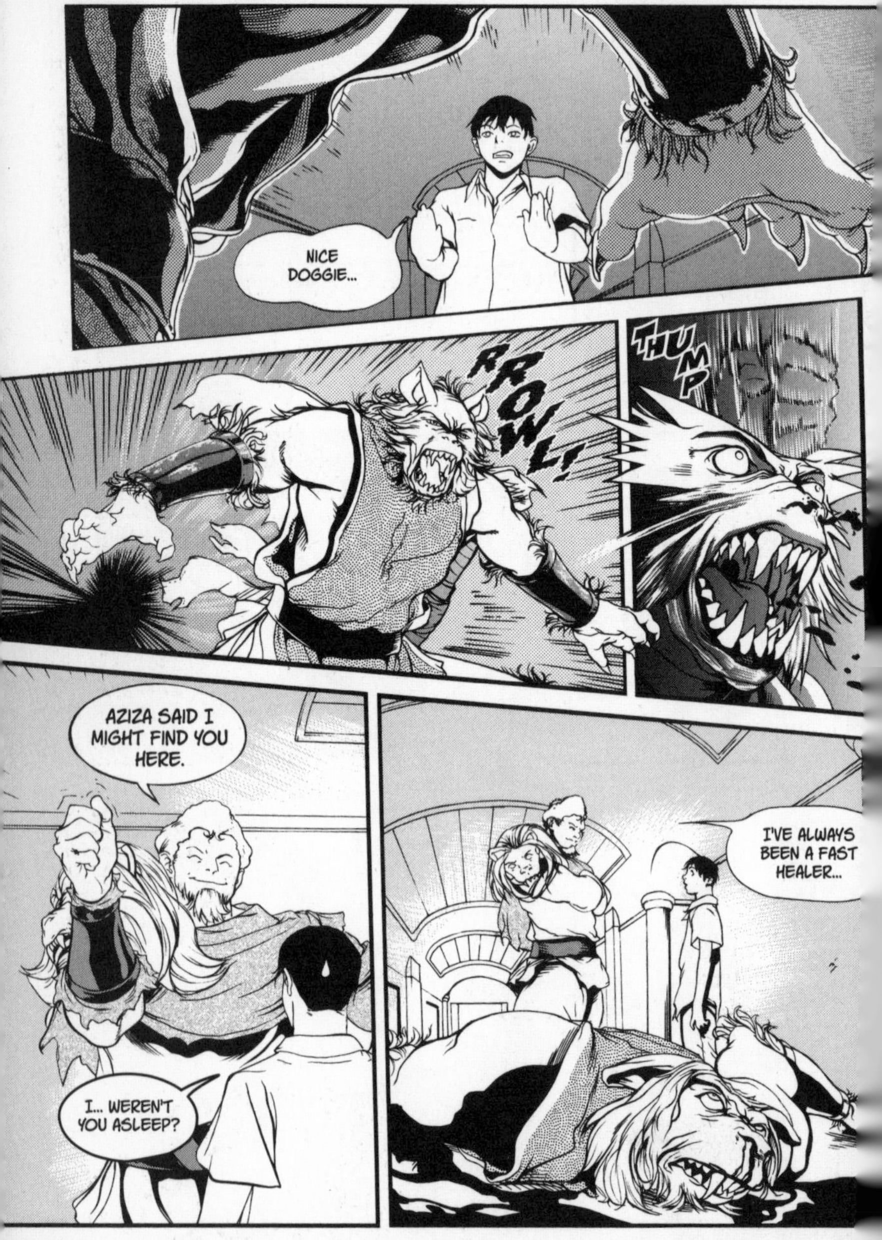
NICE DOGGIE...
RROWL!!
THUMP
AZIZA SAID I MIGHT FIND YOU HERE.
I... WEREN'T YOU ASLEEP?
I'VE ALWAYS BEEN A FAST HEALER...

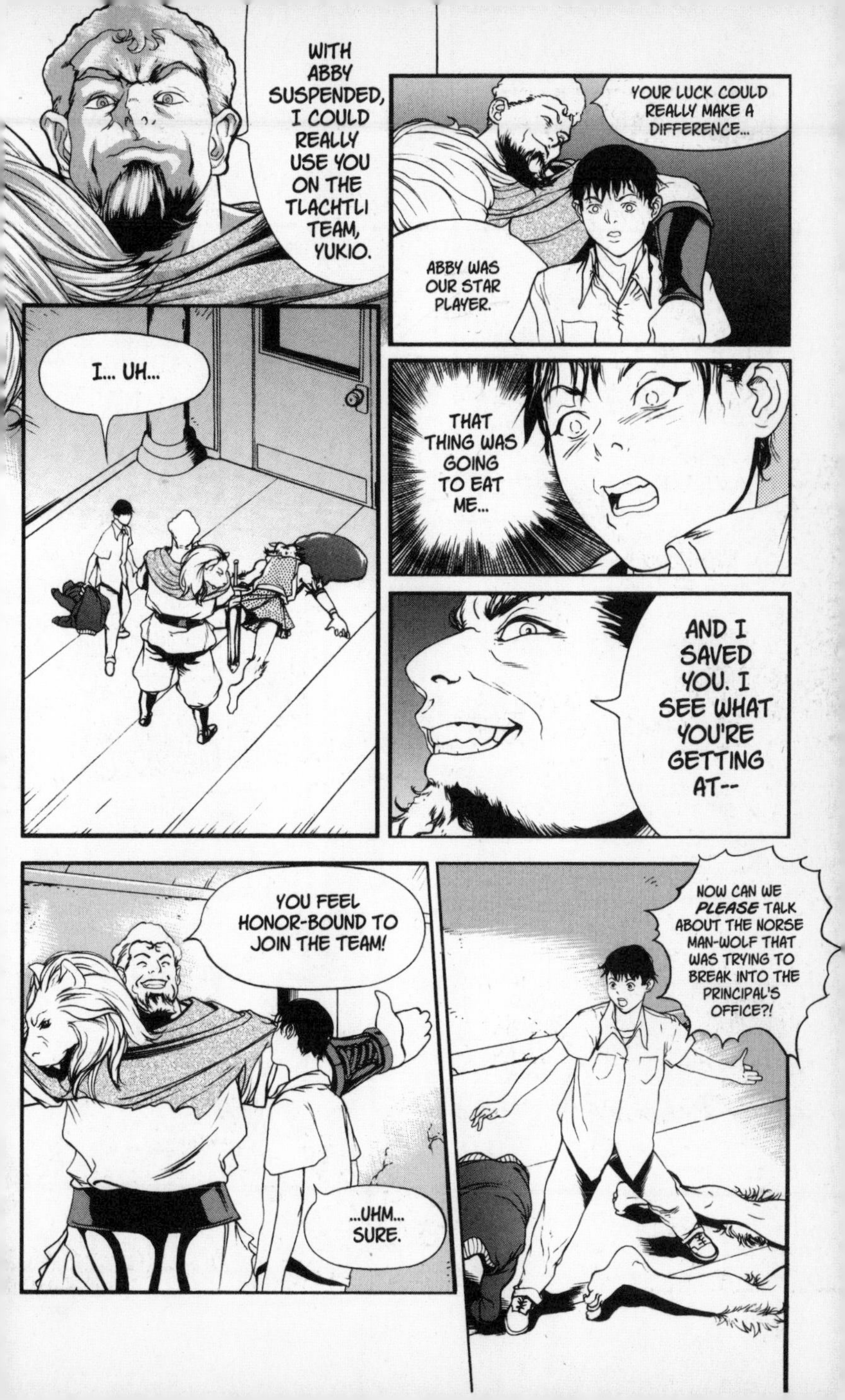
WITH ABBY SUSPENDED, I COULD REALLY USE YOU ON THE TLACHTLI TEAM, YUKIO.
YOUR LUCK COULD REALLY MAKE A DIFFERENCE...
ABBY WAS OUR STAR PLAYER.
I... UH...
THAT THING WAS GOING TO EAT ME...
AND I SAVED YOU. I SEE WHAT YOU'RE GETTING AT--
YOU FEEL HONOR-BOUND TO JOIN THE TEAM!
...UHM... SURE.
NOW CAN WE *PLEASE* TALK ABOUT THE NORSE MAN-WOLF THAT WAS TRYING TO BREAK INTO THE PRINCIPAL'S OFFICE?!

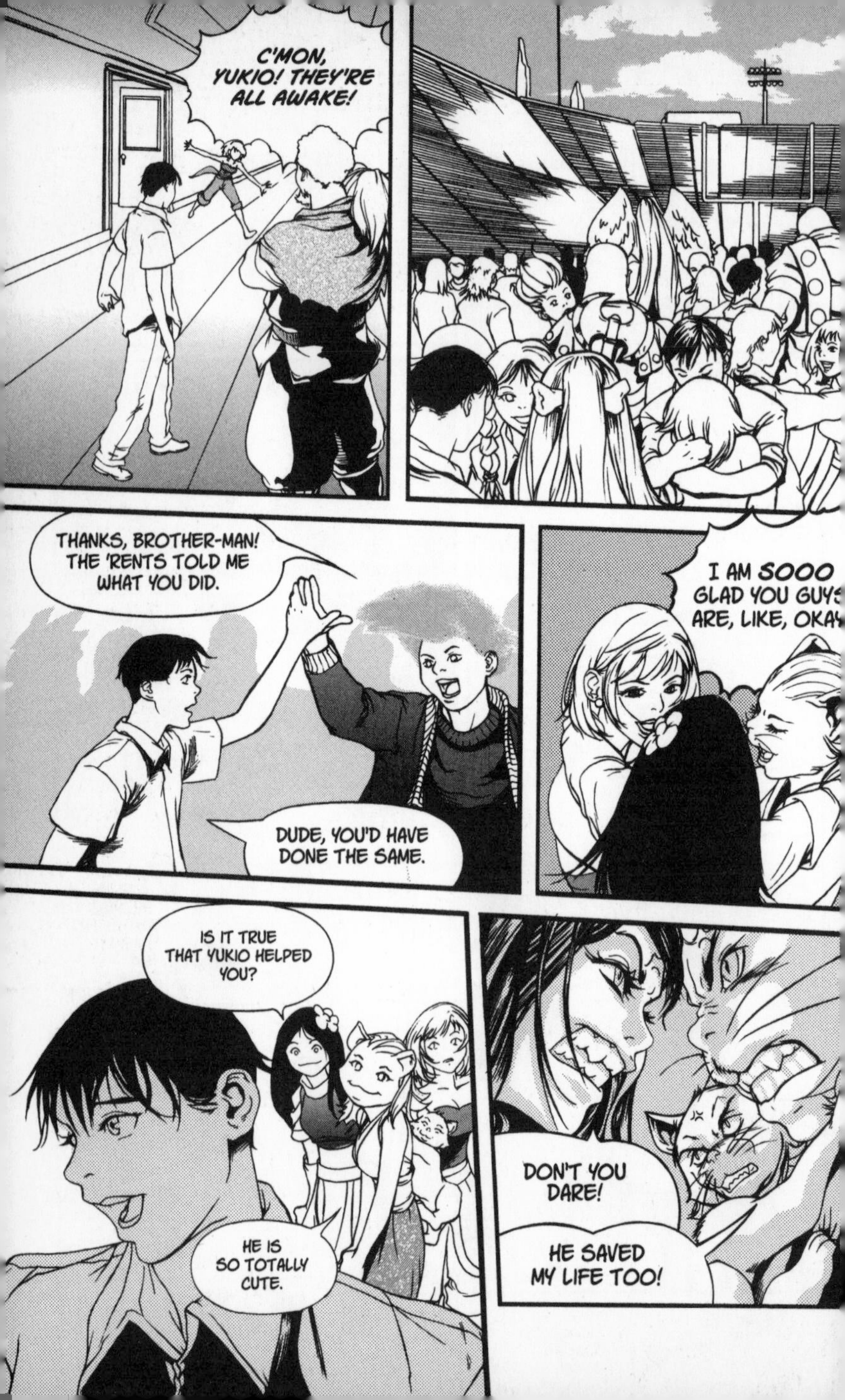
C'MON, YUKIO! THEY'RE ALL AWAKE!
THANKS, BROTHER-MAN! THE 'RENTS TOLD ME WHAT YOU DID.
DUDE, YOU'D HAVE DONE THE SAME.
I AM SOOO GLAD YOU GUYS ARE, LIKE, OKAY
IS IT TRUE THAT YUKIO HELPED YOU?
HE IS SO TOTALLY CUTE.
DON'T YOU DARE!
HE SAVED MY LIFE TOO!

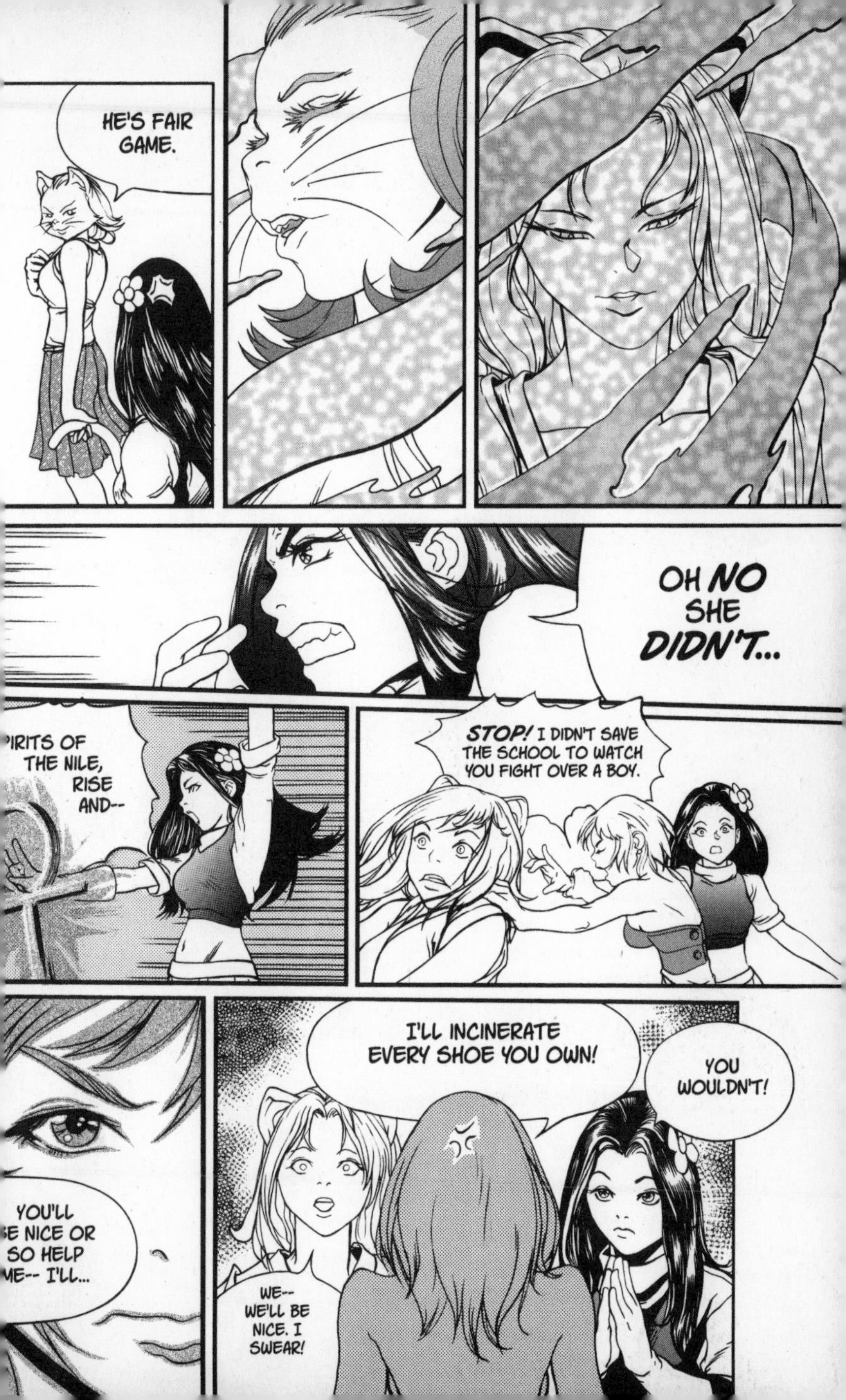
HE'S FAIR GAME.
OH NO SHE DIDN'T...
PIRITS OF THE NILE, RISE AND--
STOP! I DIDN'T SAVE THE SCHOOL TO WATCH YOU FIGHT OVER A BOY.
YOU'LL BE NICE OR SO HELP ME-- I'LL...
I'LL INCINERATE EVERY SHOE YOU OWN!
YOU WOULDN'T!
WE-- WE'LL BE NICE. I SWEAR!

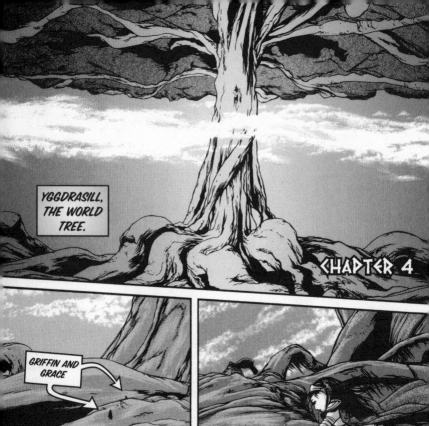

YGGDRASILL, THE WORLD TREE.

CHAPTER 4

GRIFFIN AND GRACE

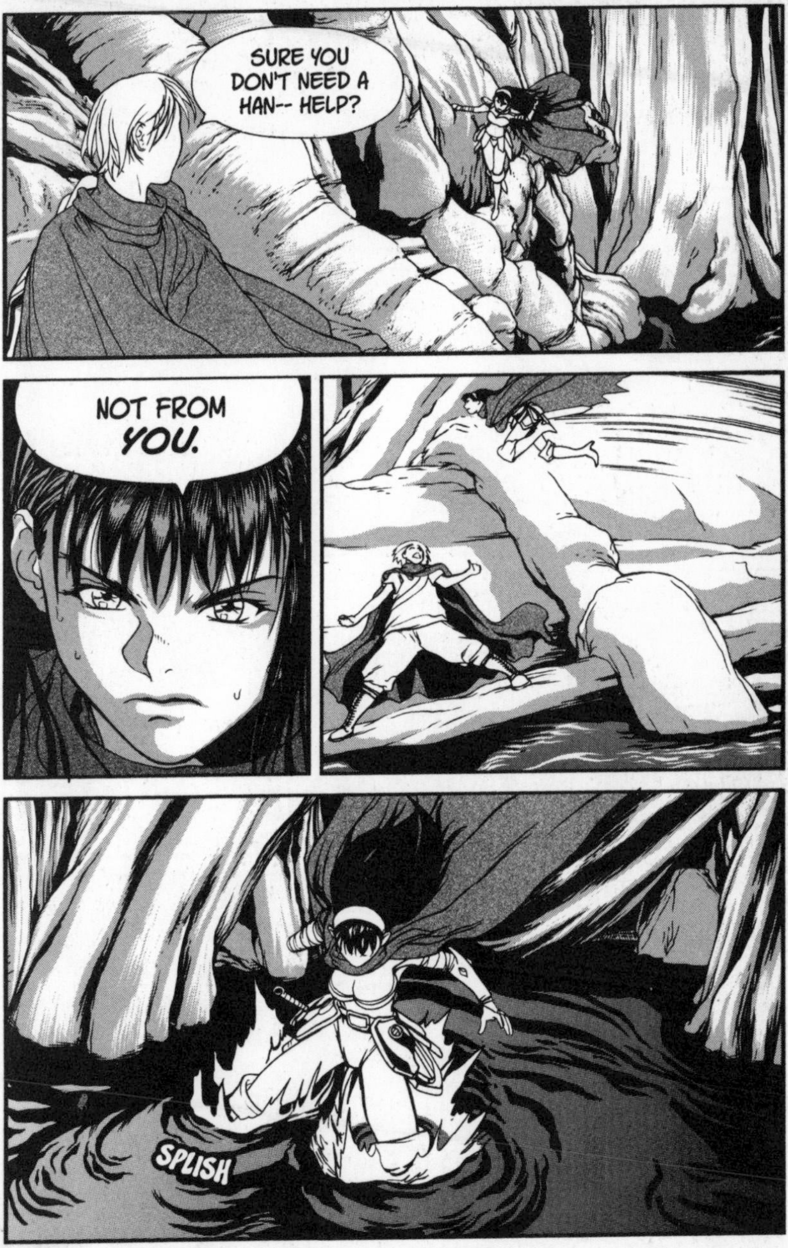
SURE YOU DON'T NEED A HAN-- HELP?
NOT FROM YOU.
SPLISH

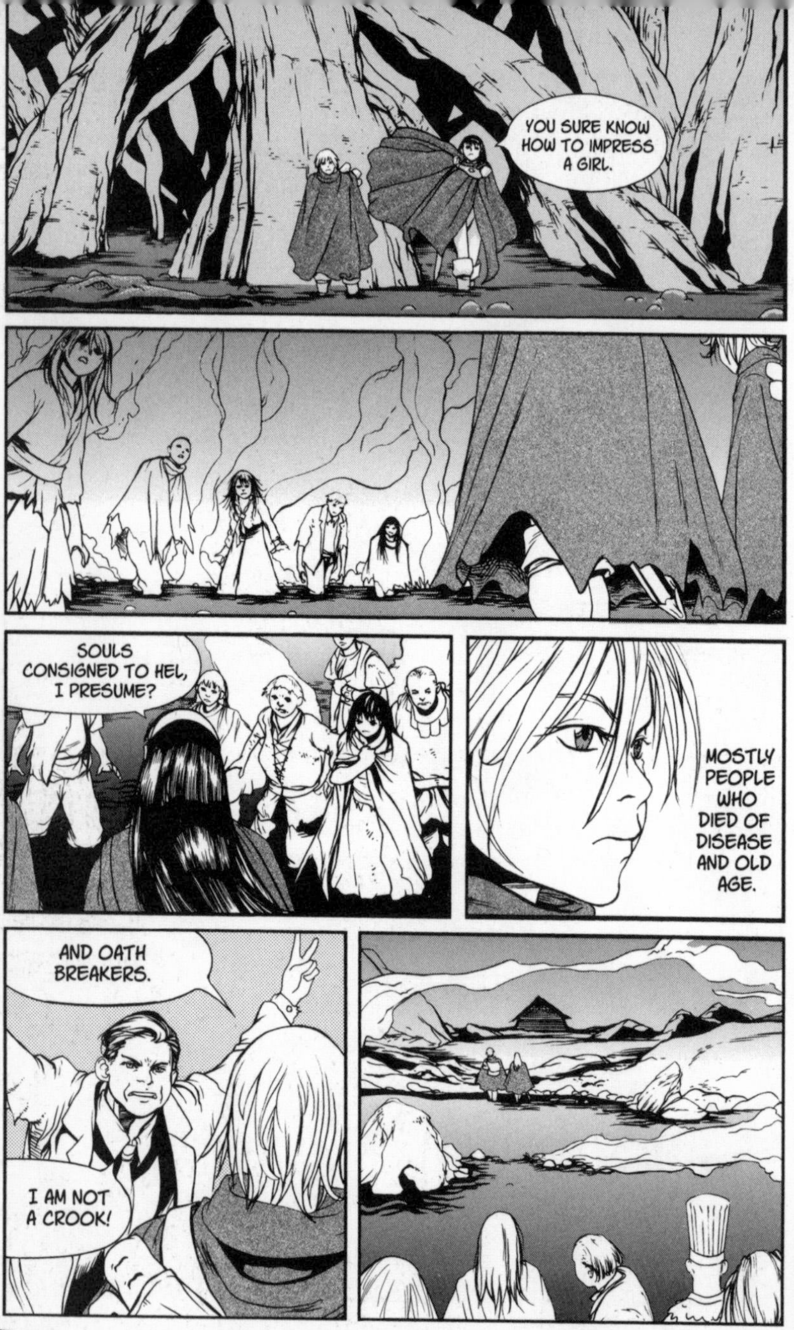
YOU SURE KNOW HOW TO IMPRESS A GIRL.
SOULS CONSIGNED TO HEL, I PRESUME?
MOSTLY PEOPLE WHO DIED OF DISEASE AND OLD AGE.
AND OATH BREAKERS.
I AM NOT A CROOK!

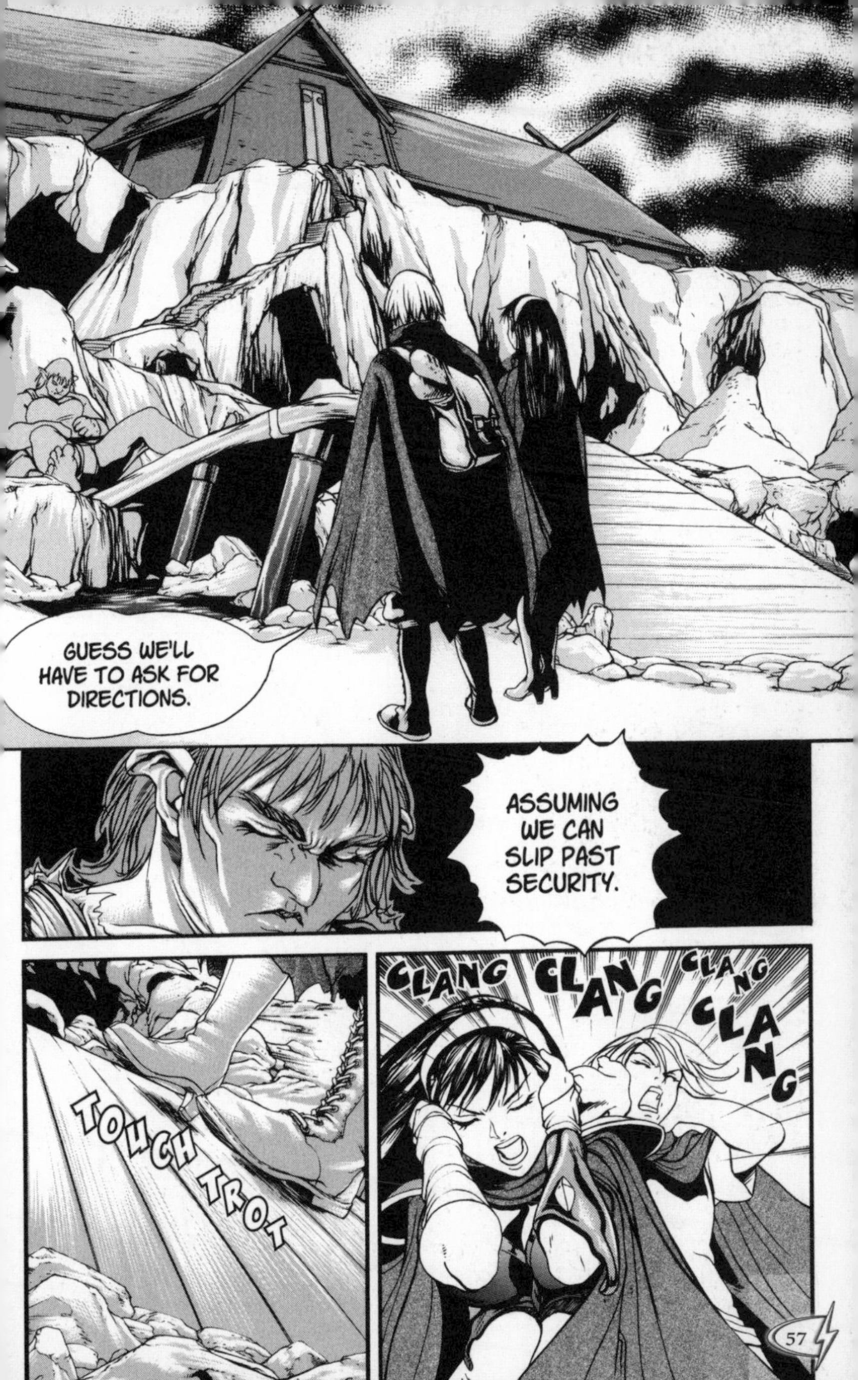
GUESS WE'LL HAVE TO ASK FOR DIRECTIONS.
ASSUMING WE CAN SLIP PAST SECURITY.
TOUCH TROT
CLANG CLANG CLANG CLANG CLANG

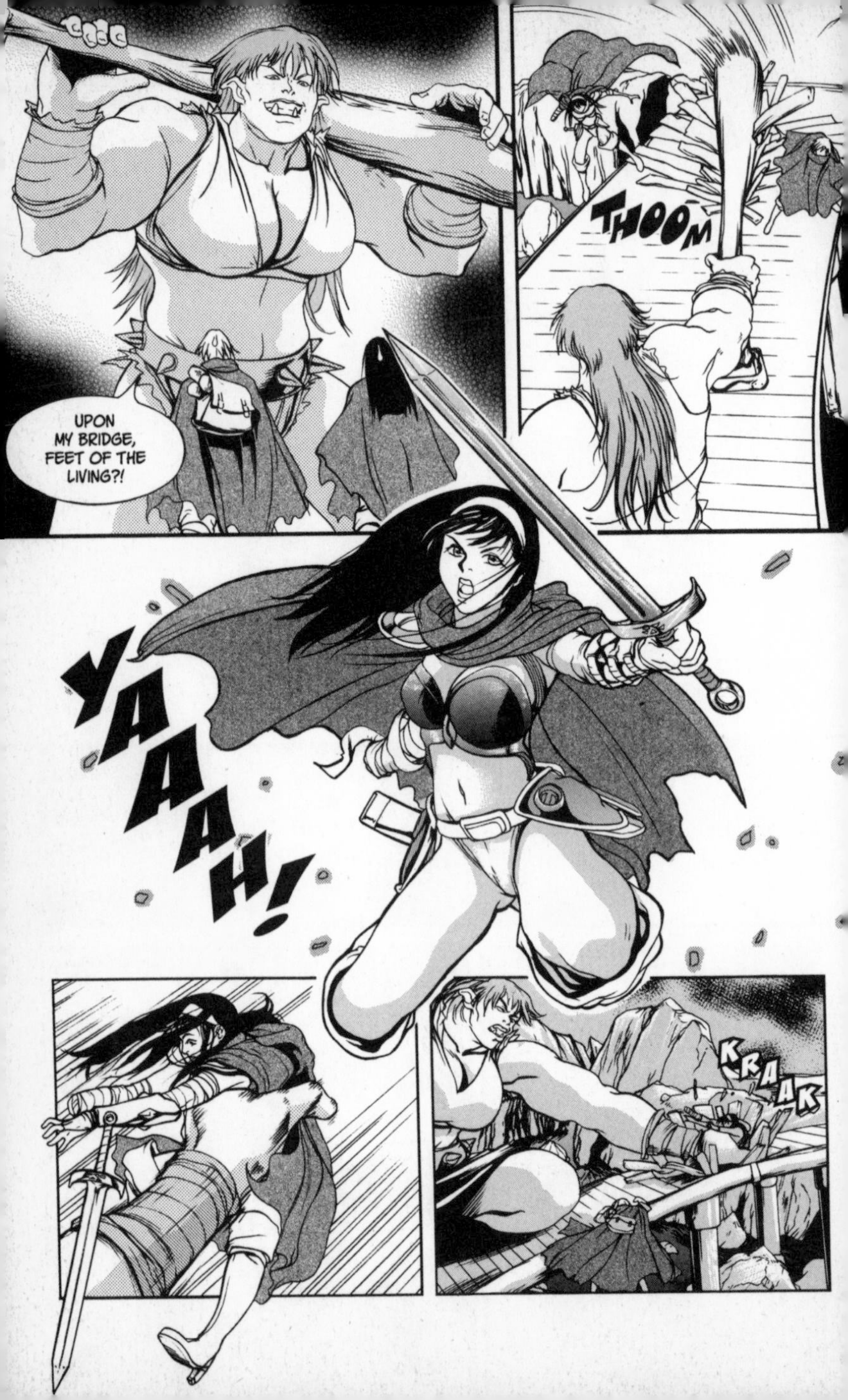
UPON MY BRIDGE, FEET OF THE LIVING?!
THOOM
YAAAAH!
KRAAK

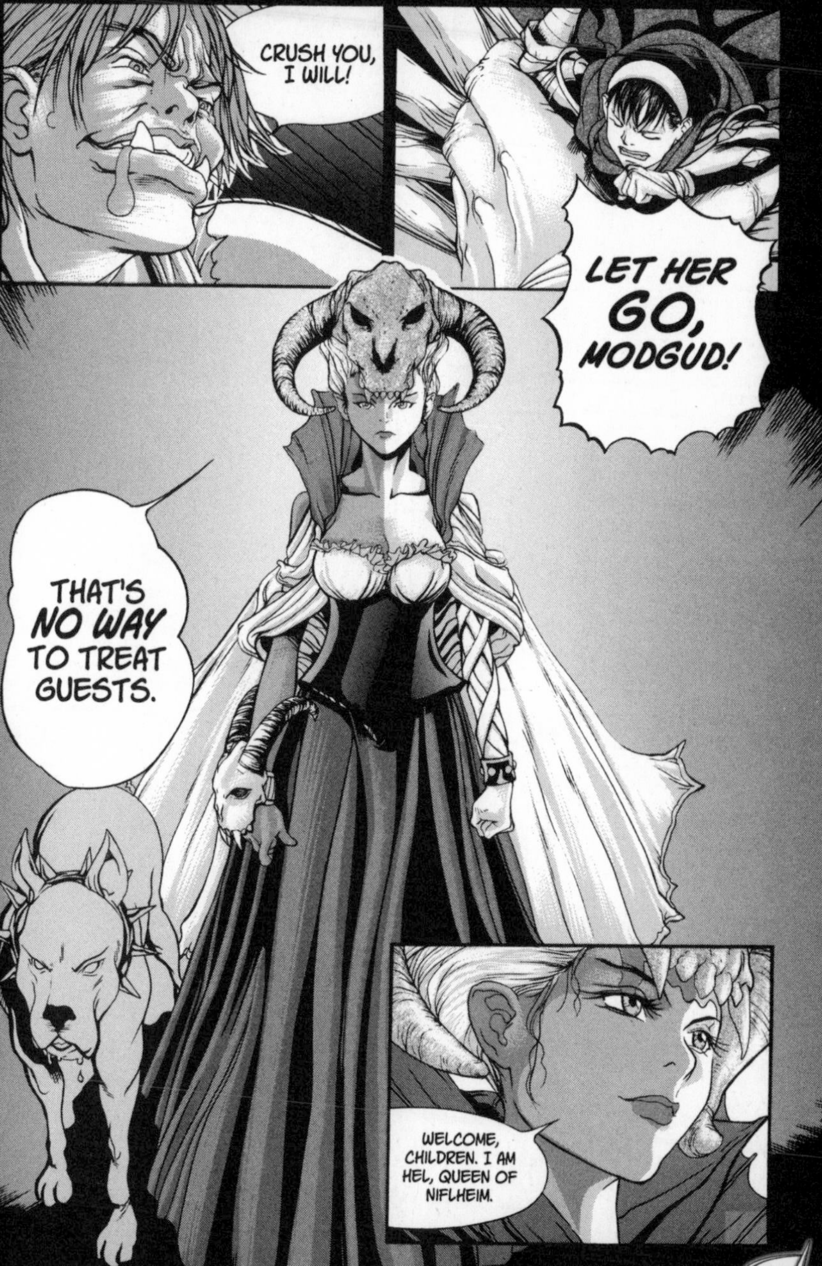

CRUSH YOU, I WILL!
LET HER GO, MODGUD!
THAT'S NO WAY TO TREAT GUESTS.
WELCOME, CHILDREN. I AM HEL, QUEEN OF NIFLHEIM.

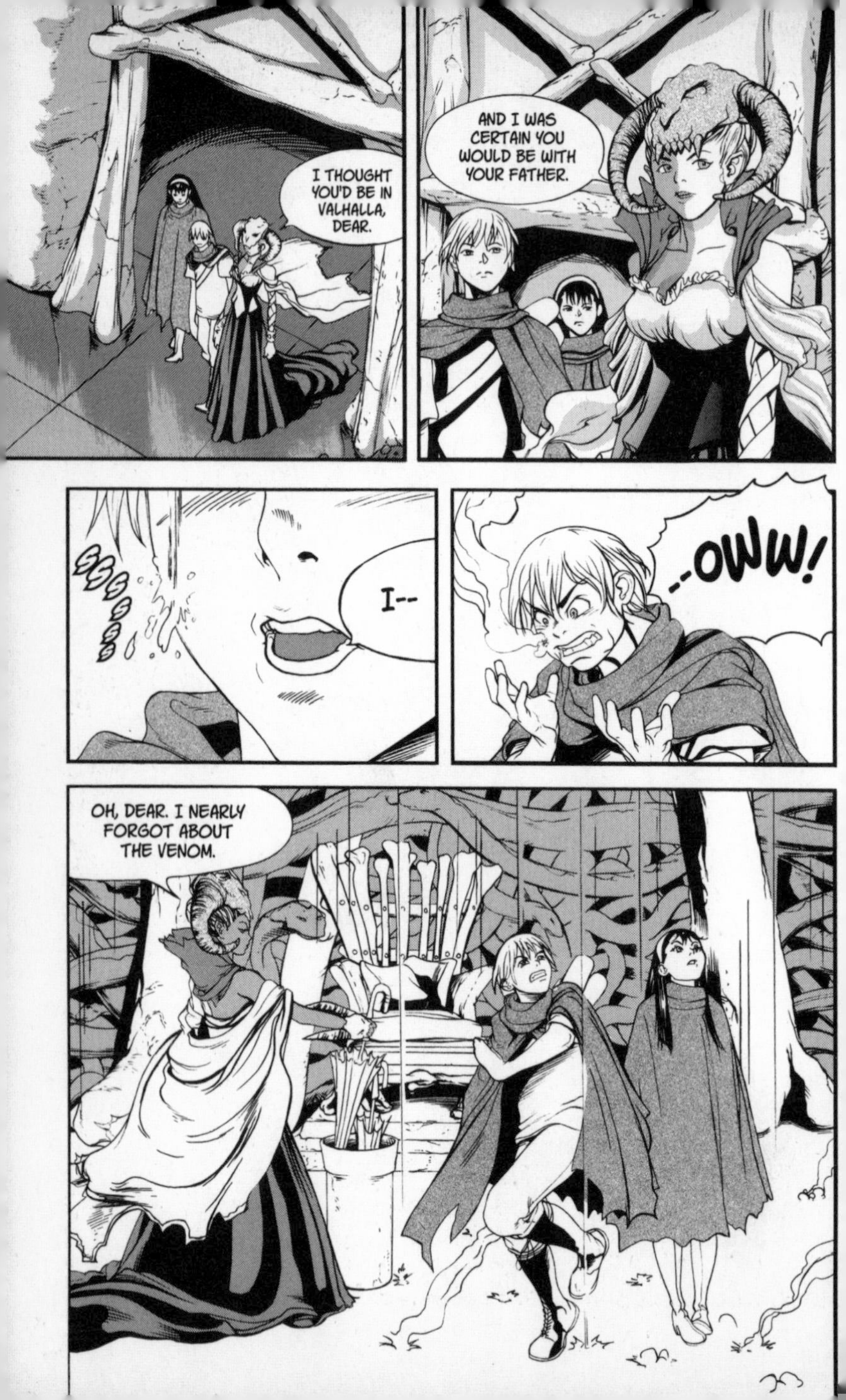
I THOUGHT YOU'D BE IN VALHALLA, DEAR.
AND I WAS CERTAIN YOU WOULD BE WITH YOUR FATHER.
SSSSSSS
I--
--OWW!
OH, DEAR. I NEARLY FORGOT ABOUT THE VENOM.

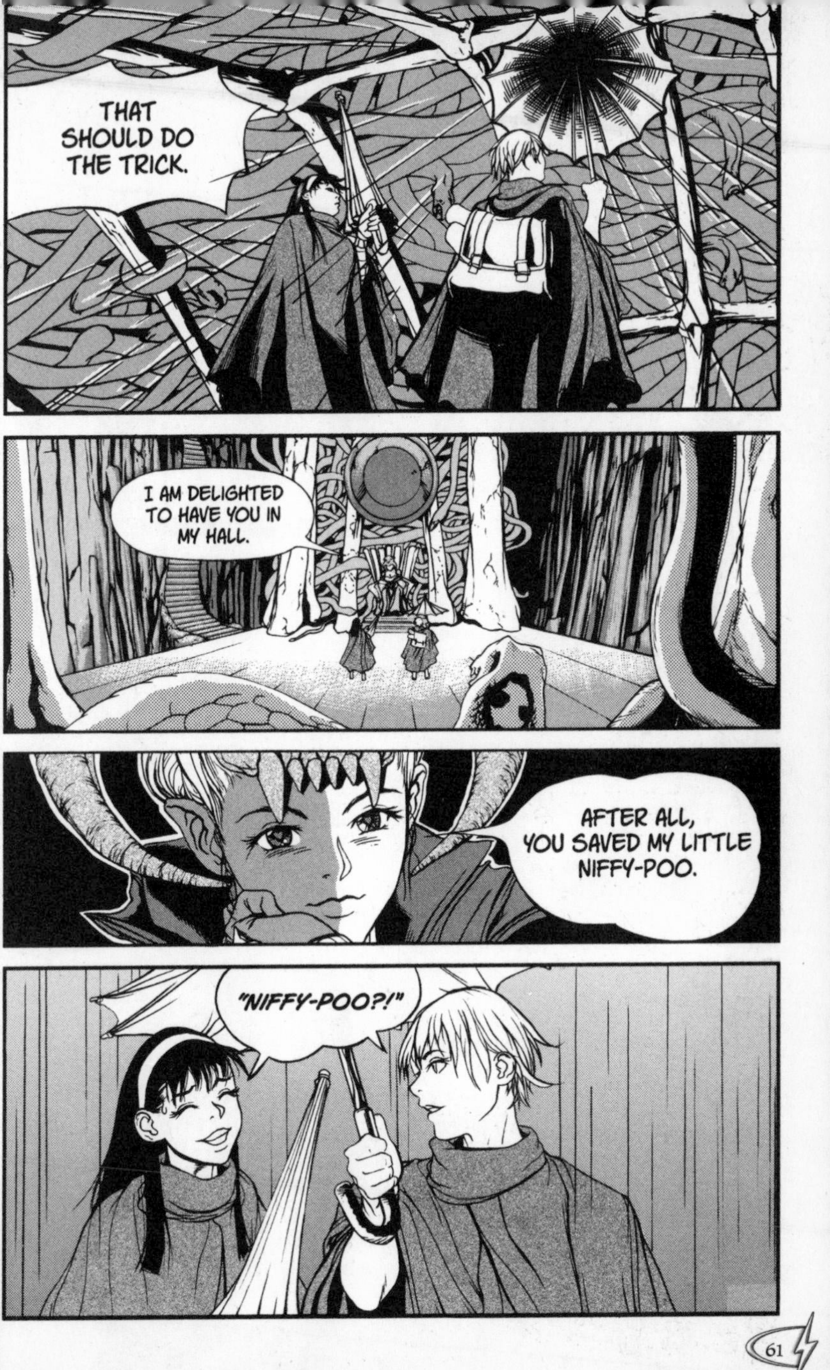
THAT SHOULD DO THE TRICK.
I AM DELIGHTED TO HAVE YOU IN MY HALL.
AFTER ALL, YOU SAVED MY LITTLE NIFFY-POO.
"NIFFY-POO?!"

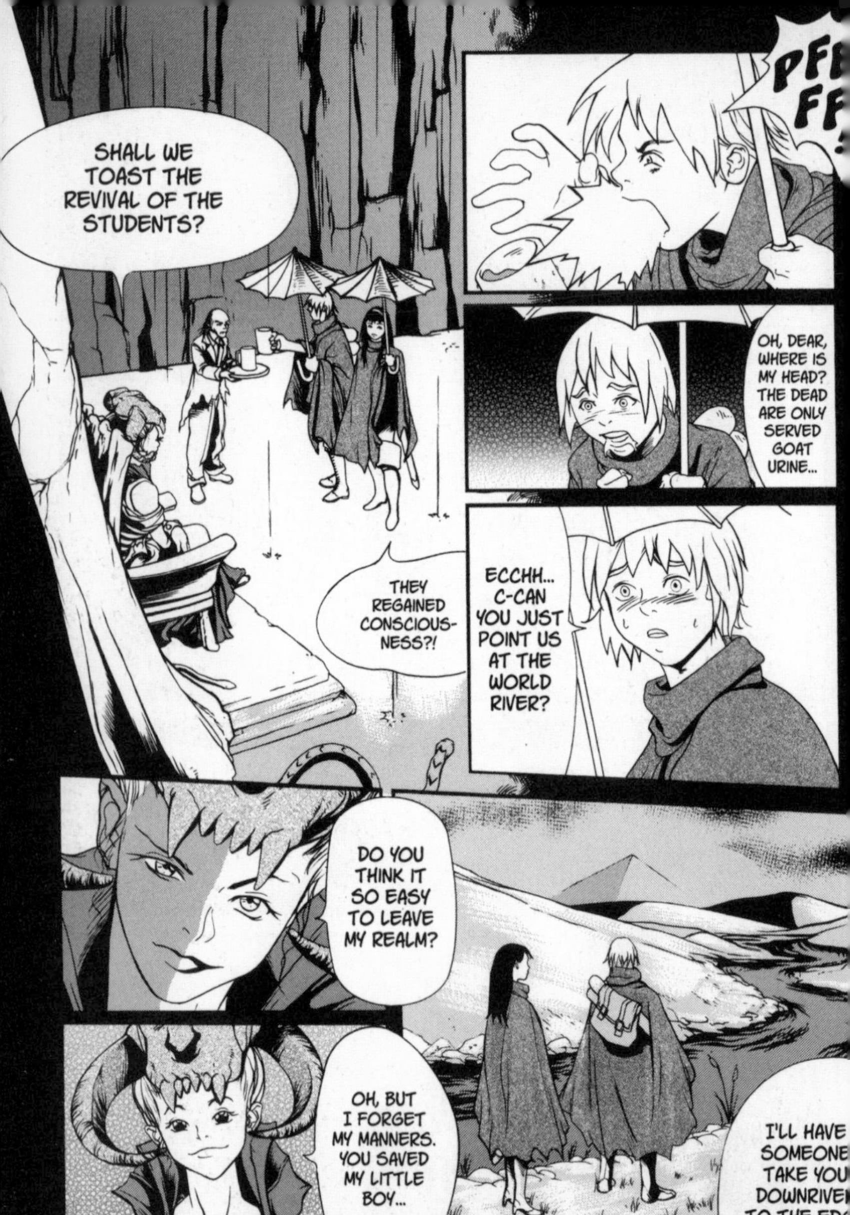
SHALL WE TOAST THE REVIVAL OF THE STUDENTS?
THEY REGAINED CONSCIOUS-NESS?!
PFF FF
OH, DEAR, WHERE IS MY HEAD? THE DEAD ARE ONLY SERVED GOAT URINE...
ECCHH... C-CAN YOU JUST POINT US AT THE WORLD RIVER?
DO YOU THINK IT SO EASY TO LEAVE MY REALM?
OH, BUT I FORGET MY MANNERS. YOU SAVED MY LITTLE BOY...
I'LL HAVE SOMEONE TAKE YOU DOWNRIVE TO THE EDG OF DUAT, T EGYPTIAN

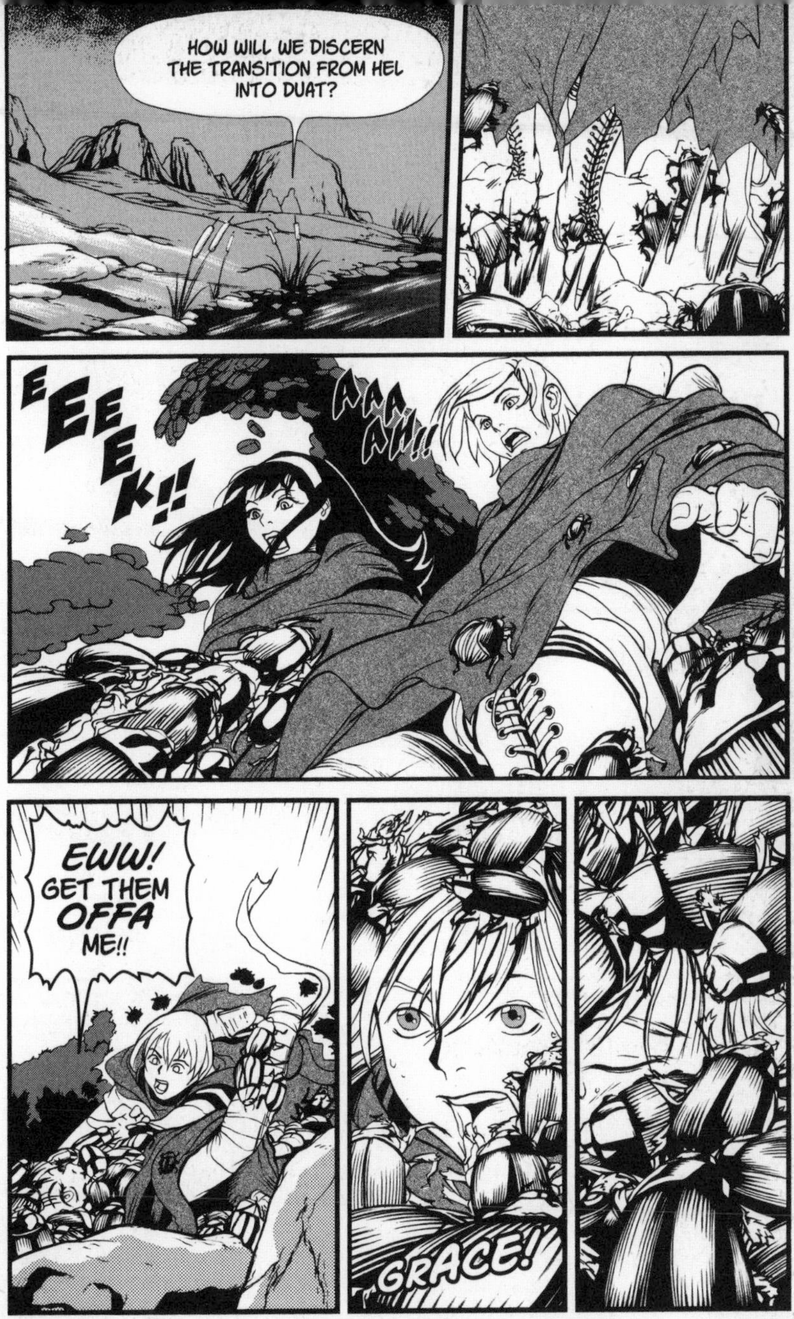
HOW WILL WE DISCERN THE TRANSITION FROM HEL INTO DUAT?
EEEEK!!
AAAAH!!
EWW! GET THEM OFFA ME!!
GRACE!

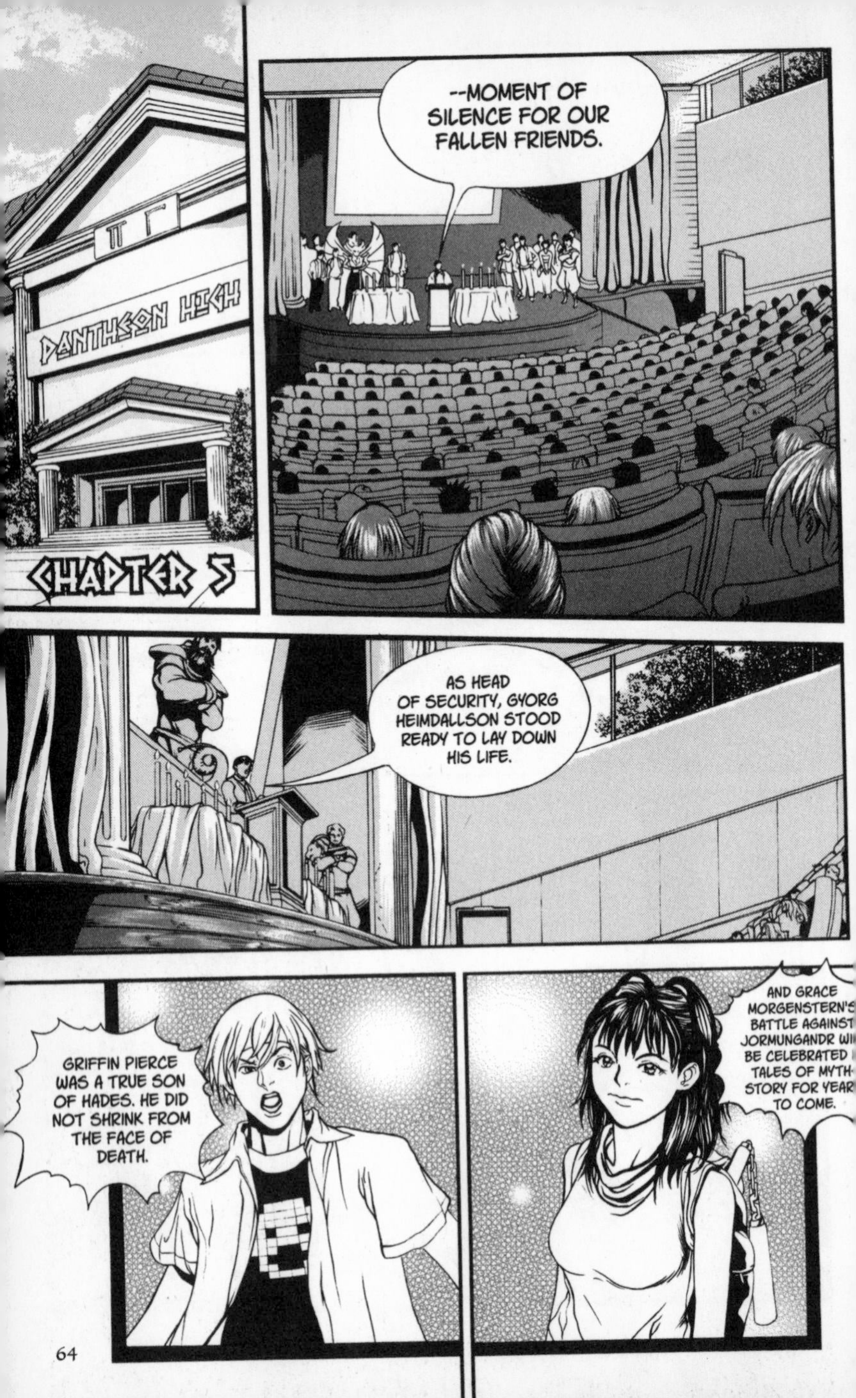
PANTHEON HIGH
CHAPTER 5
--MOMENT OF SILENCE FOR OUR FALLEN FRIENDS.
AS HEAD OF SECURITY, GYORG HEIMDALLSON STOOD READY TO LAY DOWN HIS LIFE.
GRIFFIN PIERCE WAS A TRUE SON OF HADES. HE DID NOT SHRINK FROM THE FACE OF DEATH.
AND GRACE MORGENSTERN'S BATTLE AGAINST JORMUNGANDR WI BE CELEBRATED TALES OF MYTH-STORY FOR YEAR TO COME.

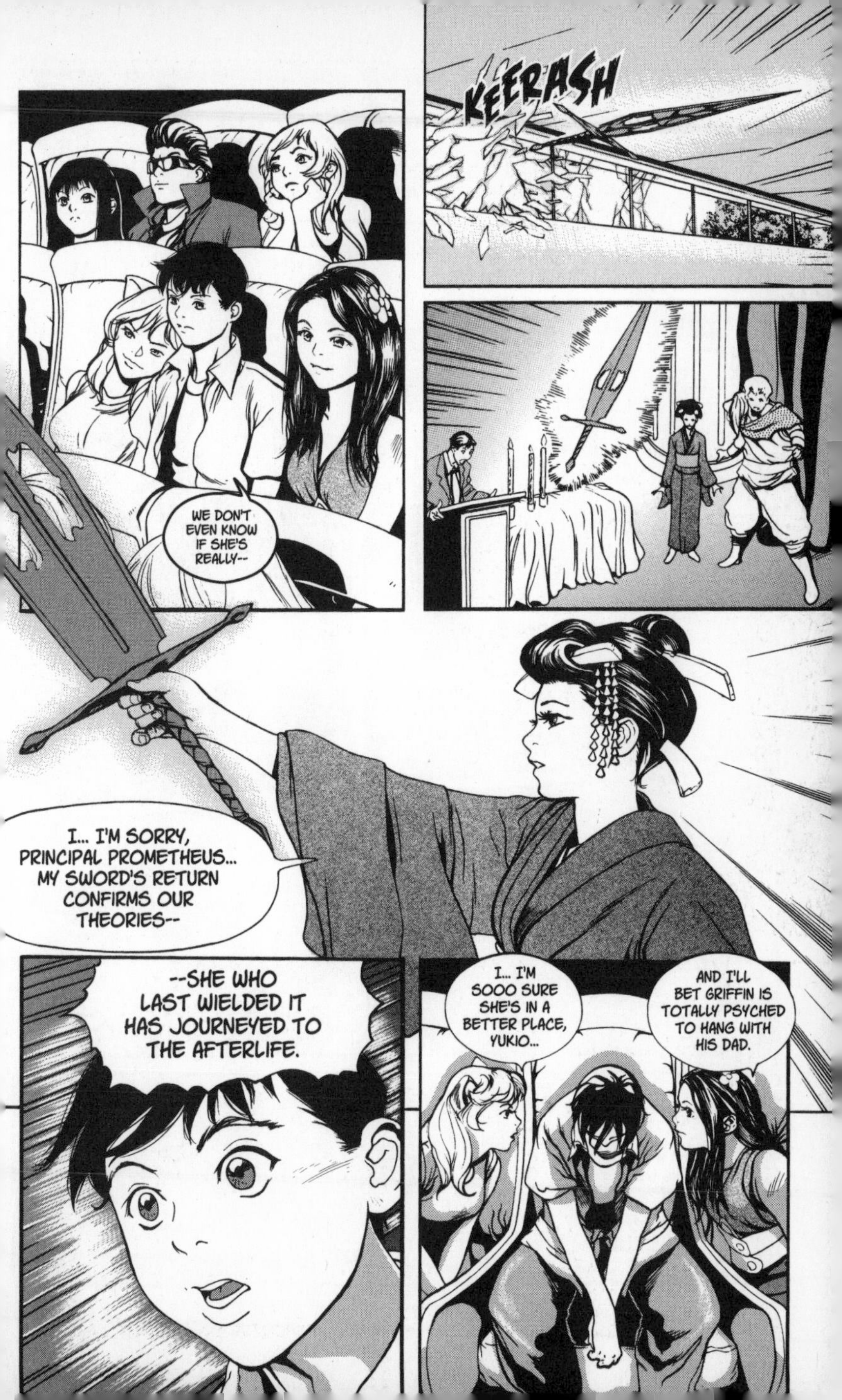
WE DON'T EVEN KNOW IF SHE'S REALLY--
KEERASH
I... I'M SORRY, PRINCIPAL PROMETHEUS... MY SWORD'S RETURN CONFIRMS OUR THEORIES--
--SHE WHO LAST WIELDED IT HAS JOURNEYED TO THE AFTERLIFE.
I... I'M SOOO SURE SHE'S IN A BETTER PLACE, YUKIO...
AND I'LL BET GRIFFIN IS TOTALLY PSYCHED TO HANG WITH HIS DAD.

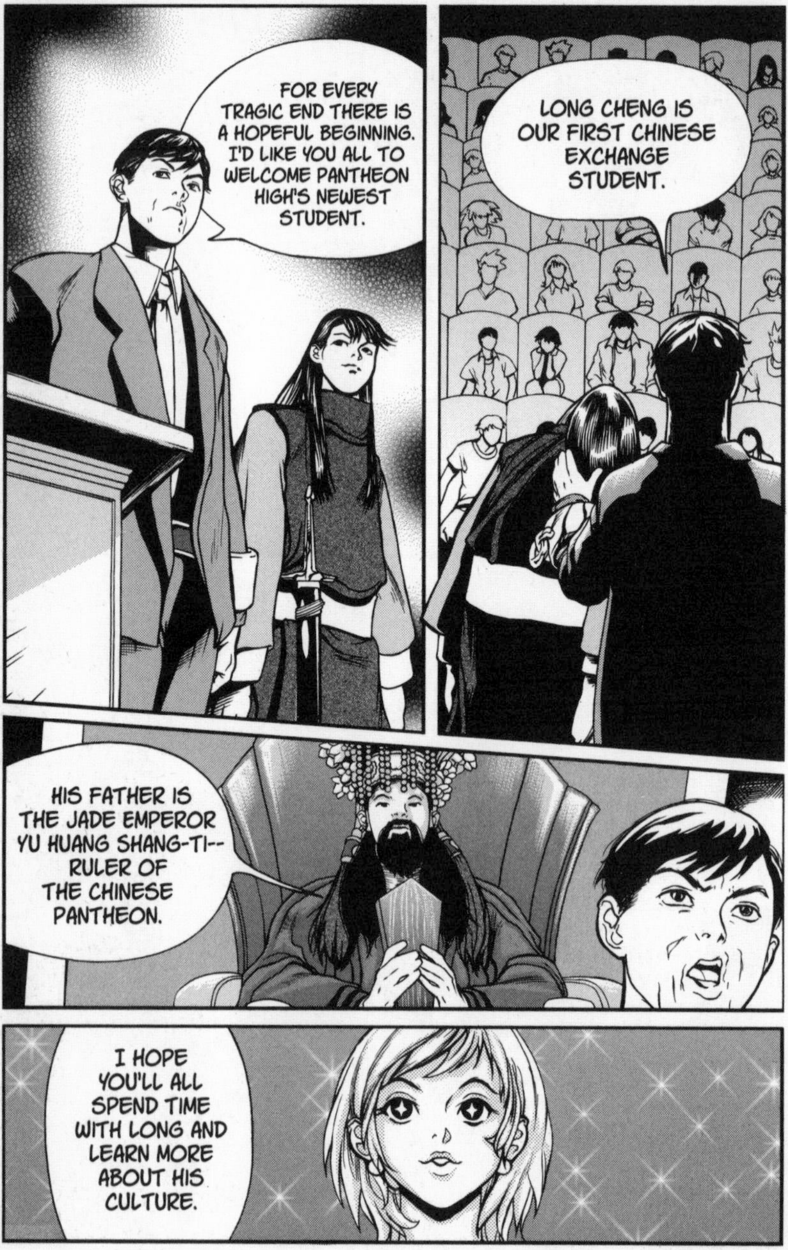
FOR EVERY TRAGIC END THERE IS A HOPEFUL BEGINNING. I'D LIKE YOU ALL TO WELCOME PANTHEON HIGH'S NEWEST STUDENT.
LONG CHENG IS OUR FIRST CHINESE EXCHANGE STUDENT.
HIS FATHER IS THE JADE EMPEROR YU HUANG SHANG-TI-- RULER OF THE CHINESE PANTHEON.
I HOPE YOU'LL ALL SPEND TIME WITH LONG AND LEARN MORE ABOUT HIS CULTURE.

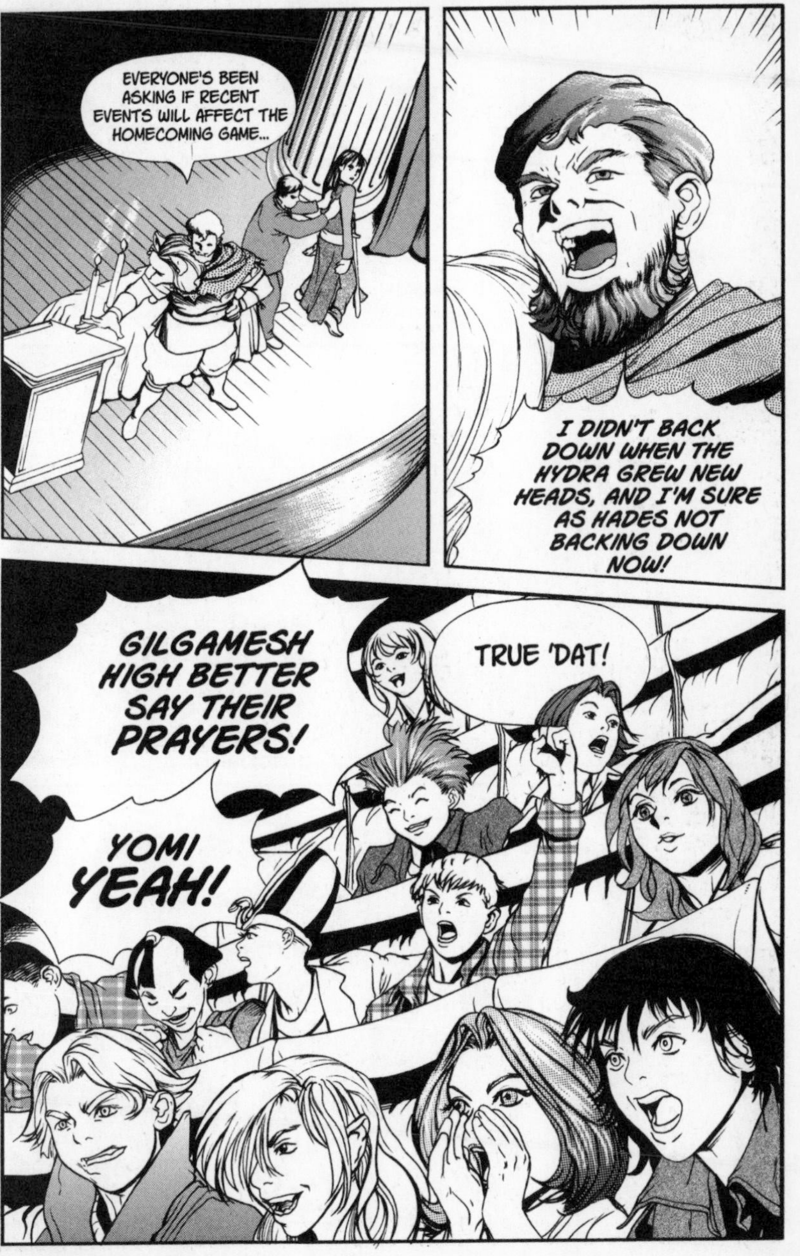
EVERYONE'S BEEN ASKING IF RECENT EVENTS WILL AFFECT THE HOMECOMING GAME...
I DIDN'T BACK DOWN WHEN THE HYDRA GREW NEW HEADS, AND I'M SURE AS HADES NOT BACKING DOWN NOW!
GILGAMESH HIGH BETTER SAY THEIR PRAYERS!
TRUE 'DAT!
YOMI YEAH!

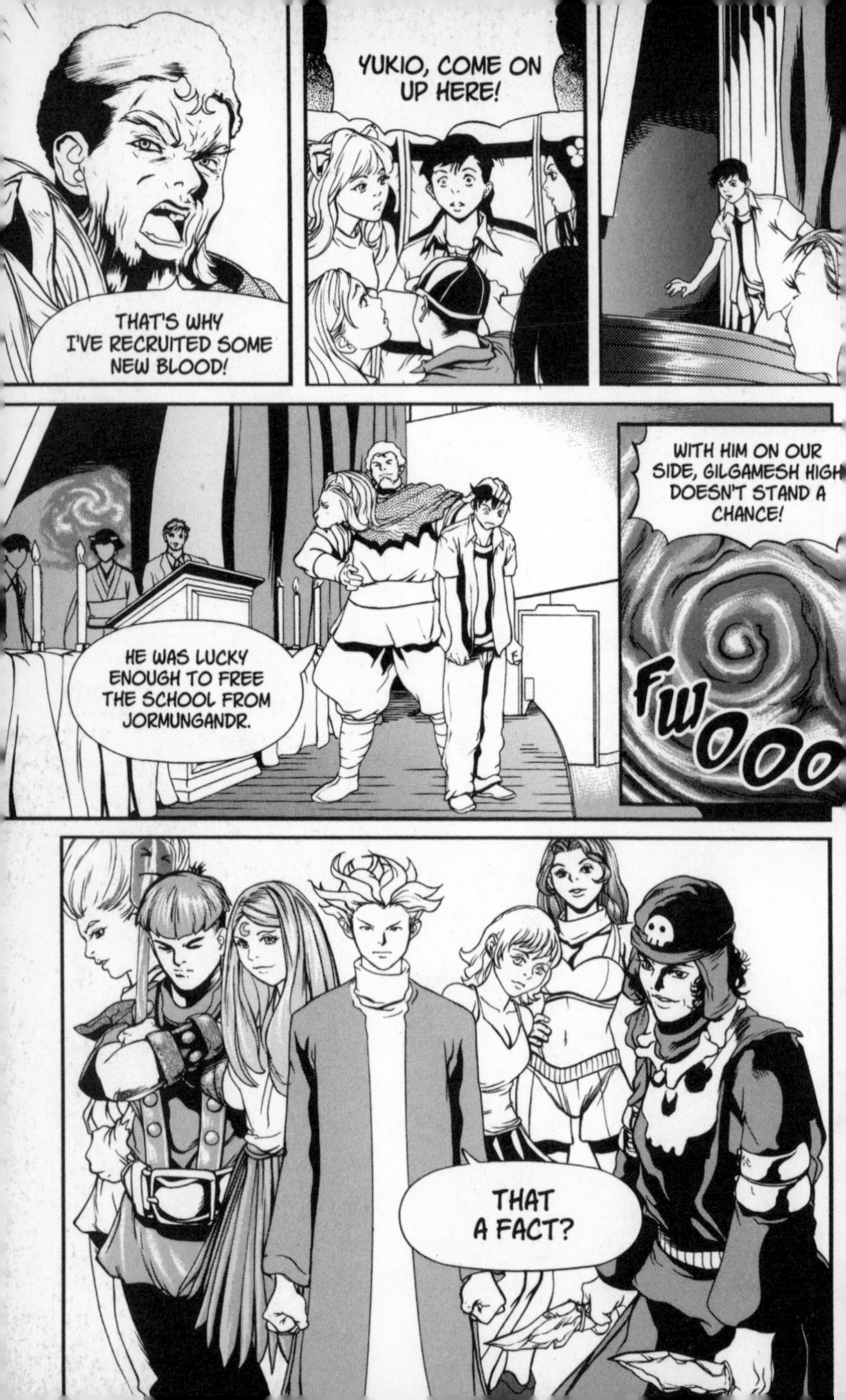
THAT'S WHY I'VE RECRUITED SOME NEW BLOOD!
YUKIO, COME ON UP HERE!
HE WAS LUCKY ENOUGH TO FREE THE SCHOOL FROM JORMUNGANDR.
WITH HIM ON OUR SIDE, GILGAMESH HIGH DOESN'T STAND A CHANCE!
FWOOO
THAT A FACT?

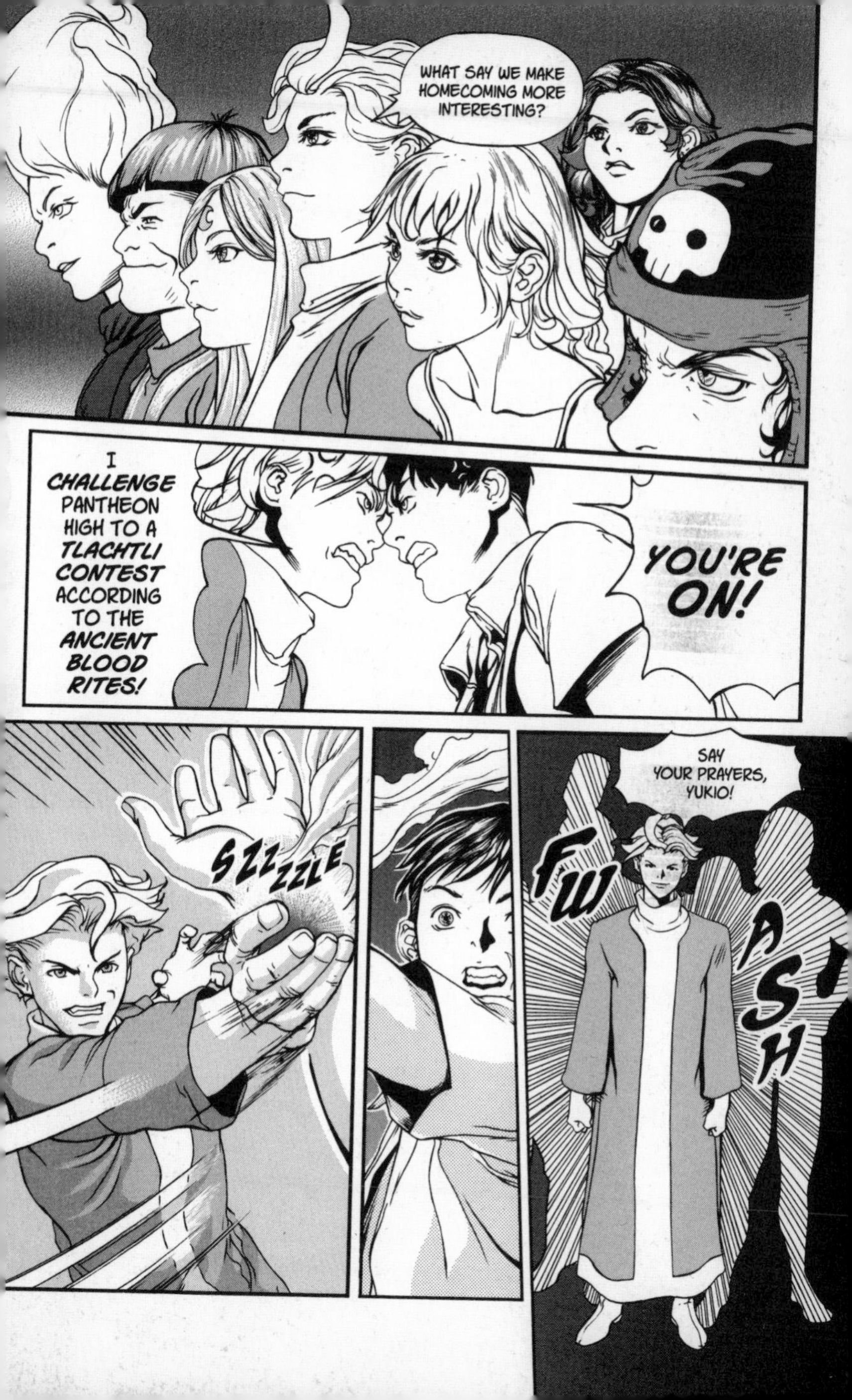
WHAT SAY WE MAKE HOMECOMING MORE INTERESTING?
I CHALLENGE PANTHEON HIGH TO A TLACHTLI CONTEST ACCORDING TO THE ANCIENT BLOOD RITES!
YOU'RE ON!
SZZZZZLE
SAY YOUR PRAYERS, YUKIO!
FWASH

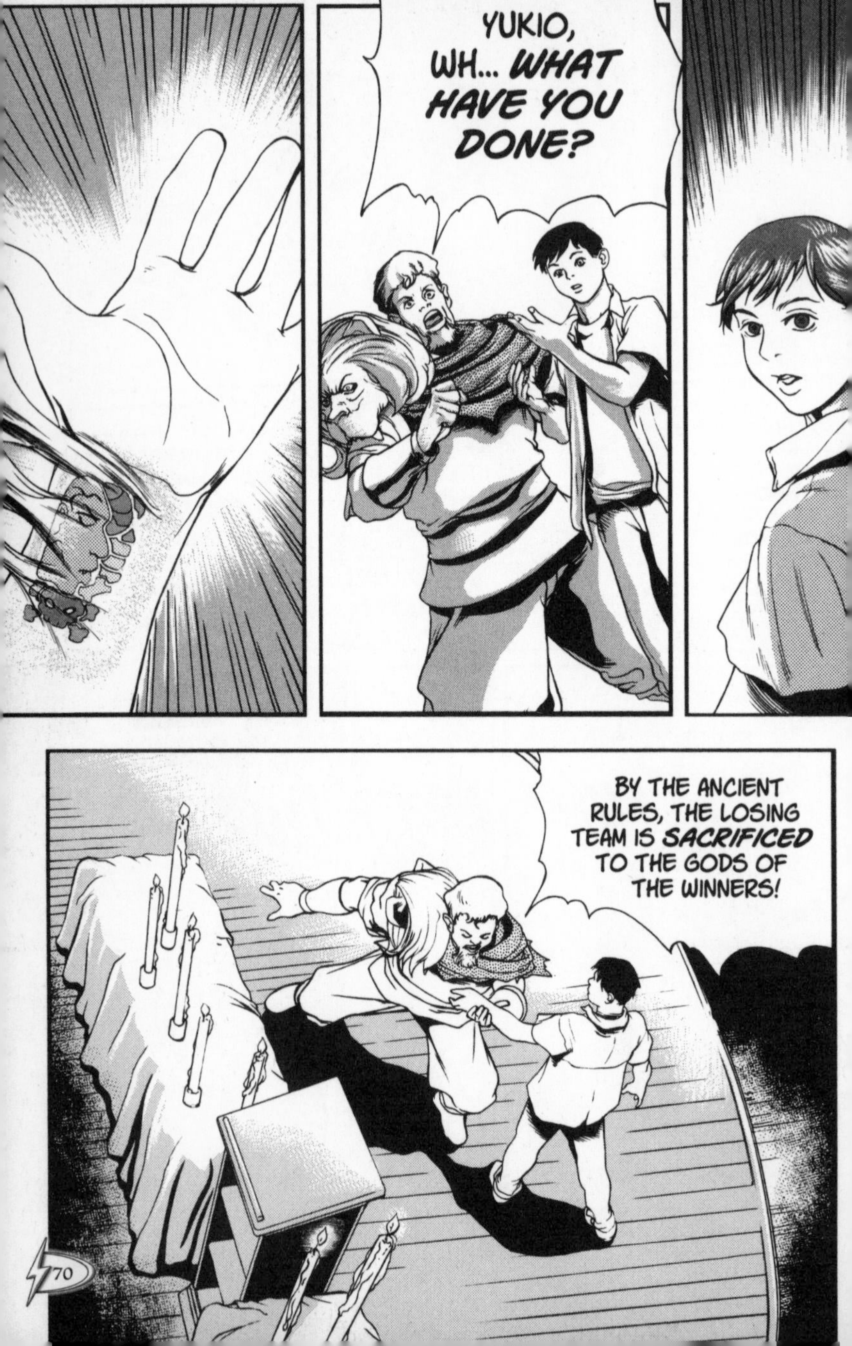

YUKIO, WH... WHAT HAVE YOU DONE?
BY THE ANCIENT RULES, THE LOSING TEAM IS SACRIFICED TO THE GODS OF THE WINNERS!

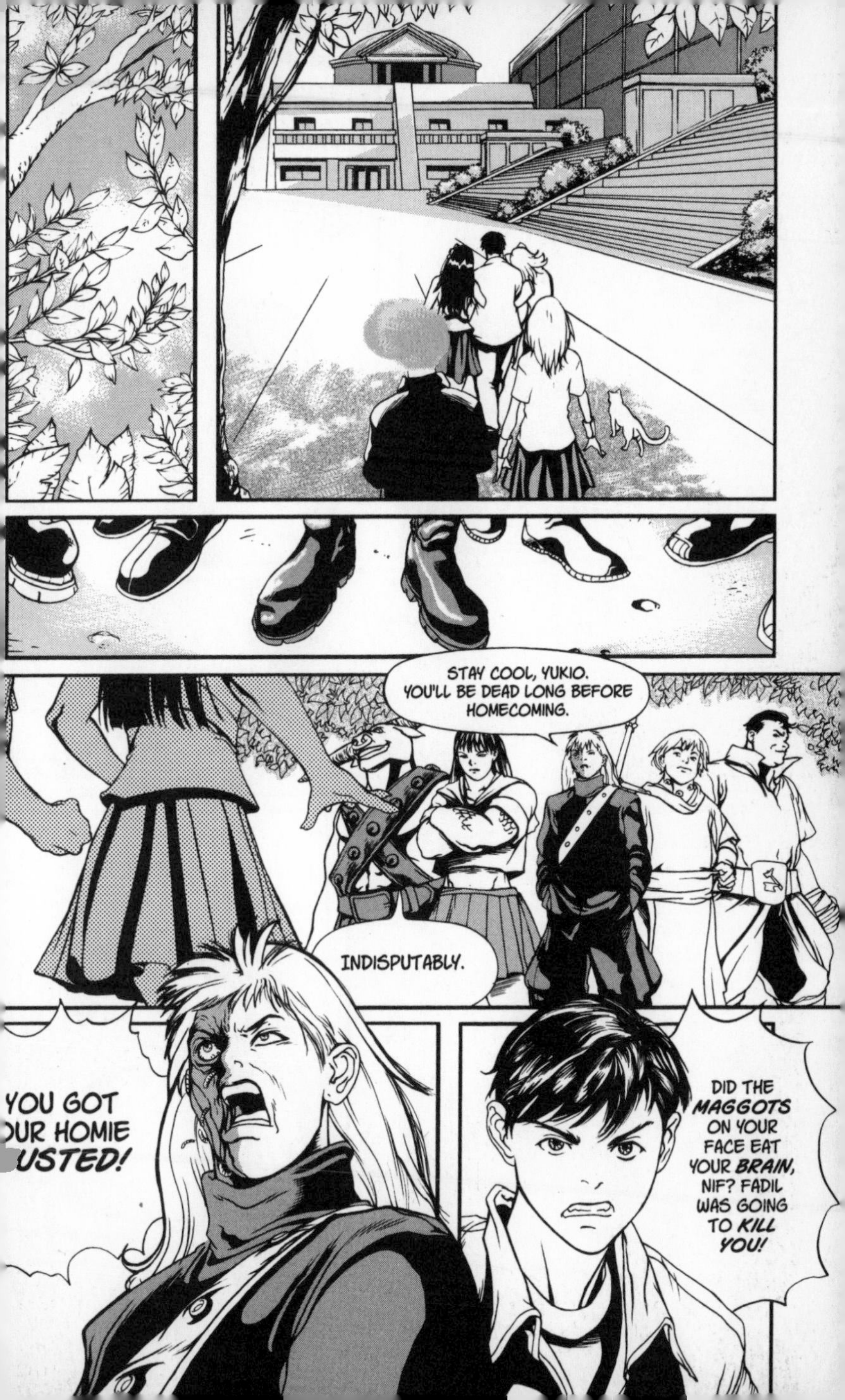
STAY COOL, YUKIO. YOU'LL BE DEAD LONG BEFORE HOMECOMING.
INDISPUTABLY.
YOU GOT OUR HOMIE BUSTED!
DID THE MAGGOTS ON YOUR FACE EAT YOUR BRAIN, NIF? FADIL WAS GOING TO KILL YOU!

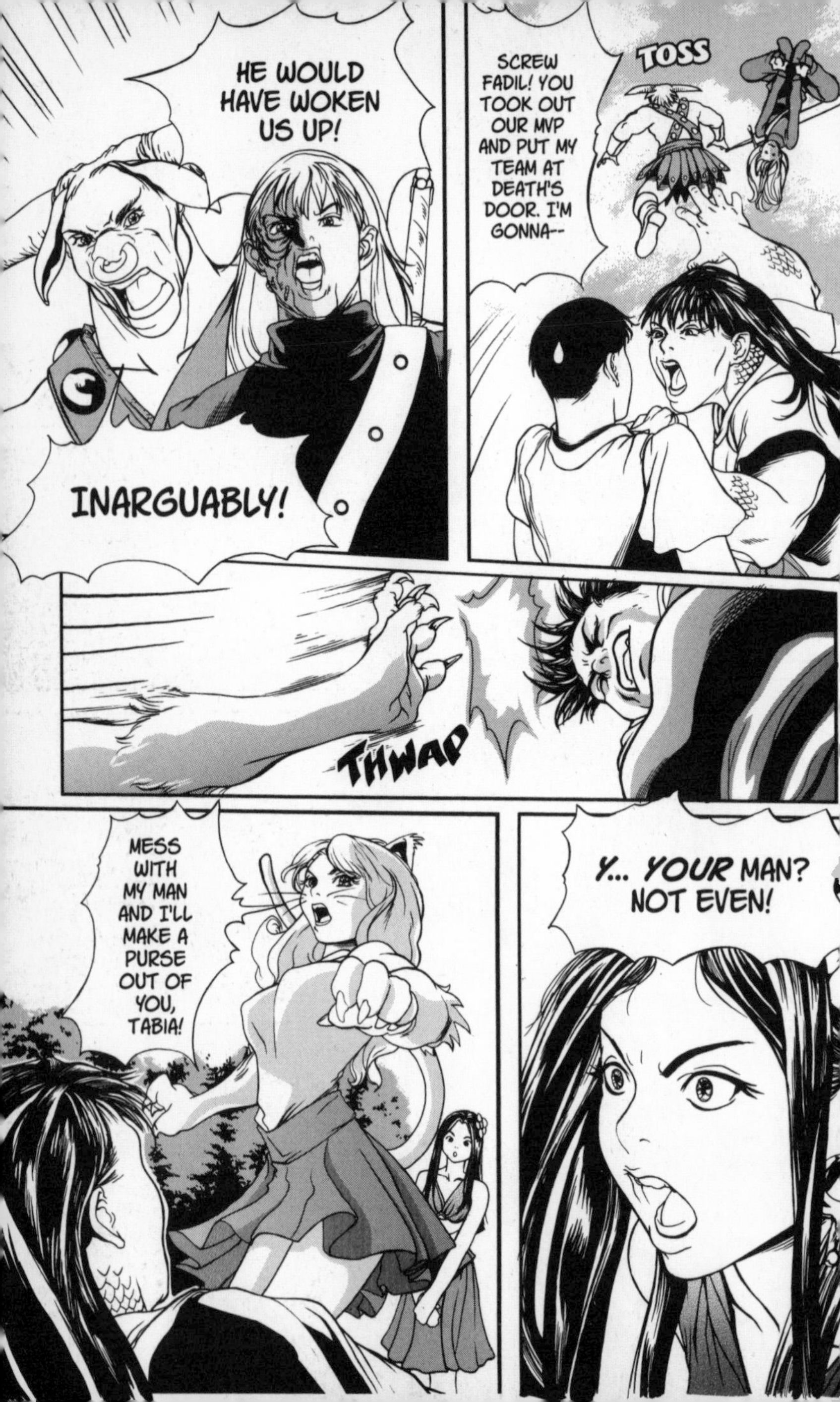
HE WOULD HAVE WOKEN US UP!
INARGUABLY!
SCREW FADIL! YOU TOOK OUT OUR MVP AND PUT MY TEAM AT DEATH'S DOOR. I'M GONNA--
TOSS
THWAP
MESS WITH MY MAN AND I'LL MAKE A PURSE OUT OF YOU, TABIA!
Y... YOUR MAN? NOT EVEN!

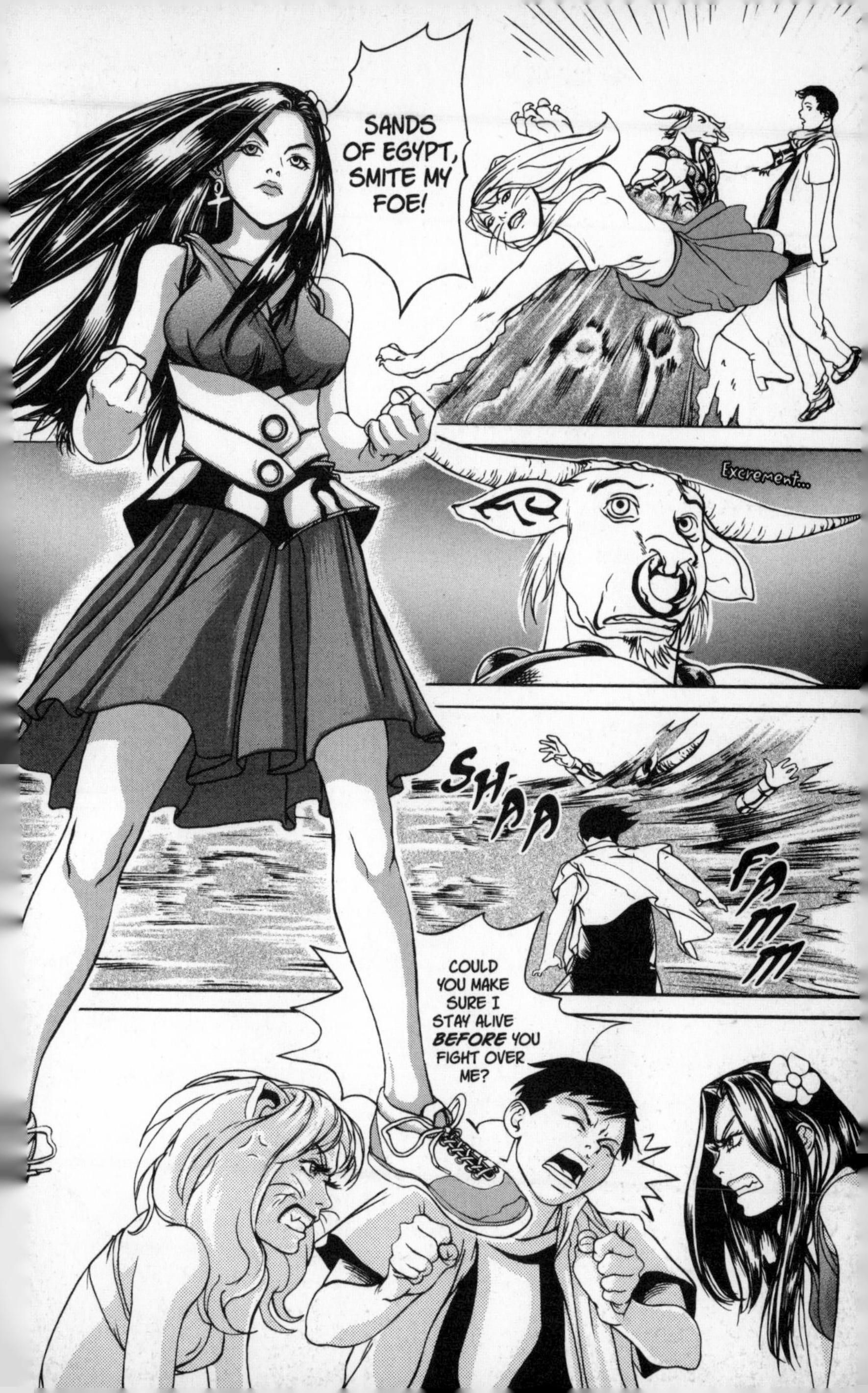
SANDS OF EGYPT, SMITE MY FOE!
Excrement...
SHAA
FAMM
COULD YOU MAKE SURE I STAY ALIVE **BEFORE** YOU FIGHT OVER ME?

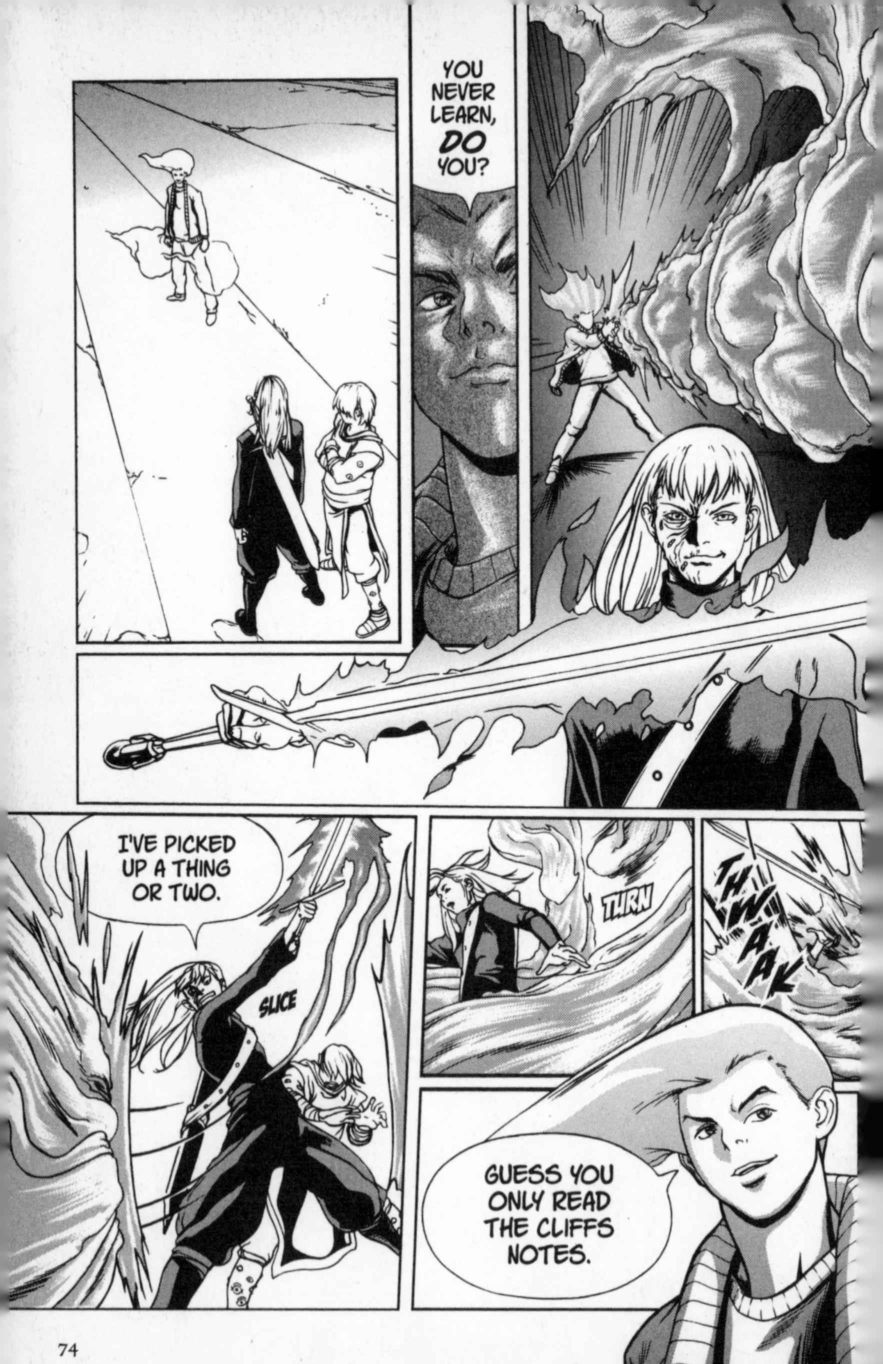
YOU NEVER LEARN, DO YOU?
I'VE PICKED UP A THING OR TWO.
SLICE
TURN
THWAAK
GUESS YOU ONLY READ THE CLIFFS NOTES.

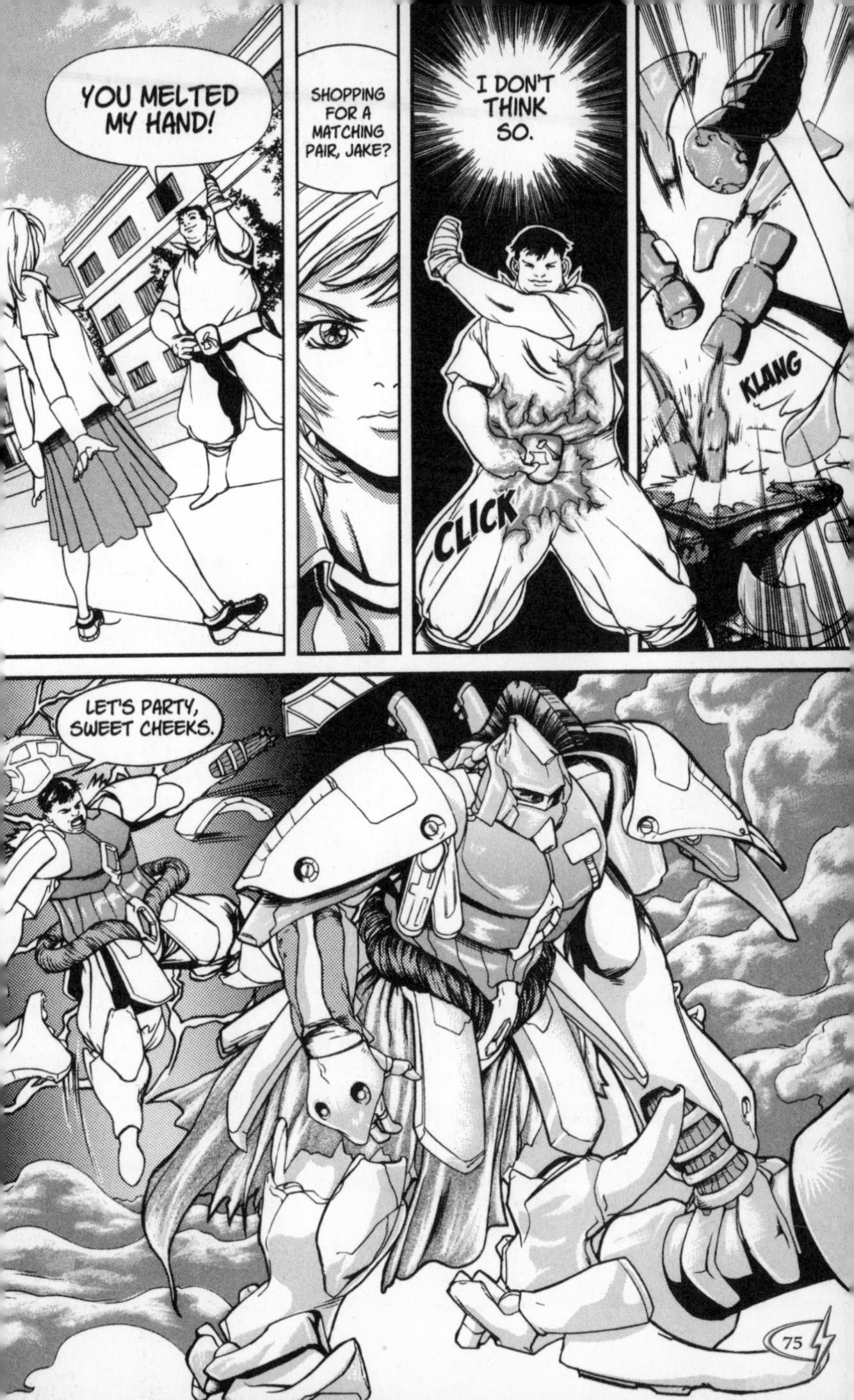
YOU MELTED MY HAND!
SHOPPING FOR A MATCHING PAIR, JAKE?
I DON'T THINK SO.
CLICK
KLANG
LET'S PARTY, SWEET CHEEKS.

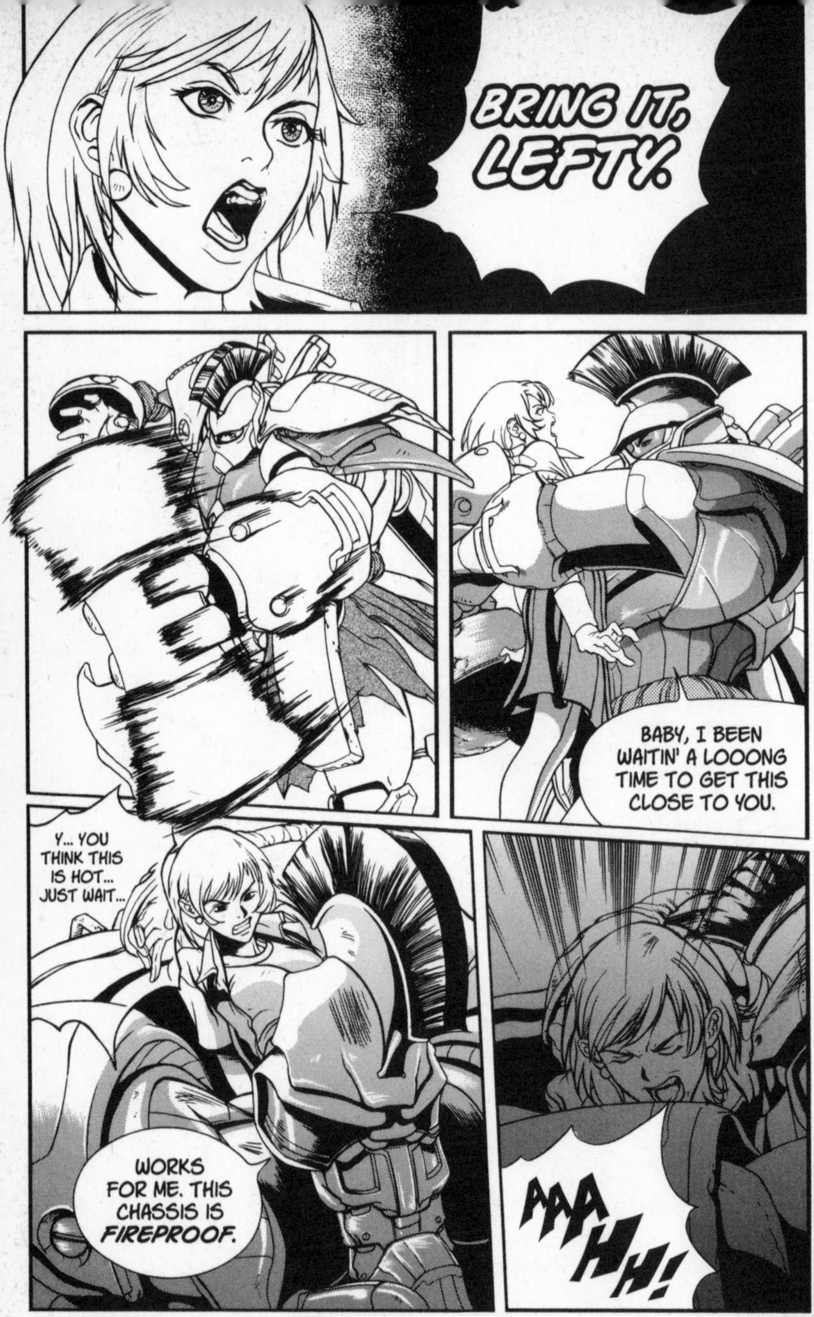
BRING IT, LEFTY.
BABY, I BEEN WAITIN' A LOOONG TIME TO GET THIS CLOSE TO YOU.
Y... YOU THINK THIS IS HOT... JUST WAIT...
WORKS FOR ME. THIS CHASSIS IS FIREPROOF.
AAAHH!

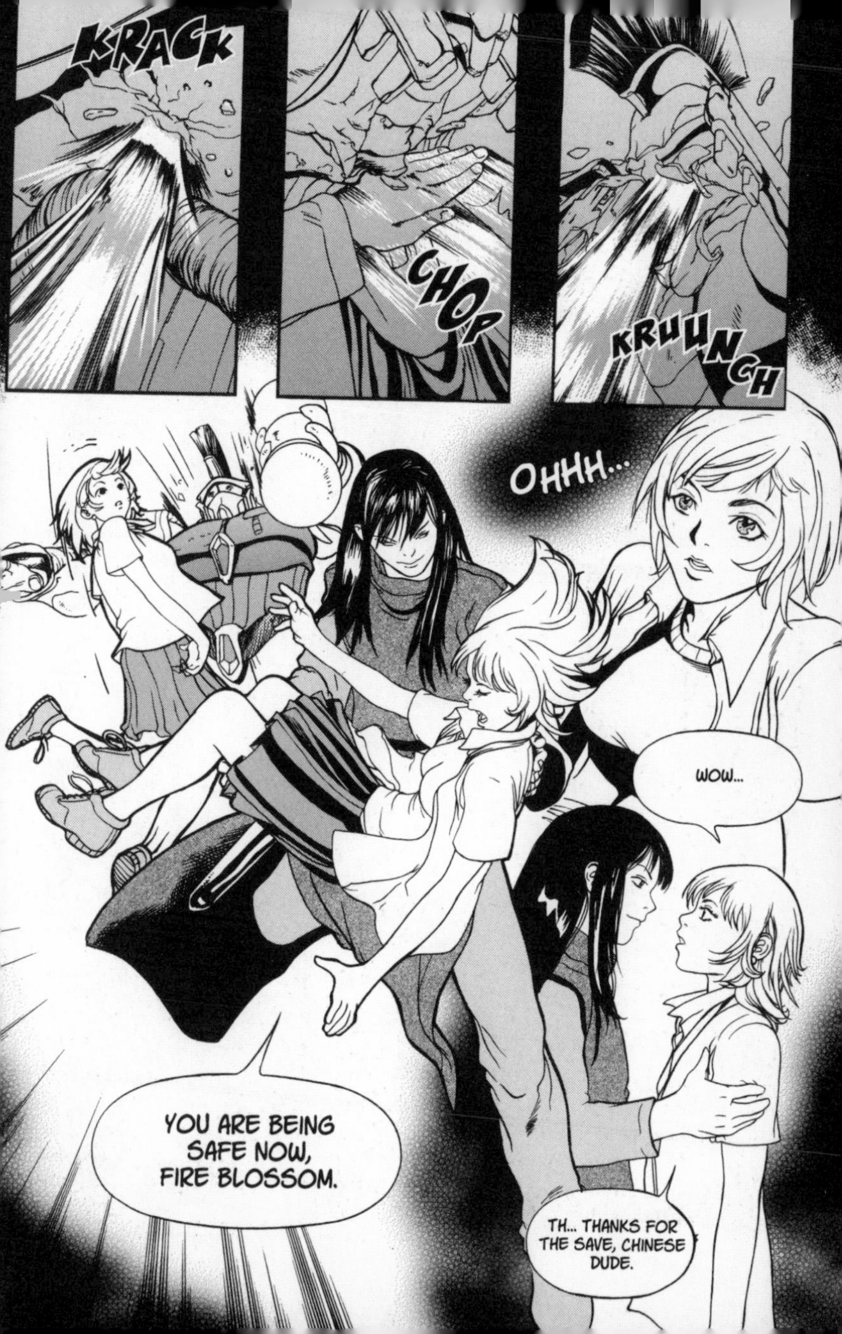
KRACK
CHOP
KRUUNCH
OHHH...
WOW...
YOU ARE BEING SAFE NOW, FIRE BLOSSOM.
TH... THANKS FOR THE SAVE, CHINESE DUDE.

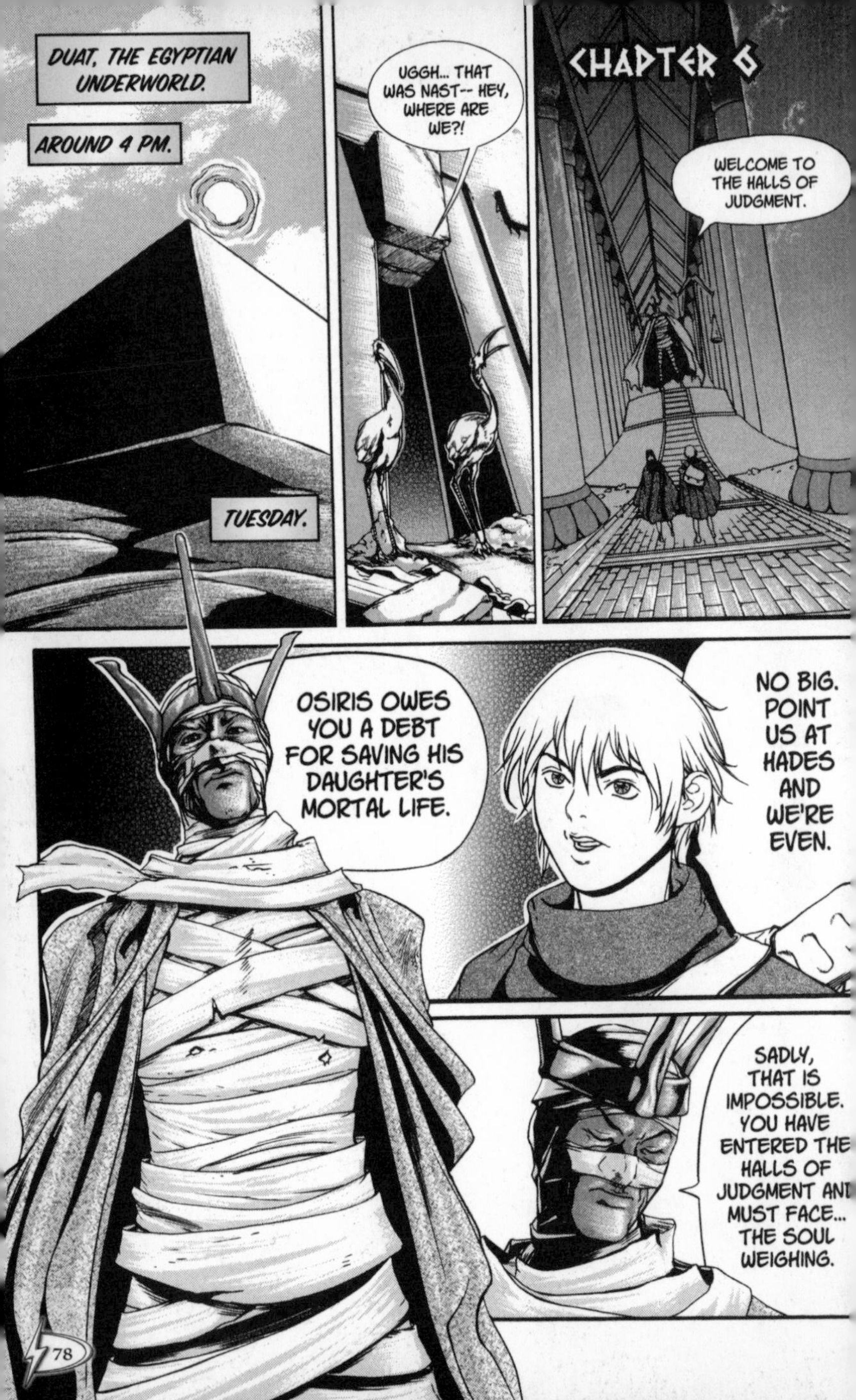
DUAT, THE EGYPTIAN UNDERWORLD.
AROUND 4 PM.
TUESDAY.
UGGH... THAT WAS NAST-- HEY, WHERE ARE WE?!
CHAPTER 6
WELCOME TO THE HALLS OF JUDGMENT.
OSIRIS OWES YOU A DEBT FOR SAVING HIS DAUGHTER'S MORTAL LIFE.
NO BIG. POINT US AT HADES AND WE'RE EVEN.
SADLY, THAT IS IMPOSSIBLE. YOU HAVE ENTERED THE HALLS OF JUDGMENT AND MUST FACE... THE SOUL WEIGHING.

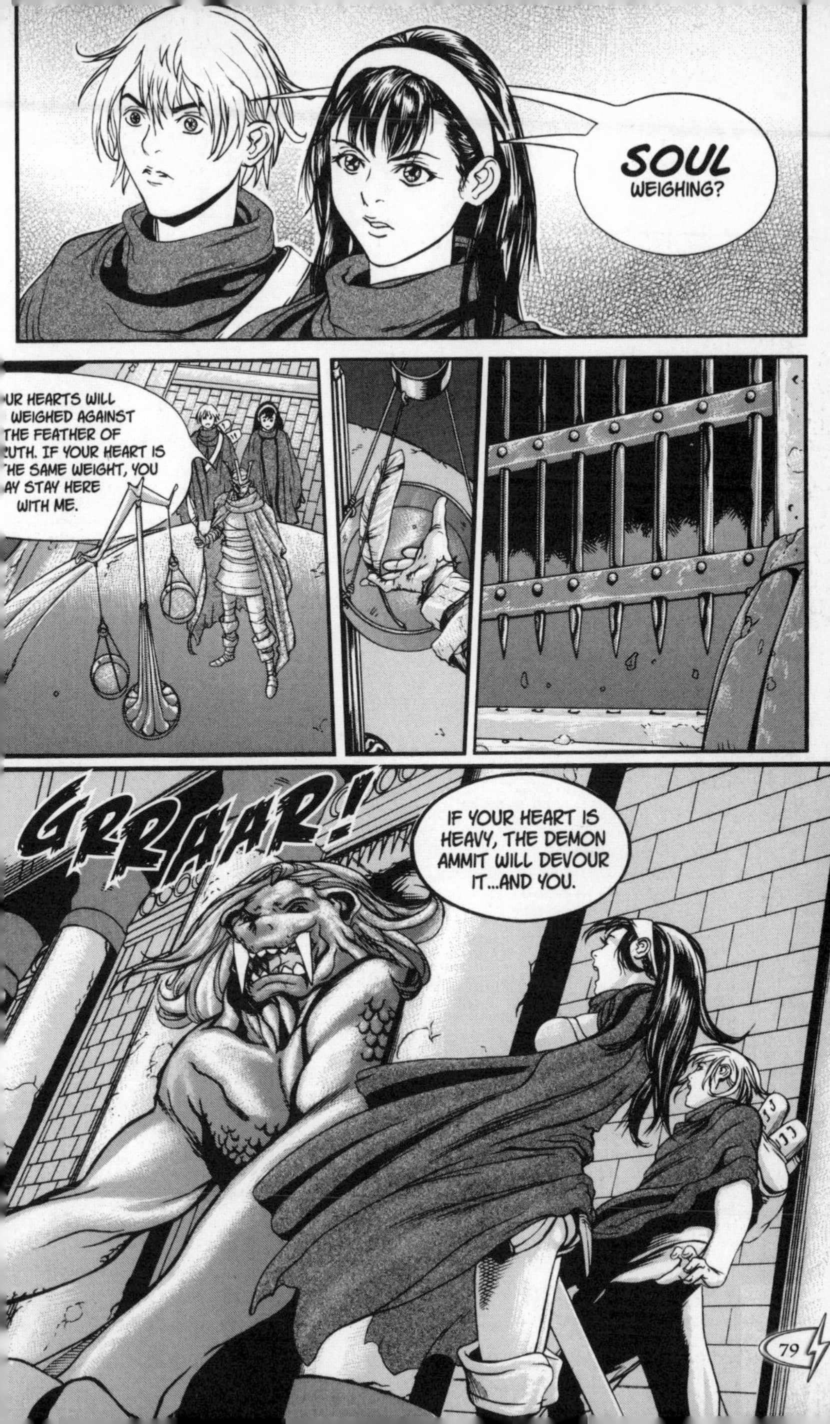
SOUL WEIGHING?
UR HEARTS WILL WEIGHED AGAINST THE FEATHER OF RUTH. IF YOUR HEART IS THE SAME WEIGHT, YOU AY STAY HERE WITH ME.
GRRAAR!
IF YOUR HEART IS HEAVY, THE DEMON AMMIT WILL DEVOUR IT...AND YOU.

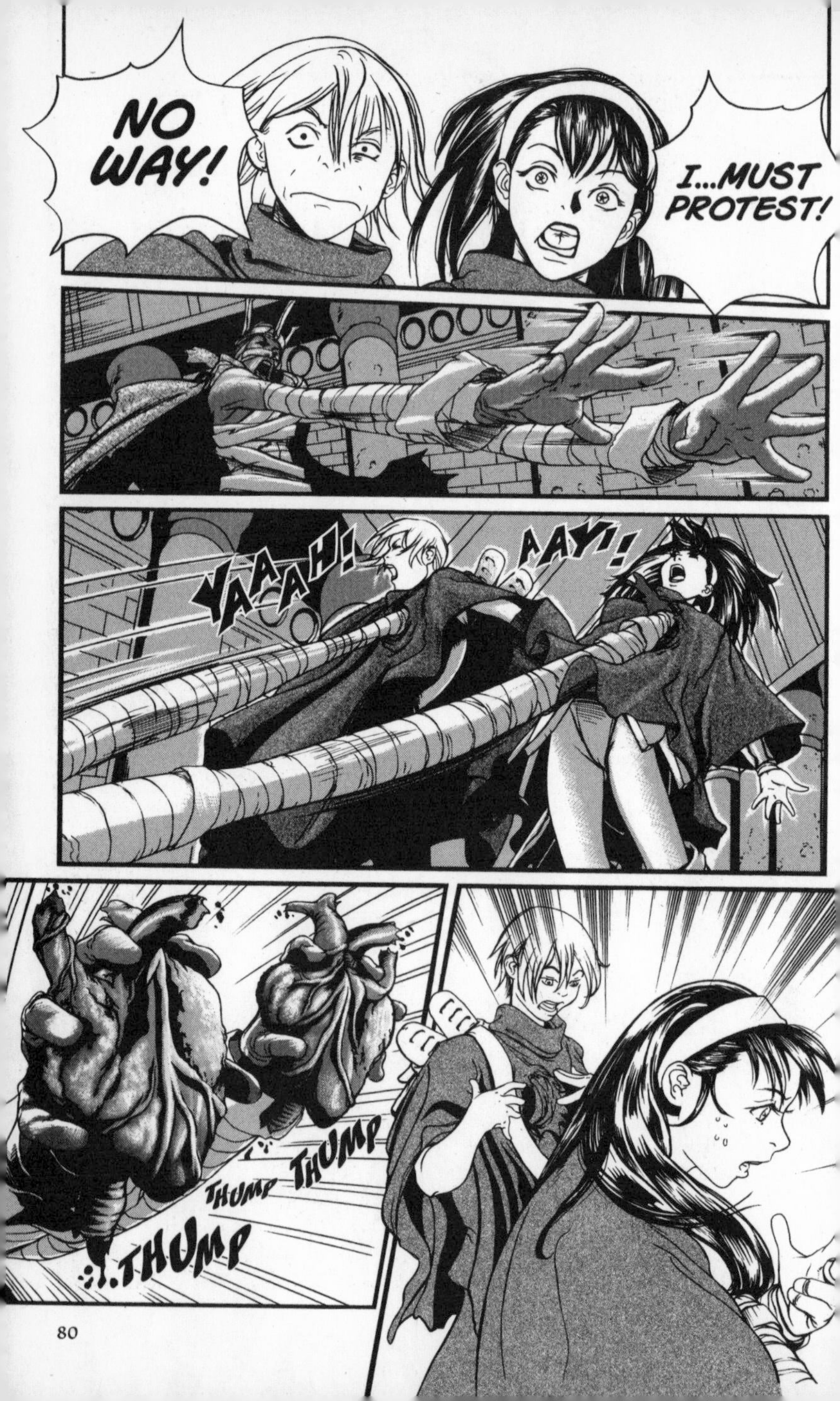

NO WAY!
I...MUST PROTEST!
YAAAH!
AAYI!
THUMP
THUMP
THUMP

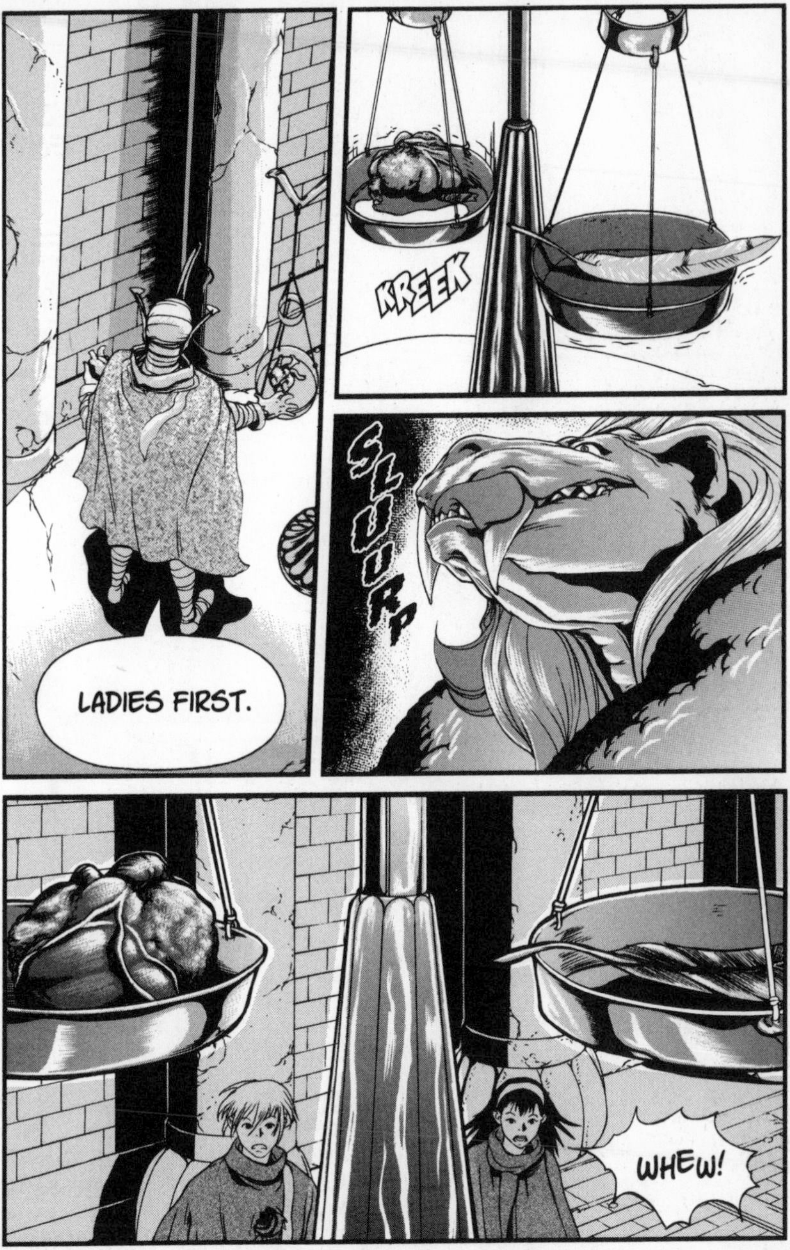
LADIES FIRST.
KREEK
SLURP
WHEW!

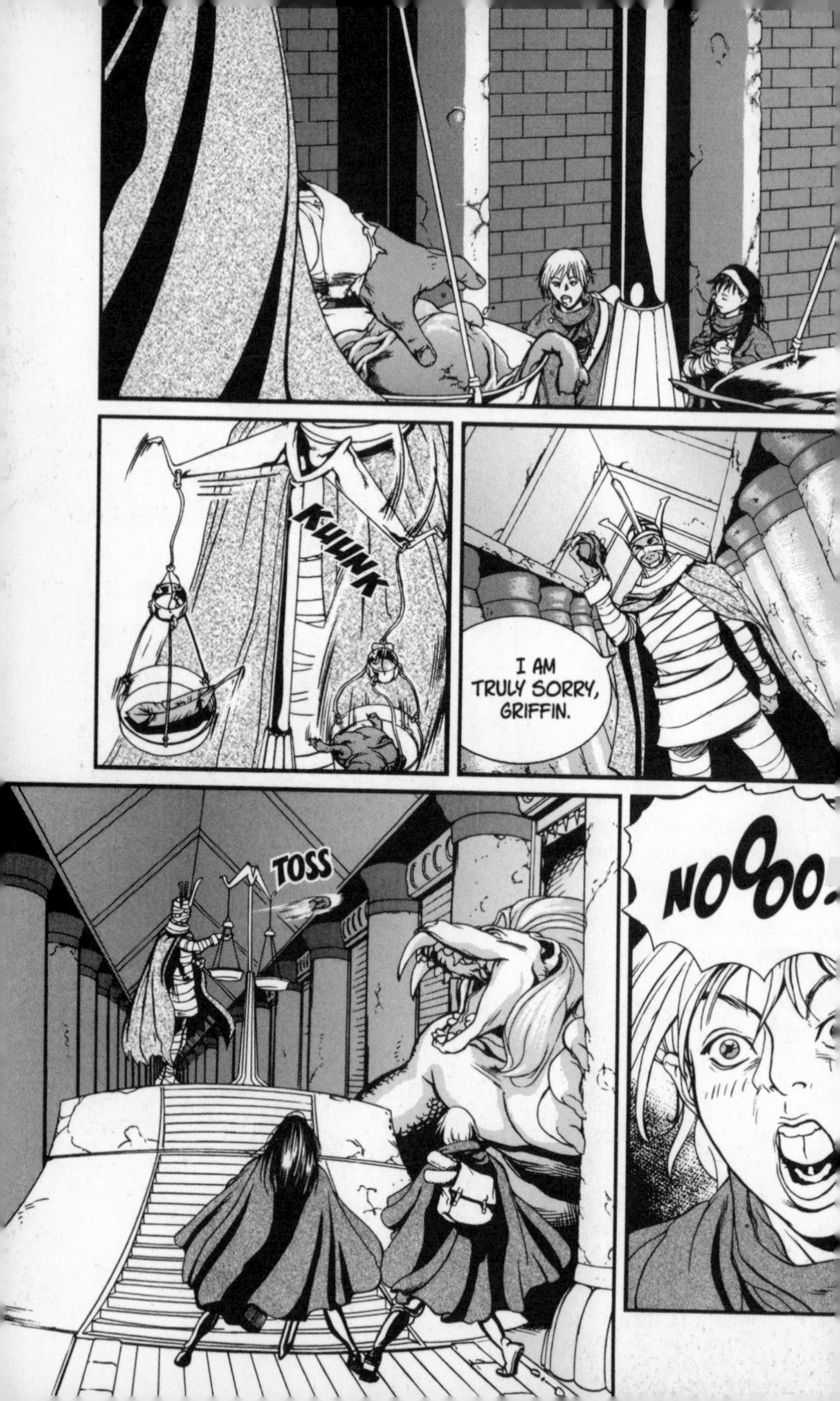
KLUNK
I AM TRULY SORRY, GRIFFIN.
TOSS
NOOOO-

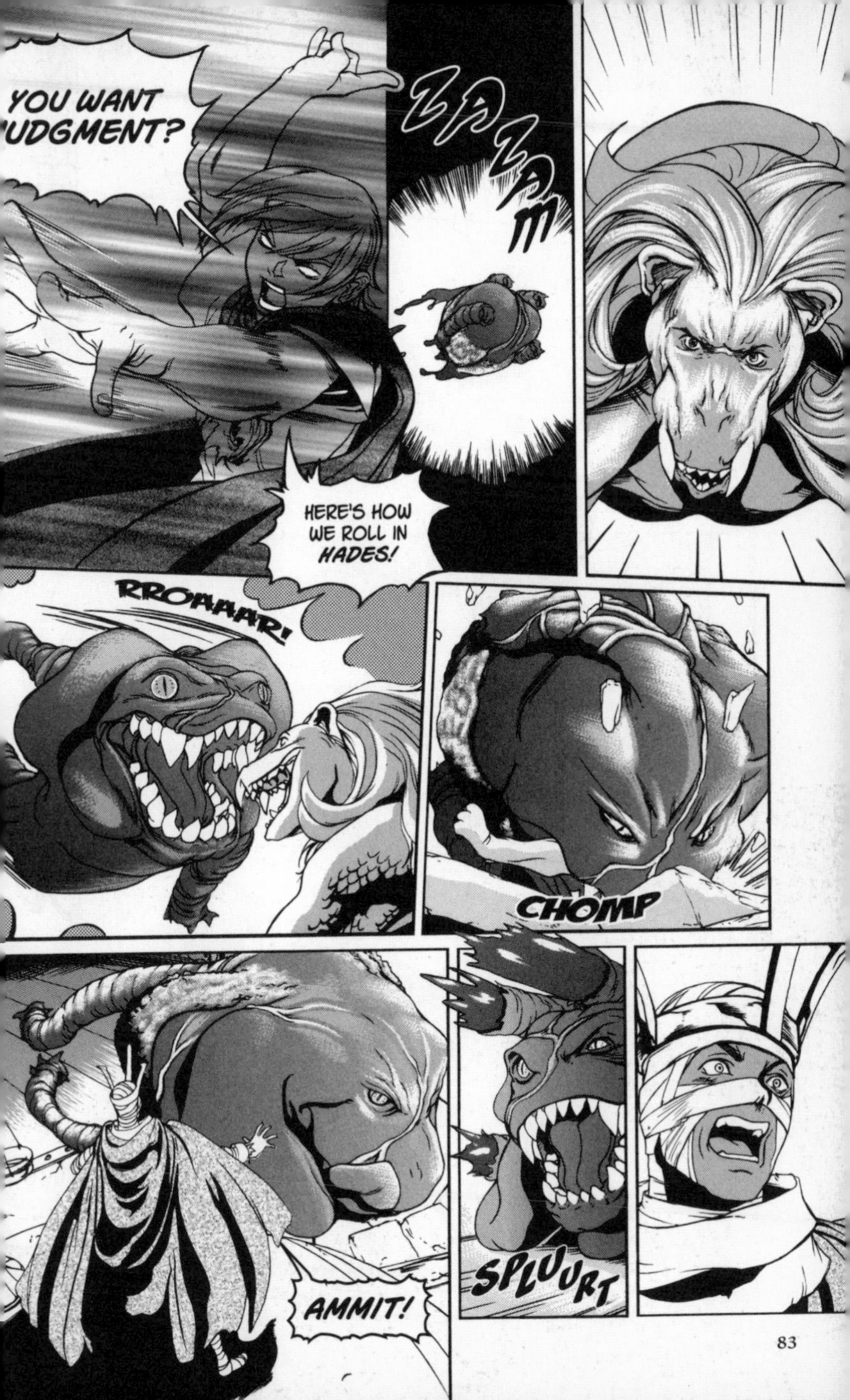

YOU WANT JUDGMENT?
ZAZAM
HERE'S HOW WE ROLL IN HADES!
RROAAAAR!
CHOMP
AMMIT!
SPLUURT

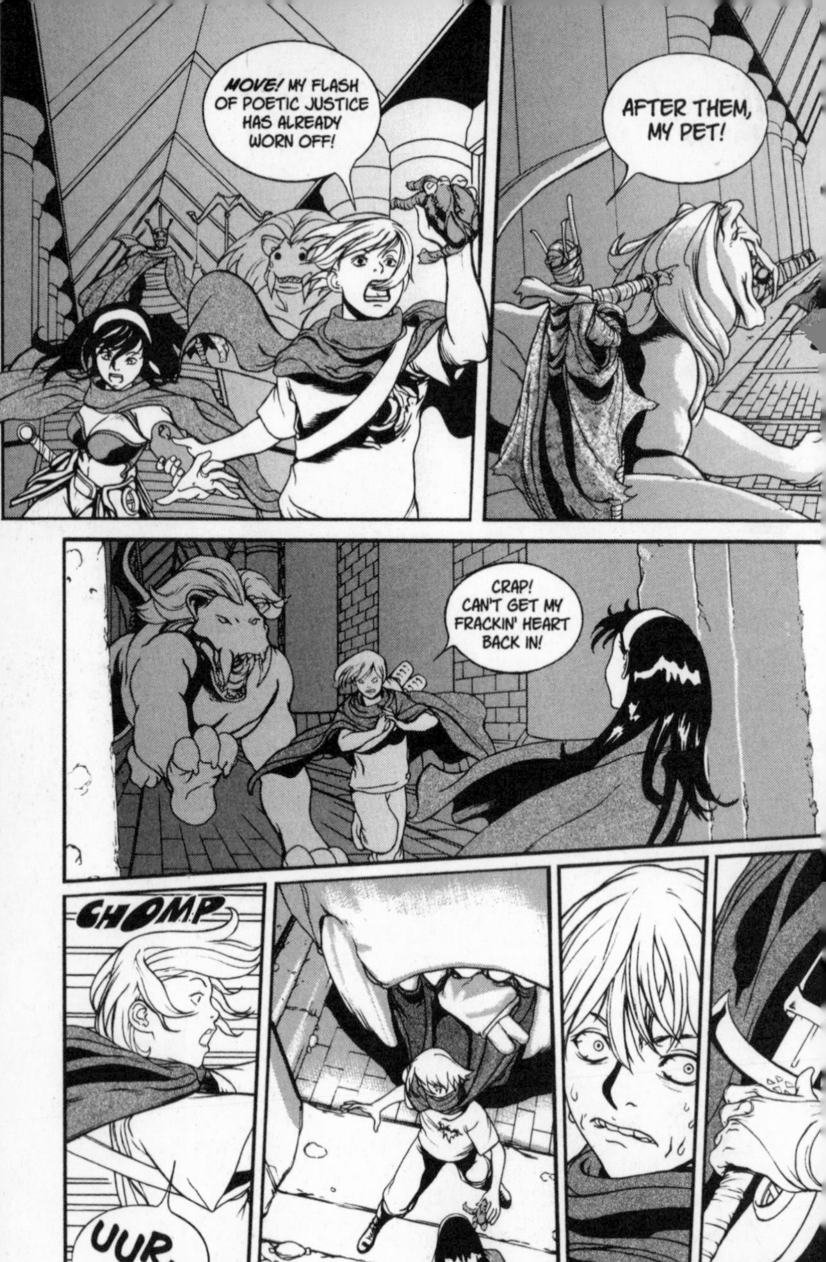

MOVE! MY FLASH OF POETIC JUSTICE HAS ALREADY WORN OFF!
AFTER THEM, MY PET!
CRAP! CAN'T GET MY FRACKIN' HEART BACK IN!
CHOMP
UURK!

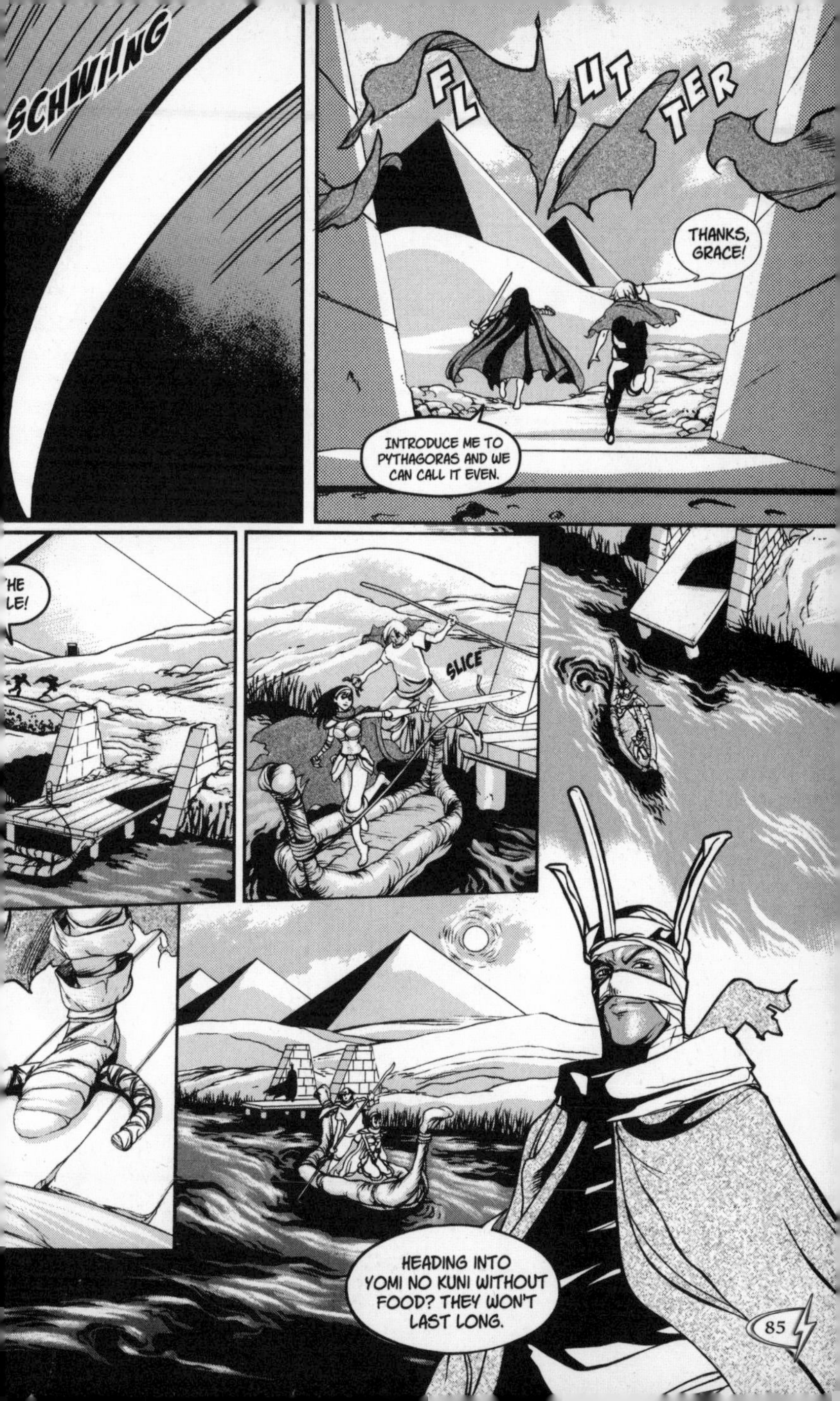
SCHWIIING
FLUTTER
THANKS, GRACE!
INTRODUCE ME TO PYTHAGORAS AND WE CAN CALL IT EVEN.
HE
LE!
SLICE
HEADING INTO YOMI NO KUNI WITHOUT FOOD? THEY WON'T LAST LONG.

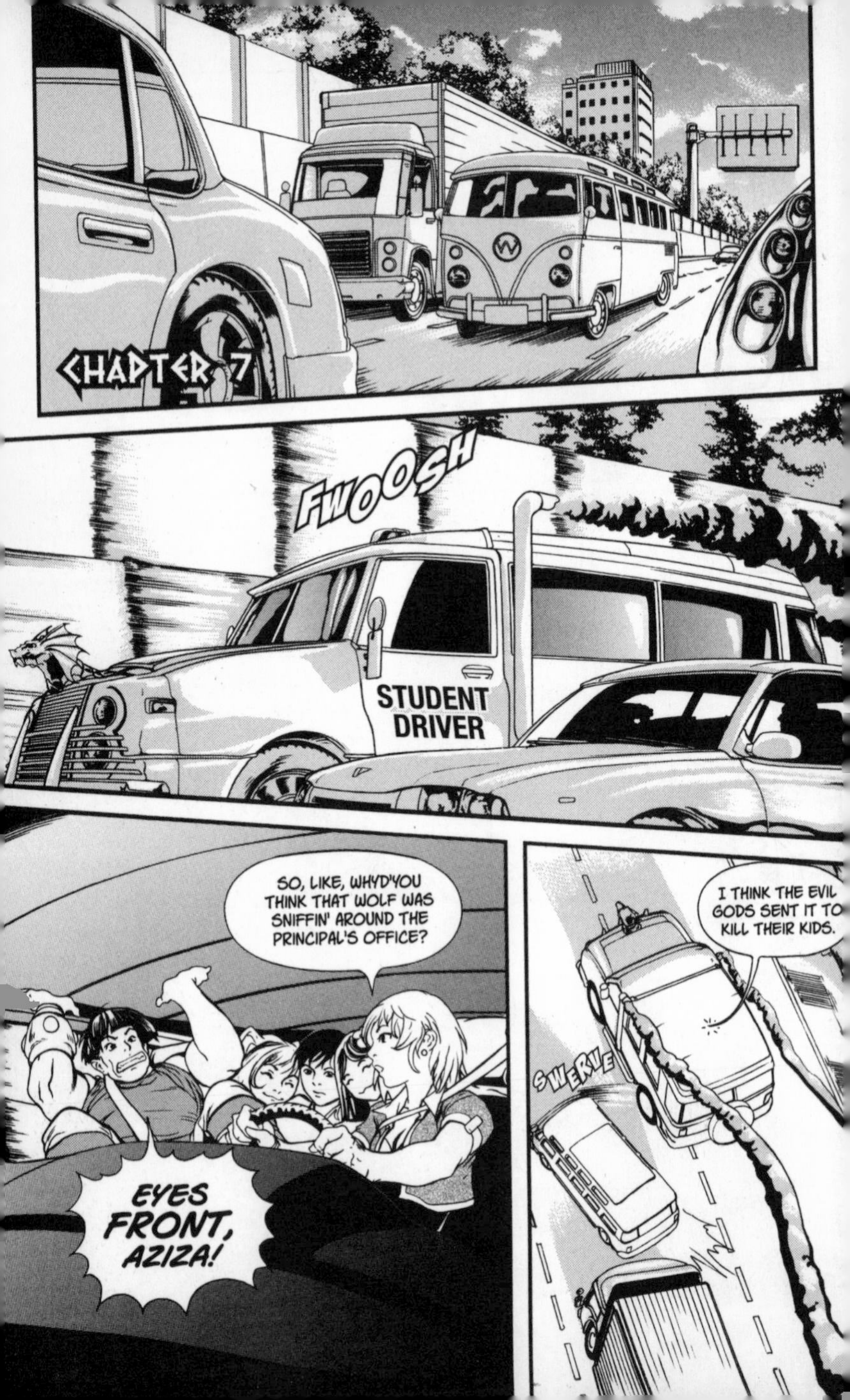
CHAPTER 7
FWOOSH
STUDENT DRIVER
SO, LIKE, WHYD'YOU THINK THAT WOLF WAS SNIFFIN' AROUND THE PRINCIPAL'S OFFICE?
EYES FRONT, AZIZA!
I THINK THE EVIL GODS SENT IT TO KILL THEIR KIDS.
SWERVE

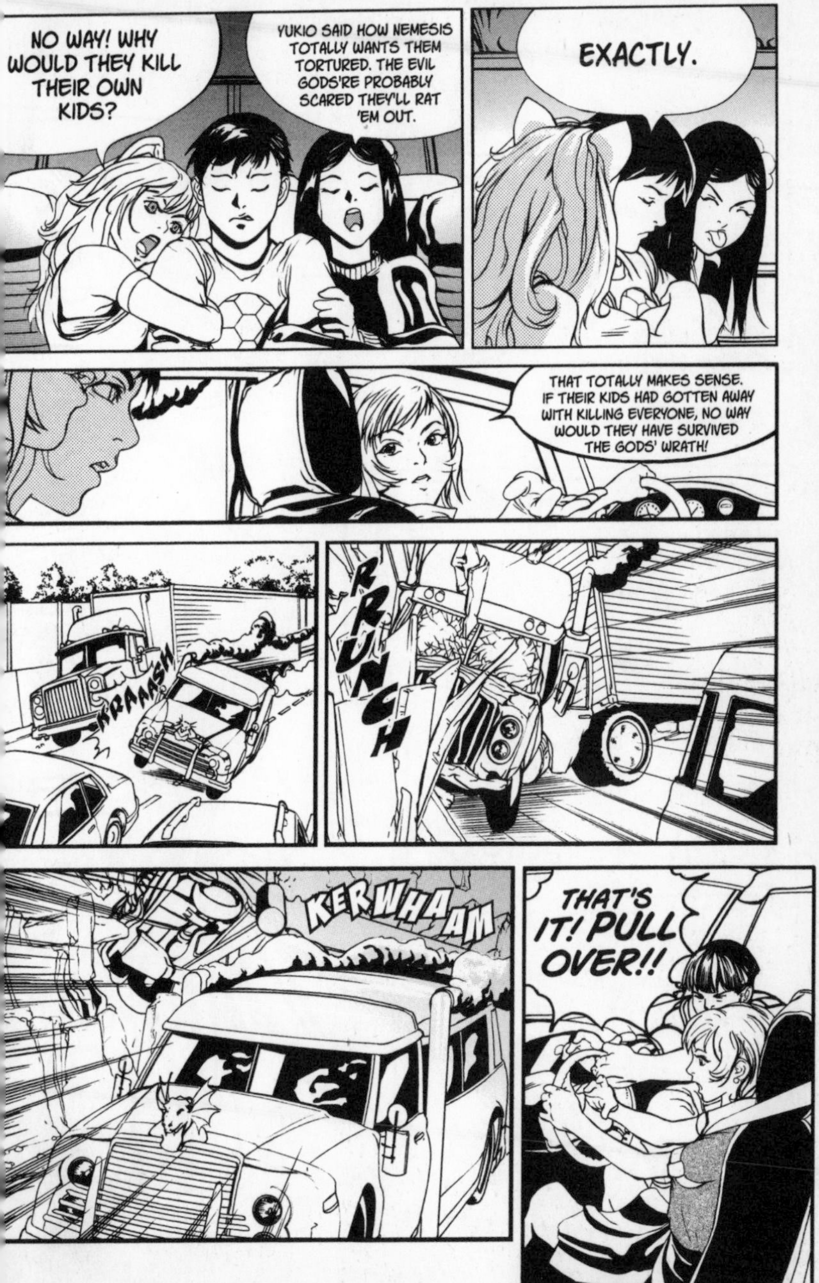
NO WAY! WHY WOULD THEY KILL THEIR OWN KIDS?
YUKIO SAID HOW NEMESIS TOTALLY WANTS THEM TORTURED. THE EVIL GODS'RE PROBABLY SCARED THEY'LL RAT 'EM OUT.
EXACTLY.
THAT TOTALLY MAKES SENSE. IF THEIR KIDS HAD GOTTEN AWAY WITH KILLING EVERYONE, NO WAY WOULD THEY HAVE SURVIVED THE GODS' WRATH!
KRAAASH
RRRUNCH
KERWHAAAM
THAT'S IT! PULL OVER!!

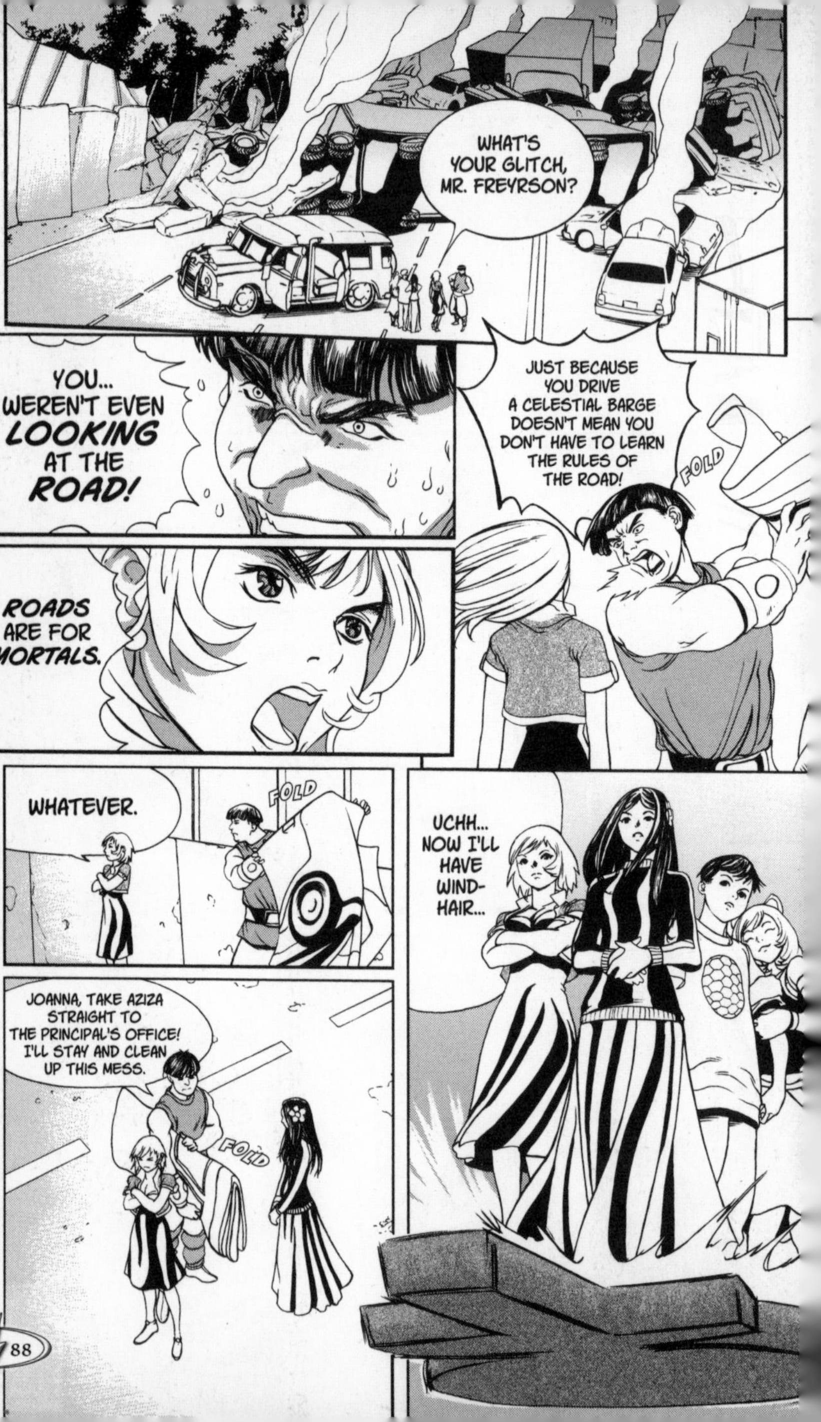
WHAT'S YOUR GLITCH, MR. FREYRSON?
YOU... WEREN'T EVEN LOOKING AT THE ROAD!
ROADS ARE FOR MORTALS.
JUST BECAUSE YOU DRIVE A CELESTIAL BARGE DOESN'T MEAN YOU DON'T HAVE TO LEARN THE RULES OF THE ROAD!
FOLD
WHATEVER.
FOLD
JOANNA, TAKE AZIZA STRAIGHT TO THE PRINCIPAL'S OFFICE! I'LL STAY AND CLEAN UP THIS MESS.
FOLD
UCHH... NOW I'LL HAVE WIND-HAIR...

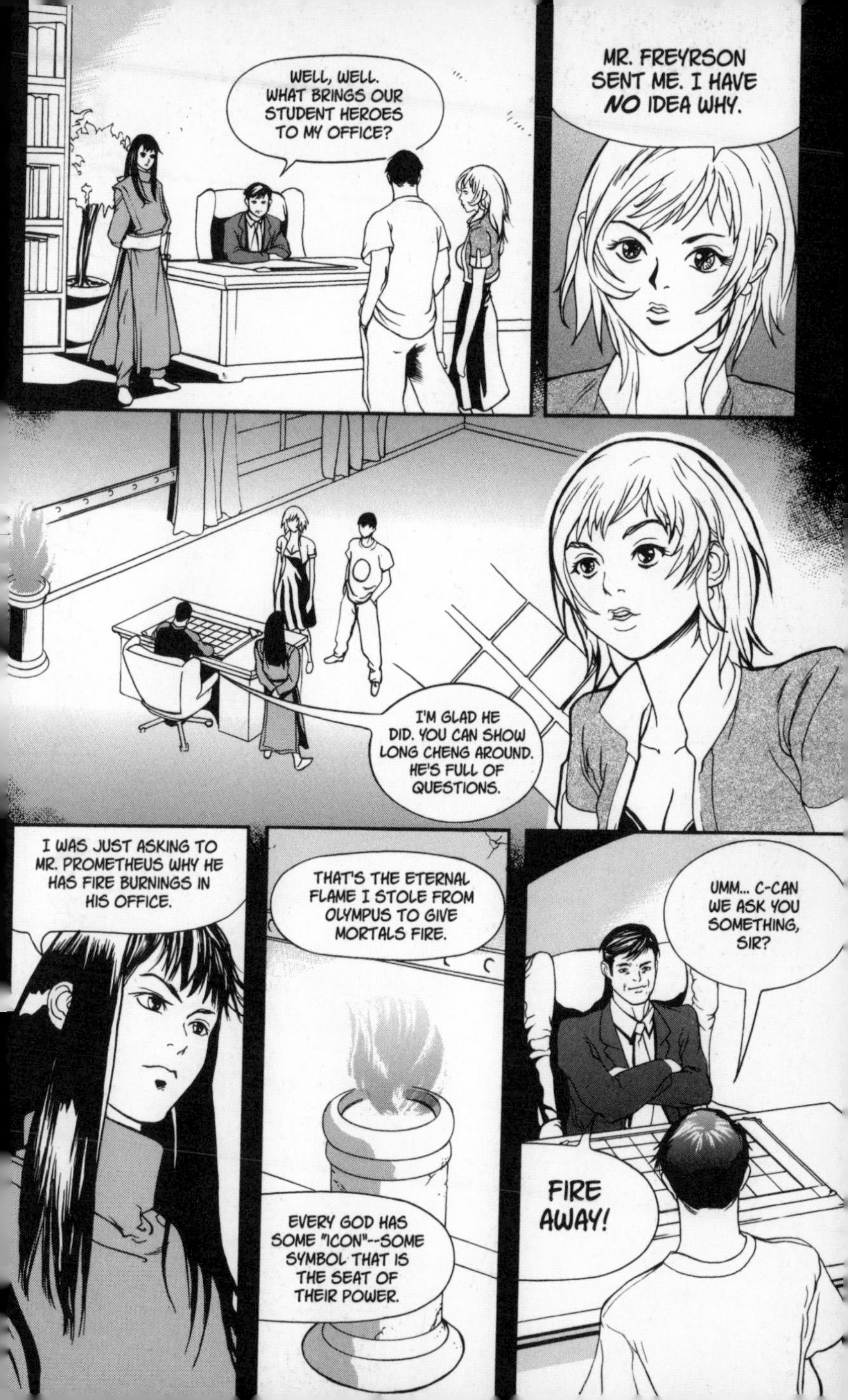
WELL, WELL. WHAT BRINGS OUR STUDENT HEROES TO MY OFFICE?
MR. FREYRSON SENT ME. I HAVE NO IDEA WHY.
I'M GLAD HE DID. YOU CAN SHOW LONG CHENG AROUND. HE'S FULL OF QUESTIONS.
I WAS JUST ASKING TO MR. PROMETHEUS WHY HE HAS FIRE BURNINGS IN HIS OFFICE.
THAT'S THE ETERNAL FLAME I STOLE FROM OLYMPUS TO GIVE MORTALS FIRE.
EVERY GOD HAS SOME "ICON"--SOME SYMBOL THAT IS THE SEAT OF THEIR POWER.
UMM... C-CAN WE ASK YOU SOMETHING, SIR?
FIRE AWAY!

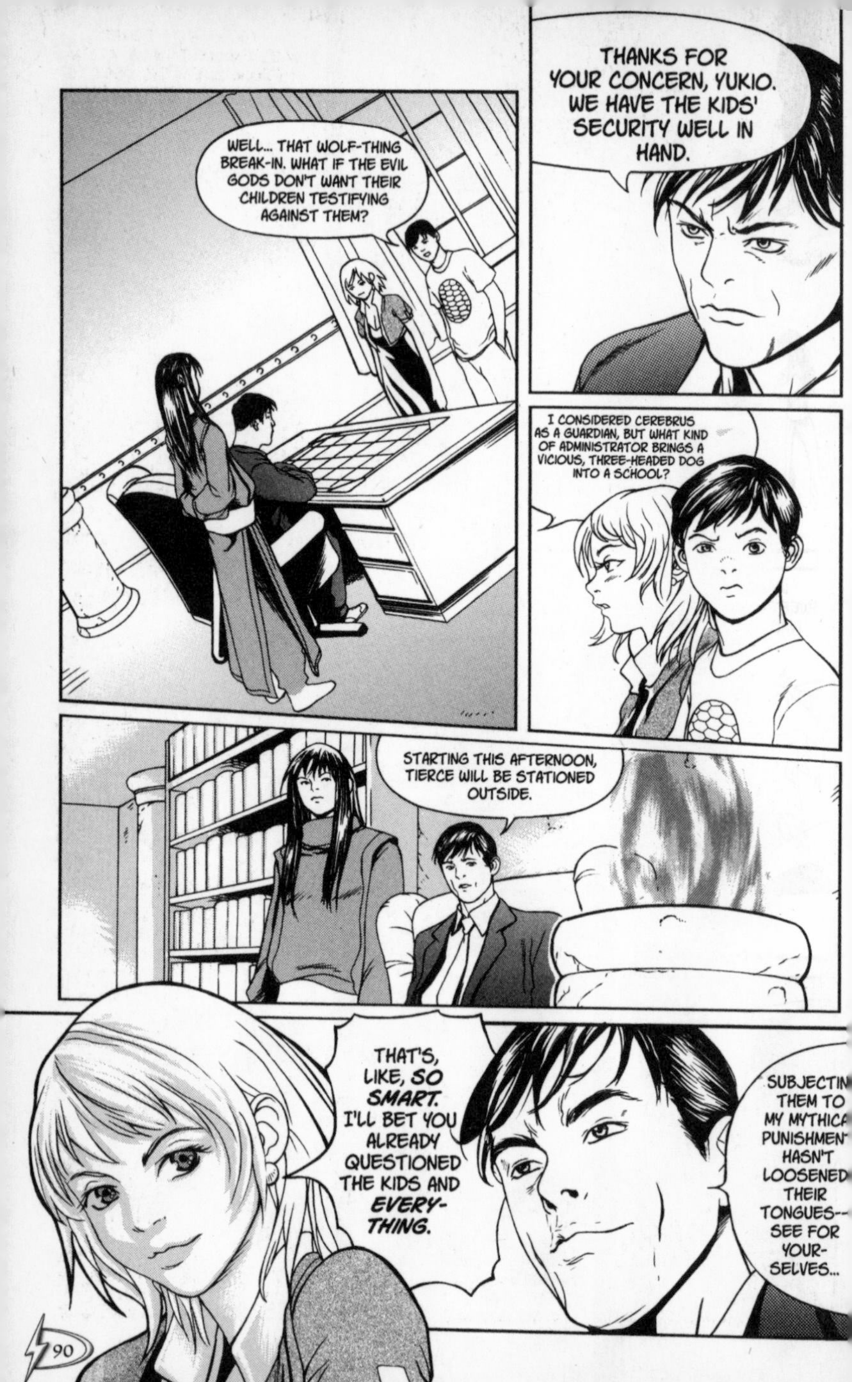
WELL... THAT WOLF-THING BREAK-IN. WHAT IF THE EVIL GODS DON'T WANT THEIR CHILDREN TESTIFYING AGAINST THEM?
THANKS FOR YOUR CONCERN, YUKIO. WE HAVE THE KIDS' SECURITY WELL IN HAND.
I CONSIDERED CEREBRUS AS A GUARDIAN, BUT WHAT KIND OF ADMINISTRATOR BRINGS A VICIOUS, THREE-HEADED DOG INTO A SCHOOL?
STARTING THIS AFTERNOON, TIERCE WILL BE STATIONED OUTSIDE.
THAT'S, LIKE, *SO SMART.* I'LL BET YOU ALREADY QUESTIONED THE KIDS AND *EVERYTHING.*
SUBJECTIN THEM TO MY MYTHICA PUNISHMEN HASN'T LOOSENED THEIR TONGUES-- SEE FOR YOUR-SELVES...

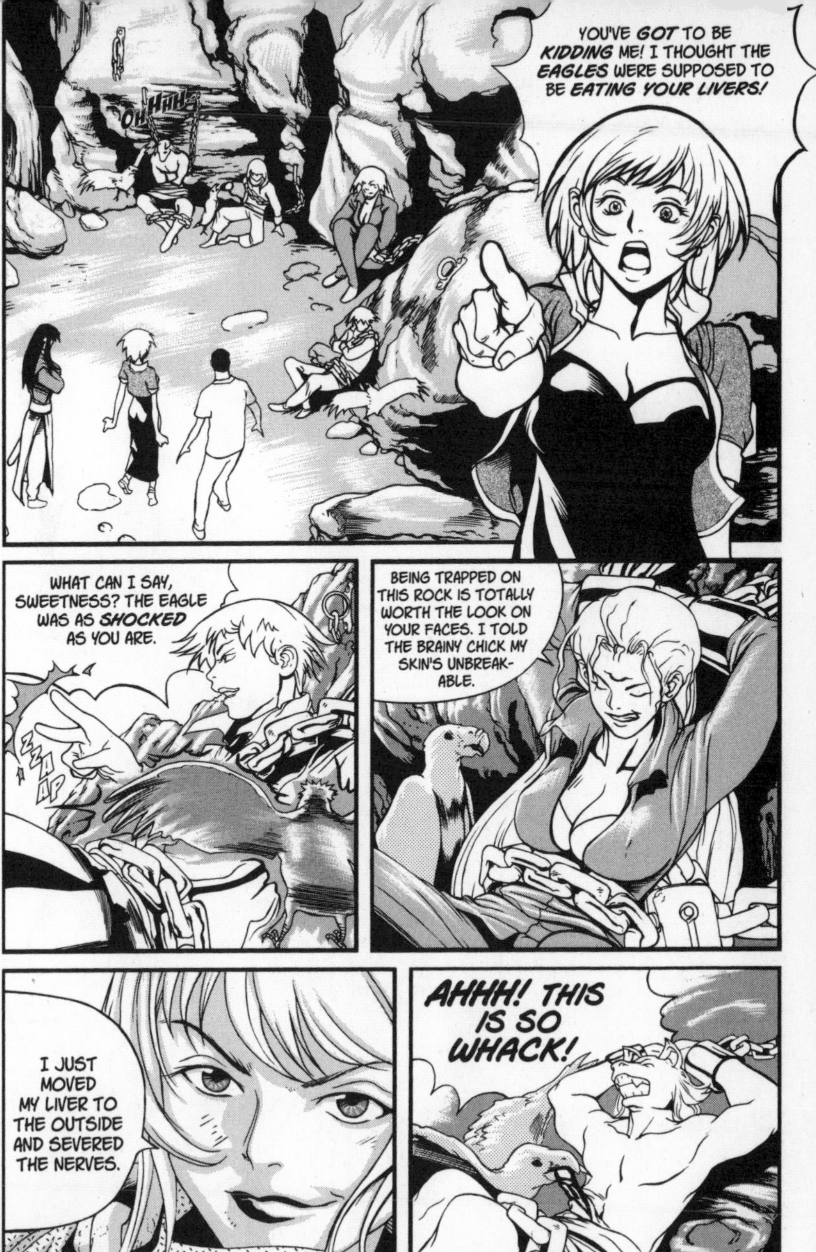
YOU'VE GOT TO BE KIDDING ME! I THOUGHT THE EAGLES WERE SUPPOSED TO BE EATING YOUR LIVERS!
WHAT CAN I SAY, SWEETNESS? THE EAGLE WAS AS SHOCKED AS YOU ARE.
BEING TRAPPED ON THIS ROCK IS TOTALLY WORTH THE LOOK ON YOUR FACES. I TOLD THE BRAINY CHICK MY SKIN'S UNBREAKABLE.
I JUST MOVED MY LIVER TO THE OUTSIDE AND SEVERED THE NERVES.
AHHH! THIS IS SO WHACK!

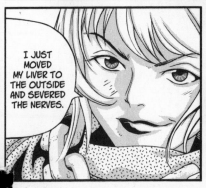

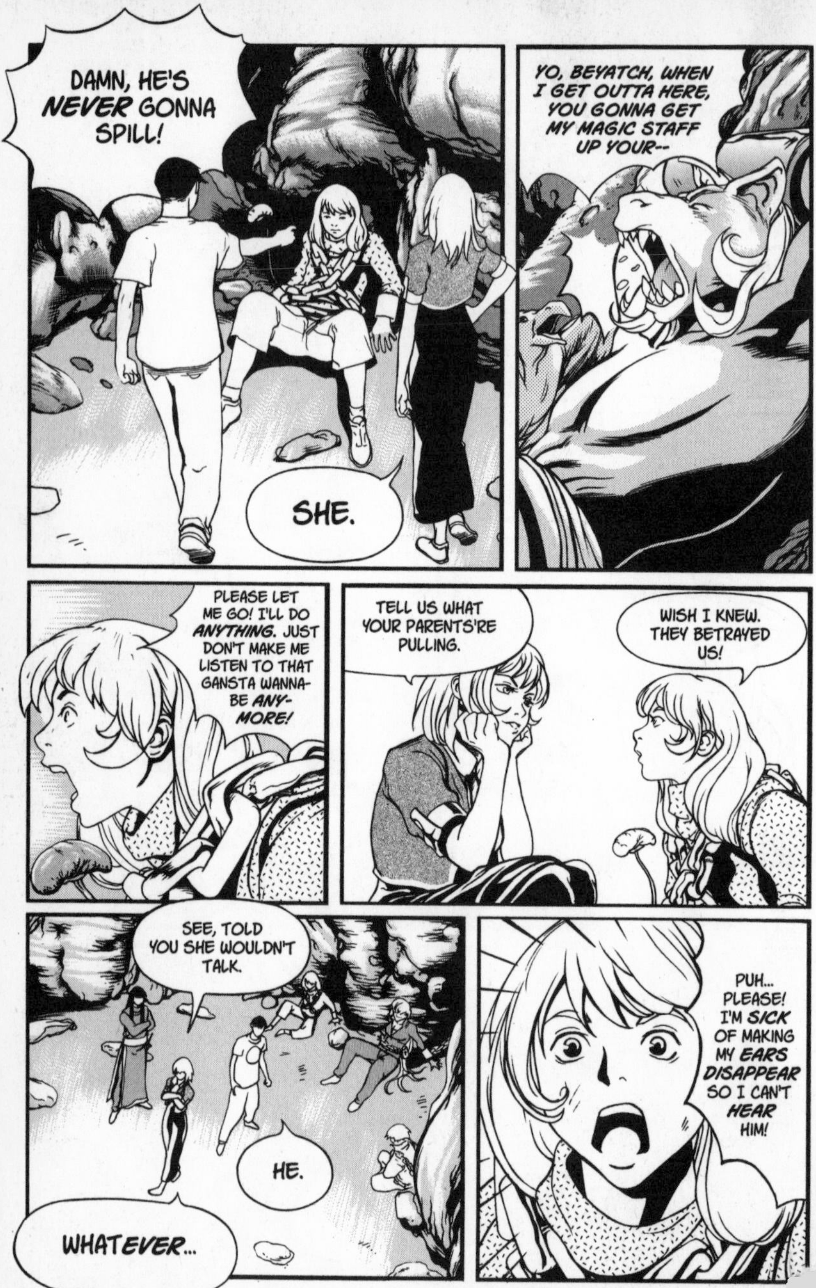
DAMN, HE'S NEVER GONNA SPILL!
SHE.
YO, BEYATCH, WHEN I GET OUTTA HERE, YOU GONNA GET MY MAGIC STAFF UP YOUR--
PLEASE LET ME GO! I'LL DO ANYTHING. JUST DON'T MAKE ME LISTEN TO THAT GANSTA WANNA-BE ANY-MORE!
TELL US WHAT YOUR PARENTS'RE PULLING.
WISH I KNEW. THEY BETRAYED US!
SEE, TOLD YOU SHE WOULDN'T TALK.
HE.
WHATEVER...
PUH... PLEASE! I'M SICK OF MAKING MY EARS DISAPPEAR SO I CAN'T HEAR HIM!

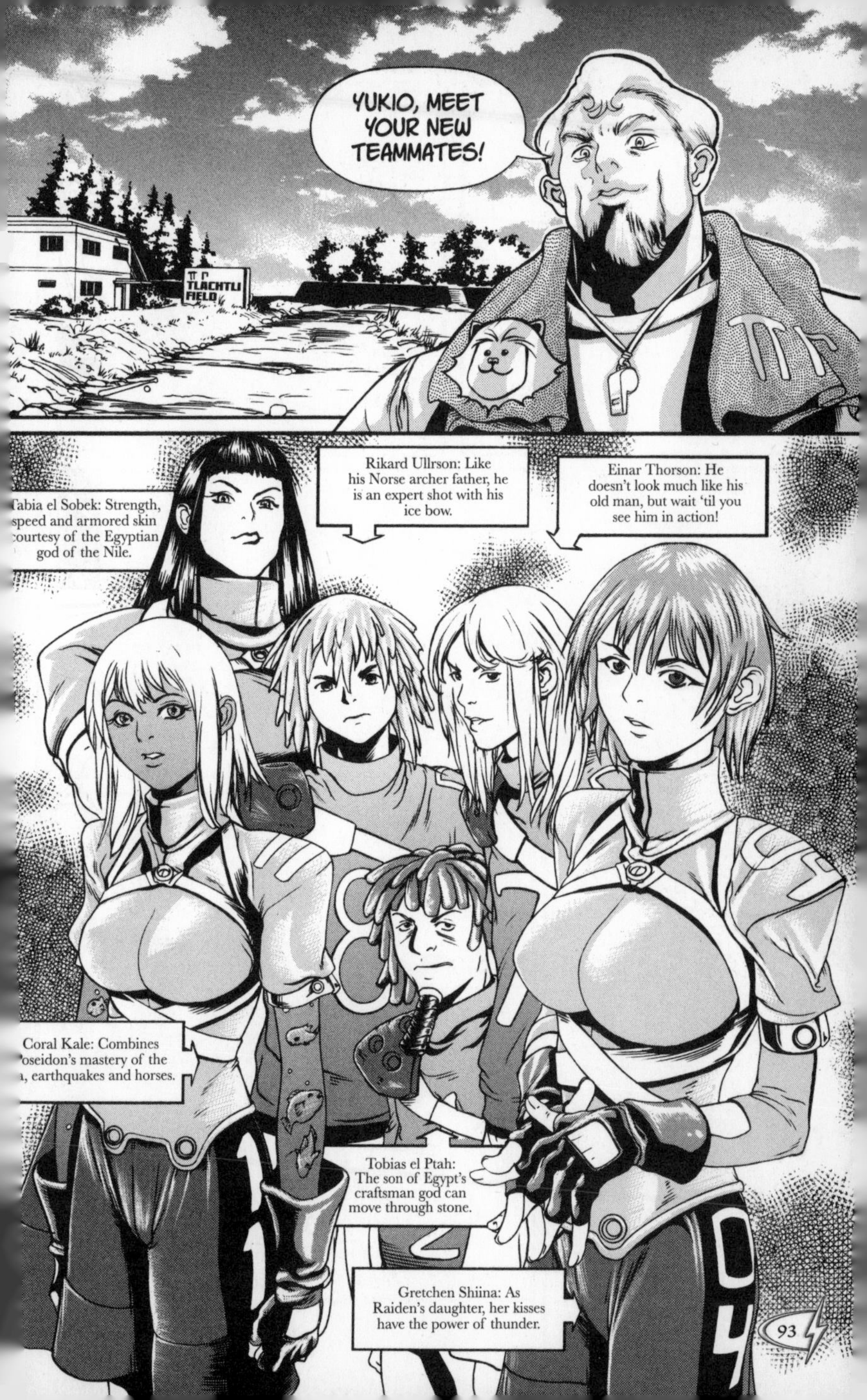
TLACHTLI FIELD
YUKIO, MEET YOUR NEW TEAMMATES!
Tabia el Sobek: Strength, speed and armored skin courtesy of the Egyptian god of the Nile.
Rikard Ullrson: Like his Norse archer father, he is an expert shot with his ice bow.
Einar Thorson: He doesn't look much like his old man, but wait 'til you see him in action!
Coral Kale: Combines Poseidon's mastery of the a, earthquakes and horses.
Tobias el Ptah: The son of Egypt's craftsman god can move through stone.
Gretchen Shiina: As Raiden's daughter, her kisses have the power of thunder.

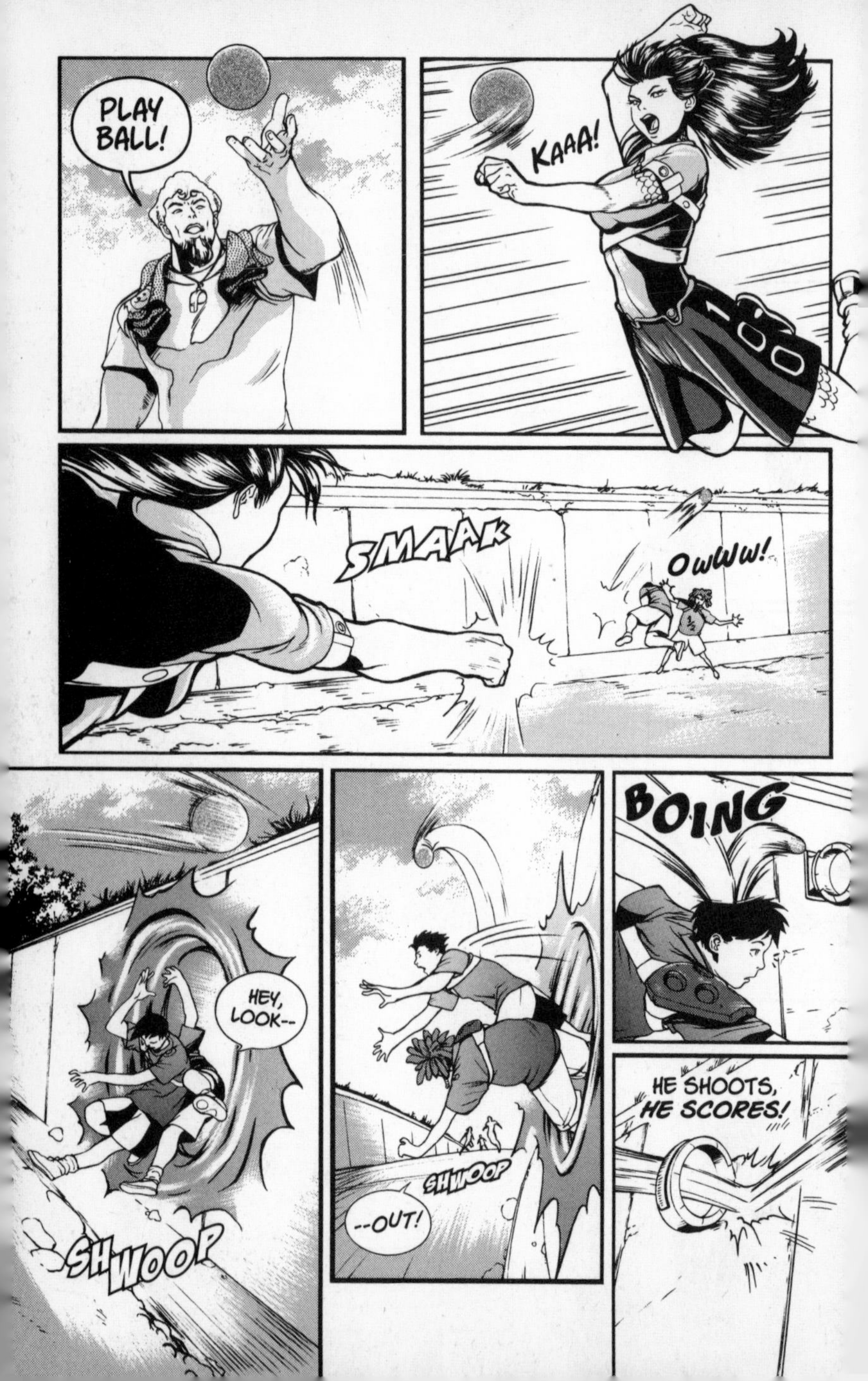
PLAY BALL!
KAAA!
SMAAK
OWWW!
HEY, LOOK--
SHWOOP
SHWOOP
--OUT!
BOING
HE SHOOTS, HE SCORES!

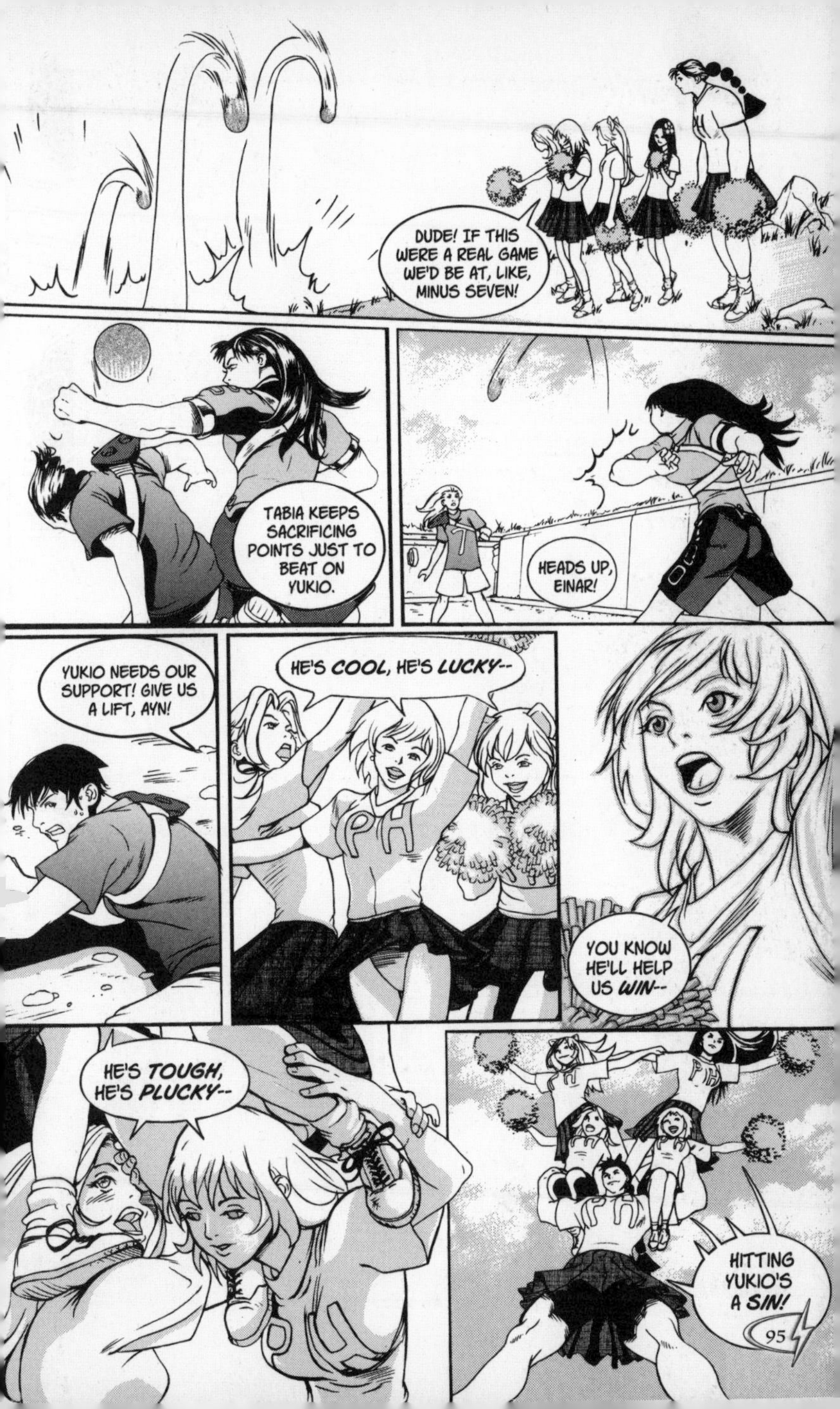
DUDE! IF THIS WERE A REAL GAME WE'D BE AT, LIKE, MINUS SEVEN!
TABIA KEEPS SACRIFICING POINTS JUST TO BEAT ON YUKIO.
HEADS UP, EINAR!
YUKIO NEEDS OUR SUPPORT! GIVE US A LIFT, AYN!
HE'S COOL, HE'S LUCKY--
YOU KNOW HE'LL HELP US WIN--
HE'S TOUGH, HE'S PLUCKY--
HITTING YUKIO'S A SIN!

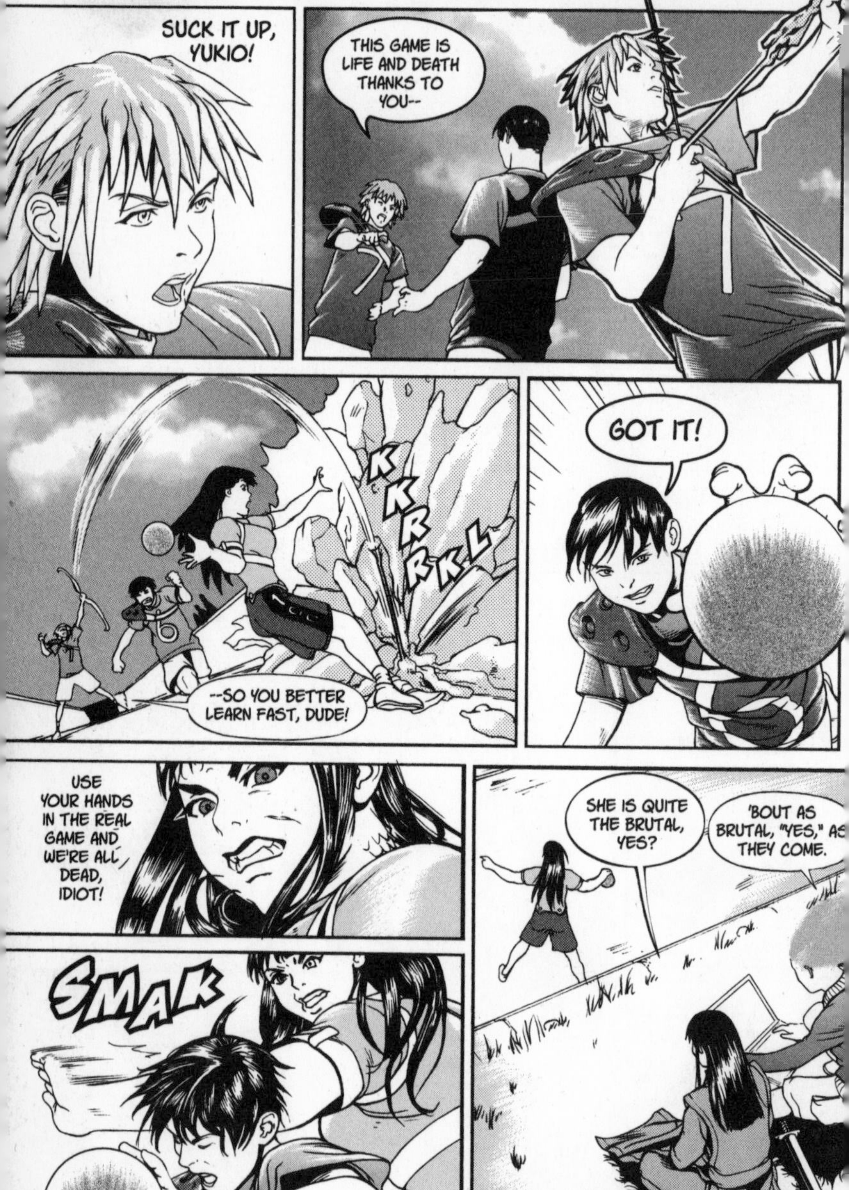

SUCK IT UP, YUKIO!
THIS GAME IS LIFE AND DEATH THANKS TO YOU--
KKRRKL
--SO YOU BETTER LEARN FAST, DUDE!
GOT IT!
USE YOUR HANDS IN THE REAL GAME AND WE'RE ALL DEAD, IDIOT!
SMAK
SHE IS QUITE THE BRUTAL, YES?
'BOUT AS BRUTAL, "YES," AS THEY COME.

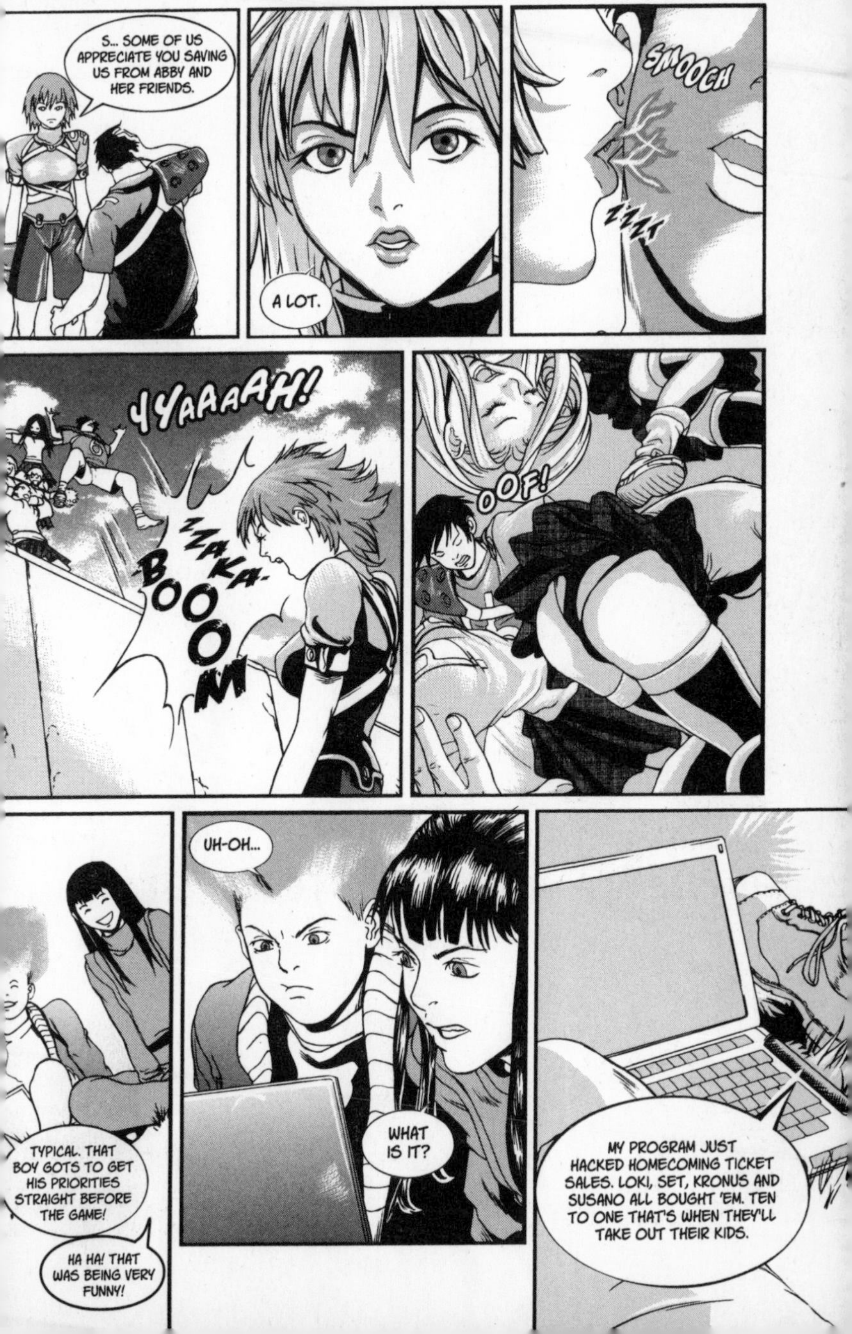
S... SOME OF US APPRECIATE YOU SAVING US FROM ABBY AND HER FRIENDS.
A LOT.
SMOOCH
ZZZT
YYAAAAAH!
ZZAKA-BOOOOM
OOF!
TYPICAL. THAT BOY GOTS TO GET HIS PRIORITIES STRAIGHT BEFORE THE GAME!
HA HA! THAT WAS BEING VERY FUNNY!
UH-OH...
WHAT IS IT?
MY PROGRAM JUST HACKED HOMECOMING TICKET SALES. LOKI, SET, KRONUS AND SUSANO ALL BOUGHT 'EM. TEN TO ONE THAT'S WHEN THEY'LL TAKE OUT THEIR KIDS.

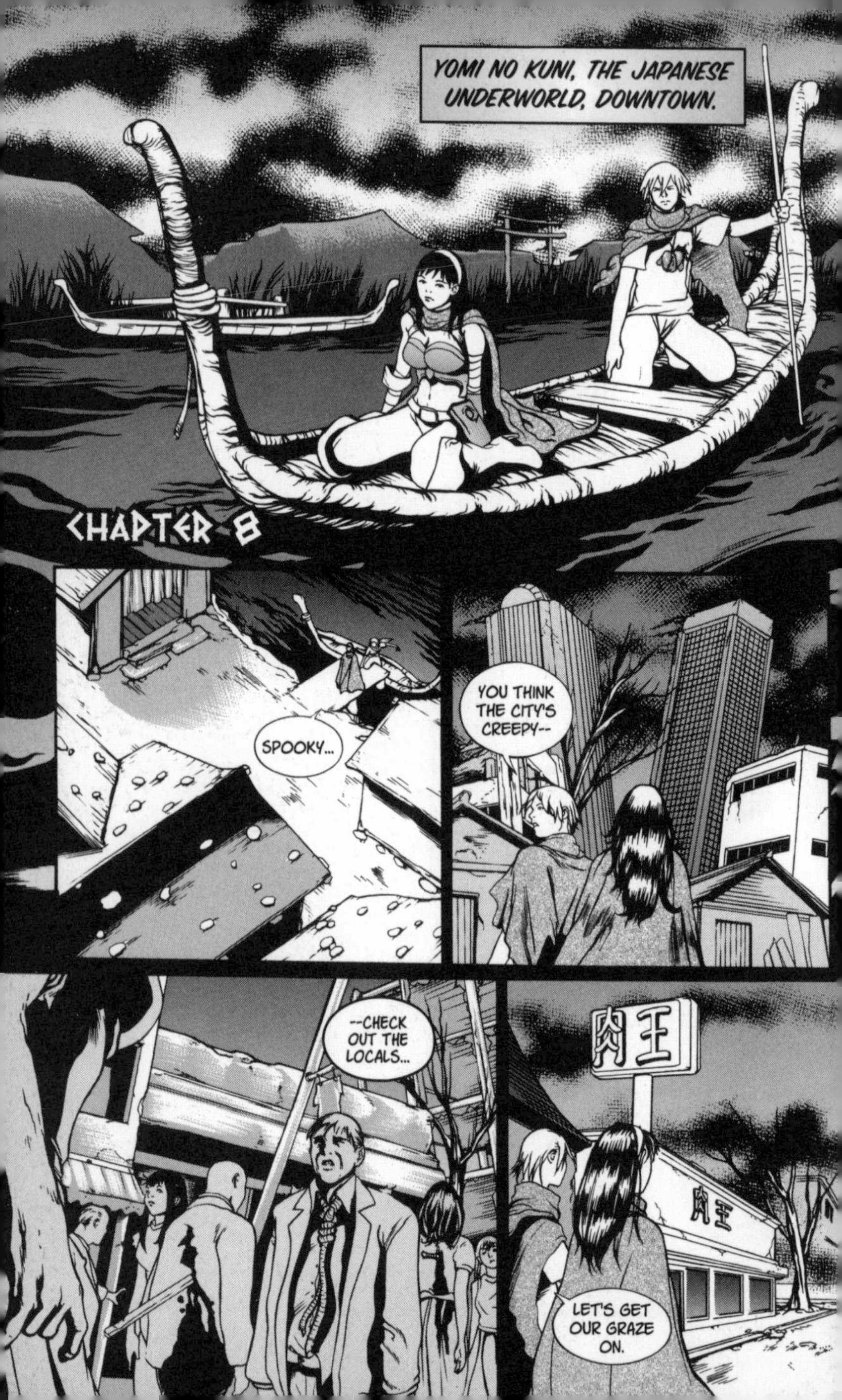
YOMI NO KUNI, THE JAPANESE UNDERWORLD, DOWNTOWN.
CHAPTER 8
SPOOKY...
YOU THINK THE CITY'S CREEPY--
--CHECK OUT THE LOCALS...
肉王
LET'S GET OUR GRAZE ON.

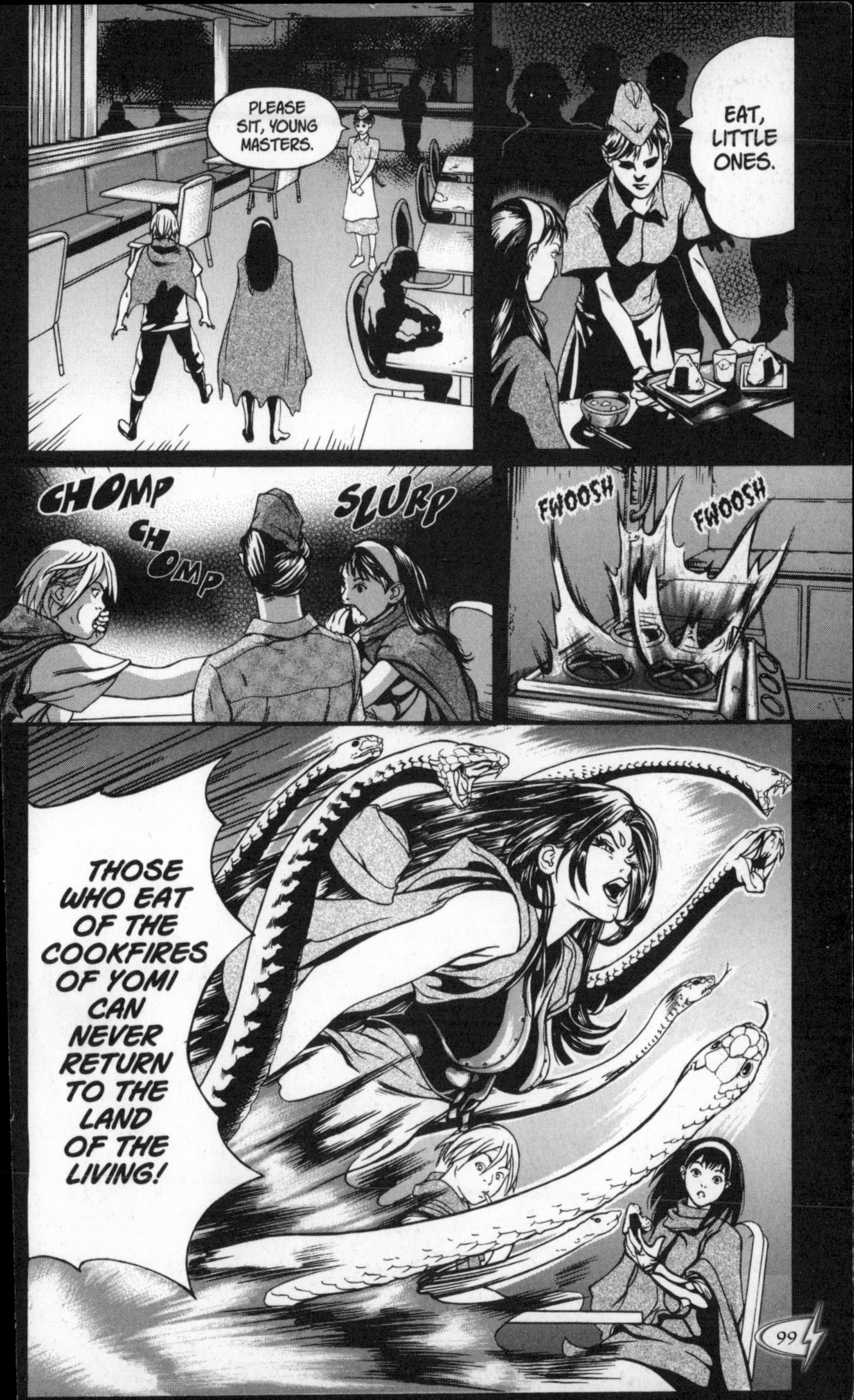
PLEASE SIT, YOUNG MASTERS.
EAT, LITTLE ONES.
CHOMP CHOMP CHOMP
SLURP
FWOOSH
FWOOSH
THOSE WHO EAT OF THE COOKFIRES OF YOMI CAN NEVER RETURN TO THE LAND OF THE LIVING!

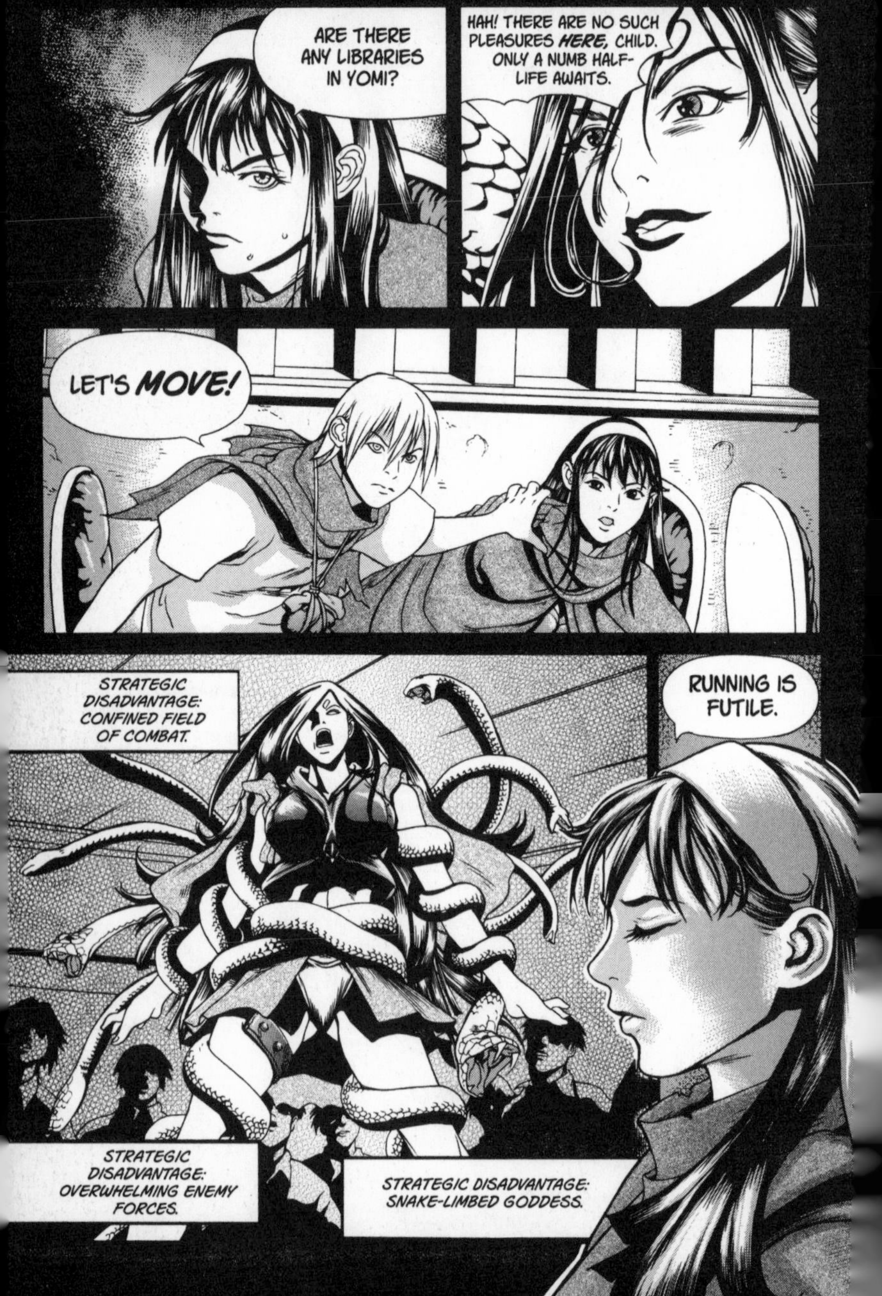
ARE THERE ANY LIBRARIES IN YOMI?
HAH! THERE ARE NO SUCH PLEASURES *HERE,* CHILD. ONLY A NUMB HALF-LIFE AWAITS.
LET'S *MOVE!*
STRATEGIC DISADVANTAGE: CONFINED FIELD OF COMBAT.
RUNNING IS FUTILE.
STRATEGIC DISADVANTAGE: OVERWHELMING ENEMY FORCES.
STRATEGIC DISADVANTAGE: SNAKE-LIMBED GODDESS.

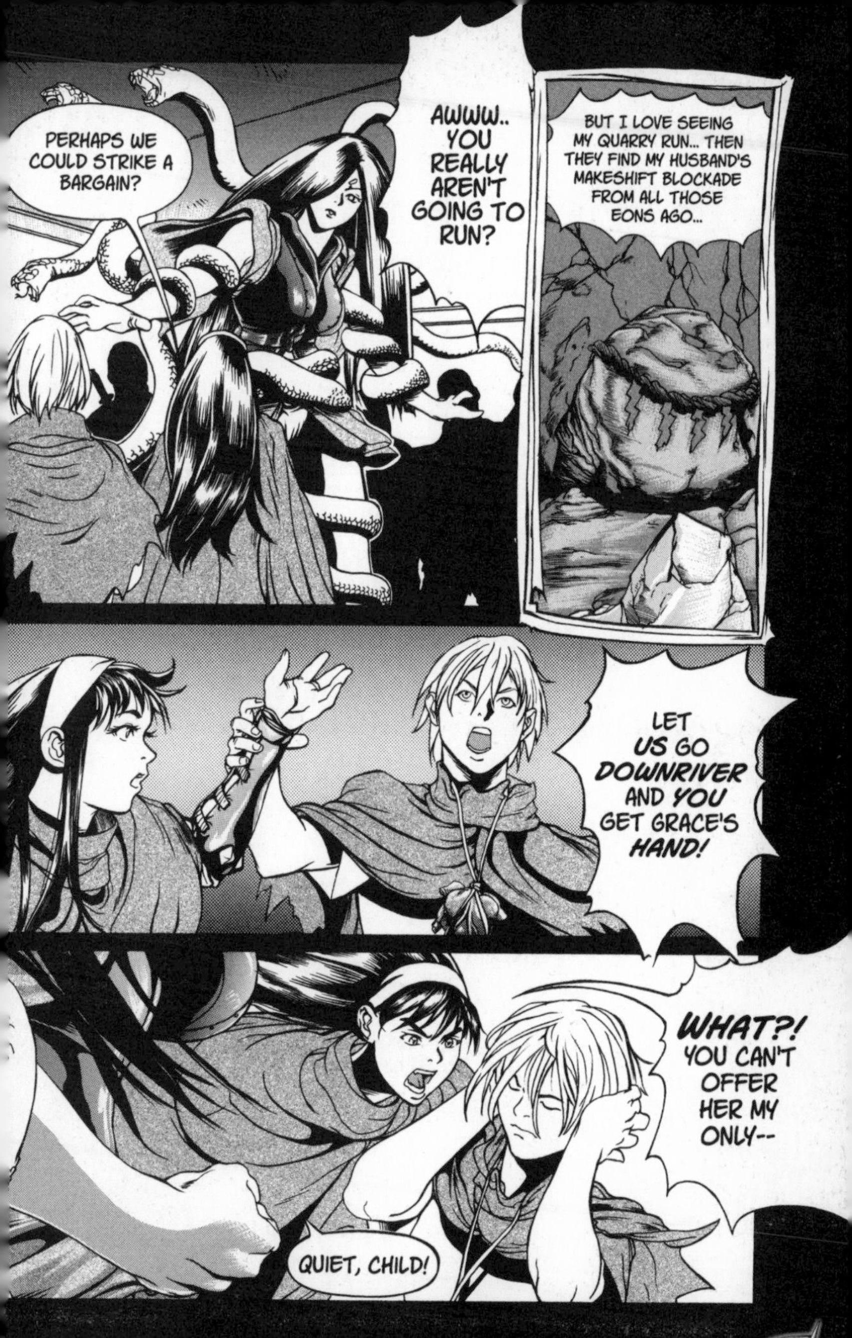
PERHAPS WE COULD STRIKE A BARGAIN?
AWWW.. YOU REALLY AREN'T GOING TO RUN?
BUT I LOVE SEEING MY QUARRY RUN... THEN THEY FIND MY HUSBAND'S MAKESHIFT BLOCKADE FROM ALL THOSE EONS AGO...
LET US GO DOWNRIVER AND YOU GET GRACE'S HAND!
WHAT?! YOU CAN'T OFFER HER MY ONLY--
QUIET, CHILD!

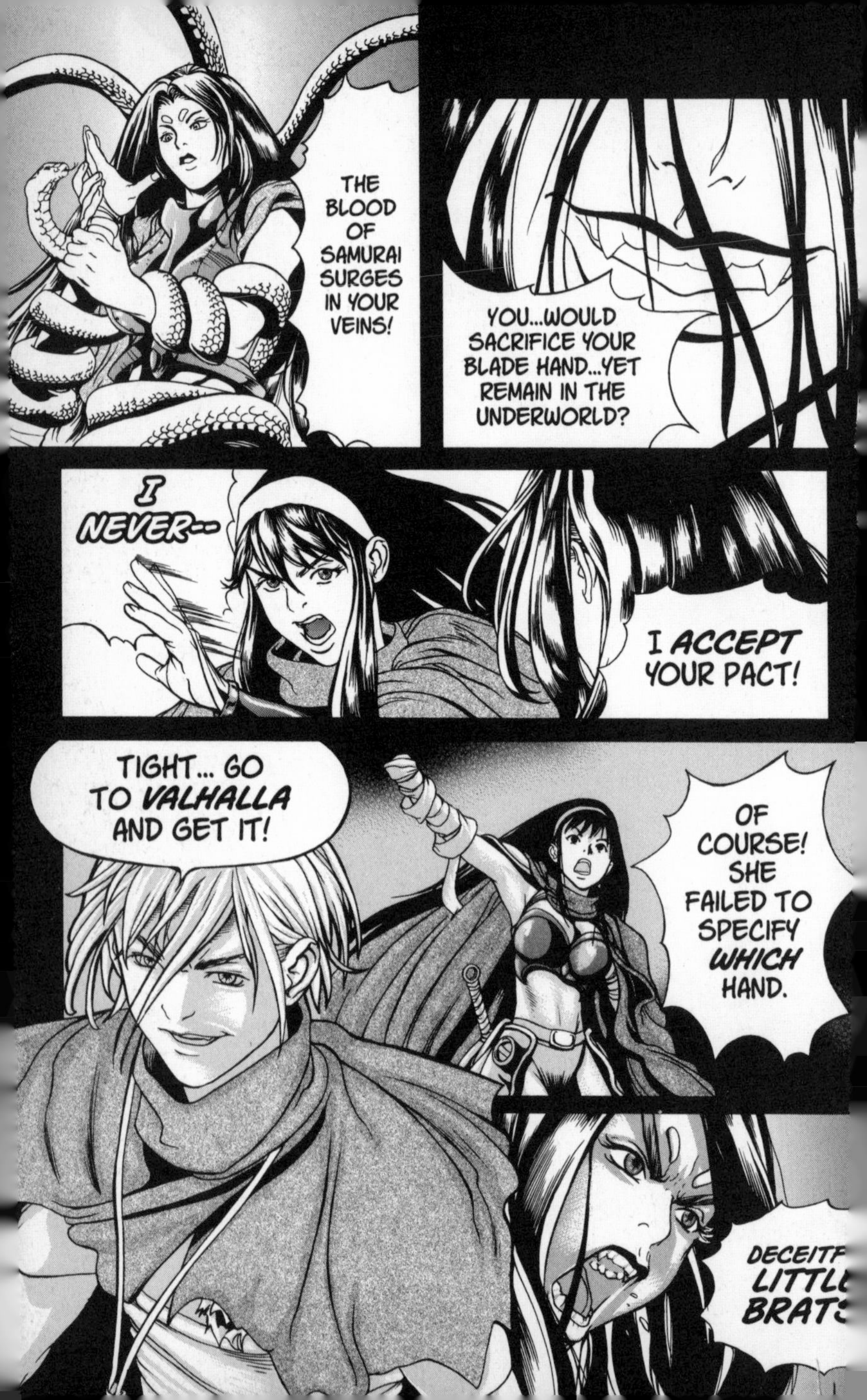
THE BLOOD OF SAMURAI SURGES IN YOUR VEINS!
YOU...WOULD SACRIFICE YOUR BLADE HAND...YET REMAIN IN THE UNDERWORLD?
I NEVER--
I ACCEPT YOUR PACT!
TIGHT... GO TO VALHALLA AND GET IT!
OF COURSE! SHE FAILED TO SPECIFY WHICH HAND.
DECEITF LITTL BRATS

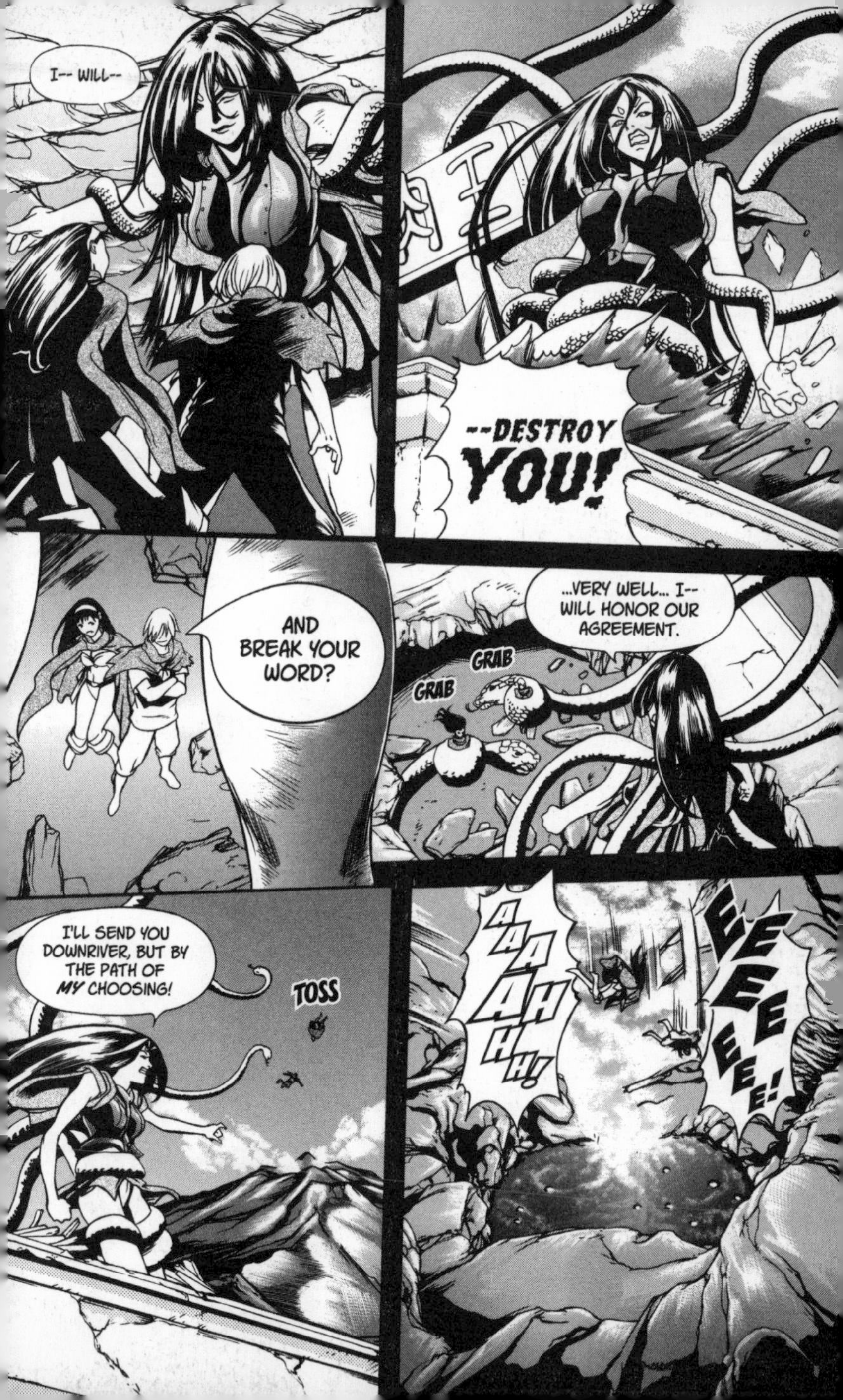
I-- WILL--
--DESTROY YOU!
AND BREAK YOUR WORD?
...VERY WELL... I-- WILL HONOR OUR AGREEMENT.
GRAB
GRAB
I'LL SEND YOU DOWNRIVER, BUT BY THE PATH OF *MY* CHOOSING!
TOSS
AAAAHHH!
EEEEEEE!

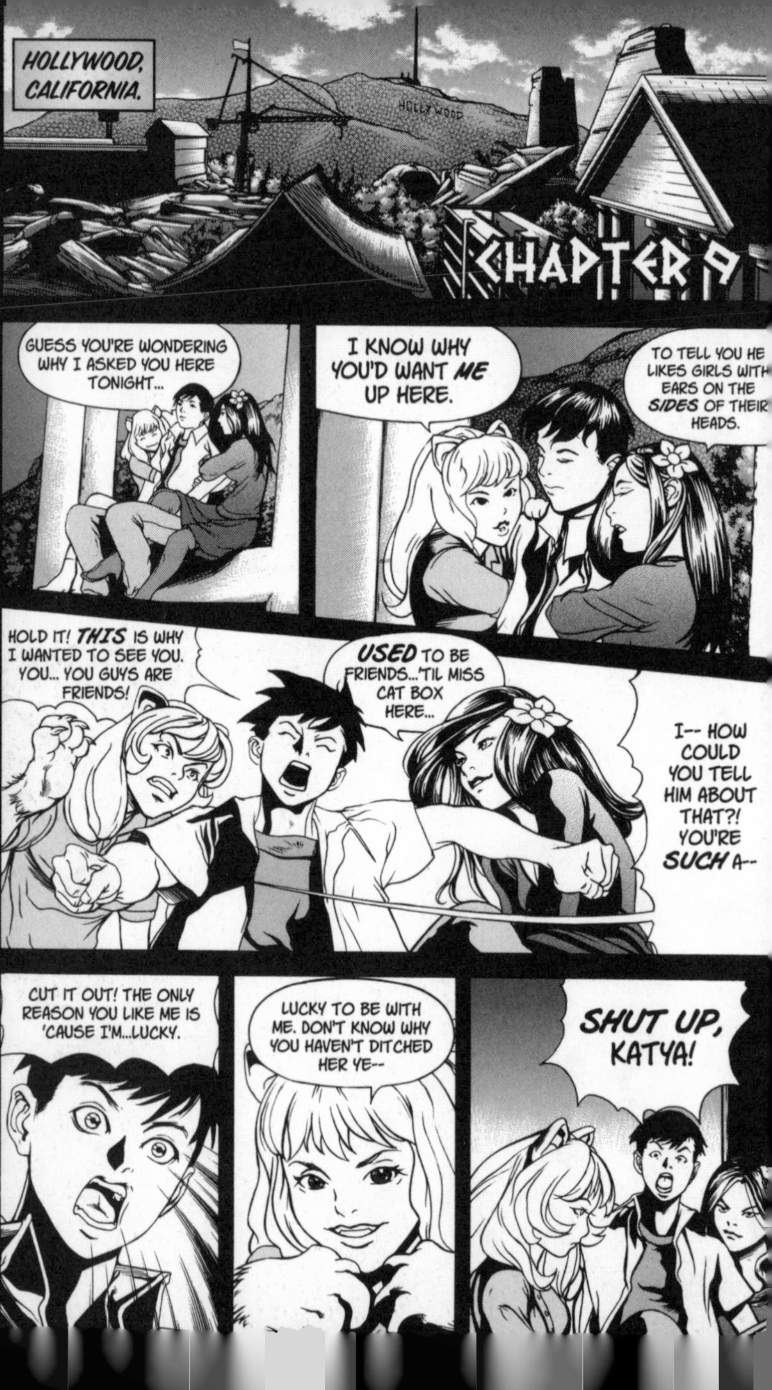
HOLLYWOOD, CALIFORNIA.
HOLLYWOOD
CHAPTER 9
GUESS YOU'RE WONDERING WHY I ASKED YOU HERE TONIGHT...
I KNOW WHY YOU'D WANT ME UP HERE.
TO TELL YOU HE LIKES GIRLS WITH EARS ON THE SIDES OF THEIR HEADS.
HOLD IT! THIS IS WHY I WANTED TO SEE YOU. YOU... YOU GUYS ARE FRIENDS!
USED TO BE FRIENDS...'TIL MISS CAT BOX HERE...
I-- HOW COULD YOU TELL HIM ABOUT THAT?! YOU'RE SUCH A--
CUT IT OUT! THE ONLY REASON YOU LIKE ME IS 'CAUSE I'M...LUCKY.
LUCKY TO BE WITH ME. DON'T KNOW WHY YOU HAVEN'T DITCHED HER YE--
SHUT UP, KATYA!

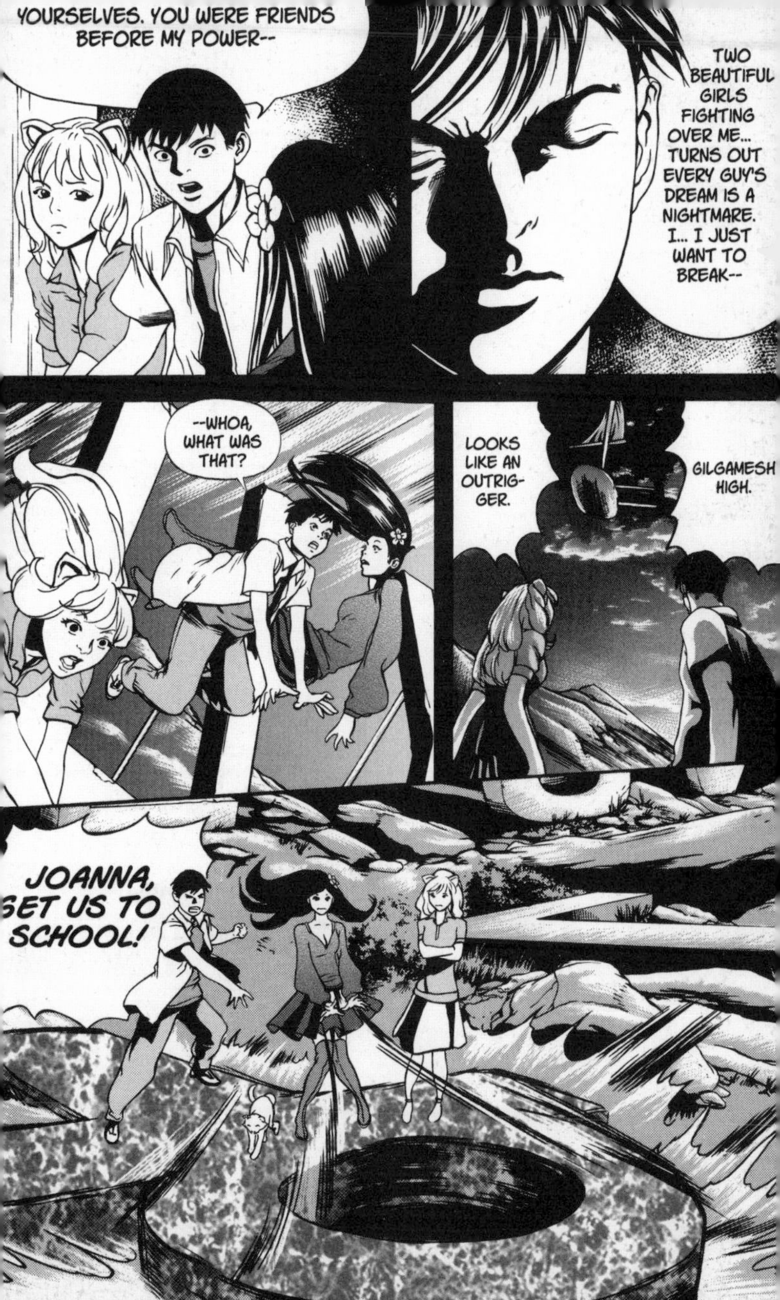
YOURSELVES. YOU WERE FRIENDS BEFORE MY POWER--
TWO BEAUTIFUL GIRLS FIGHTING OVER ME... TURNS OUT EVERY GUY'S DREAM IS A NIGHTMARE. I... I JUST WANT TO BREAK--
--WHOA, WHAT WAS THAT?
LOOKS LIKE AN OUTRIG-GER.
GILGAMESH HIGH.
JOANNA, GET US TO SCHOOL!

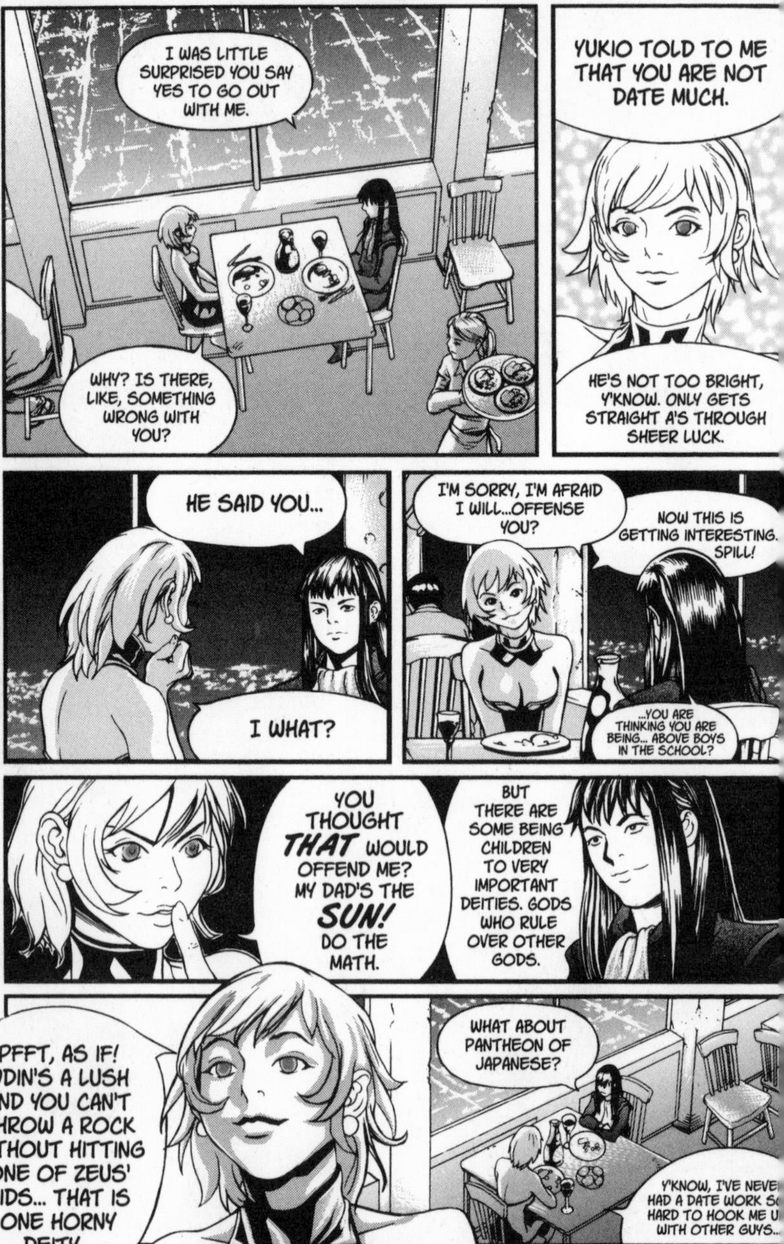
I WAS LITTLE SURPRISED YOU SAY YES TO GO OUT WITH ME.
WHY? IS THERE, LIKE, SOMETHING WRONG WITH YOU?
YUKIO TOLD TO ME THAT YOU ARE NOT DATE MUCH.
HE'S NOT TOO BRIGHT, Y'KNOW. ONLY GETS STRAIGHT A'S THROUGH SHEER LUCK.
HE SAID YOU...
I WHAT?
I'M SORRY, I'M AFRAID I WILL...OFFENSE YOU?
NOW THIS IS GETTING INTERESTING. SPILL!
...YOU ARE THINKING YOU ARE BEING... ABOVE BOYS IN THE SCHOOL?
YOU THOUGHT THAT WOULD OFFEND ME? MY DAD'S THE SUN! DO THE MATH.
BUT THERE ARE SOME BEING CHILDREN TO VERY IMPORTANT DEITIES. GODS WHO RULE OVER OTHER GODS.
PFFT, AS IF! ODIN'S A LUSH AND YOU CAN'T THROW A ROCK WITHOUT HITTING ONE OF ZEUS' KIDS... THAT IS ONE HORNY DEITY...
WHAT ABOUT PANTHEON OF JAPANESE?
Y'KNOW, I'VE NEVE HAD A DATE WORK S HARD TO HOOK ME U WITH OTHER GUYS...

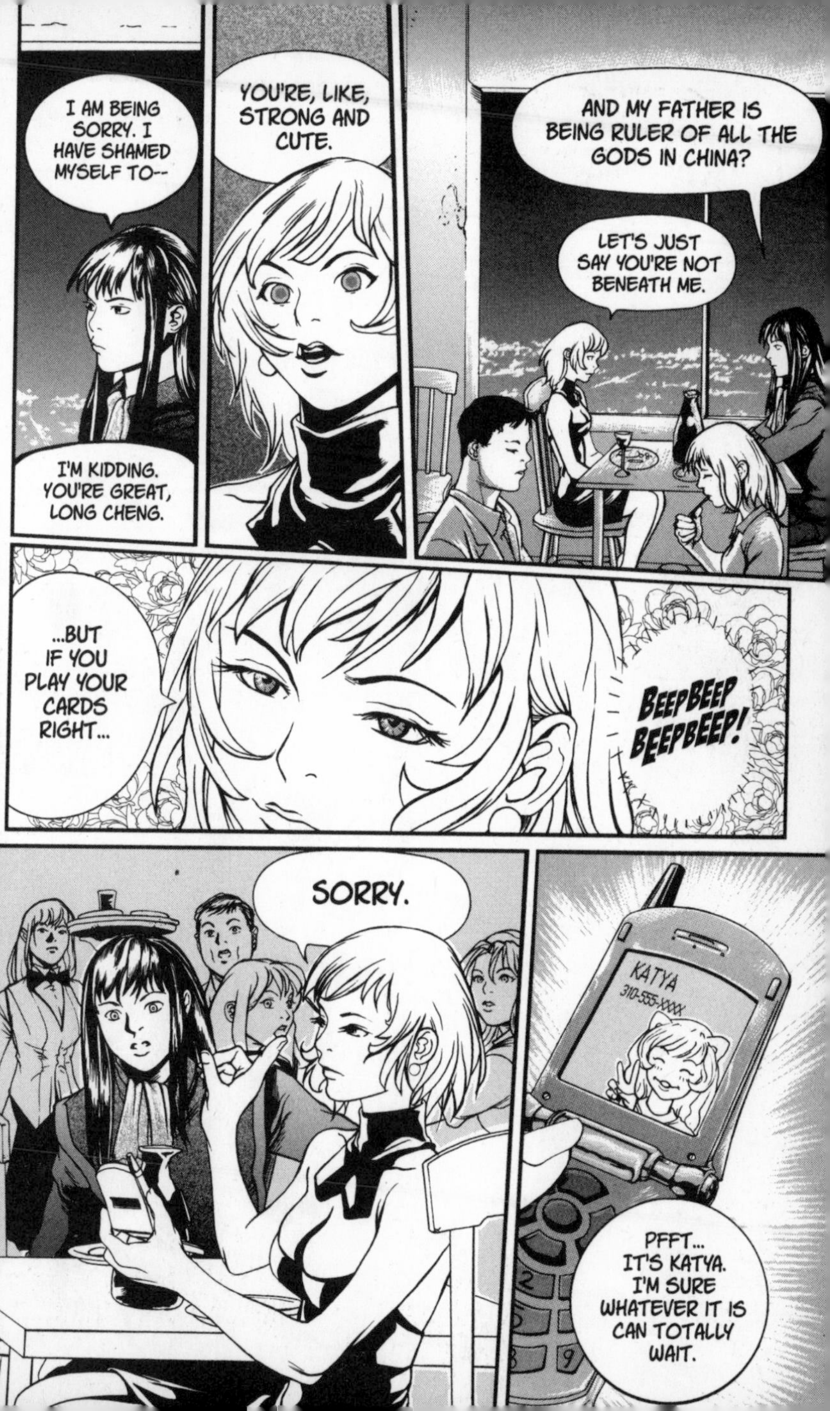

I AM BEING SORRY. I HAVE SHAMED MYSELF TO--
I'M KIDDING. YOU'RE GREAT, LONG CHENG.
YOU'RE, LIKE, STRONG AND CUTE.
AND MY FATHER IS BEING RULER OF ALL THE GODS IN CHINA?
LET'S JUST SAY YOU'RE NOT BENEATH ME.
...BUT IF YOU PLAY YOUR CARDS RIGHT...
BEEPBEEP BEEPBEEP!
SORRY.
KATYA
310-555-XXXX
PFFT... IT'S KATYA. I'M SURE WHATEVER IT IS CAN TOTALLY WAIT.

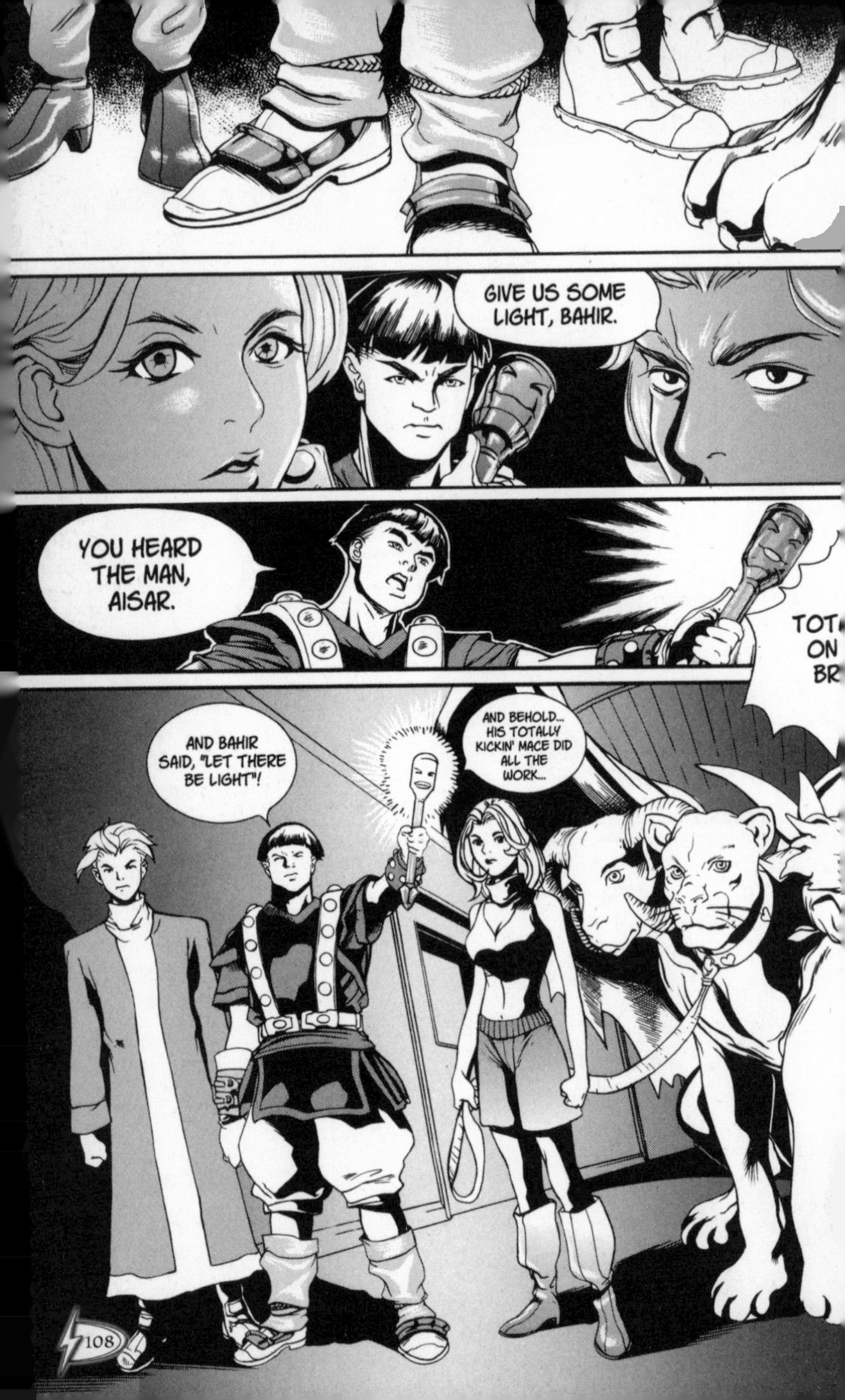
GIVE US SOME LIGHT, BAHIR.
YOU HEARD THE MAN, AISAR.
AND BAHIR SAID, "LET THERE BE LIGHT"!
AND BEHOLD... HIS TOTALLY KICKIN' MACE DID ALL THE WORK...

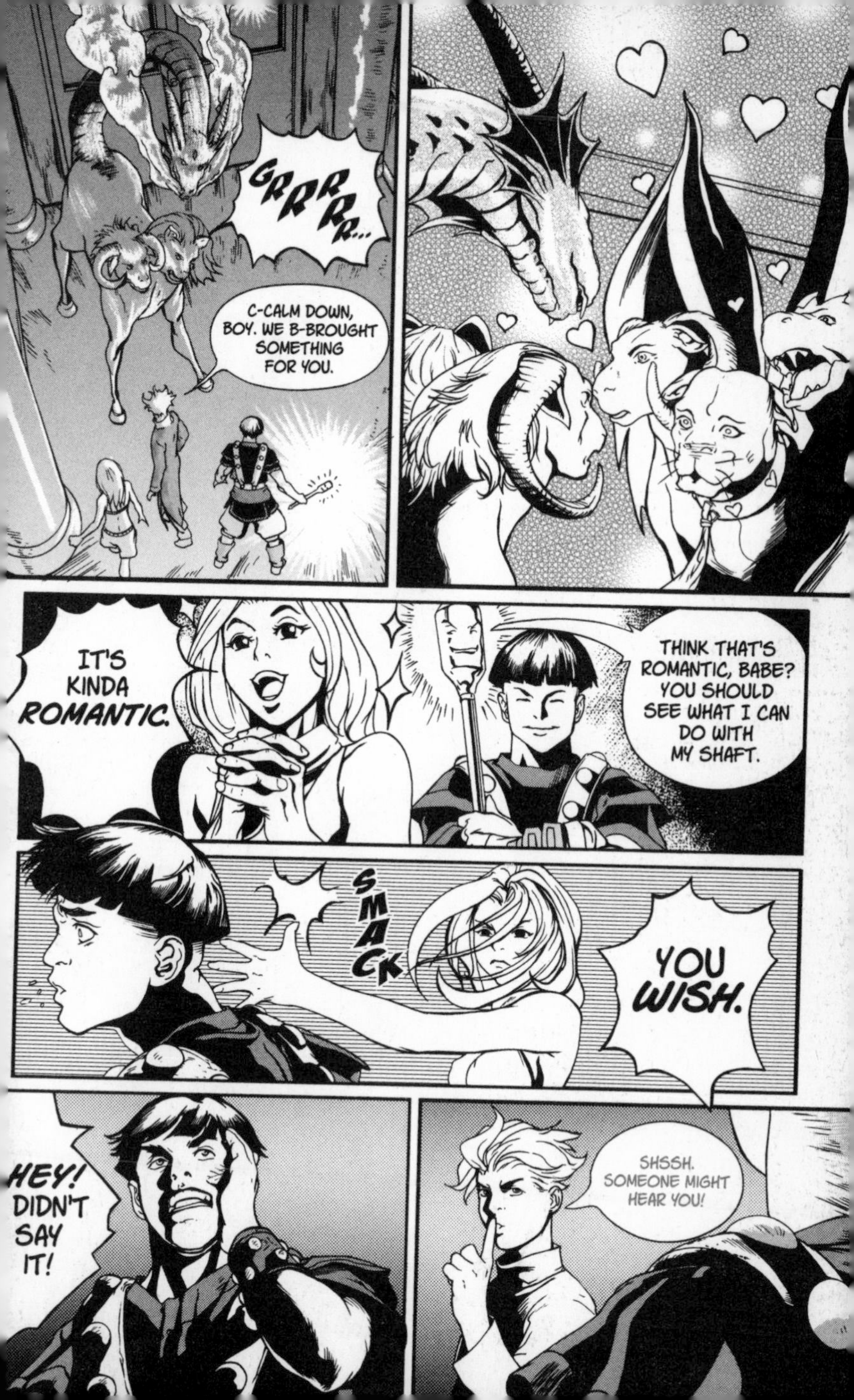
GRRRRR...
C-CALM DOWN, BOY. WE B-BROUGHT SOMETHING FOR YOU.
IT'S KINDA ROMANTIC.
THINK THAT'S ROMANTIC, BABE? YOU SHOULD SEE WHAT I CAN DO WITH MY SHAFT.
SMACK
YOU WISH.
HEY! DIDN'T SAY IT!
SHSSH. SOMEONE MIGHT HEAR YOU!

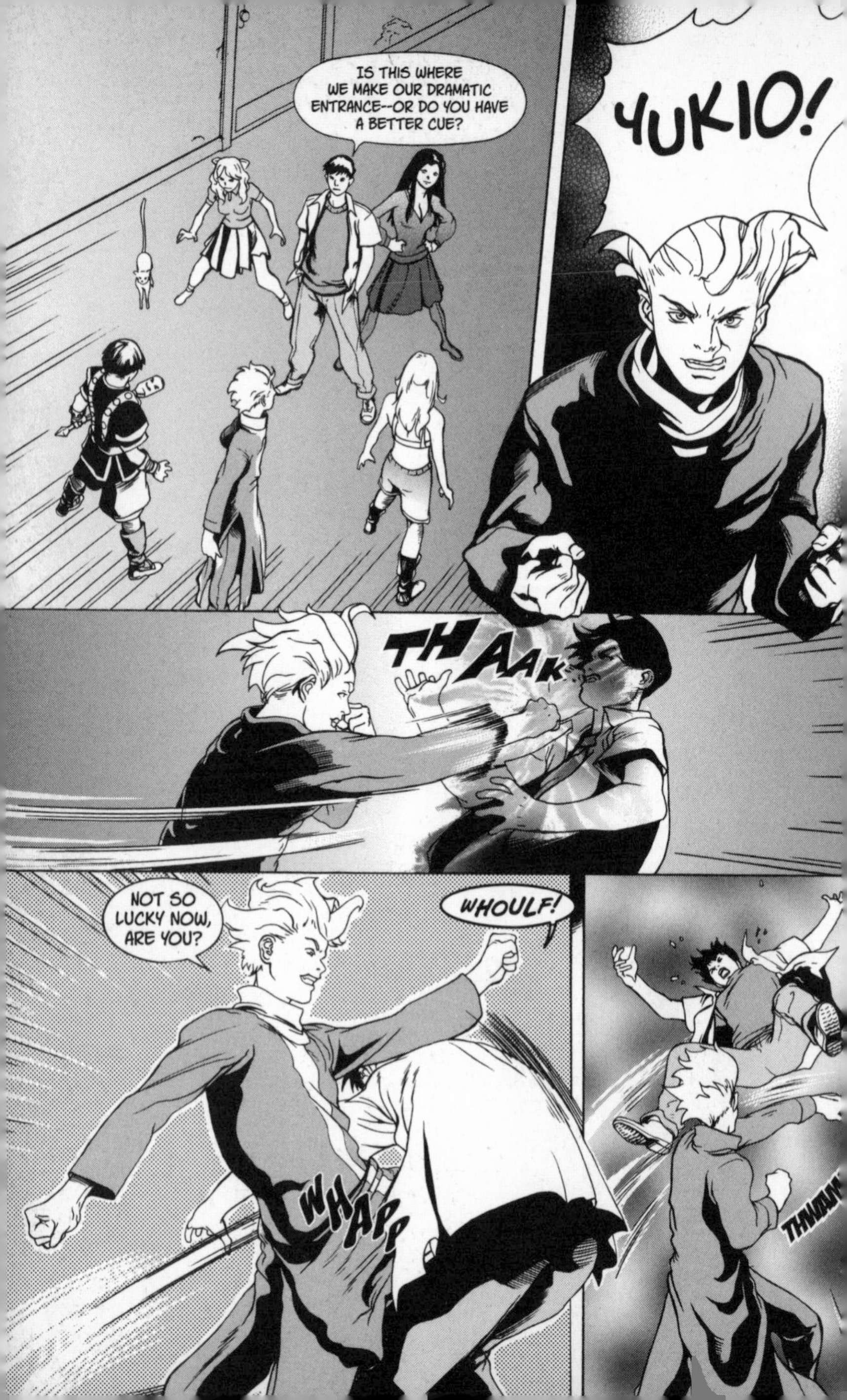
IS THIS WHERE WE MAKE OUR DRAMATIC ENTRANCE--OR DO YOU HAVE A BETTER CUE?
YUKIO!
THAAK
NOT SO LUCKY NOW, ARE YOU?
WHOULF!
WHAPP
THWAM

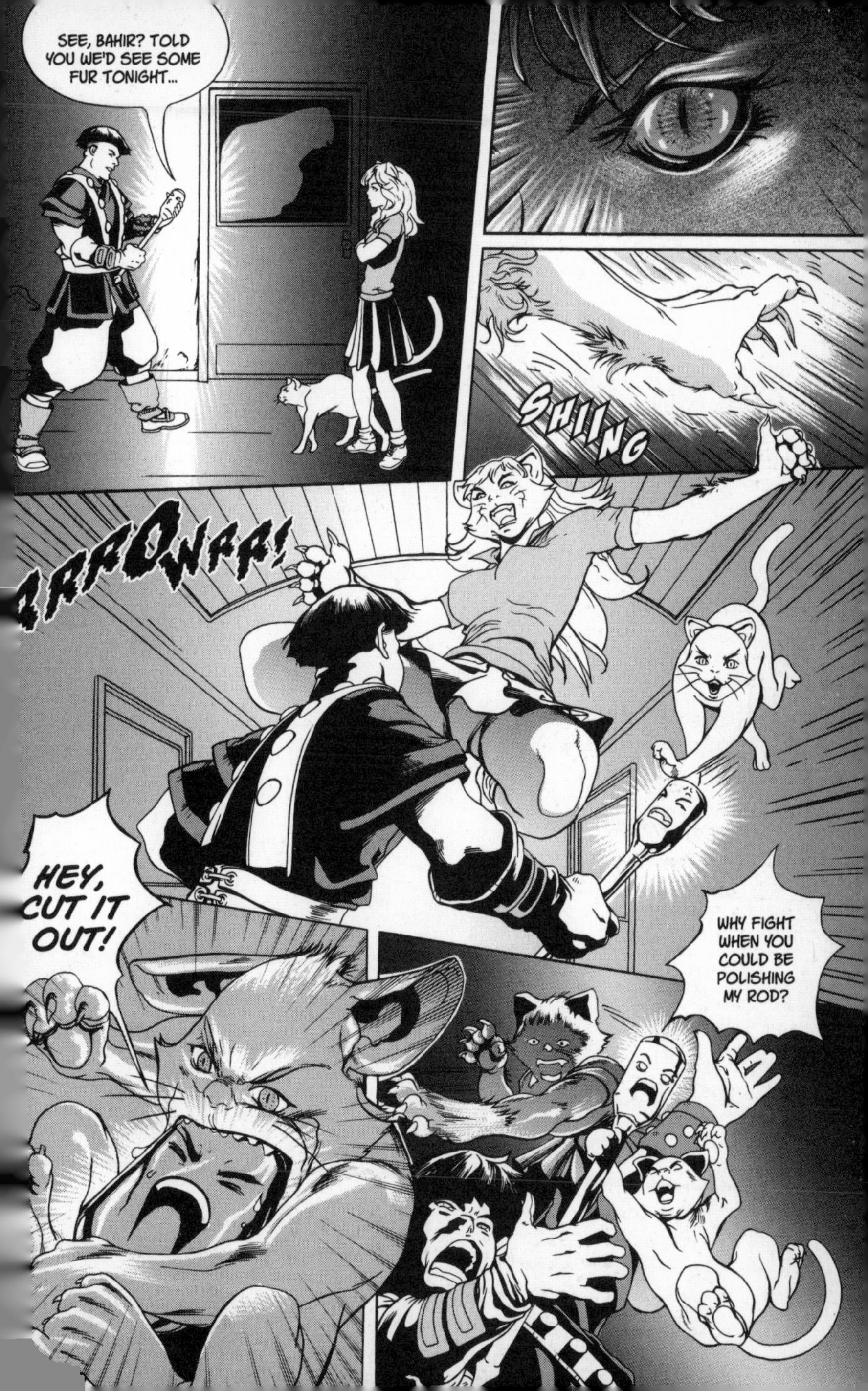
SEE, BAHIR? TOLD YOU WE'D SEE SOME FUR TONIGHT...
SHIING
ZRRROWRR!
HEY, CUT IT OUT!
WHY FIGHT WHEN YOU COULD BE POLISHING MY ROD?

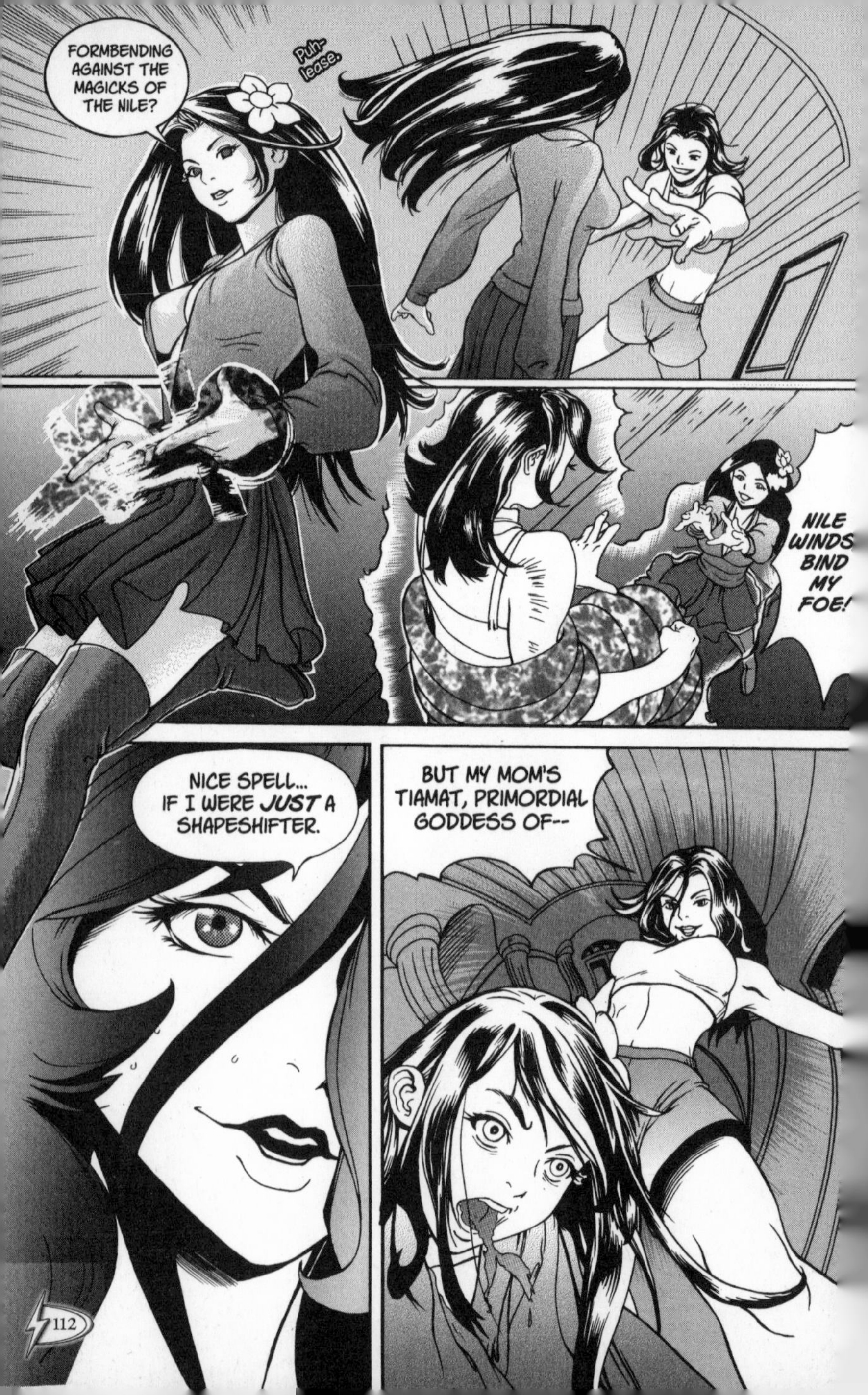
FORMBENDING AGAINST THE MAGICKS OF THE NILE?
Puh-lease.
NILE WINDS BIND MY FOE!
NICE SPELL... IF I WERE *JUST* A SHAPESHIFTER.
BUT MY MOM'S TIAMAT, PRIMORDIAL GODDESS OF--

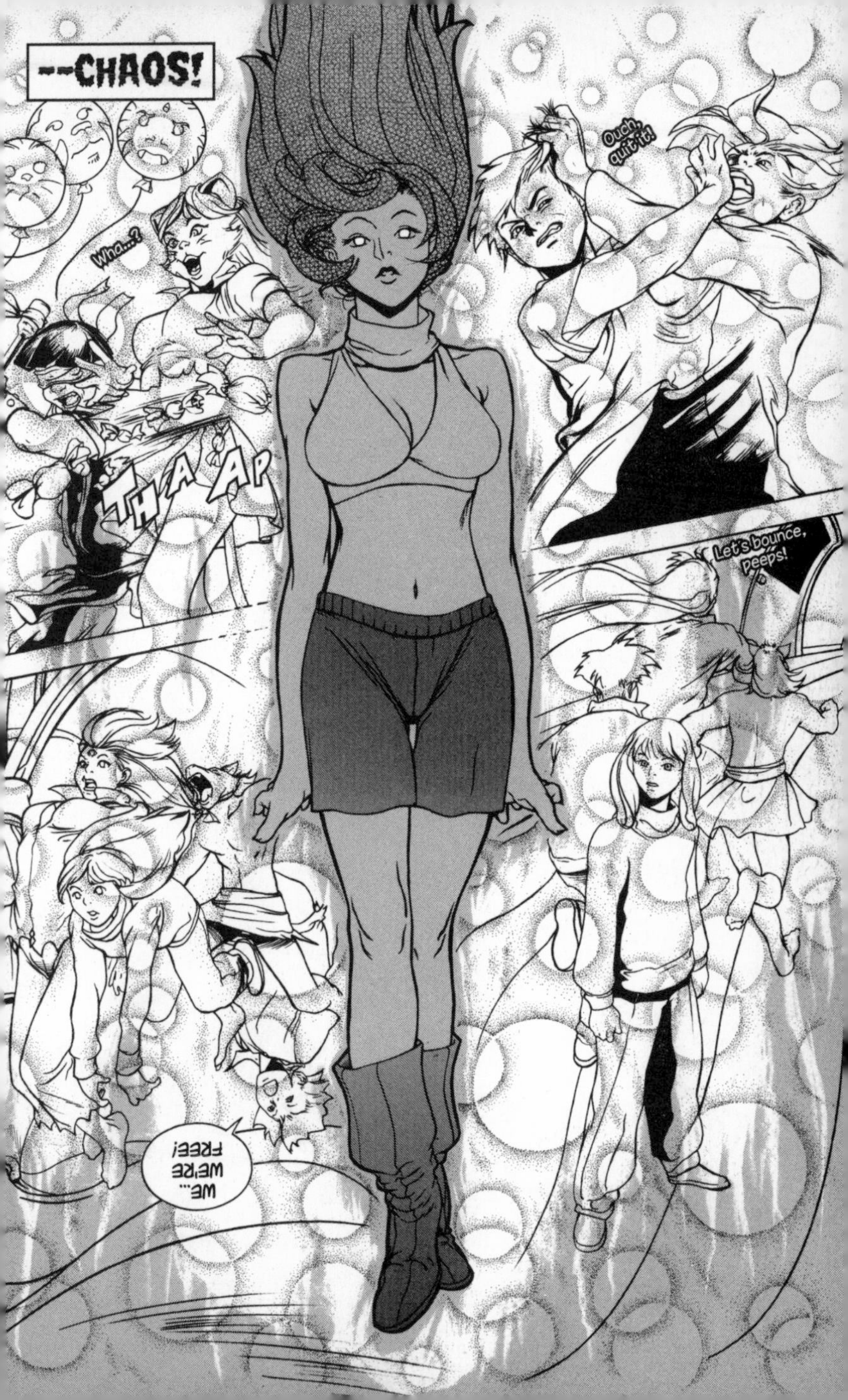
--CHAOS!
Wha...?
THAAP
Ouch, quit it!
Let's bounce, peeps!
WE... WE'RE FREE!

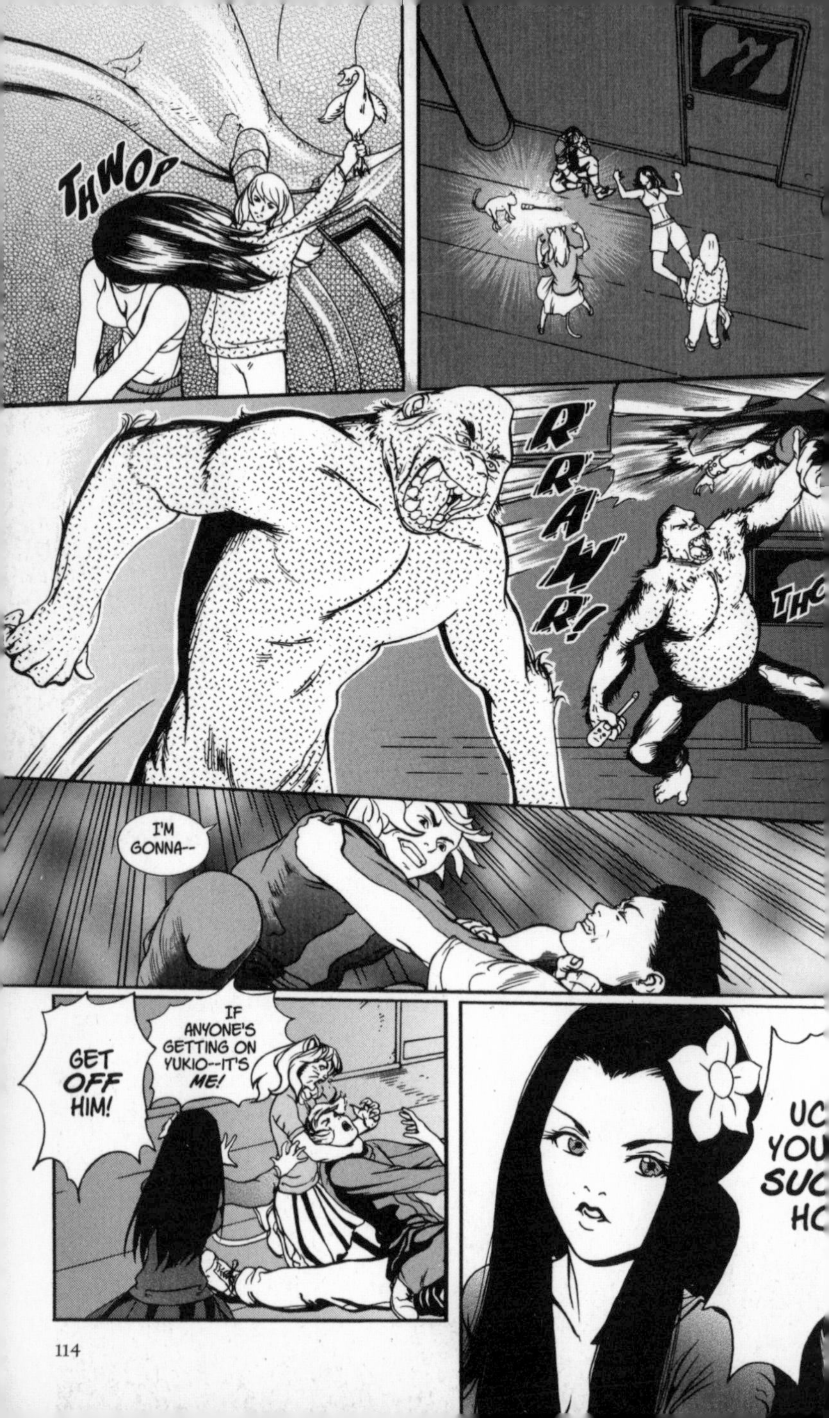
THWOP
RRAWR!
I'M GONNA--
GET OFF HIM!
IF ANYONE'S GETTING ON YUKIO--IT'S ME!

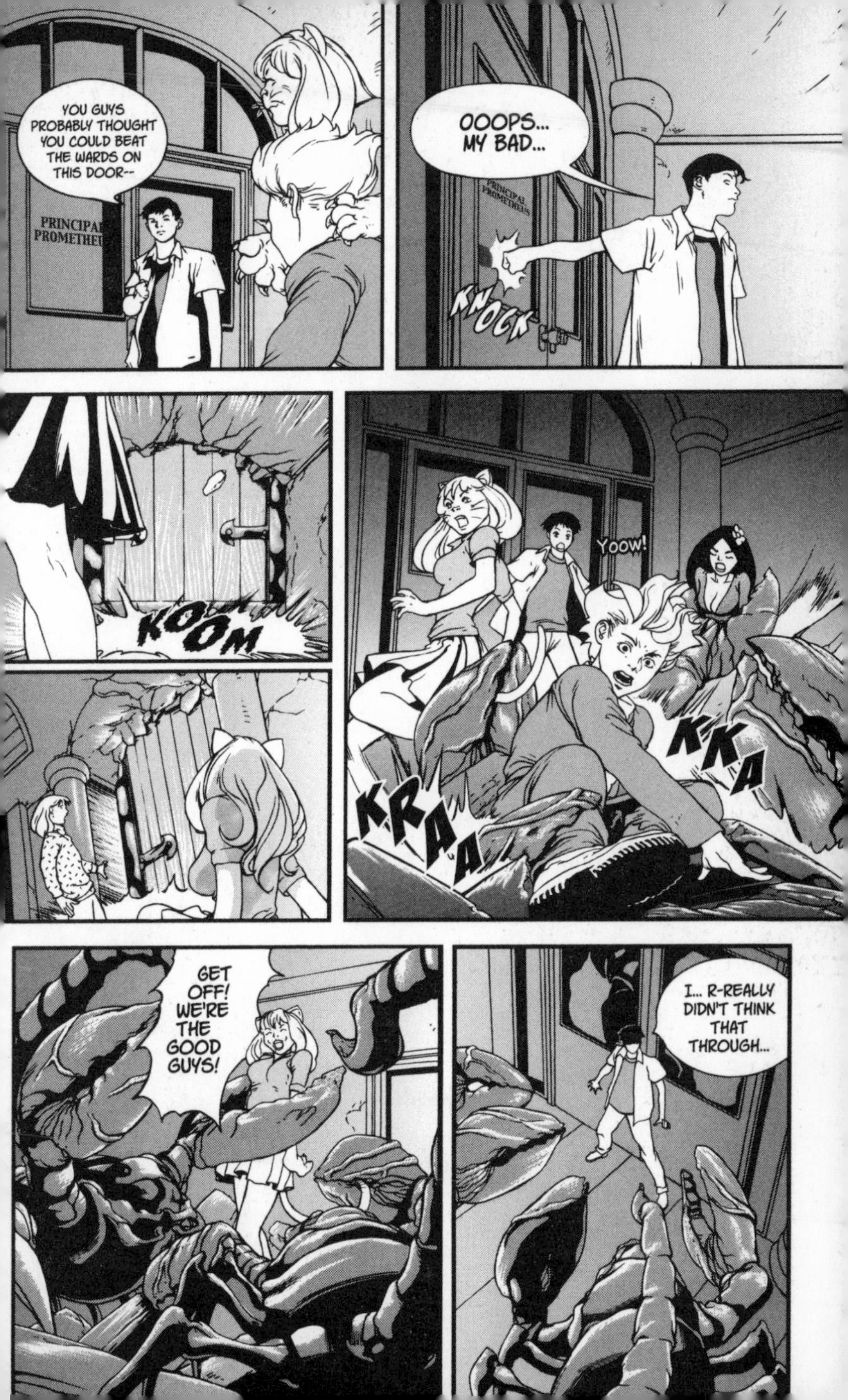
YOU GUYS PROBABLY THOUGHT YOU COULD BEAT THE WARDS ON THIS DOOR--
PRINCIPAL PROMETHEUS
OOOPS... MY BAD...
PRINCIPAL PROMETHEUS
KNOCK
KOOM
YOOW!
KRAAA
KKA
GET OFF! WE'RE THE GOOD GUYS!
I... R-REALLY DIDN'T THINK THAT THROUGH...

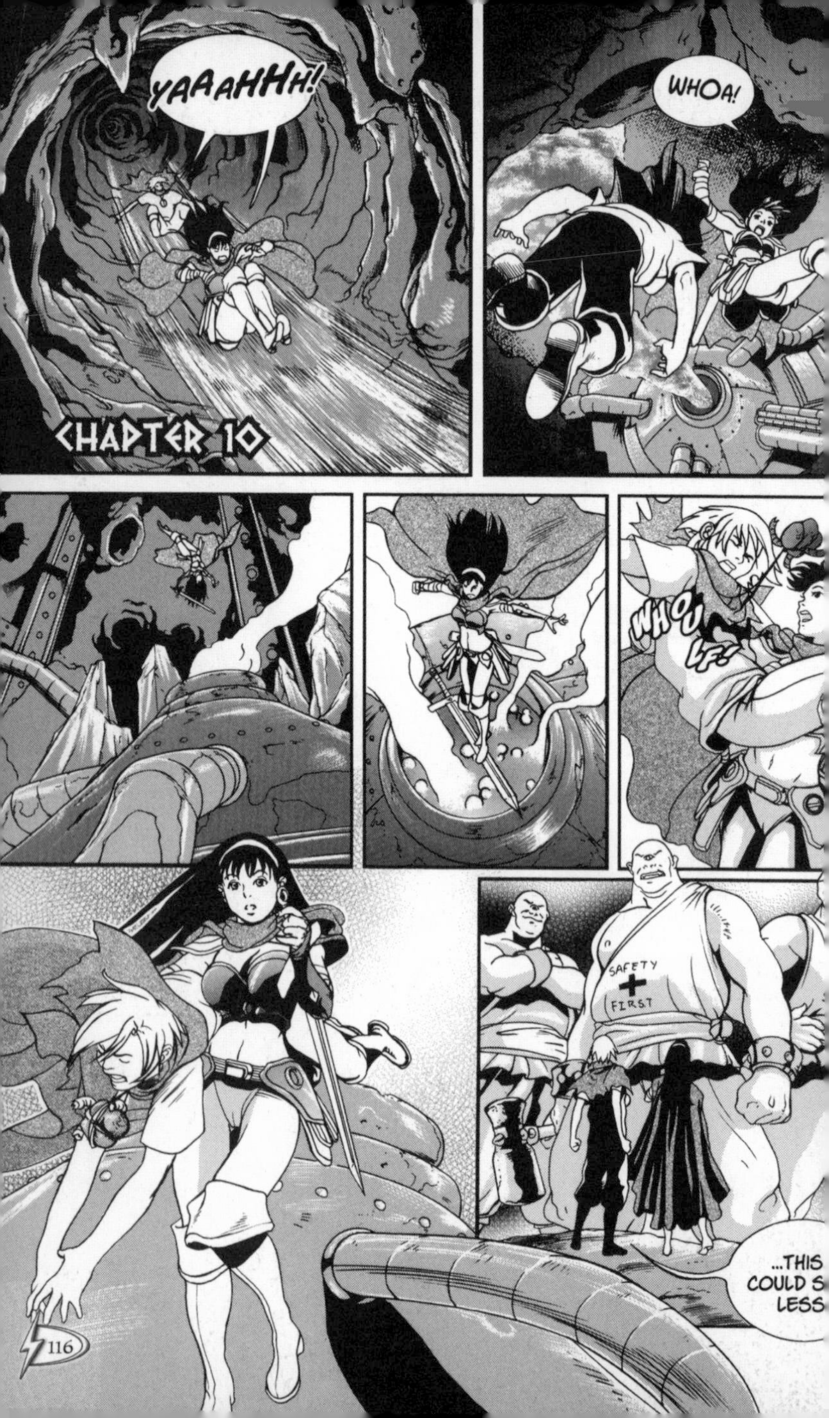
YAAAHHH!
CHAPTER 10
WHOA!
WHOUF!
SAFETY FIRST
...THIS COULD S LESS

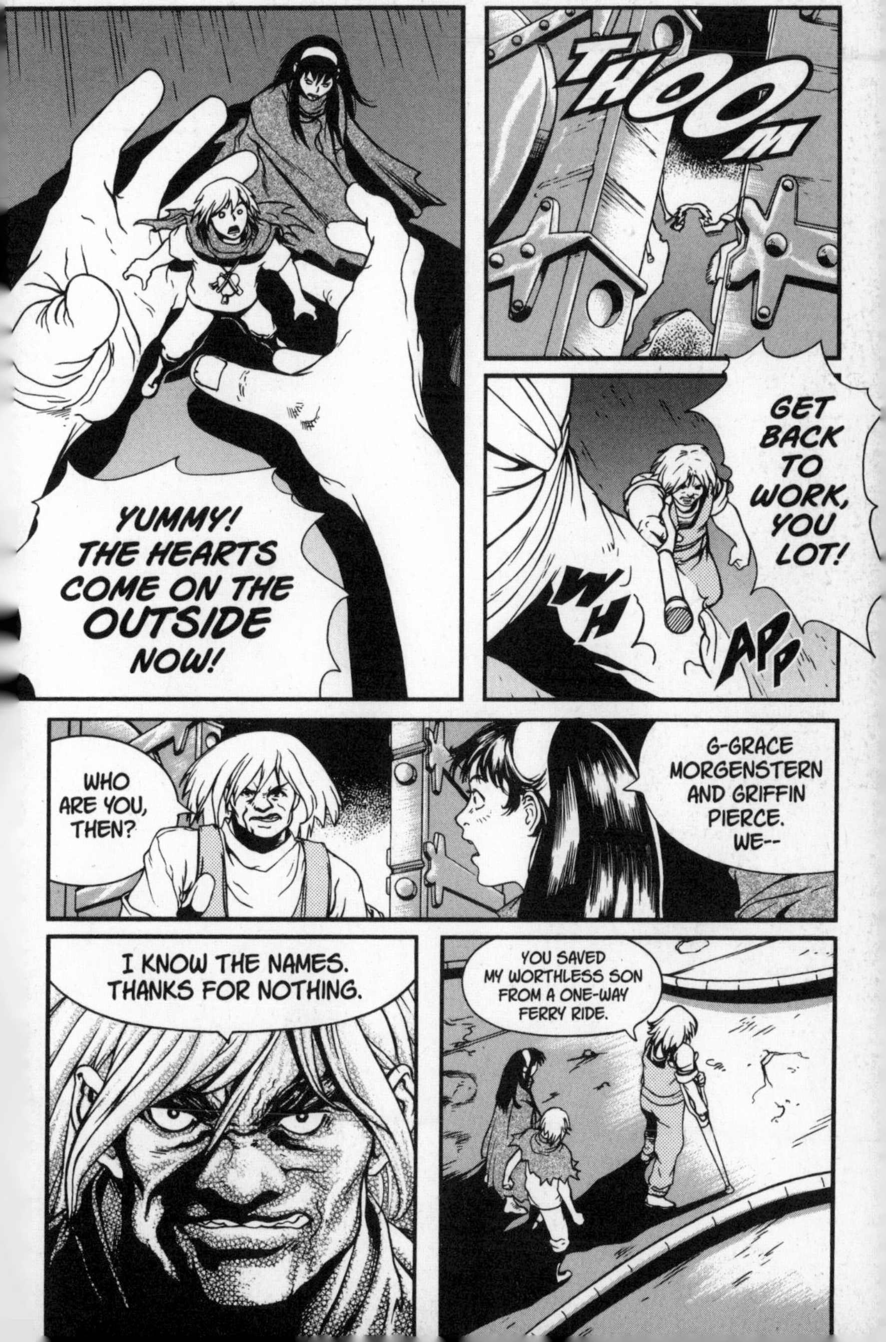
YUMMY! THE HEARTS COME ON THE OUTSIDE NOW!
THOOM
GET BACK TO WORK, YOU LOT!
WHAPP
WHO ARE YOU, THEN?
G-GRACE MORGENSTERN AND GRIFFIN PIERCE. WE--
I KNOW THE NAMES. THANKS FOR NOTHING.
YOU SAVED MY WORTHLESS SON FROM A ONE-WAY FERRY RIDE.

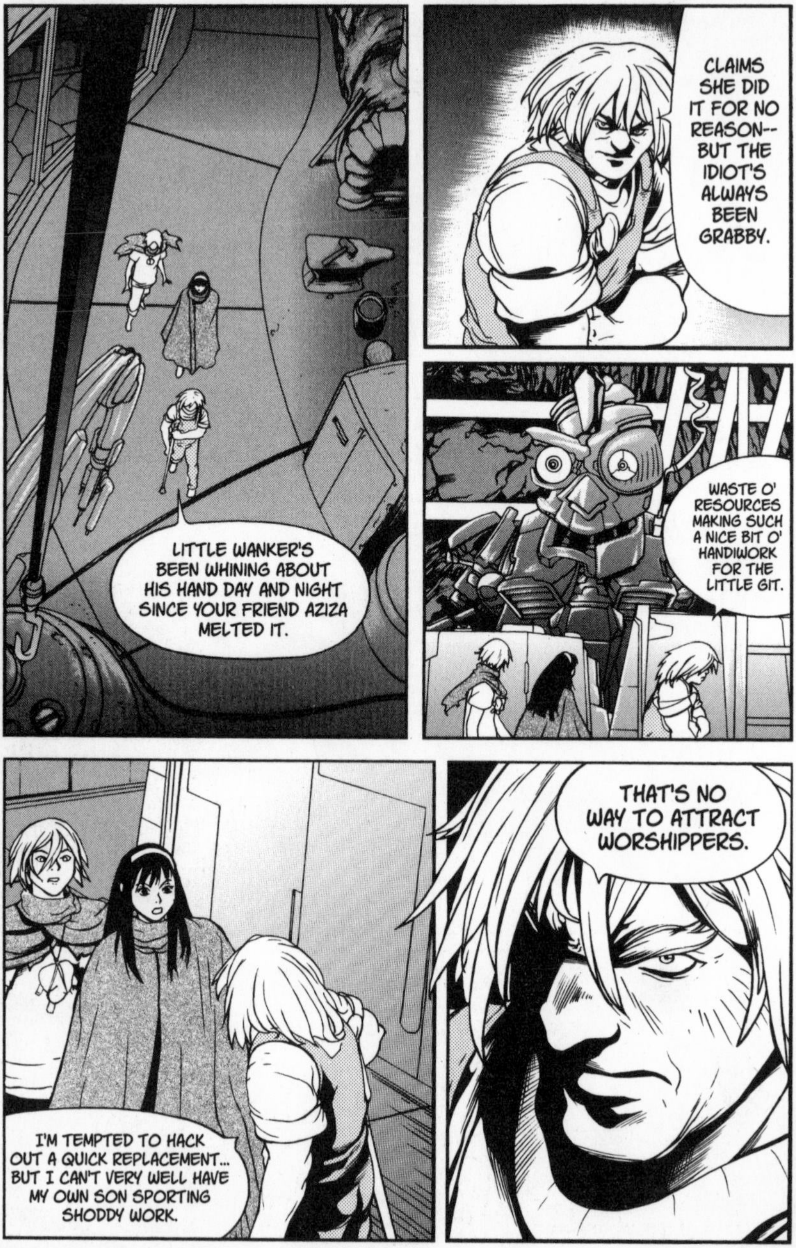
LITTLE WANKER'S BEEN WHINING ABOUT HIS HAND DAY AND NIGHT SINCE YOUR FRIEND AZIZA MELTED IT.
CLAIMS SHE DID IT FOR NO REASON-- BUT THE IDIOT'S ALWAYS BEEN GRABBY.
WASTE O' RESOURCES MAKING SUCH A NICE BIT O' HANDIWORK FOR THE LITTLE GIT.
I'M TEMPTED TO HACK OUT A QUICK REPLACEMENT... BUT I CAN'T VERY WELL HAVE MY OWN SON SPORTING SHODDY WORK.
THAT'S NO WAY TO ATTRACT WORSHIPPERS.

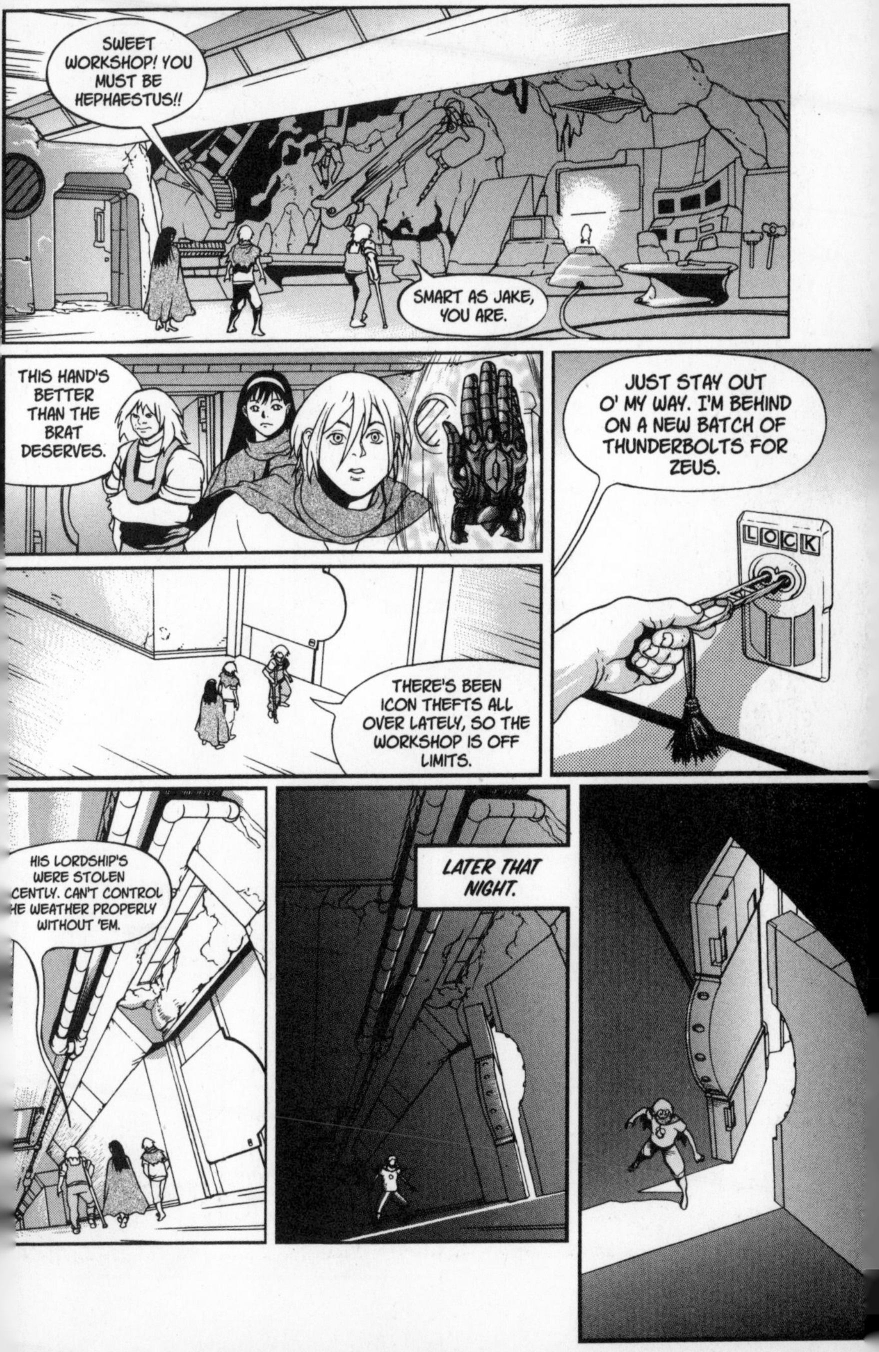
SWEET WORKSHOP! YOU MUST BE HEPHAESTUS!!
SMART AS JAKE, YOU ARE.
THIS HAND'S BETTER THAN THE BRAT DESERVES.
THERE'S BEEN ICON THEFTS ALL OVER LATELY, SO THE WORKSHOP IS OFF LIMITS.
JUST STAY OUT O' MY WAY. I'M BEHIND ON A NEW BATCH OF THUNDERBOLTS FOR ZEUS.
LOCK
HIS LORDSHIP'S WERE STOLEN CENTLY. CAN'T CONTROL HE WEATHER PROPERLY WITHOUT 'EM.
LATER THAT NIGHT.

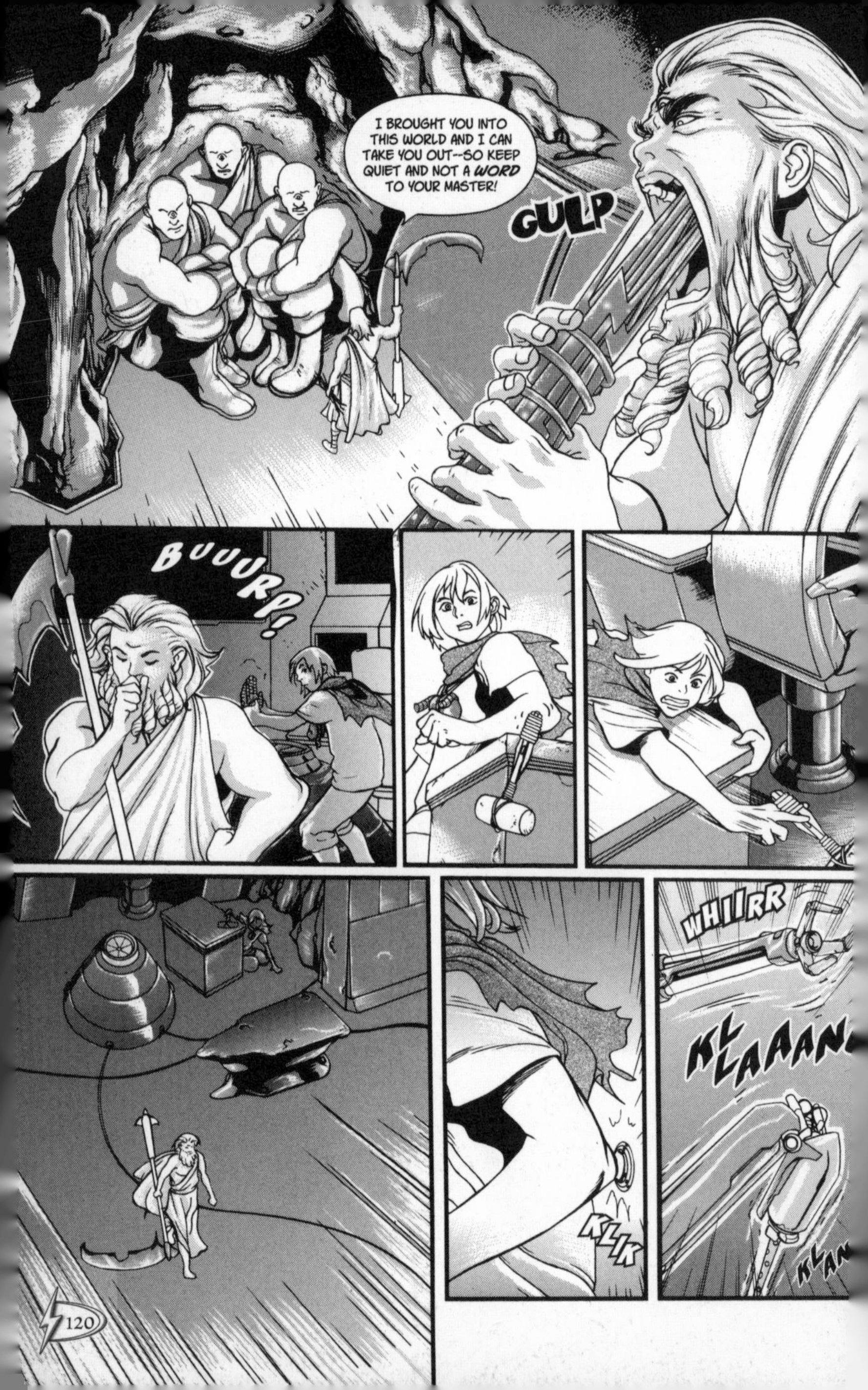
I BROUGHT YOU INTO THIS WORLD AND I CAN TAKE YOU OUT--SO KEEP QUIET AND NOT A ***WORD*** TO YOUR MASTER!
GULP
BUUURP!!
KLIK
WHIIRR
KL LAAAN
KL AN

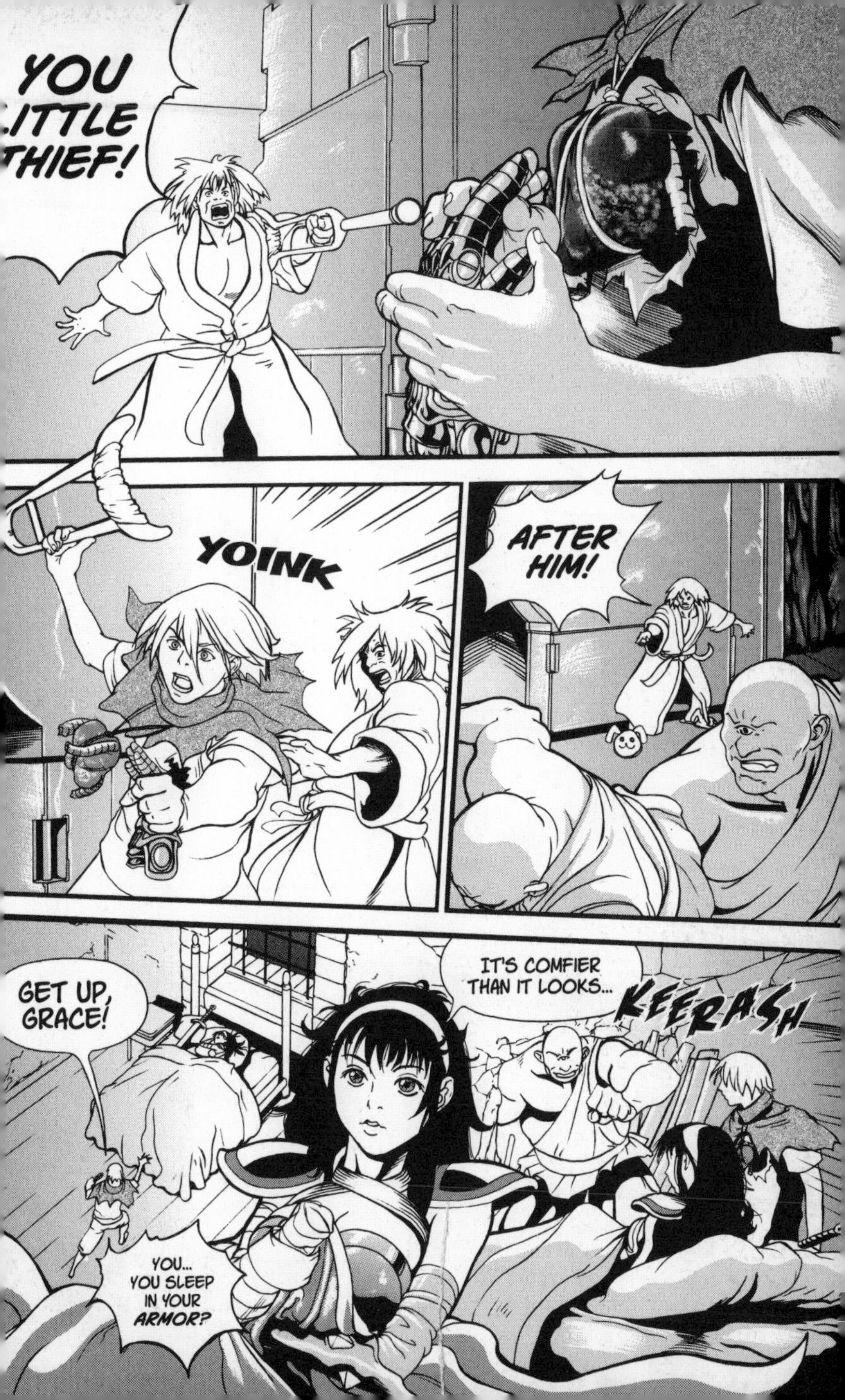
YOU LITTLE THIEF!
YOINK
AFTER HIM!
GET UP, GRACE!
IT'S COMFIER THAN IT LOOKS...
KEERASH
YOU... YOU SLEEP IN YOUR ARMOR?

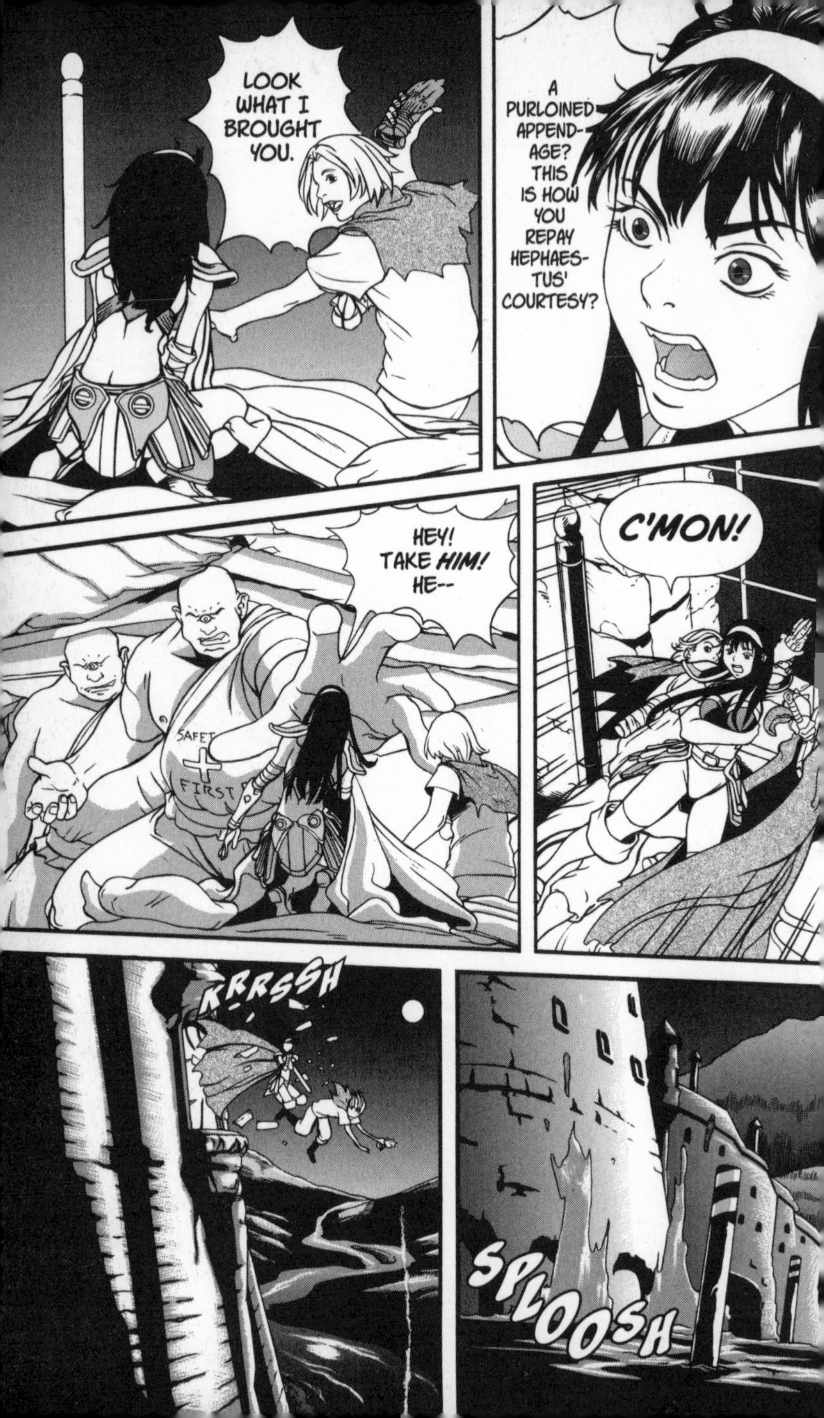
LOOK WHAT I BROUGHT YOU.
A PURLOINED APPEND-AGE? THIS IS HOW YOU REPAY HEPHAES-TUS' COURTESY?
HEY! TAKE *HIM*! HE--
SAFETY FIRST
C'MON!
KRRSSH
SPLOOSH

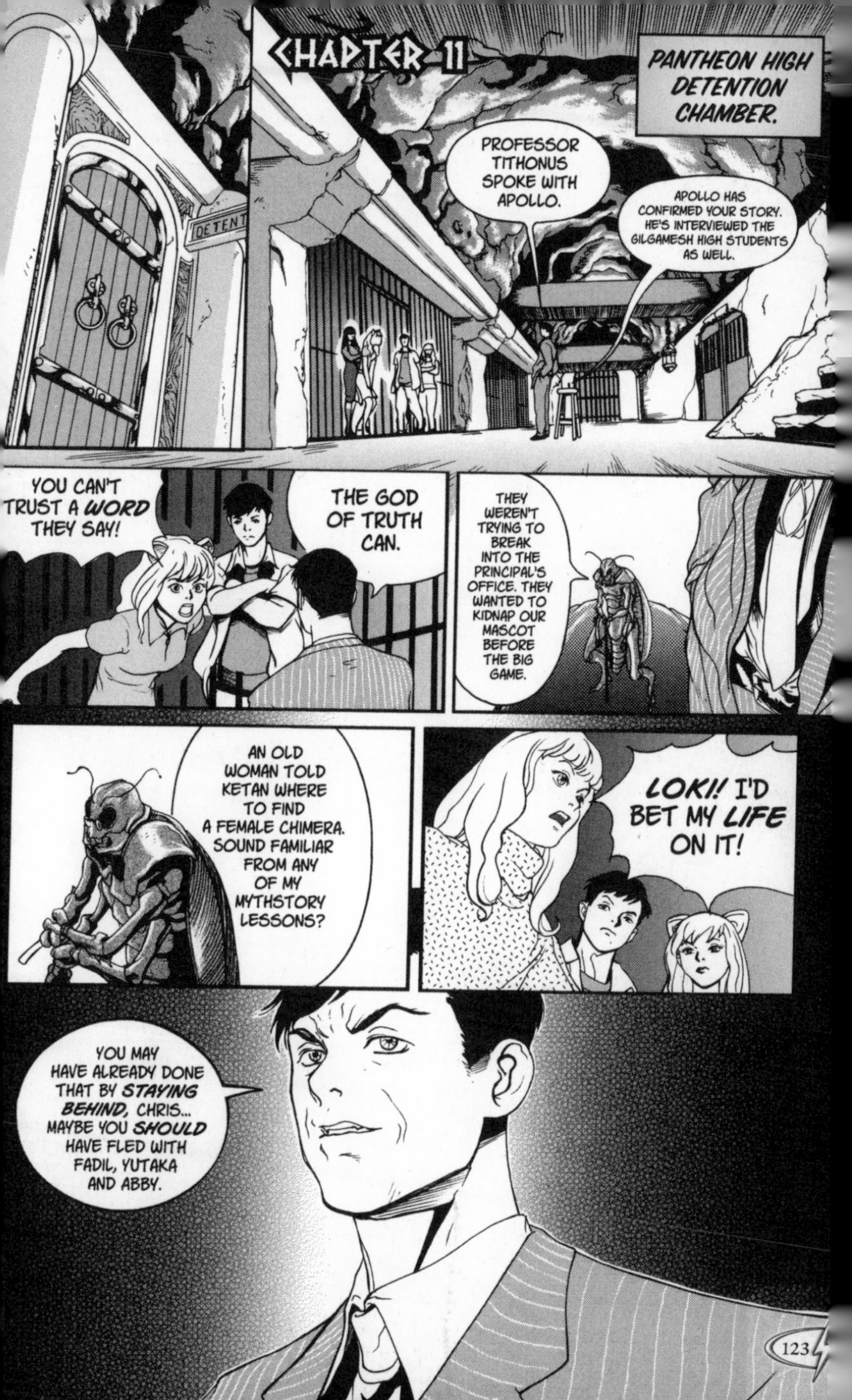
CHAPTER 11
PANTHEON HIGH DETENTION CHAMBER.
DETENT
PROFESSOR TITHONUS SPOKE WITH APOLLO.
APOLLO HAS CONFIRMED YOUR STORY. HE'S INTERVIEWED THE GILGAMESH HIGH STUDENTS AS WELL.
YOU CAN'T TRUST A *WORD* THEY SAY!
THE GOD OF TRUTH CAN.
THEY WEREN'T TRYING TO BREAK INTO THE PRINCIPAL'S OFFICE. THEY WANTED TO KIDNAP OUR MASCOT BEFORE THE BIG GAME.
AN OLD WOMAN TOLD KETAN WHERE TO FIND A FEMALE CHIMERA. SOUND FAMILIAR FROM ANY OF MY MYTHSTORY LESSONS?
LOKI! I'D BET MY *LIFE* ON IT!
YOU MAY HAVE ALREADY DONE THAT BY *STAYING BEHIND,* CHRIS... MAYBE YOU *SHOULD* HAVE FLED WITH FADIL, YUTAKA AND ABBY.

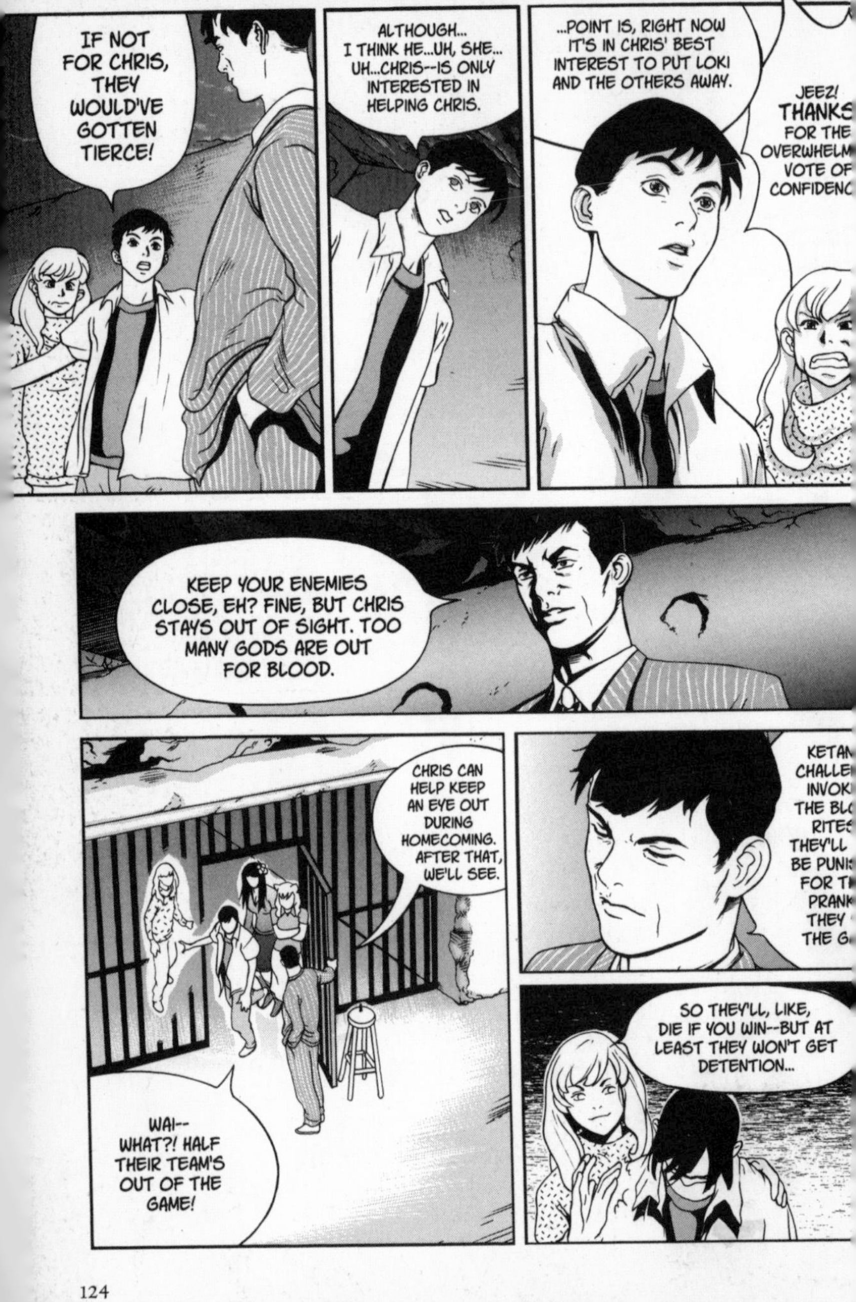
IF NOT FOR CHRIS, THEY WOULD'VE GOTTEN TIERCE!
ALTHOUGH... I THINK HE...UH, SHE... UH...CHRIS--IS ONLY INTERESTED IN HELPING CHRIS.
...POINT IS, RIGHT NOW IT'S IN CHRIS' BEST INTEREST TO PUT LOKI AND THE OTHERS AWAY.
JEEZ! THANKS FOR THE OVERWHELM VOTE OF CONFIDENC
KEEP YOUR ENEMIES CLOSE, EH? FINE, BUT CHRIS STAYS OUT OF SIGHT. TOO MANY GODS ARE OUT FOR BLOOD.
CHRIS CAN HELP KEEP AN EYE OUT DURING HOMECOMING. AFTER THAT, WE'LL SEE.
WAI-- WHAT?! HALF THEIR TEAM'S OUT OF THE GAME!
KETAN CHALLE INVOK THE BL RITES THEY'LL BE PUNIS FOR T PRANK THEY THE G
SO THEY'LL, LIKE, DIE IF YOU WIN--BUT AT LEAST THEY WON'T GET DETENTION...

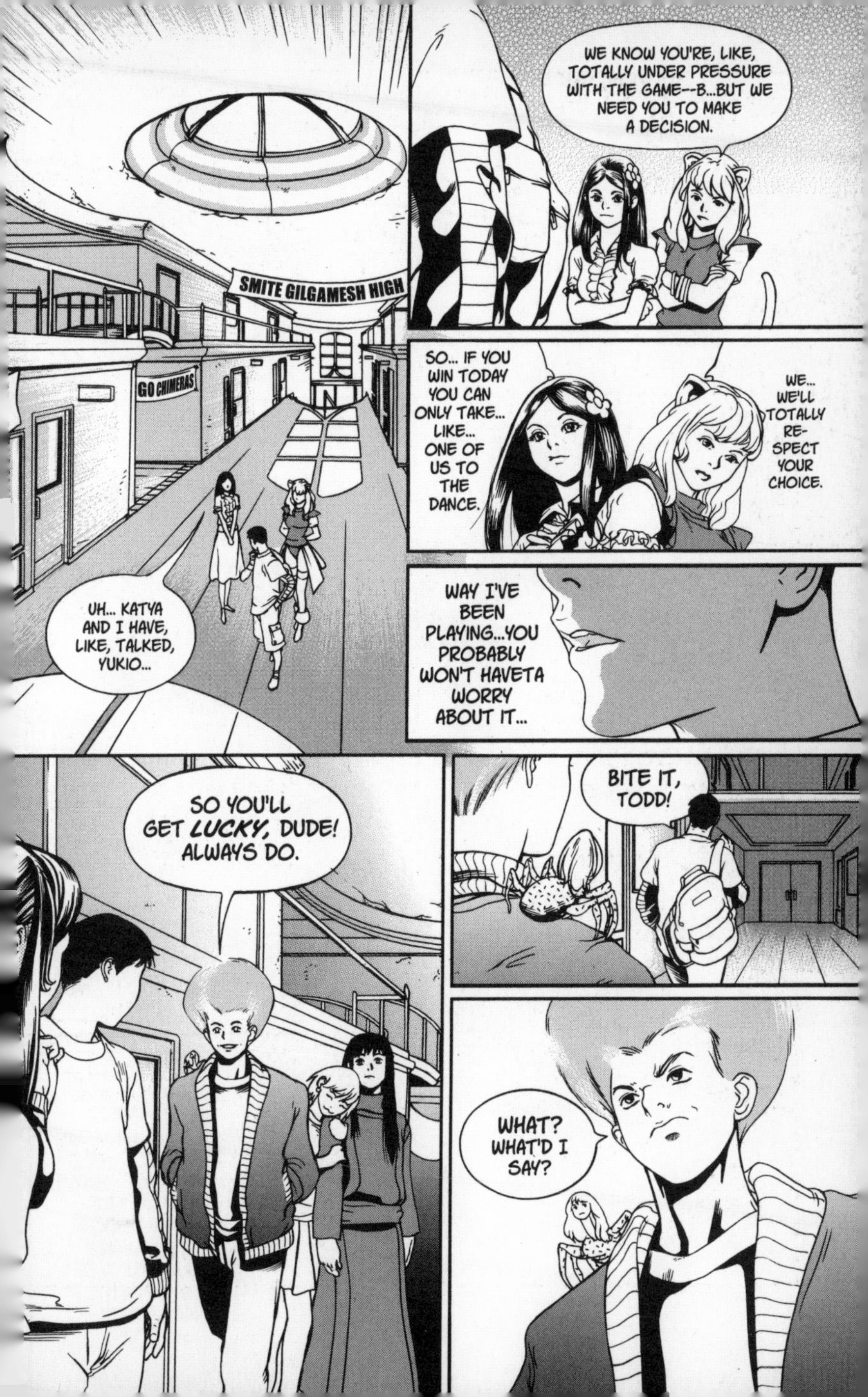
SMITE GILGAMESH HIGH
GO CHIMERAS
UH... KATYA AND I HAVE, LIKE, TALKED, YUKIO...
WE KNOW YOU'RE, LIKE, TOTALLY UNDER PRESSURE WITH THE GAME--B...BUT WE NEED YOU TO MAKE A DECISION.
SO... IF YOU WIN TODAY YOU CAN ONLY TAKE... LIKE... ONE OF US TO THE DANCE.
WE... WE'LL TOTALLY RE-SPECT YOUR CHOICE.
WAY I'VE BEEN PLAYING...YOU PROBABLY WON'T HAVETA WORRY ABOUT IT...
SO YOU'LL GET *LUCKY,* DUDE! ALWAYS DO.
BITE IT, TODD!
WHAT? WHAT'D I SAY?

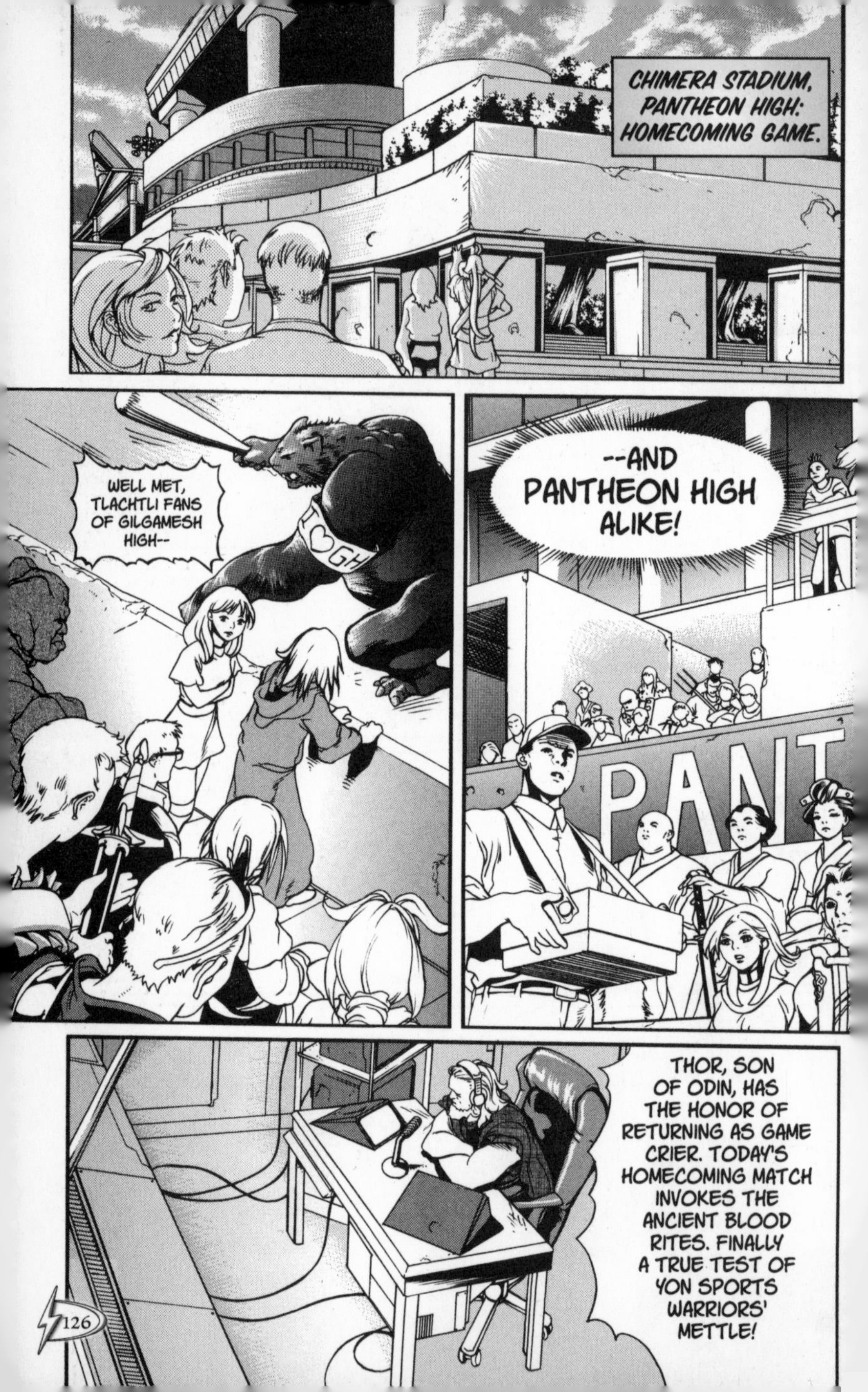

CHIMERA STADIUM, PANTHEON HIGH: HOMECOMING GAME.
WELL MET, TLACHTLI FANS OF GILGAMESH HIGH--
I ♥ GH
--AND PANTHEON HIGH ALIKE!
PANT
THOR, SON OF ODIN, HAS THE HONOR OF RETURNING AS GAME CRIER. TODAY'S HOMECOMING MATCH INVOKES THE ANCIENT BLOOD RITES. FINALLY A TRUE TEST OF YON SPORTS WARRIORS' METTLE!

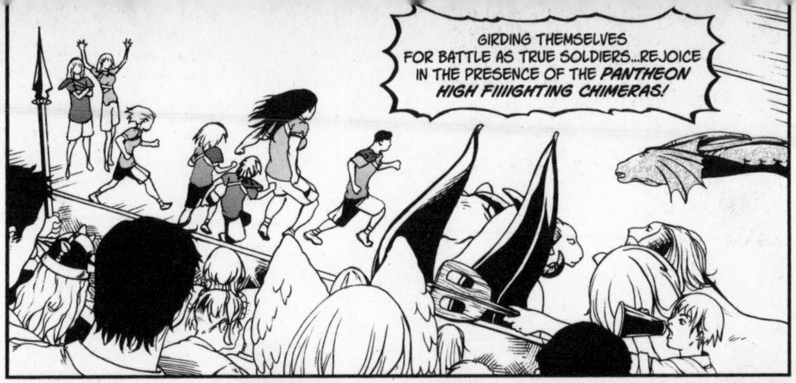
GIRDING THEMSELVES FOR BATTLE AS TRUE SOLDIERS...REJOICE IN THE PRESENCE OF THE *PANTHEON HIGH FIIIIGHTING CHIMERAS!*

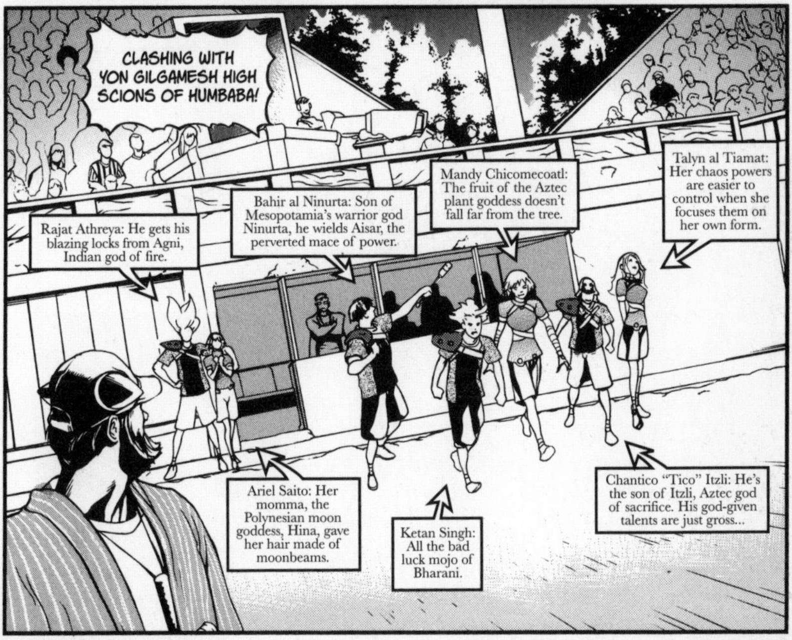
CLASHING WITH YON GILGAMESH HIGH SCIONS OF HUMBABA!
Rajat Athreya: He gets his blazing locks from Agni, Indian god of fire.
Bahir al Ninurta: Son of Mesopotamia's warrior god Ninurta, he wields Aisar, the perverted mace of power.
Mandy Chicomecoatl: The fruit of the Aztec plant goddess doesn't fall far from the tree.
Talyn al Tiamat: Her chaos powers are easier to control when she focuses them on her own form.
Ariel Saito: Her momma, the Polynesian moon goddess, Hina, gave her hair made of moonbeams.
Ketan Singh: All the bad luck mojo of Bharani.
Chantico "Tico" Itzli: He's the son of Itzli, Aztec god of sacrifice. His god-given talents are just gross...

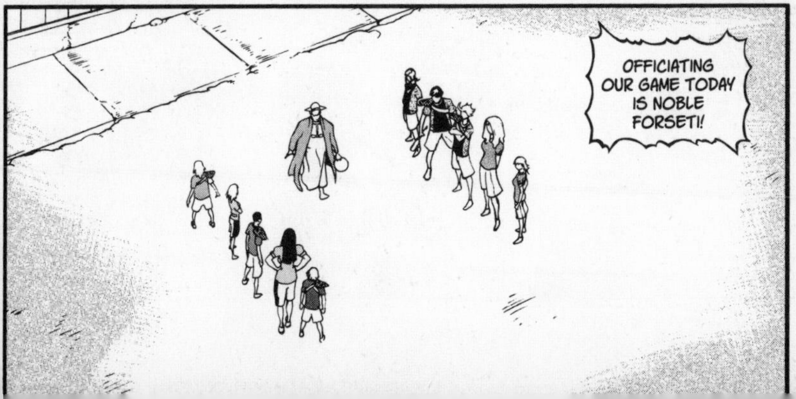
OFFICIATING OUR GAME TODAY IS NOBLE FORSETI!

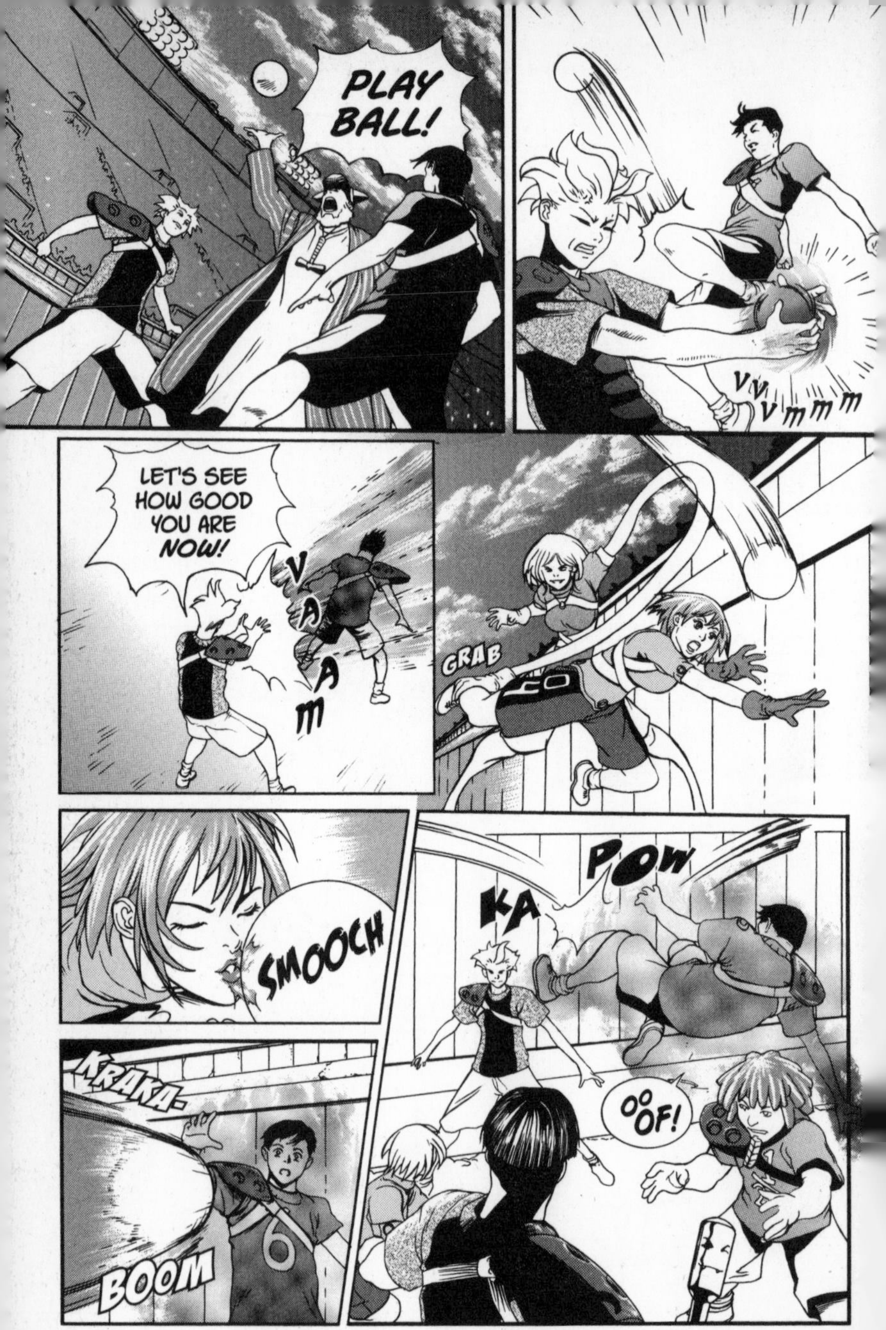
PLAY BALL!
VVVVMMMM
LET'S SEE HOW GOOD YOU ARE NOW!
VAAM
GRAB
SMOOCH
KA
POW
KRAKA-
BOOM
OOOF!

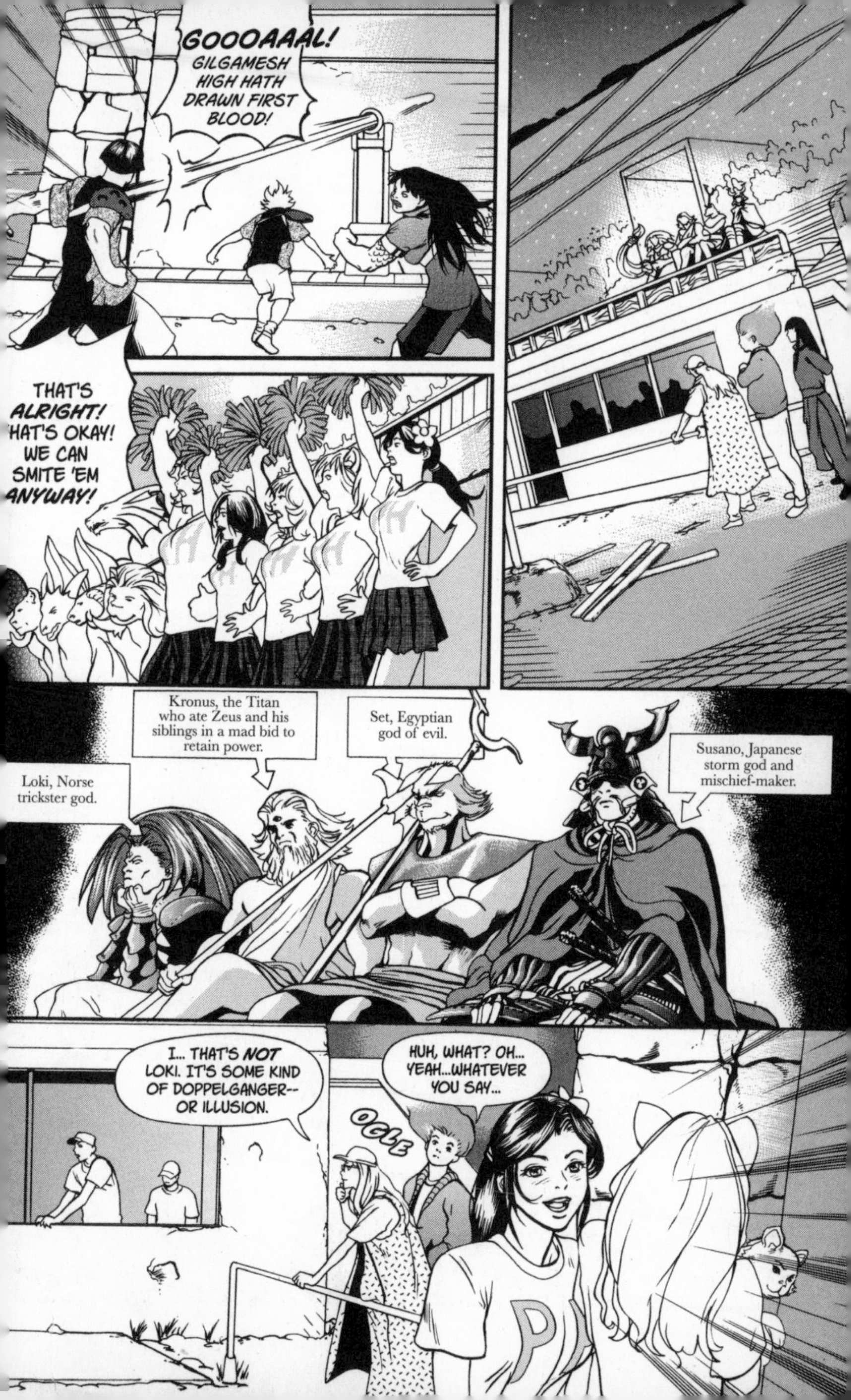
GOOOAAAL! GILGAMESH HIGH HATH DRAWN FIRST BLOOD!
THAT'S ALRIGHT! THAT'S OKAY! WE CAN SMITE 'EM ANYWAY!
Loki, Norse trickster god.
Kronus, the Titan who ate Zeus and his siblings in a mad bid to retain power.
Set, Egyptian god of evil.
Susano, Japanese storm god and mischief-maker.
I... THAT'S NOT LOKI. IT'S SOME KIND OF DOPPELGANGER-- OR ILLUSION.
OGLE
HUH, WHAT? OH... YEAH...WHATEVER YOU SAY...

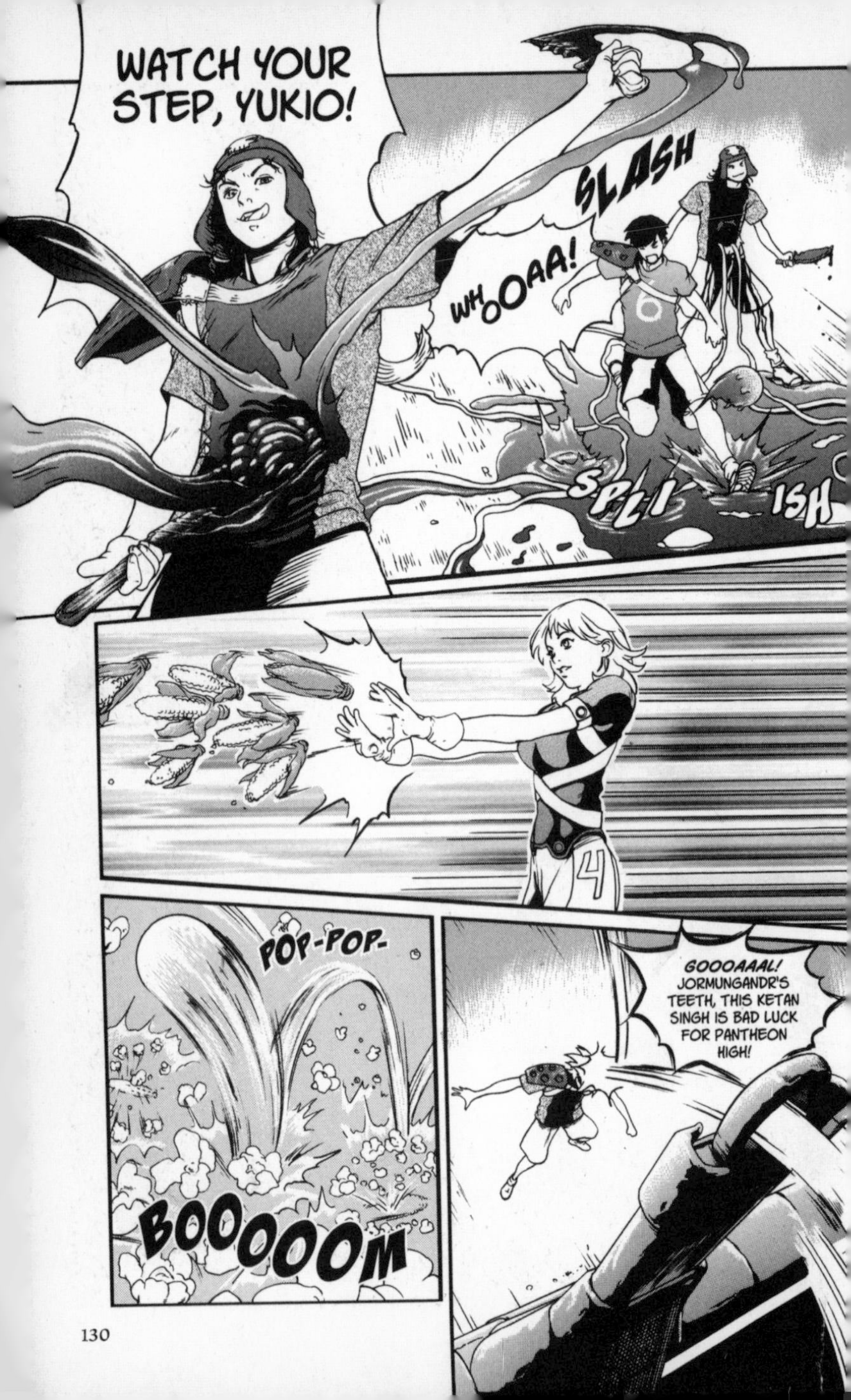
WATCH YOUR STEP, YUKIO!
SLASH
WHOOAA!
SPLI-ISH
POP-POP-
BOOOOOM
GOOOAAAL! JORMUNGANDR'S TEETH, THIS KETAN SINGH IS BAD LUCK FOR PANTHEON HIGH!

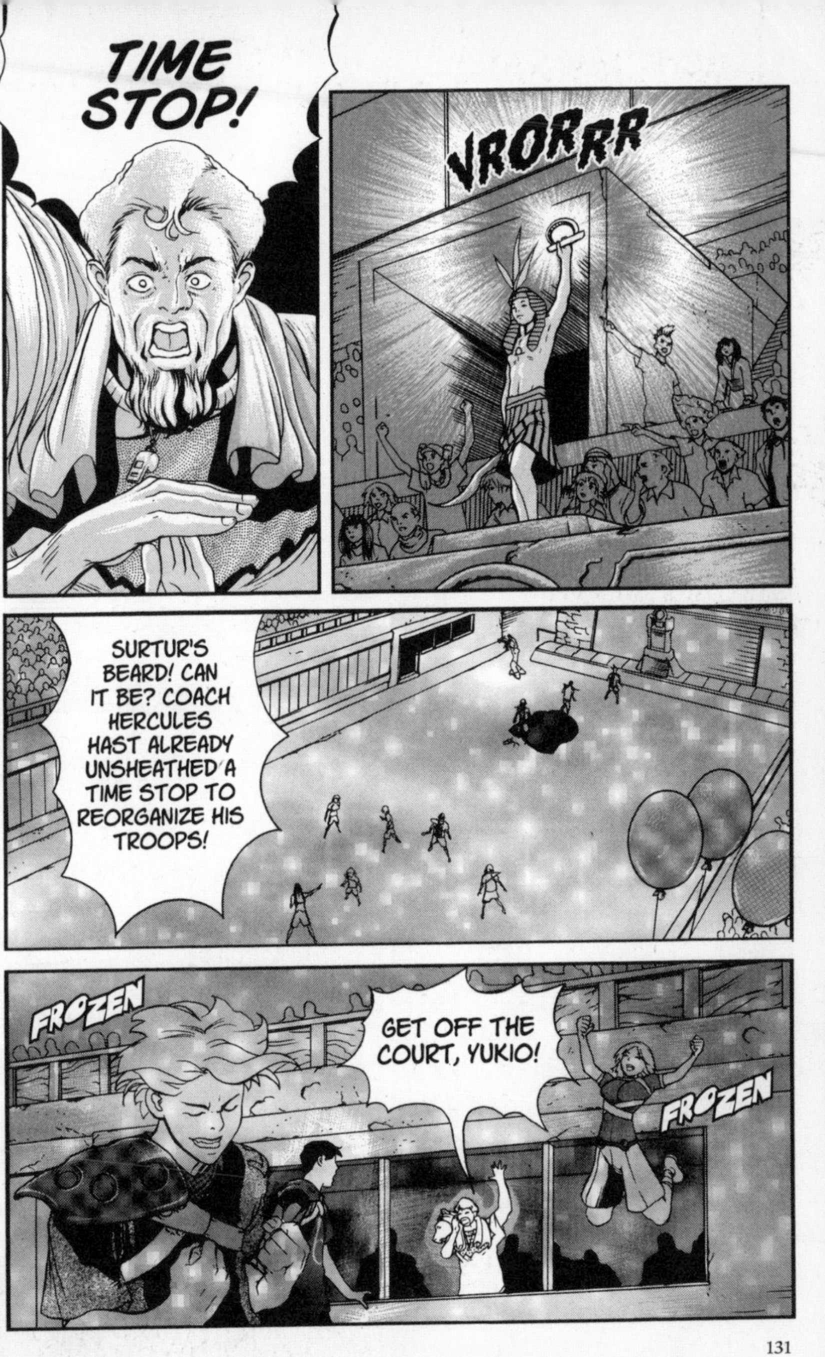
TIME STOP!
VRORRR
SURTUR'S BEARD! CAN IT BE? COACH HERCULES HAST ALREADY UNSHEATHED A TIME STOP TO REORGANIZE HIS TROOPS!
FROZEN
GET OFF THE COURT, YUKIO!
FROZEN

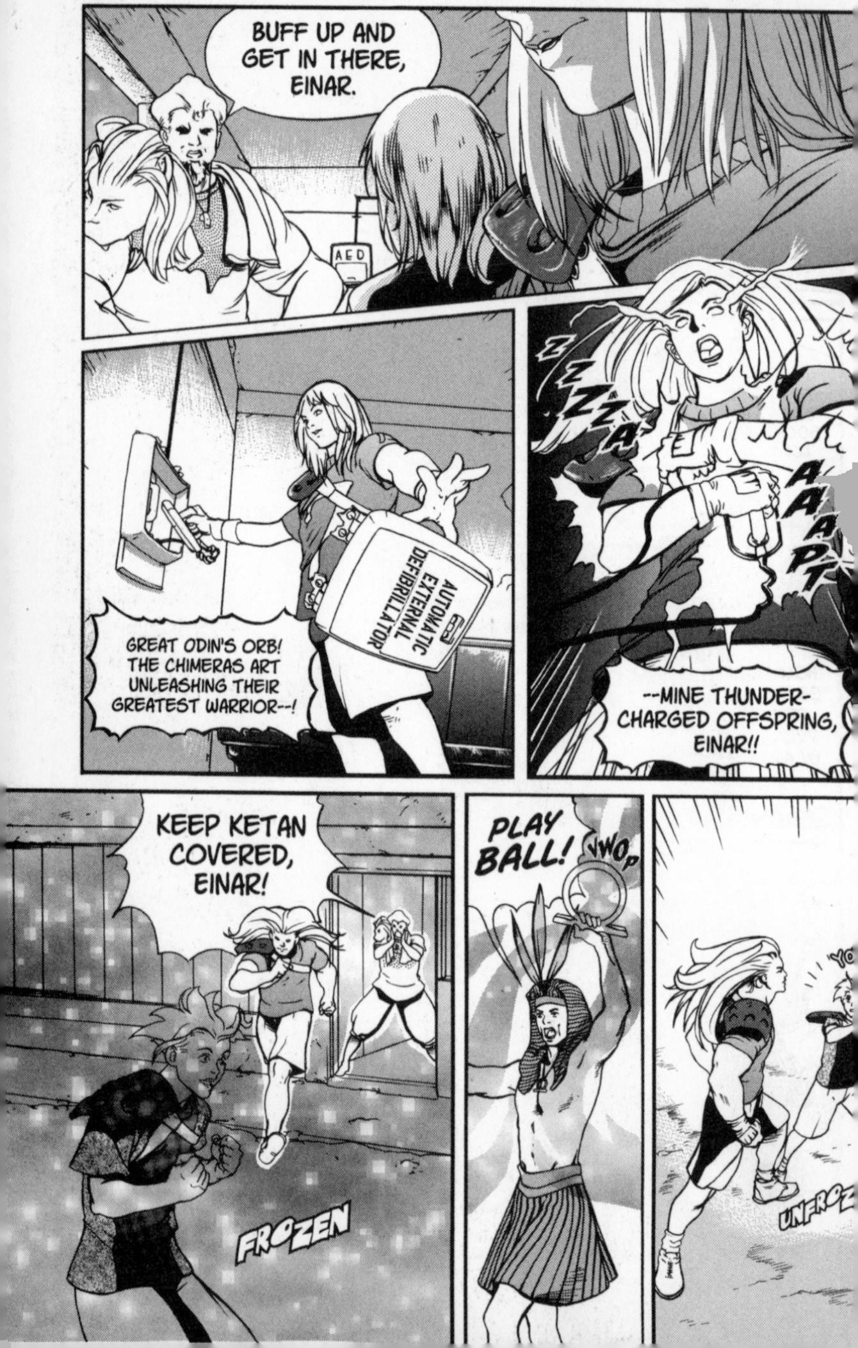
BUFF UP AND GET IN THERE, EINAR.
AED
AUTOMATIC EXTERNAL DEFIBRILLATOR
GREAT ODIN'S ORB! THE CHIMERAS ART UNLEASHING THEIR GREATEST WARRIOR--!
ZZZZA
AAAAPT
--MINE THUNDER-CHARGED OFFSPRING, EINAR!!
KEEP KETAN COVERED, EINAR!
FROZEN
PLAY BALL!
VWOp

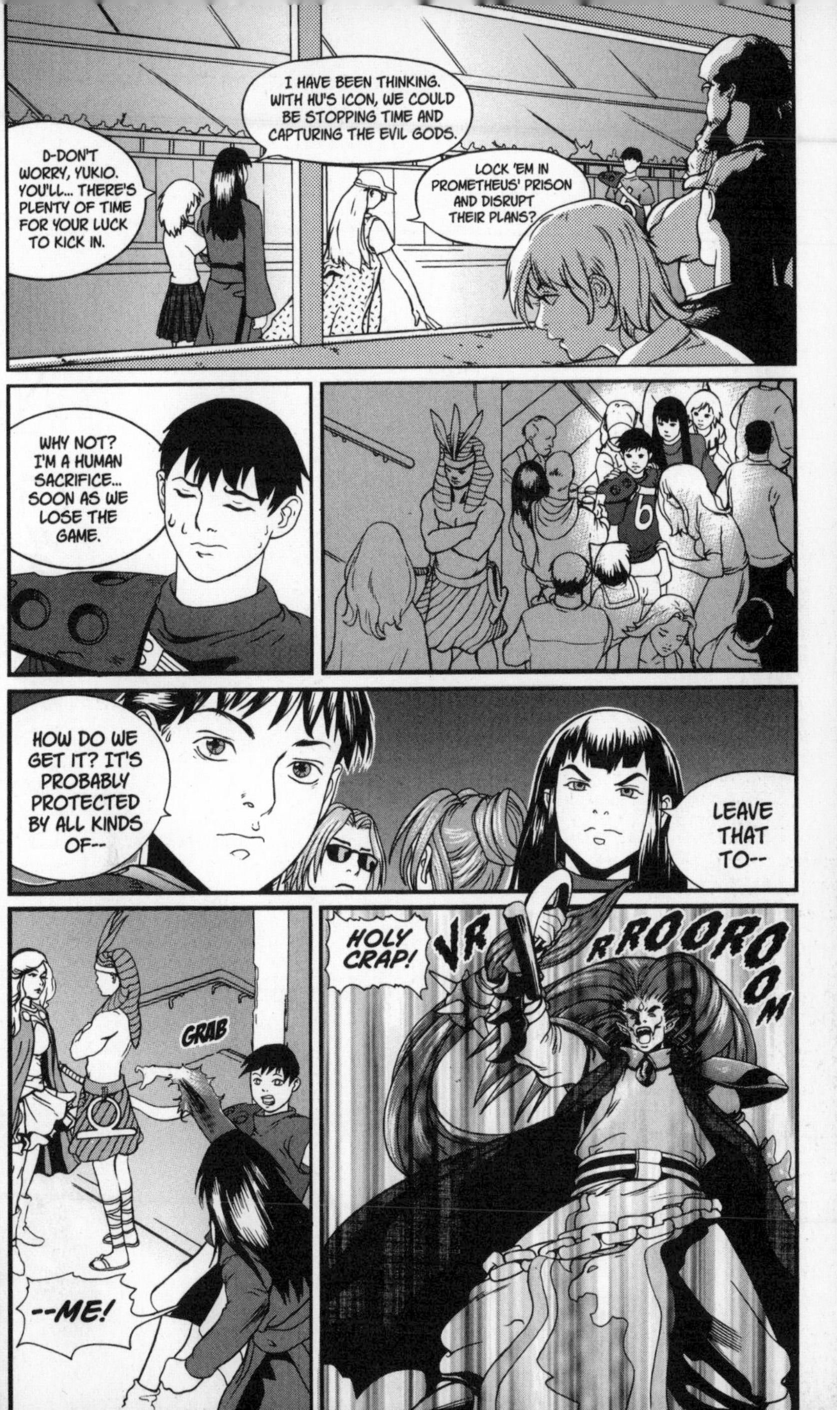
D-DON'T WORRY, YUKIO. YOU'LL... THERE'S PLENTY OF TIME FOR YOUR LUCK TO KICK IN.
I HAVE BEEN THINKING. WITH HU'S ICON, WE COULD BE STOPPING TIME AND CAPTURING THE EVIL GODS.
LOCK 'EM IN PROMETHEUS' PRISON AND DISRUPT THEIR PLANS?
WHY NOT? I'M A HUMAN SACRIFICE... SOON AS WE LOSE THE GAME.
HOW DO WE GET IT? IT'S PROBABLY PROTECTED BY ALL KINDS OF--
LEAVE THAT TO--
GRAB
--ME!
HOLY CRAP!
VRRROOROOOM

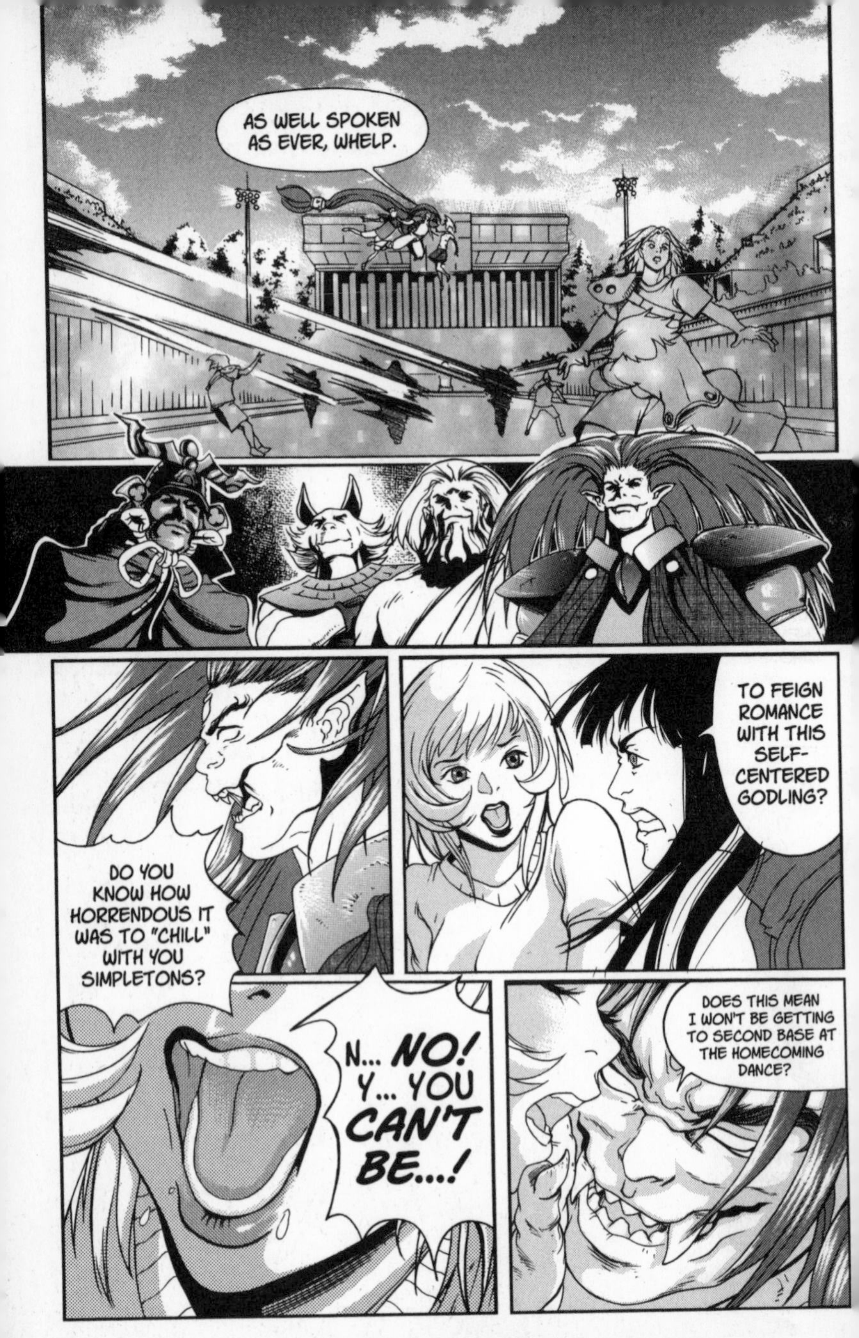
AS WELL SPOKEN AS EVER, WHELP.
DO YOU KNOW HOW HORRENDOUS IT WAS TO "CHILL" WITH YOU SIMPLETONS?
TO FEIGN ROMANCE WITH THIS SELF-CENTERED GODLING?
N... NO! Y... YOU CAN'T BE...!
DOES THIS MEAN I WON'T BE GETTING TO SECOND BASE AT THE HOMECOMING DANCE?

THE PROPHECY SAYS, "FOUR NEOPHYTES STAND ASTRIDE THE PATH." WE LED OUR CHILDREN TO *BELIEVE* THEY WERE ~~STINED~~ FOR ~~ER~~ SO THAT ~~COULD~~ *RE-* ~~VE~~ EVERY ~~DENT~~ FROM ~~E~~ PLAYING FIELD.

THEN IT SEEMED THE "FOUR" MIGHT BE YOU AND YOUR FRIENDS... THAT IS, UNTIL MY *PRECIOUS JORMUNGANDR* DEVOURED TWO OF YOU...

EVEN THEN, YOU INTERFERED WITH OUR PLANS. YOU THOUGHT WE WANTED OUR CHILDREN *DEAD* WHEN ALL WE WANTED WAS THE *ETERNAL FLAME* IN PROMETHEUS' OFFICE.

BUT NO MATTER. THE GODS HAVE BEEN *WEAKENED* BY OUR THEFT OF THEIR *ICONS*...

...AND *MANY* OF THEIR FOLLOWERS HAVE TURNED THEIR FAITH TO *US*.

WE WILL MURDER ~~O~~UR KIN WITH THEIR ~~O~~WN WEAPONS, THEN ~~D~~ESTROY GILGAMESH ~~I~~GH AND THE OTHER ~~PA~~NTHEONS! SOON ~~T~~HERE WILL BE NONE ~~F~~OR THE MORTALS ~~T~~O WORSHIP-- BUT *US*!

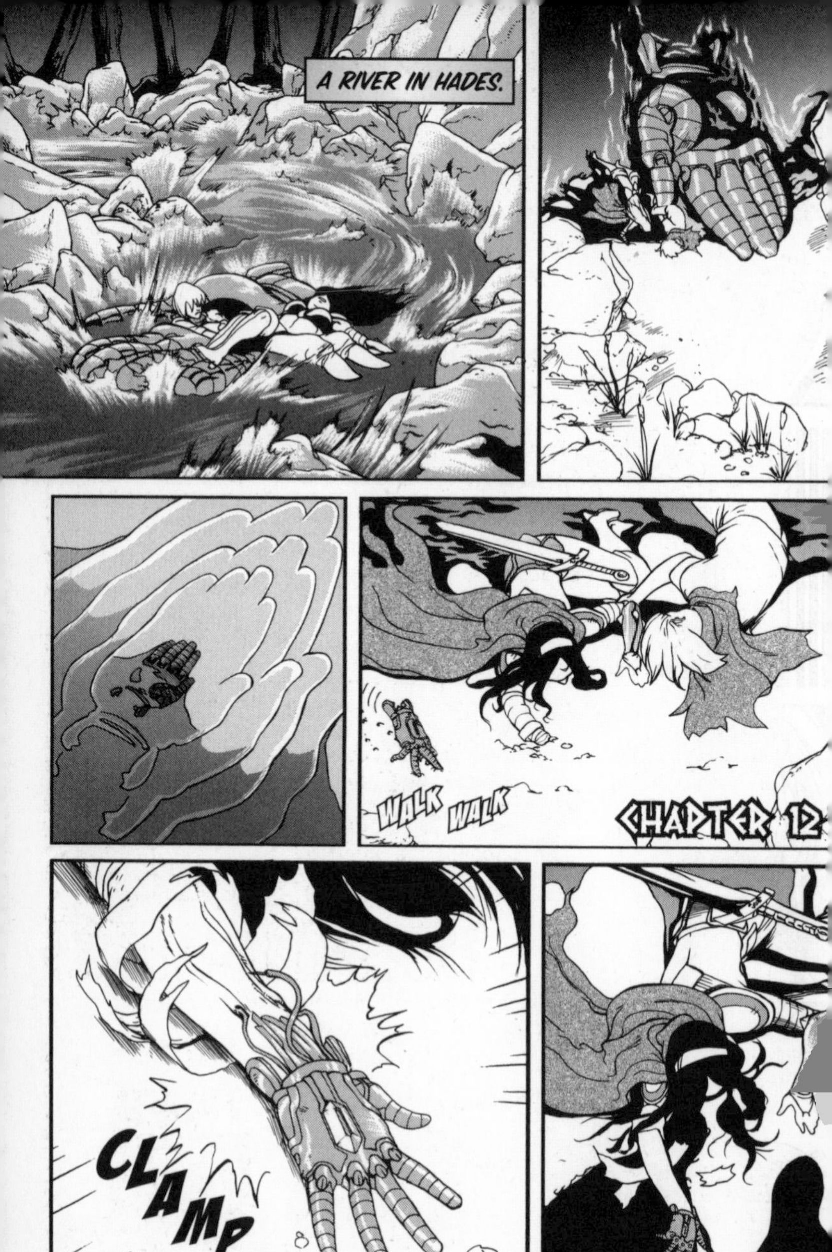
A RIVER IN HADES.
WALK
WALK
CHAPTER 12
CLAMP

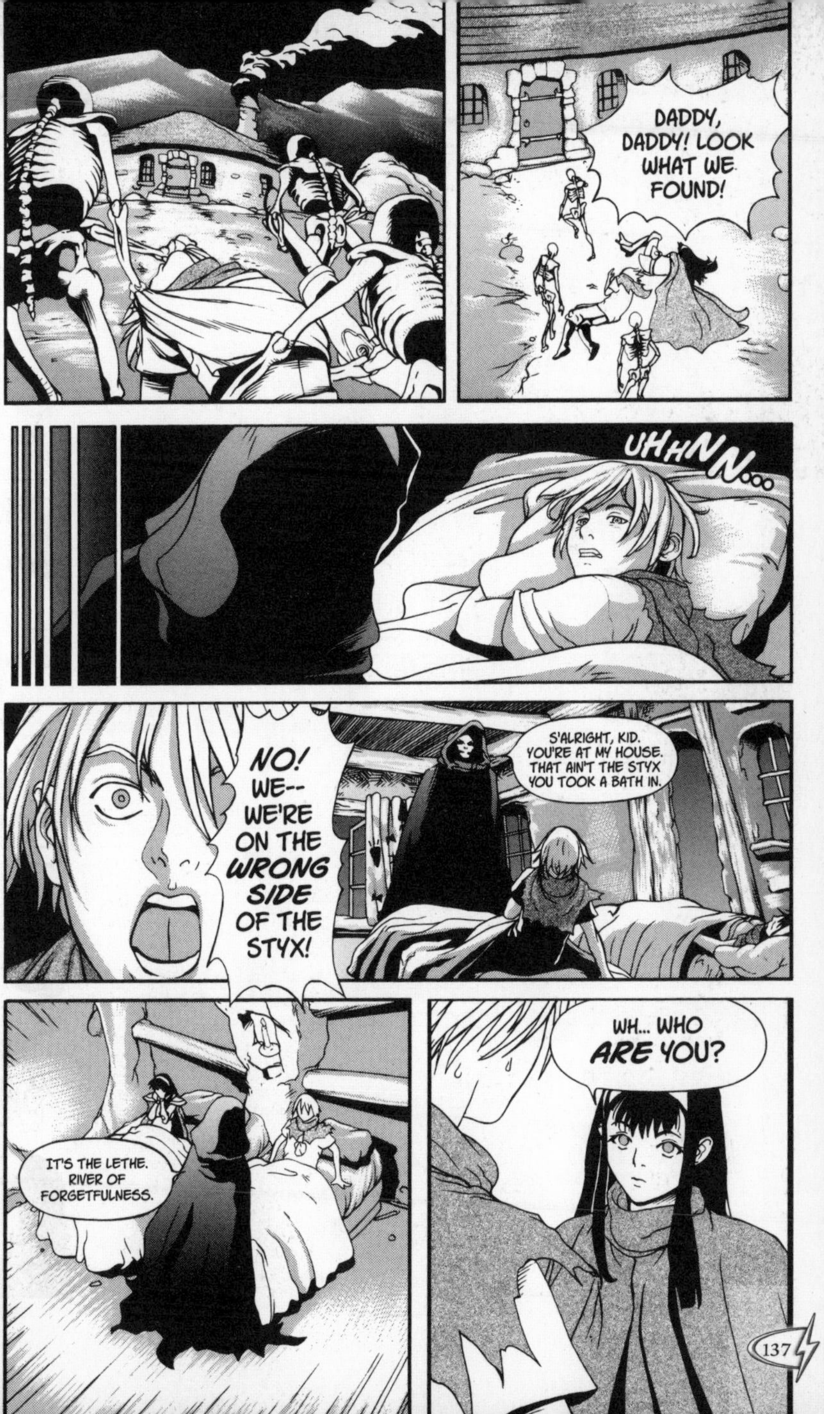
DADDY, DADDY! LOOK WHAT WE FOUND!
UHHNNN...
NO! WE-- WE'RE ON THE WRONG SIDE OF THE STYX!
S'ALRIGHT, KID. YOU'RE AT MY HOUSE. THAT AIN'T THE STYX YOU TOOK A BATH IN.
IT'S THE LETHE. RIVER OF FORGETFULNESS.
WH... WHO ARE YOU?

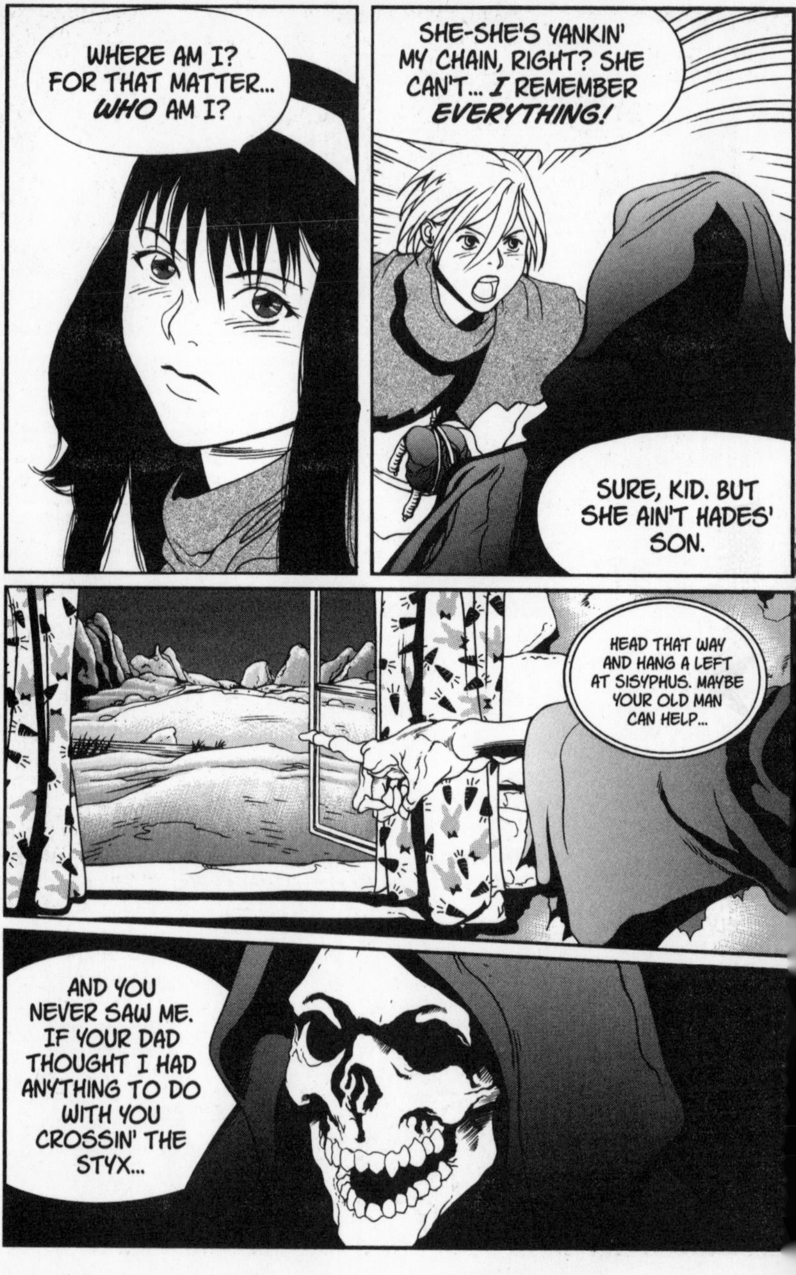
WHERE AM I? FOR THAT MATTER... WHO AM I?
SHE-SHE'S YANKIN' MY CHAIN, RIGHT? SHE CAN'T... I REMEMBER EVERYTHING!
SURE, KID. BUT SHE AIN'T HADES' SON.
HEAD THAT WAY AND HANG A LEFT AT SISYPHUS. MAYBE YOUR OLD MAN CAN HELP...
AND YOU NEVER SAW ME. IF YOUR DAD THOUGHT I HAD ANYTHING TO DO WITH YOU CROSSIN' THE STYX...

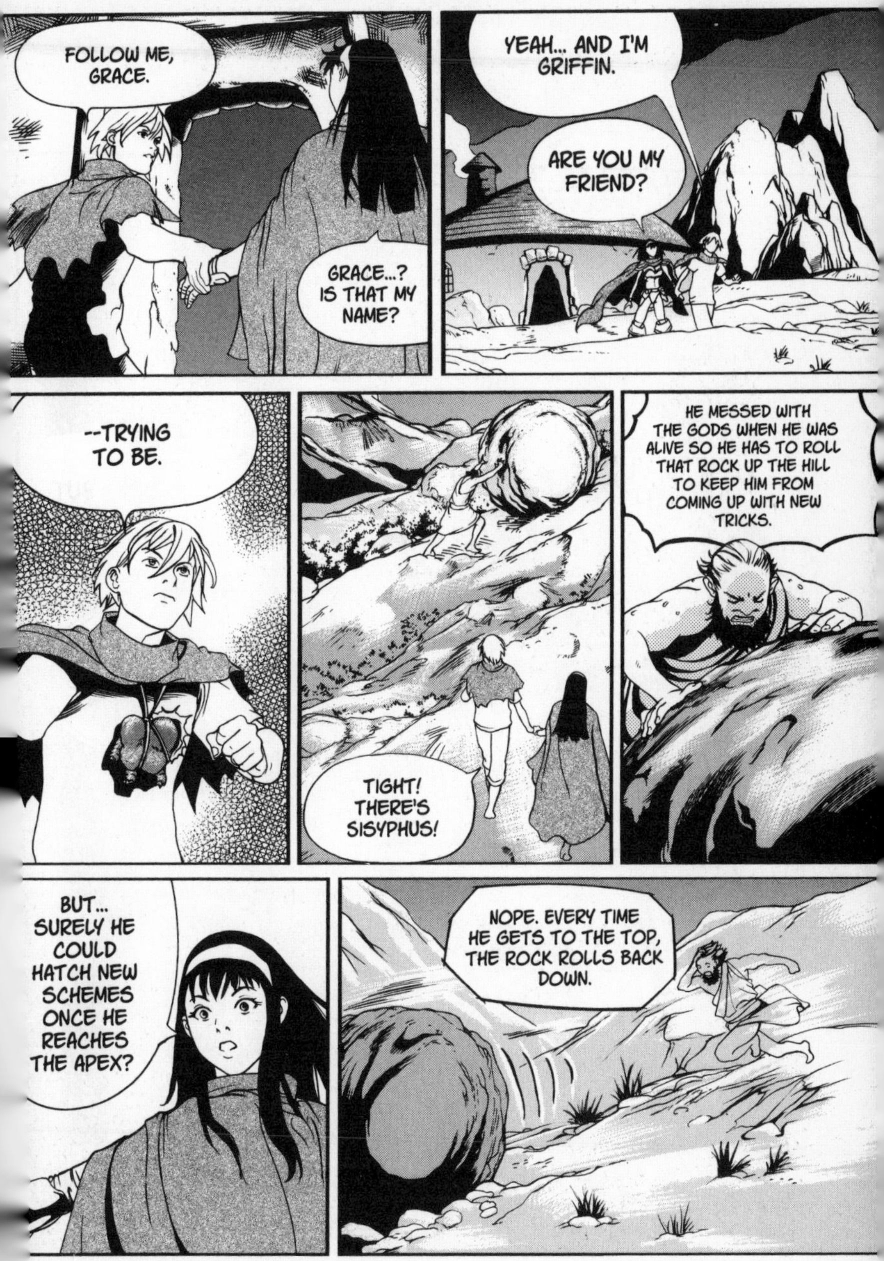
FOLLOW ME, GRACE.
GRACE...? IS THAT MY NAME?
YEAH... AND I'M GRIFFIN.
ARE YOU MY FRIEND?
--TRYING TO BE.
TIGHT! THERE'S SISYPHUS!
HE MESSED WITH THE GODS WHEN HE WAS ALIVE SO HE HAS TO ROLL THAT ROCK UP THE HILL TO KEEP HIM FROM COMING UP WITH NEW TRICKS.
BUT... SURELY HE COULD HATCH NEW SCHEMES ONCE HE REACHES THE APEX?
NOPE. EVERY TIME HE GETS TO THE TOP, THE ROCK ROLLS BACK DOWN.

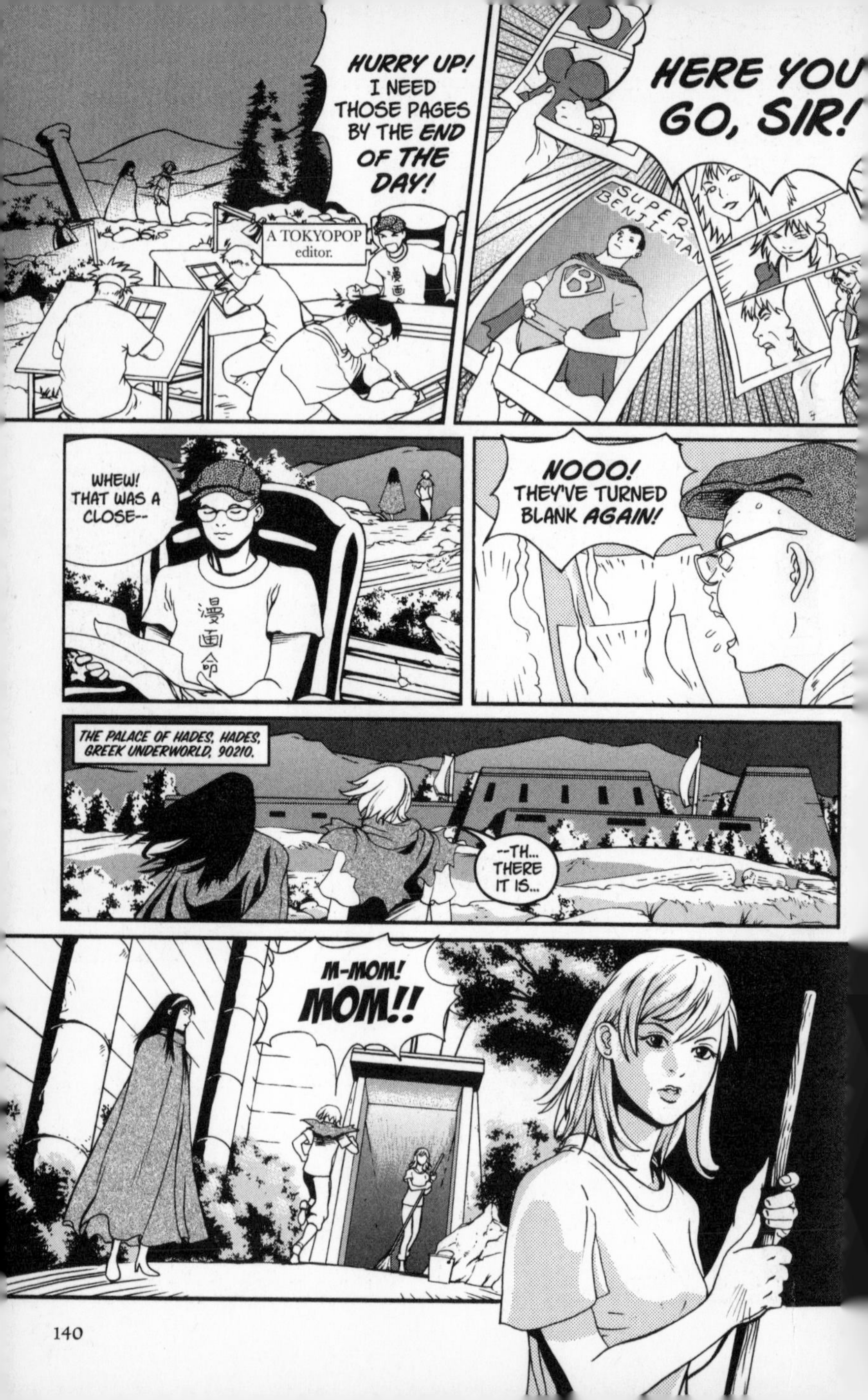
HURRY UP! I NEED THOSE PAGES BY THE END OF THE DAY!
A TOKYOPOP editor.
HERE YOU GO, SIR!
SUPER BENJI-MAN
WHEW! THAT WAS A CLOSE--
NOOO! THEY'VE TURNED BLANK AGAIN!
THE PALACE OF HADES, HADES, GREEK UNDERWORLD, 90210.
--TH... THERE IT IS...
M-MOM! MOM!!

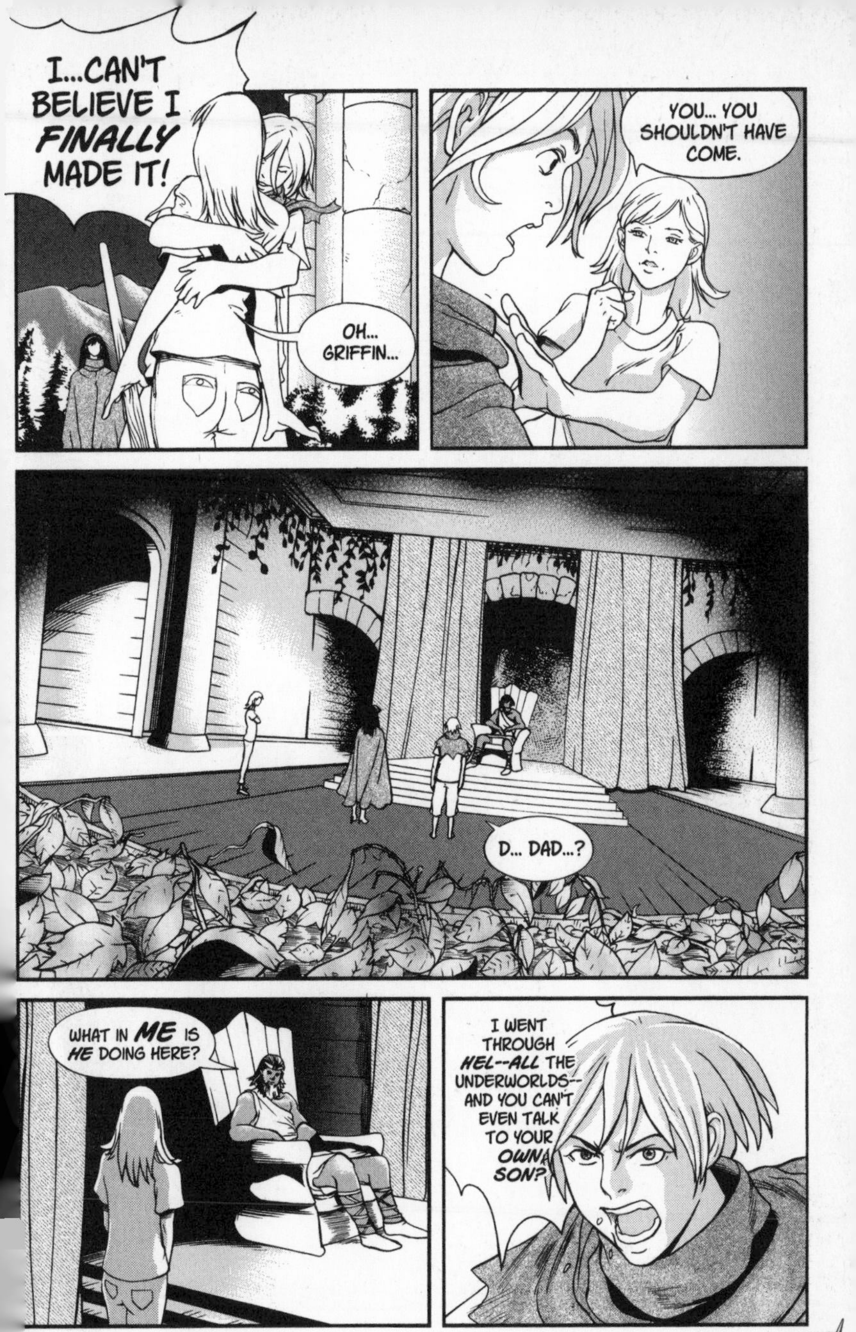
I...CAN'T BELIEVE I FINALLY MADE IT!
OH... GRIFFIN...
YOU... YOU SHOULDN'T HAVE COME.
D... DAD...?
WHAT IN ME IS HE DOING HERE?
I WENT THROUGH HEL--ALL THE UNDERWORLDS--AND YOU CAN'T EVEN TALK TO YOUR OWN SON?

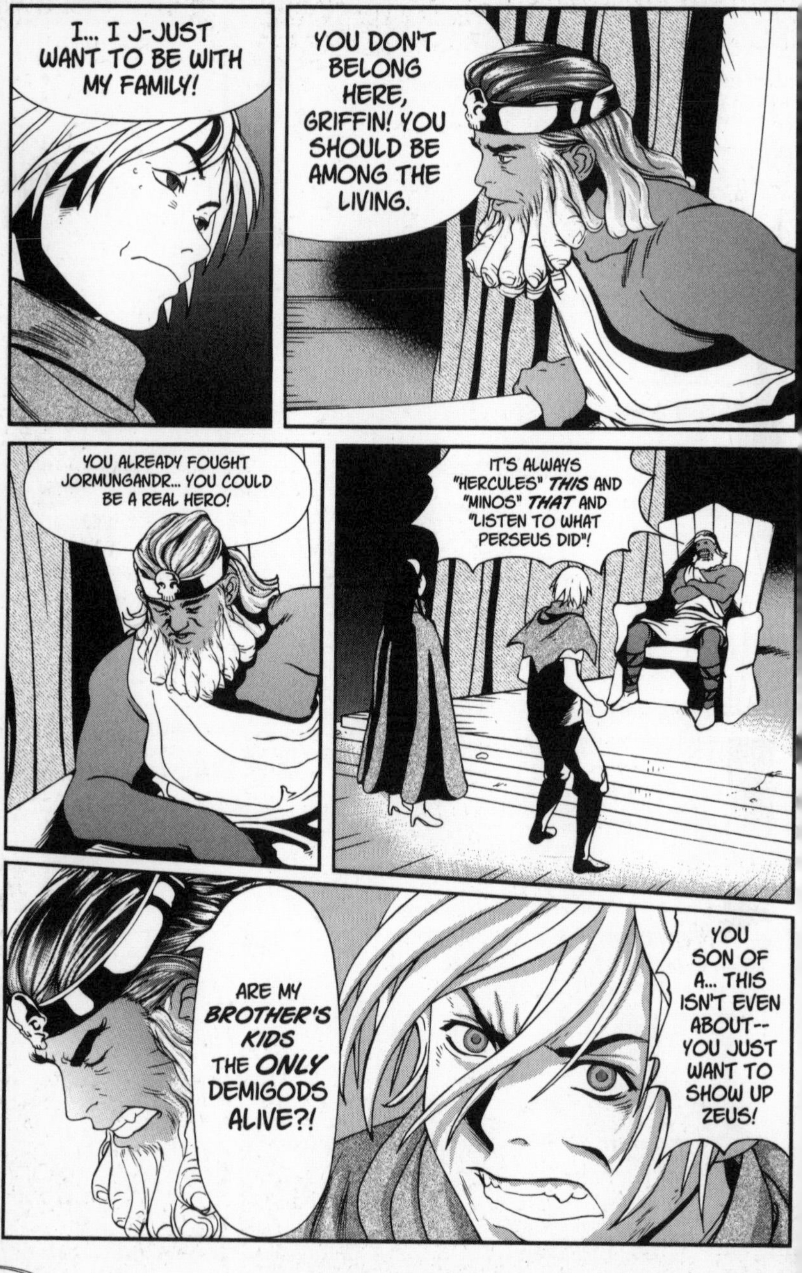

I... I J-JUST WANT TO BE WITH MY FAMILY!
YOU DON'T BELONG HERE, GRIFFIN! YOU SHOULD BE AMONG THE LIVING.
YOU ALREADY FOUGHT JORMUNGANDR... YOU COULD BE A REAL HERO!
IT'S ALWAYS "HERCULES" *THIS* AND "MINOS" *THAT* AND "LISTEN TO WHAT PERSEUS DID"!
ARE MY *BROTHER'S KIDS* THE *ONLY* DEMIGODS ALIVE?!
YOU SON OF A... THIS ISN'T EVEN ABOUT-- YOU JUST WANT TO SHOW UP ZEUS!

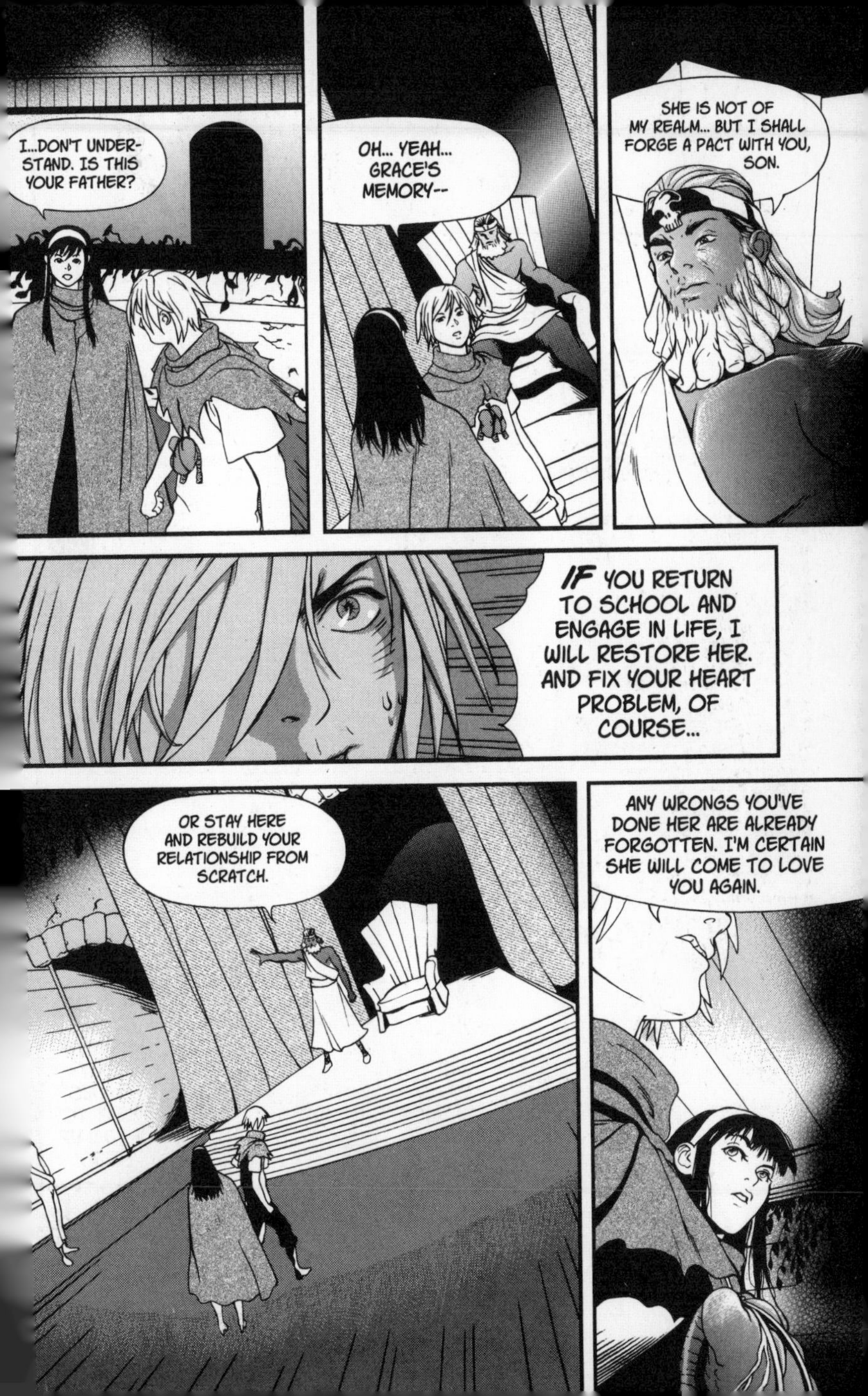
I...DON'T UNDER-STAND. IS THIS YOUR FATHER?
OH... YEAH... GRACE'S MEMORY--
SHE IS NOT OF MY REALM... BUT I SHALL FORGE A PACT WITH YOU, SON.
IF YOU RETURN TO SCHOOL AND ENGAGE IN LIFE, I WILL RESTORE HER. AND FIX YOUR HEART PROBLEM, OF COURSE...
OR STAY HERE AND REBUILD YOUR RELATIONSHIP FROM SCRATCH.
ANY WRONGS YOU'VE DONE HER ARE ALREADY FORGOTTEN. I'M CERTAIN SHE WILL COME TO LOVE YOU AGAIN.

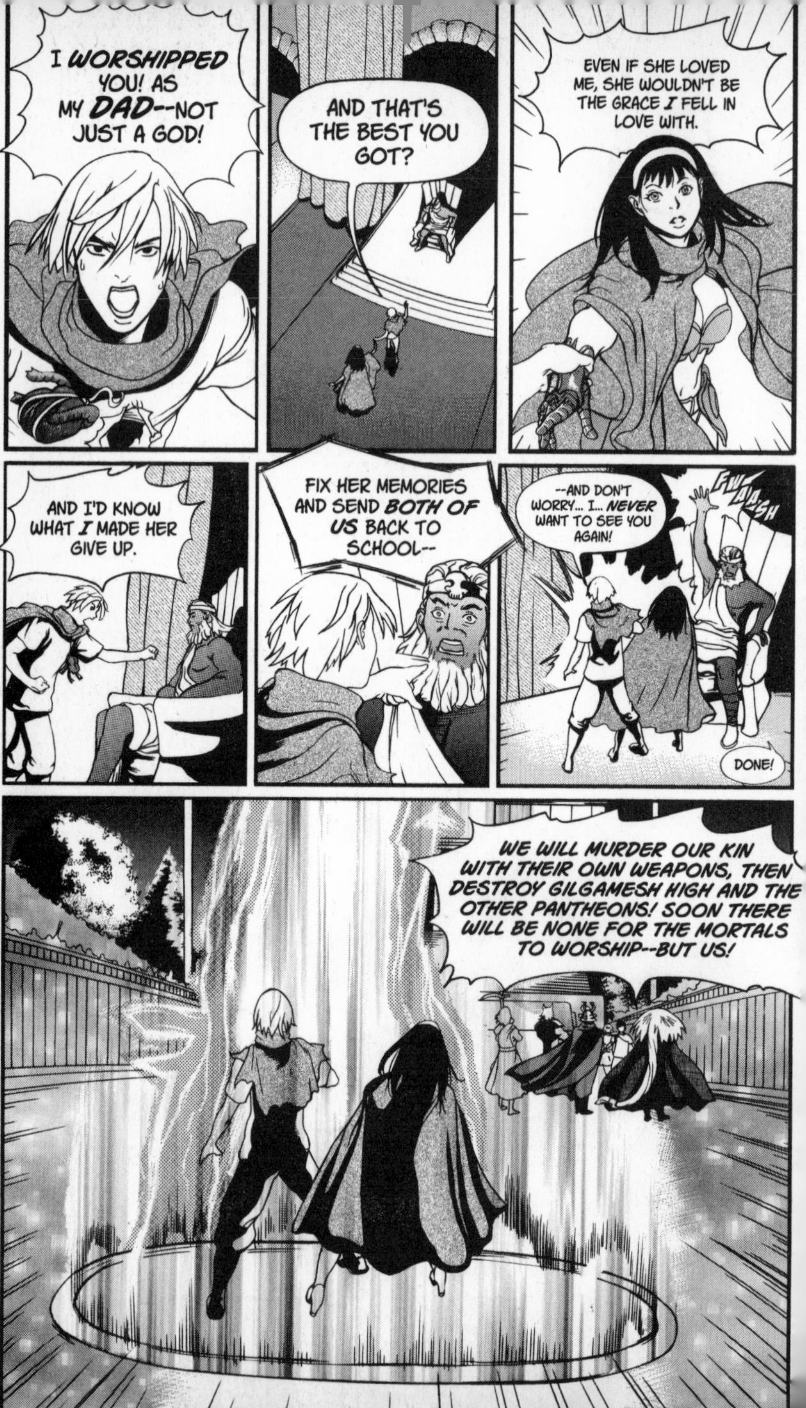
I WORSHIPPED YOU! AS MY DAD--NOT JUST A GOD!
AND THAT'S THE BEST YOU GOT?
EVEN IF SHE LOVED ME, SHE WOULDN'T BE THE GRACE I FELL IN LOVE WITH.
AND I'D KNOW WHAT I MADE HER GIVE UP.
FIX HER MEMORIES AND SEND BOTH OF US BACK TO SCHOOL--
--AND DON'T WORRY... I... NEVER WANT TO SEE YOU AGAIN!
FWAASH
DONE!
WE WILL MURDER OUR KIN WITH THEIR OWN WEAPONS, THEN DESTROY GILGAMESH HIGH AND THE OTHER PANTHEONS! SOON THERE WILL BE NONE FOR THE MORTALS TO WORSHIP--BUT US!

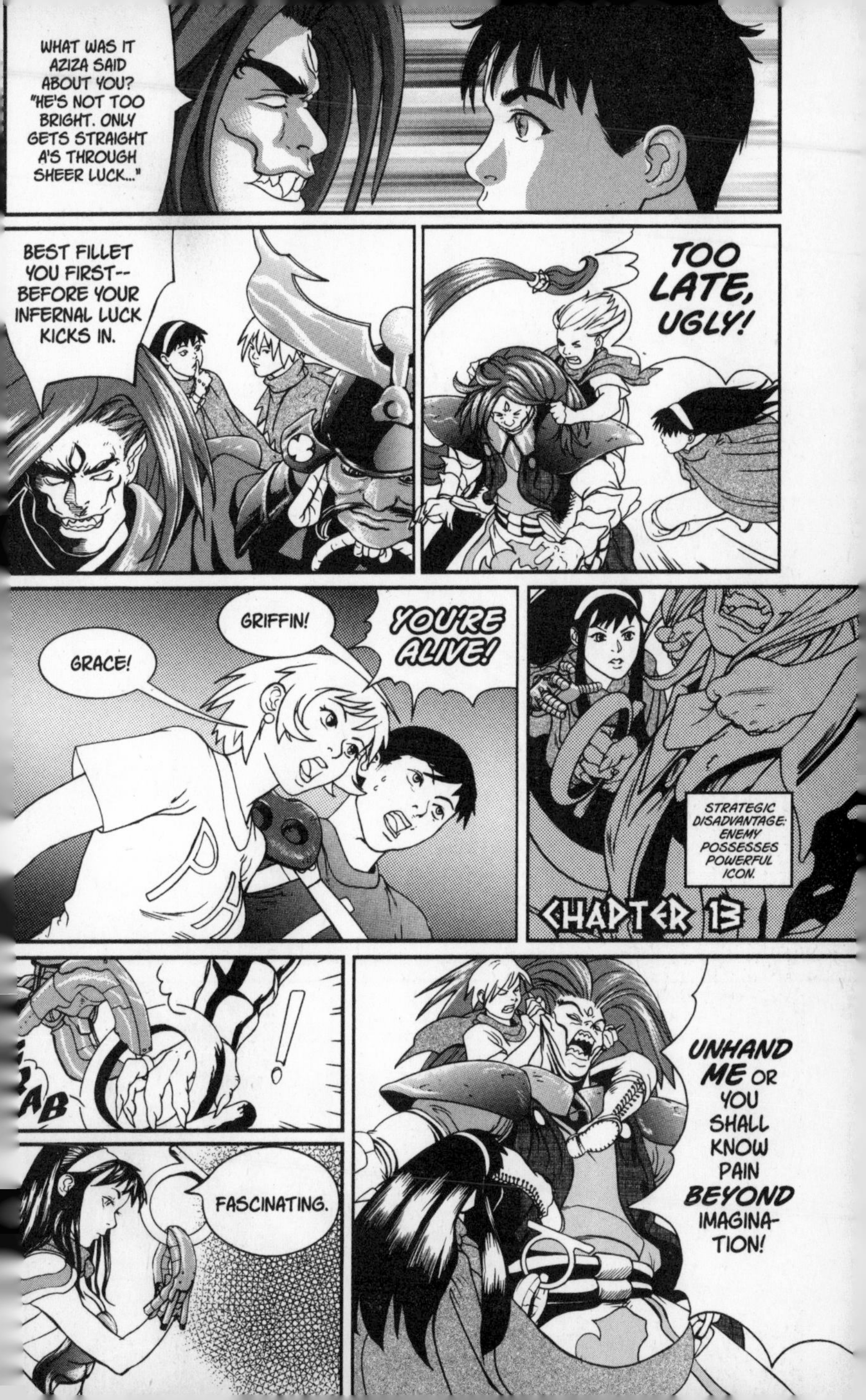
WHAT WAS IT AZIZA SAID ABOUT YOU? "HE'S NOT TOO BRIGHT. ONLY GETS STRAIGHT A'S THROUGH SHEER LUCK..."
BEST FILLET YOU FIRST-- BEFORE YOUR INFERNAL LUCK KICKS IN.
TOO LATE, UGLY!
GRIFFIN!
GRACE!
YOU'RE ALIVE!
STRATEGIC DISADVANTAGE: ENEMY POSSESSES POWERFUL ICON.
CHAPTER 13
FASCINATING.
UNHAND ME OR YOU SHALL KNOW PAIN BEYOND IMAGINATION!

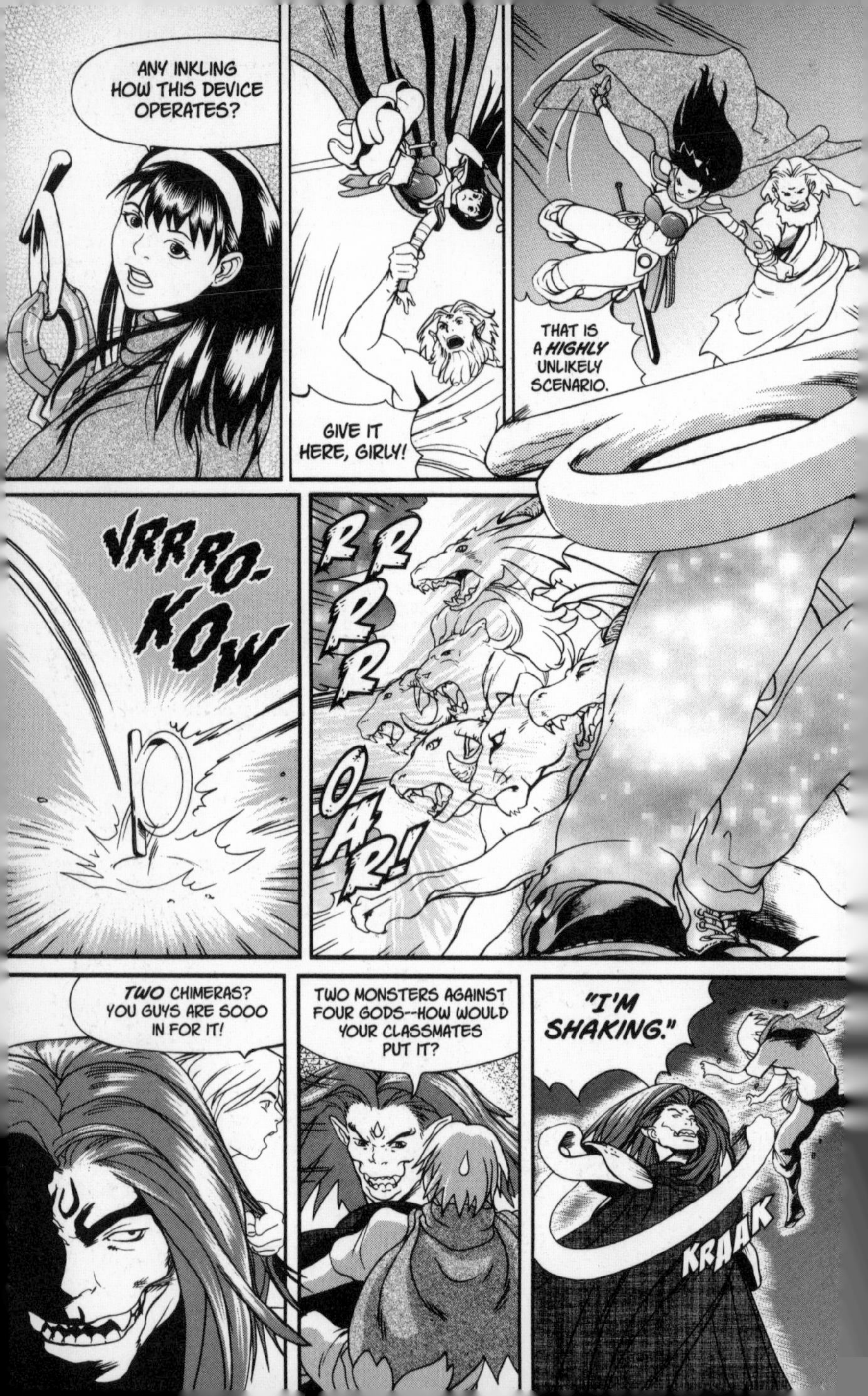
ANY INKLING HOW THIS DEVICE OPERATES?
GIVE IT HERE, GIRLY!
THAT IS A *HIGHLY* UNLIKELY SCENARIO.
VRRRO-KOW
RRRRR-OAR!
TWO CHIMERAS? YOU GUYS ARE SOOO IN FOR IT!
TWO MONSTERS AGAINST FOUR GODS--HOW WOULD YOUR CLASSMATES PUT IT?
"I'M SHAKING."
KRAAK

WHAAA!
OOOF!
VRRRO-
KOW
AROO?
ROAR!
GRRRAR!
BITE
THAAK
YIPE!

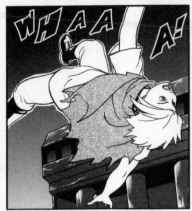

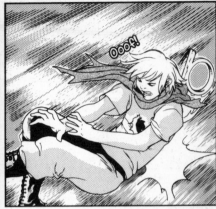

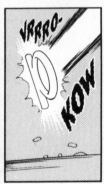

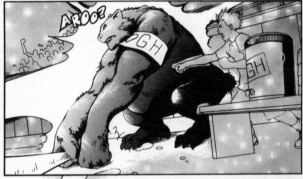

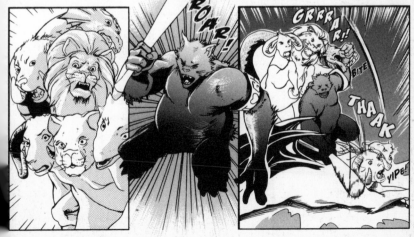

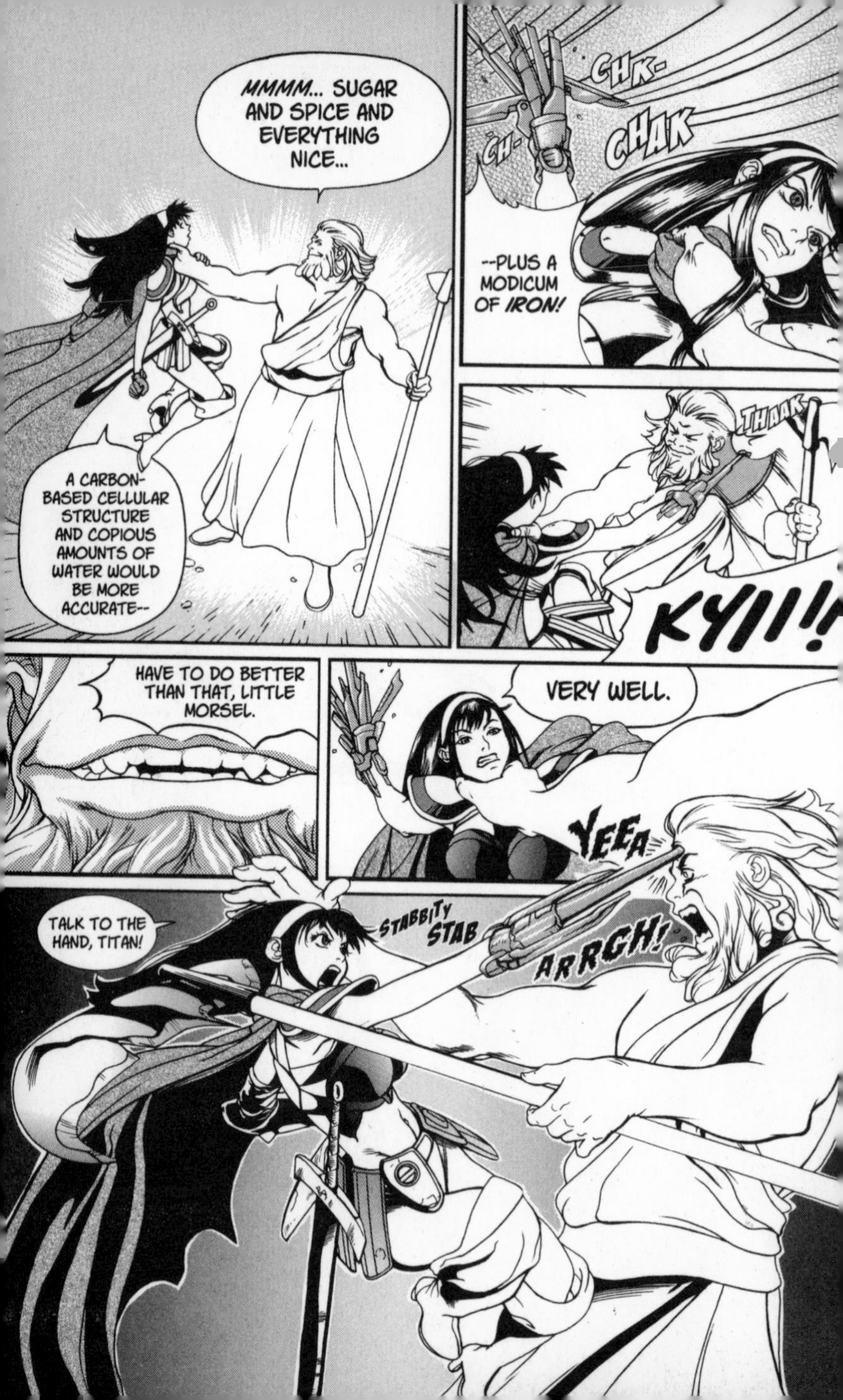
MMMM... SUGAR AND SPICE AND EVERYTHING NICE...
A CARBON-BASED CELLULAR STRUCTURE AND COPIOUS AMOUNTS OF WATER WOULD BE MORE ACCURATE--
CHK-
CH-
CHAK
--PLUS A MODICUM OF IRON!
THAAK
KYII!!
HAVE TO DO BETTER THAN THAT, LITTLE MORSEL.
VERY WELL.
YEEA
TALK TO THE HAND, TITAN!
STABBITY STAB
ARRGH!

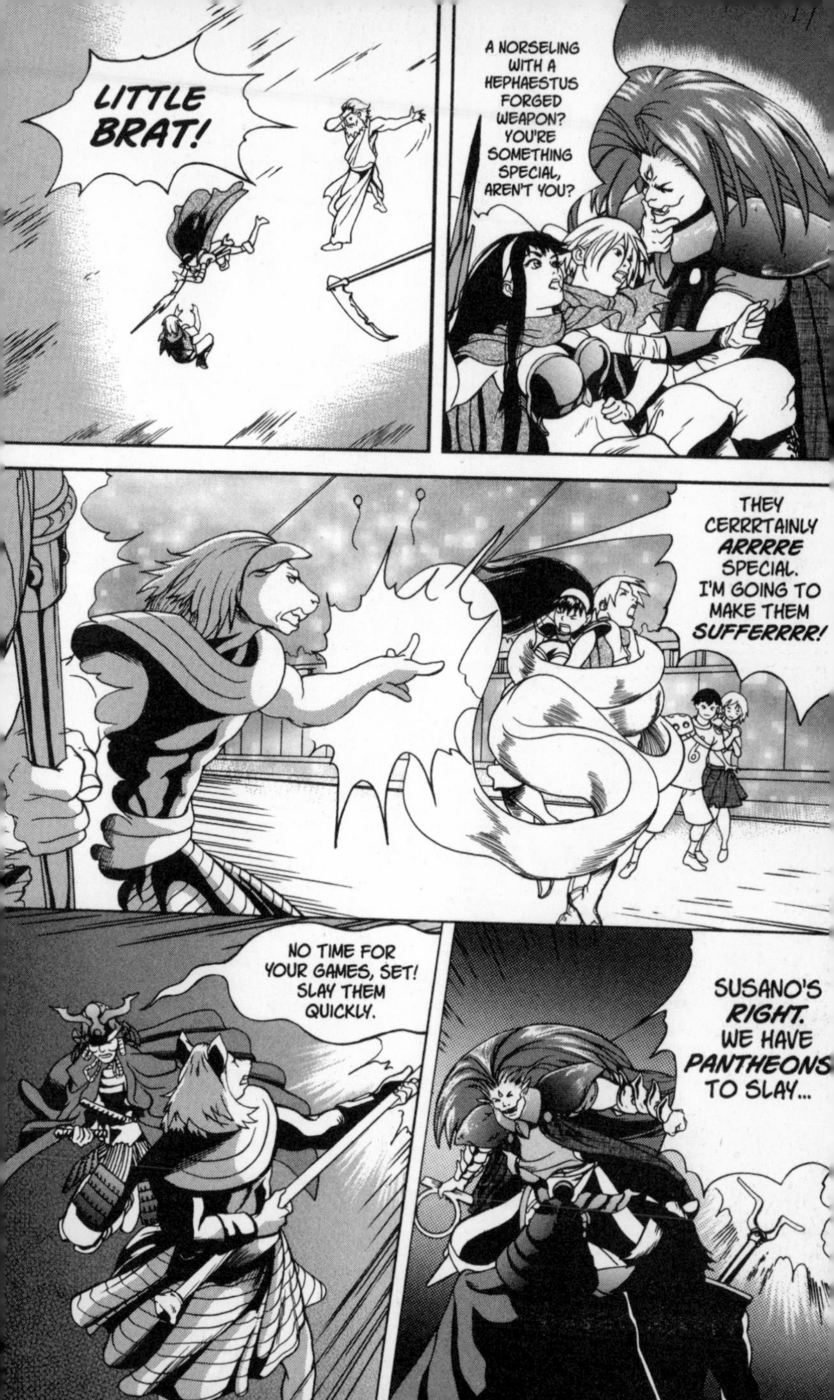
LITTLE BRAT!
A NORSELING WITH A HEPHAESTUS FORGED WEAPON? YOU'RE SOMETHING SPECIAL, AREN'T YOU?
THEY CERRRTAINLY ARRRRE SPECIAL. I'M GOING TO MAKE THEM SUFFERRRR!
NO TIME FOR YOUR GAMES, SET! SLAY THEM QUICKLY.
SUSANO'S RIGHT. WE HAVE PANTHEONS TO SLAY...

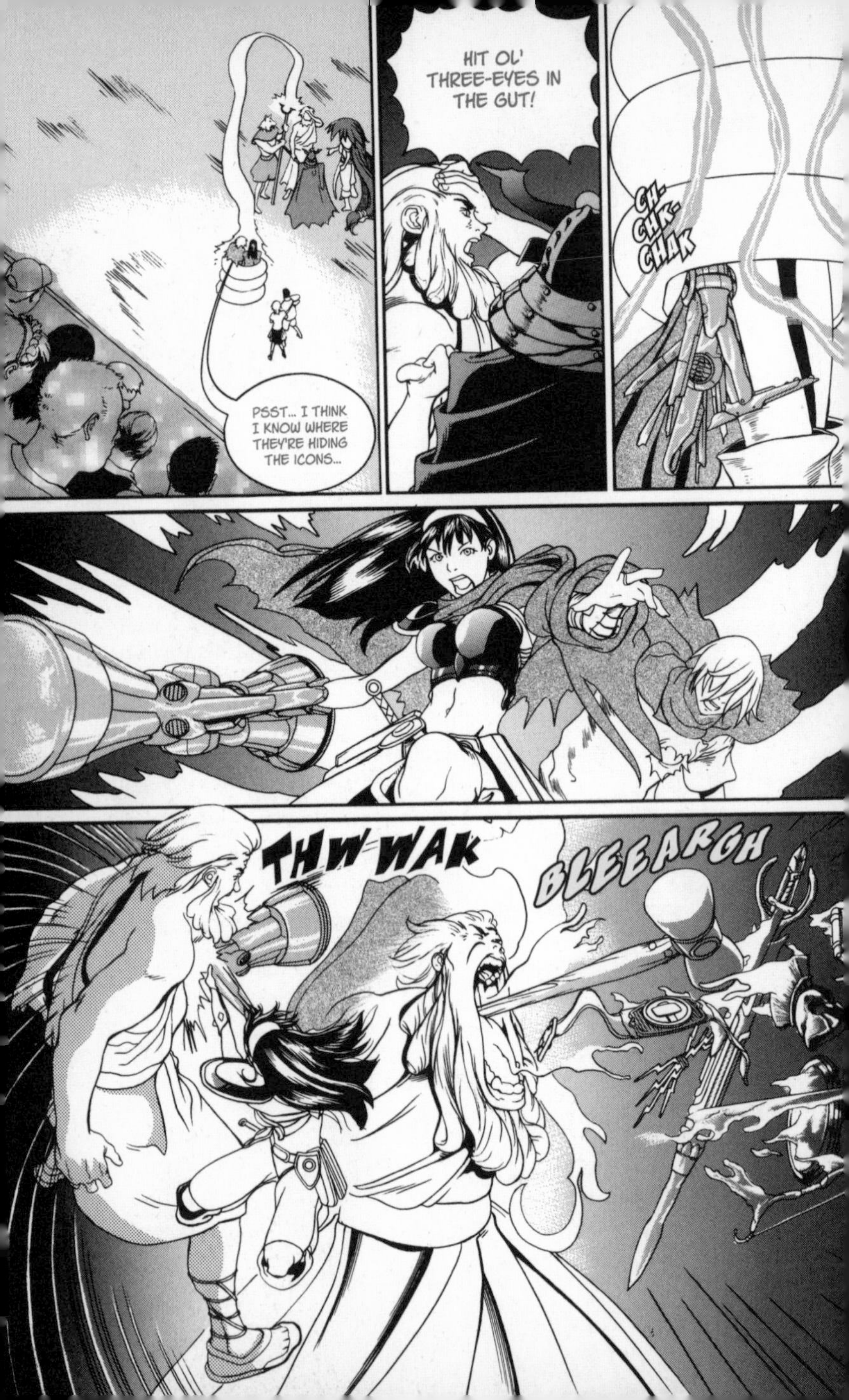
PSST... I THINK I KNOW WHERE THEY'RE HIDING THE ICONS...
HIT OL' THREE-EYES IN THE GUT!
CH-CHK-CHAK
THW WAK
BLEEARGH

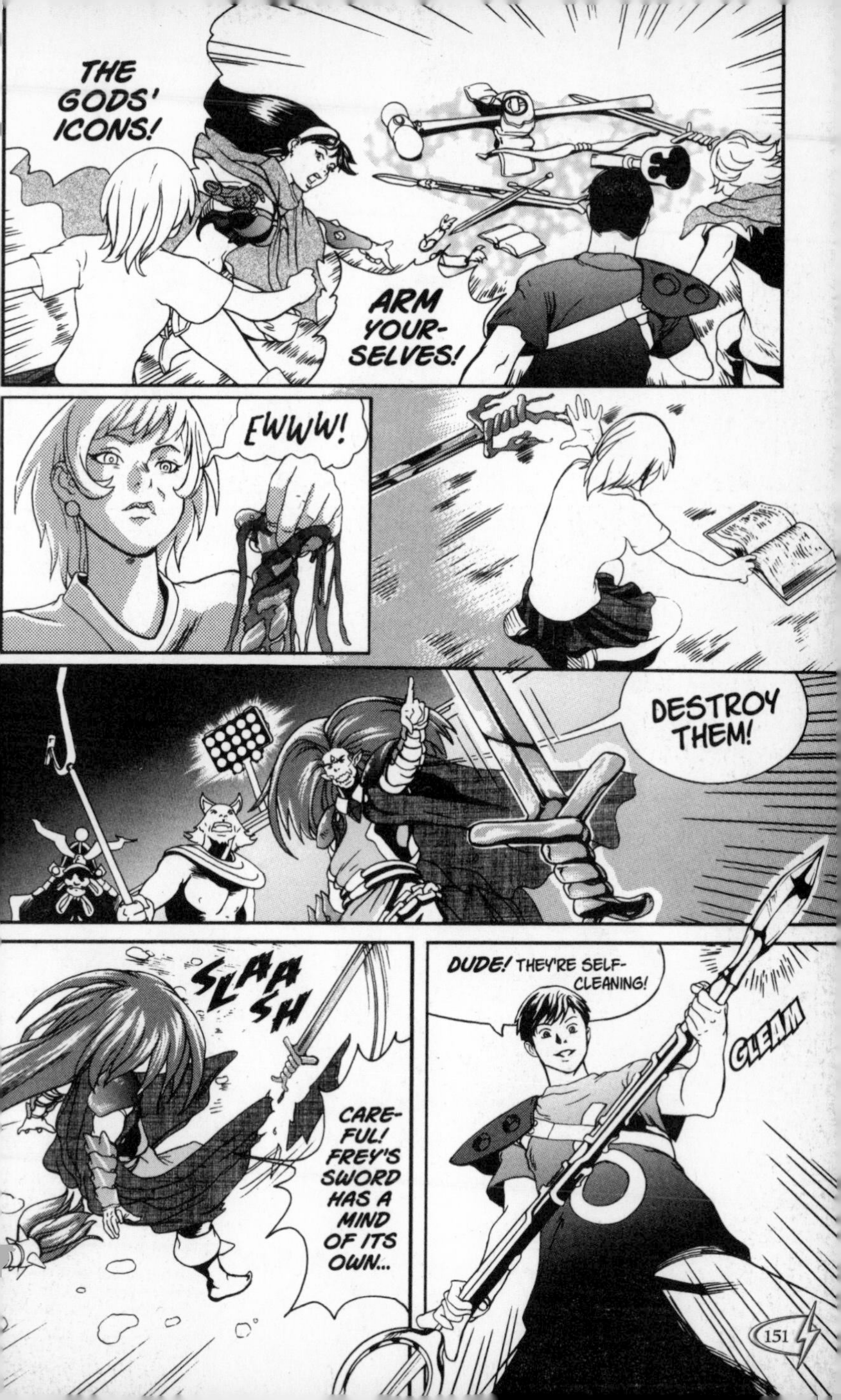
THE GODS' ICONS!
ARM YOURSELVES!
EWWW!
DESTROY THEM!
SLAASH
CAREFUL! FREY'S SWORD HAS A MIND OF ITS OWN...
DUDE! THEY'RE SELF-CLEANING!
GLEAM

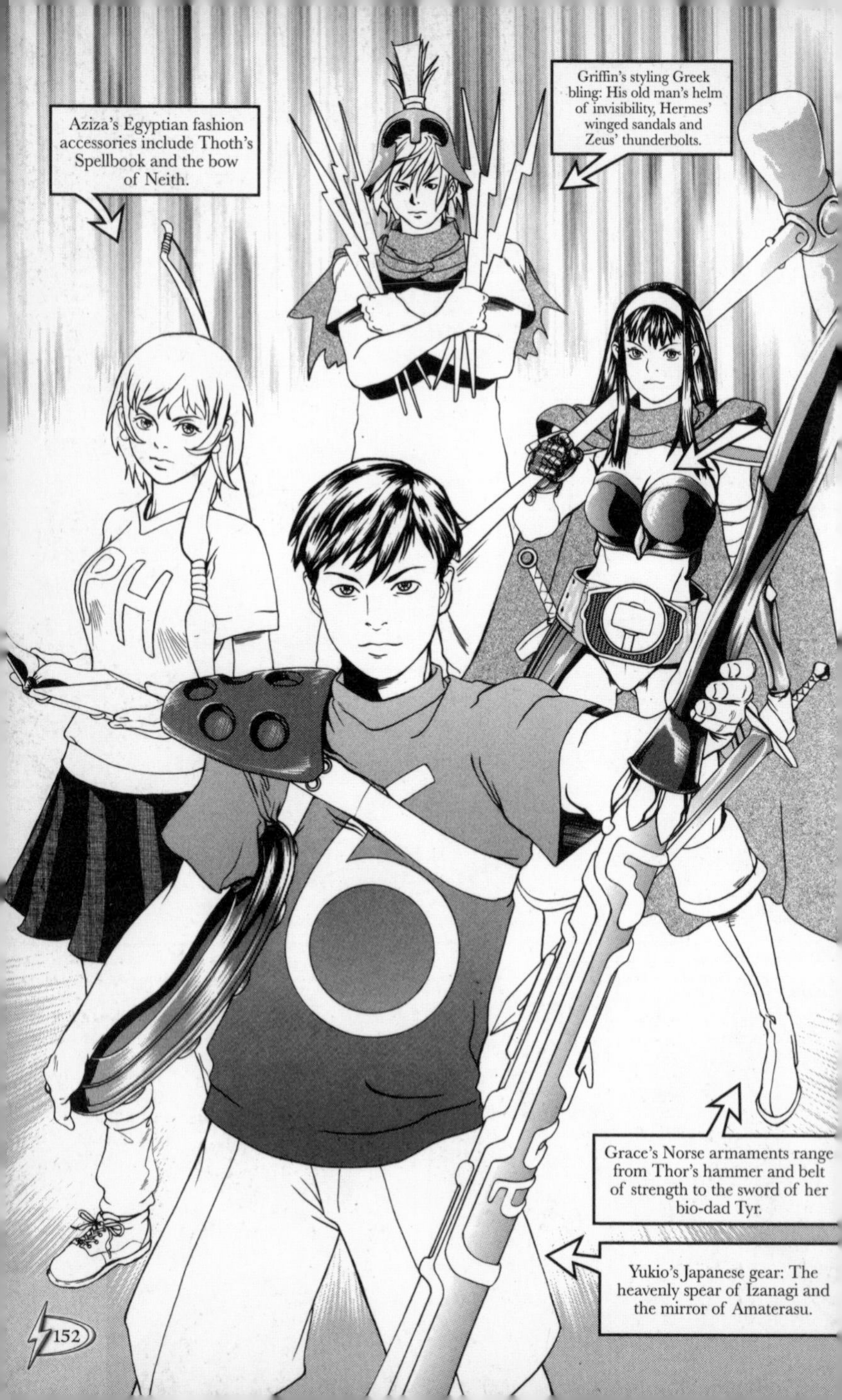
Aziza's Egyptian fashion accessories include Thoth's Spellbook and the bow of Neith.
Griffin's styling Greek bling: His old man's helm of invisibility, Hermes' winged sandals and Zeus' thunderbolts.
PH
Grace's Norse armaments range from Thor's hammer and belt of strength to the sword of her bio-dad Tyr.
Yukio's Japanese gear: The heavenly spear of Izanagi and the mirror of Amaterasu.

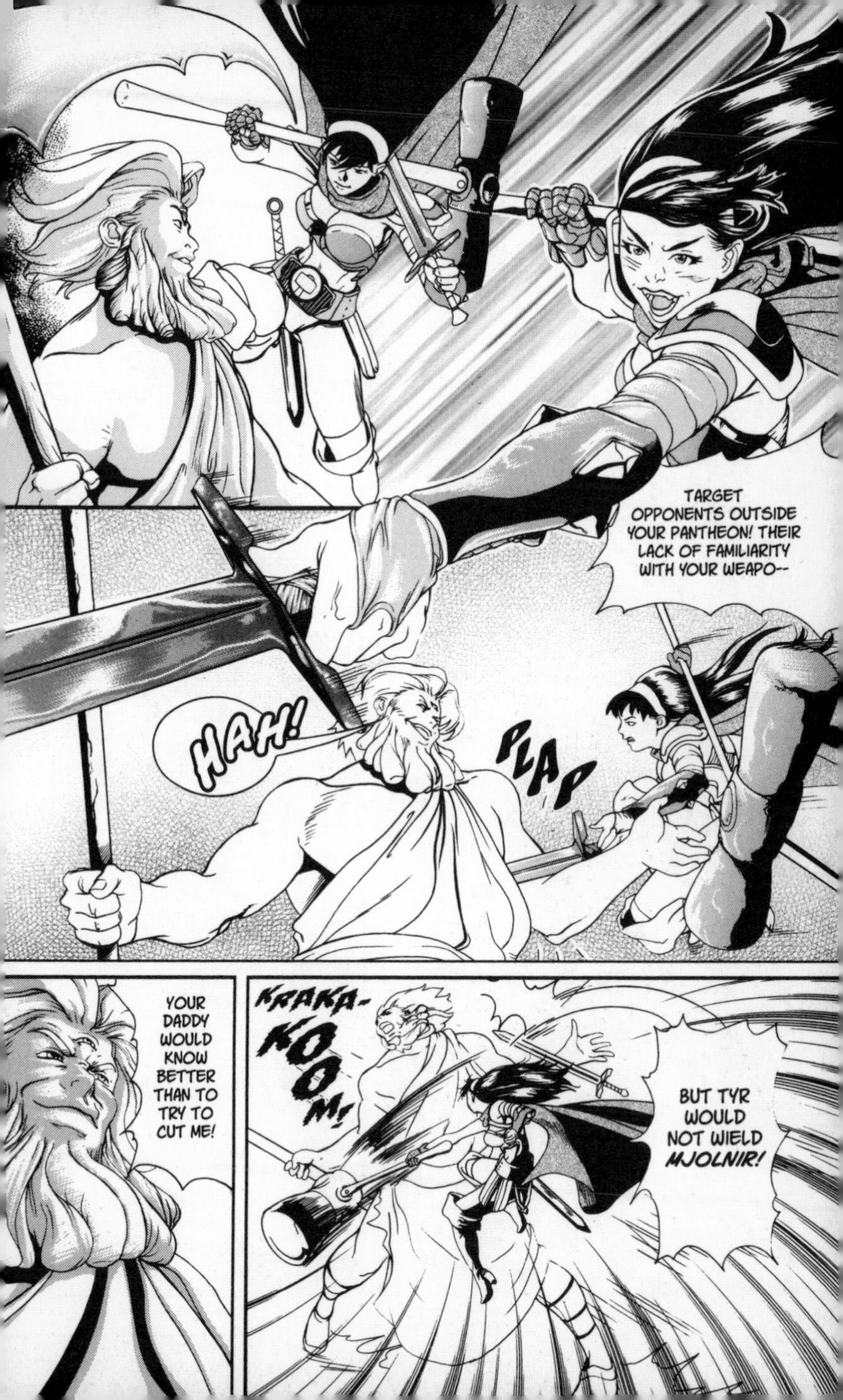
TARGET OPPONENTS OUTSIDE YOUR PANTHEON! THEIR LACK OF FAMILIARITY WITH YOUR WEAPO--
HAH!
PLAP
YOUR DADDY WOULD KNOW BETTER THAN TO TRY TO CUT ME!
KRAKA-KOOM!
BUT TYR WOULD NOT WIELD *MJOLNIR!*

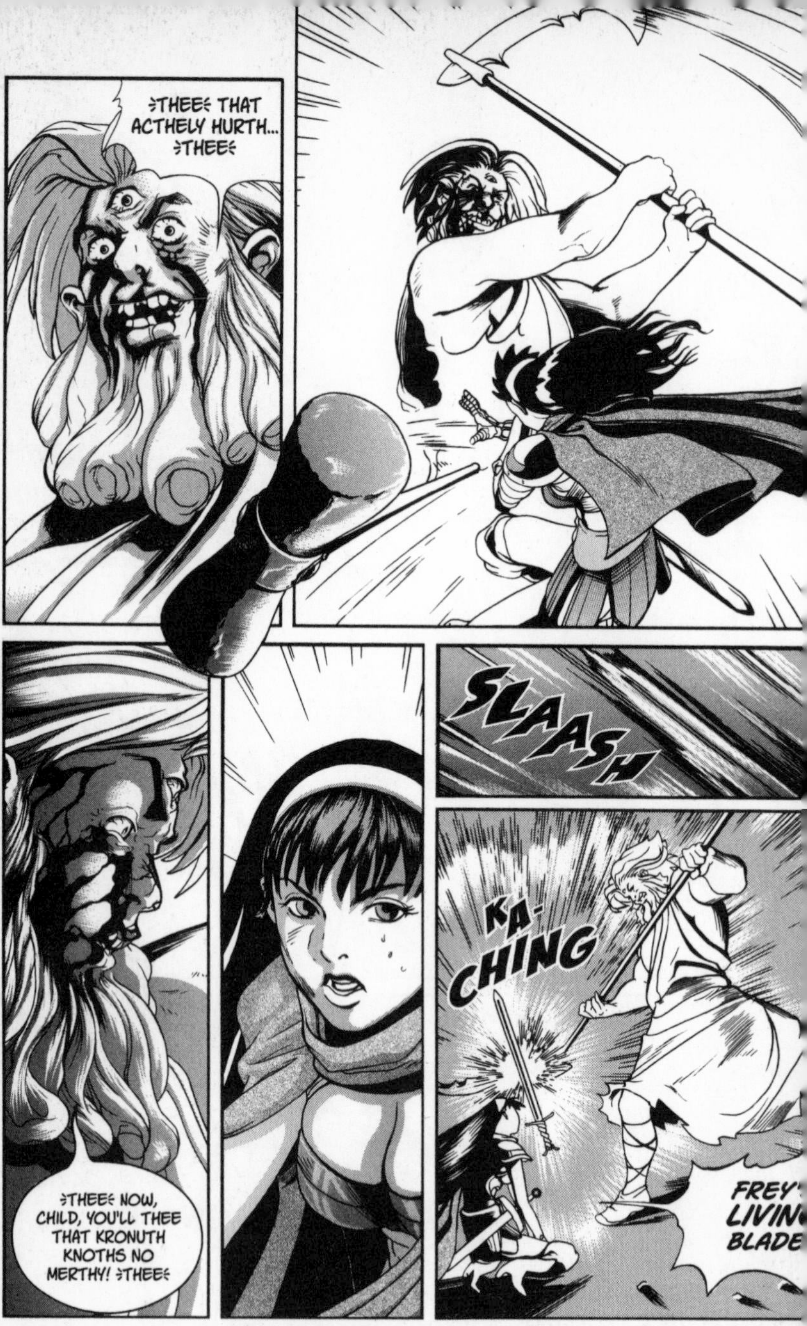

∋THEE∈ THAT ACTHELY HURTH... ∋THEE∈
∋THEE∈ NOW, CHILD, YOU'LL THEE THAT KRONUTH KNOTHS NO MERTHY! ∋THEE∈
SLAASH
KA-CHING
FREY'S LIVING BLADE

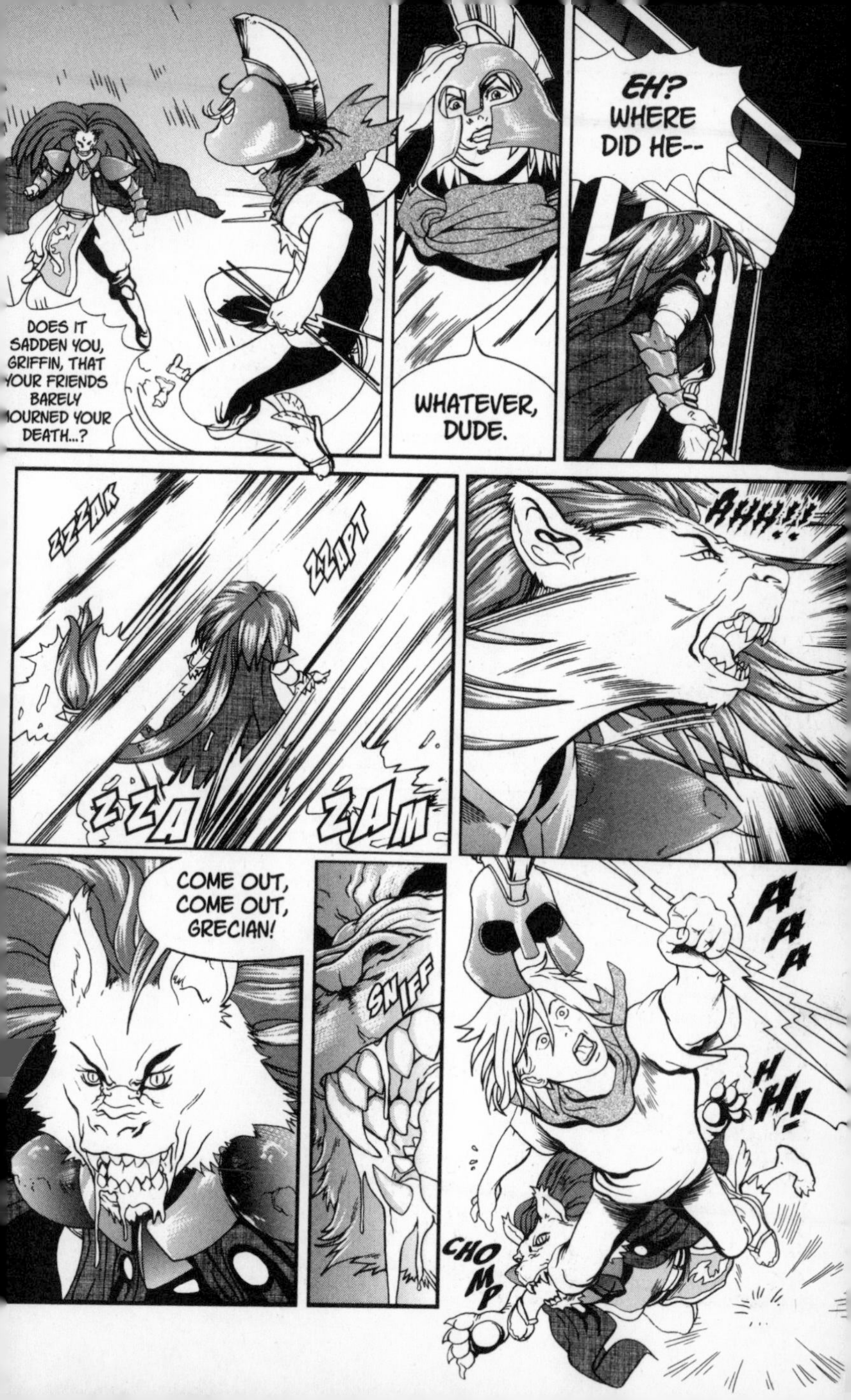
DOES IT SADDEN YOU, GRIFFIN, THAT YOUR FRIENDS BARELY MOURNED YOUR DEATH...?
WHATEVER, DUDE.
EH? WHERE DID HE--
ZZZAK
ZZAPT
ZZA
ZAM
AHH!!!
COME OUT, COME OUT, GRECIAN!
SNIFF
AAAHH!
CHOMP

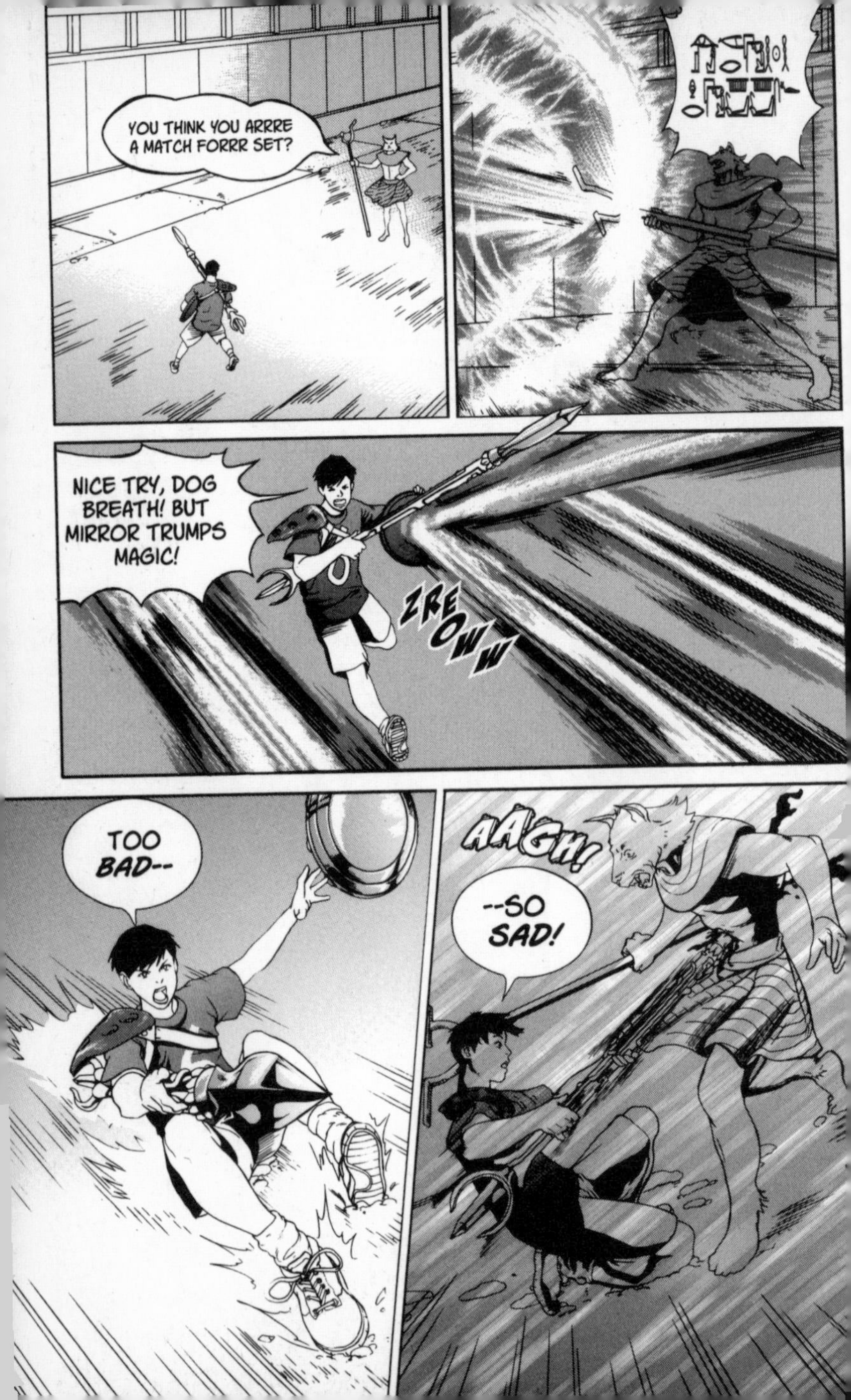
YOU THINK YOU ARRRE A MATCH FORRR SET?
NICE TRY, DOG BREATH! BUT MIRROR TRUMPS MAGIC!
ZREOWW
TOO BAD--
AAGH!
--SO SAD!

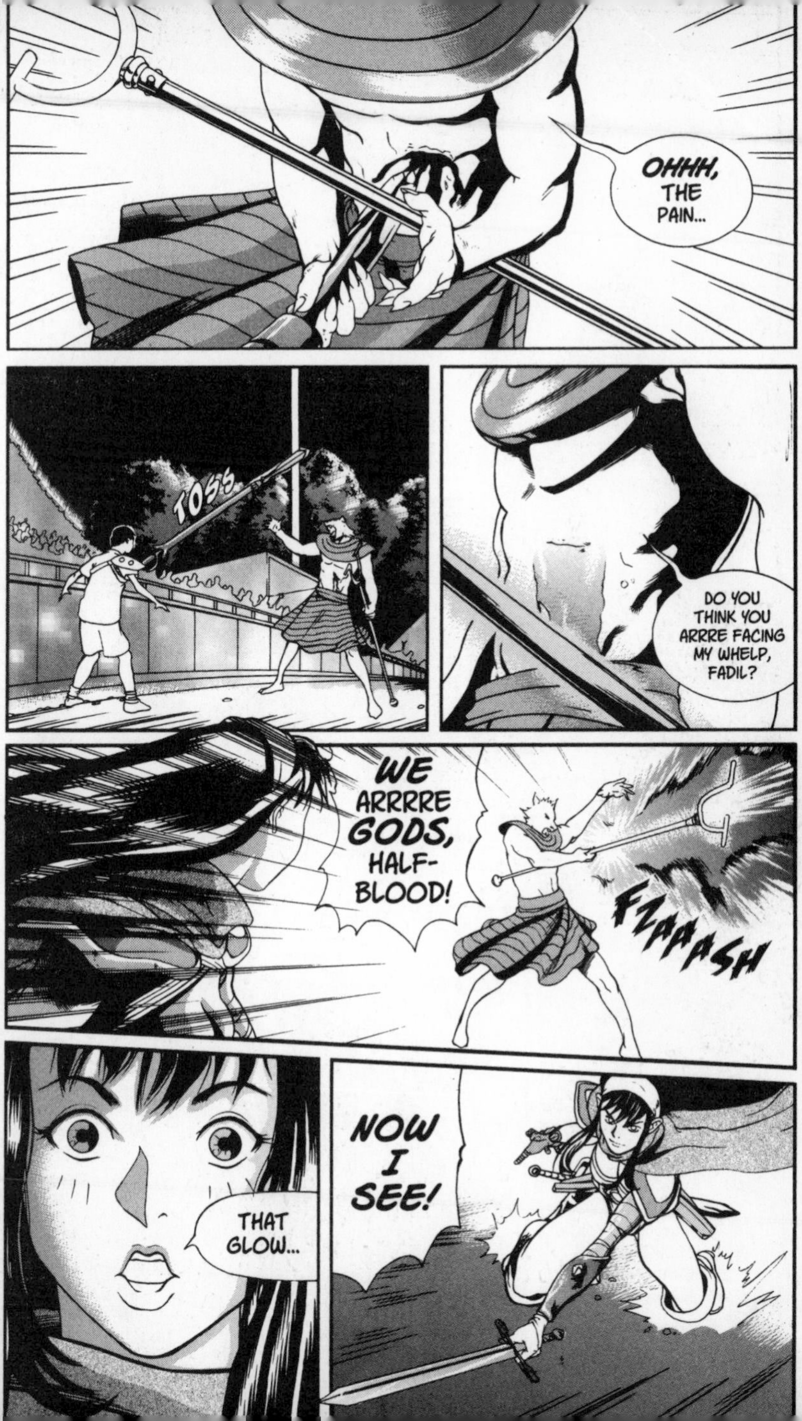
OHHH, THE PAIN...
TOSS
DO YOU THINK YOU ARRRE FACING MY WHELP, FADIL?
WE ARRRRE GODS, HALF-BLOOD!
FZAAASH
THAT GLOW...
NOW I SEE!

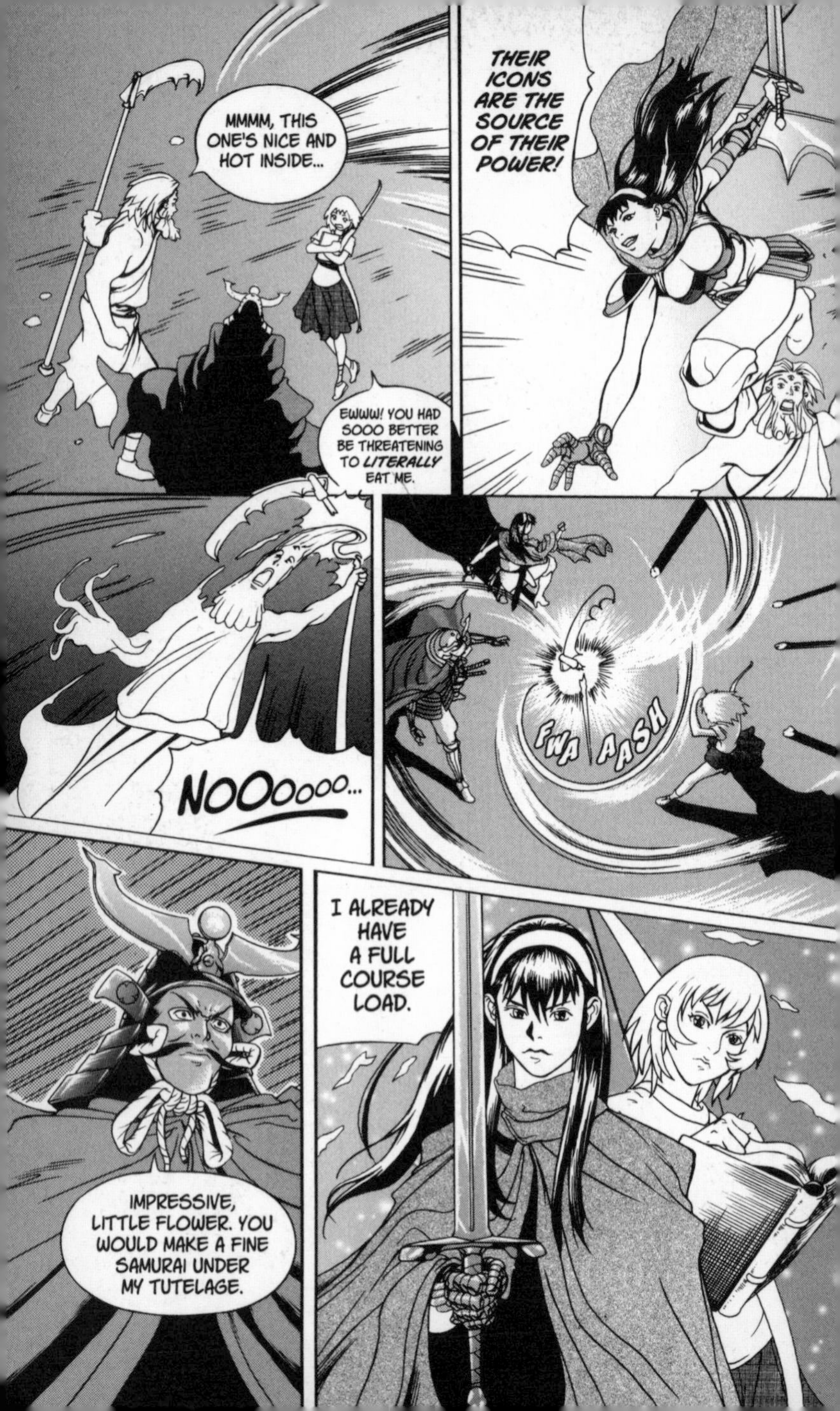
MMMM, THIS ONE'S NICE AND HOT INSIDE...
EWWW! YOU HAD SOOO BETTER BE THREATENING TO *LITERALLY* EAT ME.
THEIR ICONS ARE THE SOURCE OF THEIR POWER!
NOOooooo...
FWAAASH
IMPRESSIVE, LITTLE FLOWER. YOU WOULD MAKE A FINE SAMURAI UNDER MY TUTELAGE.
I ALREADY HAVE A FULL COURSE LOAD.

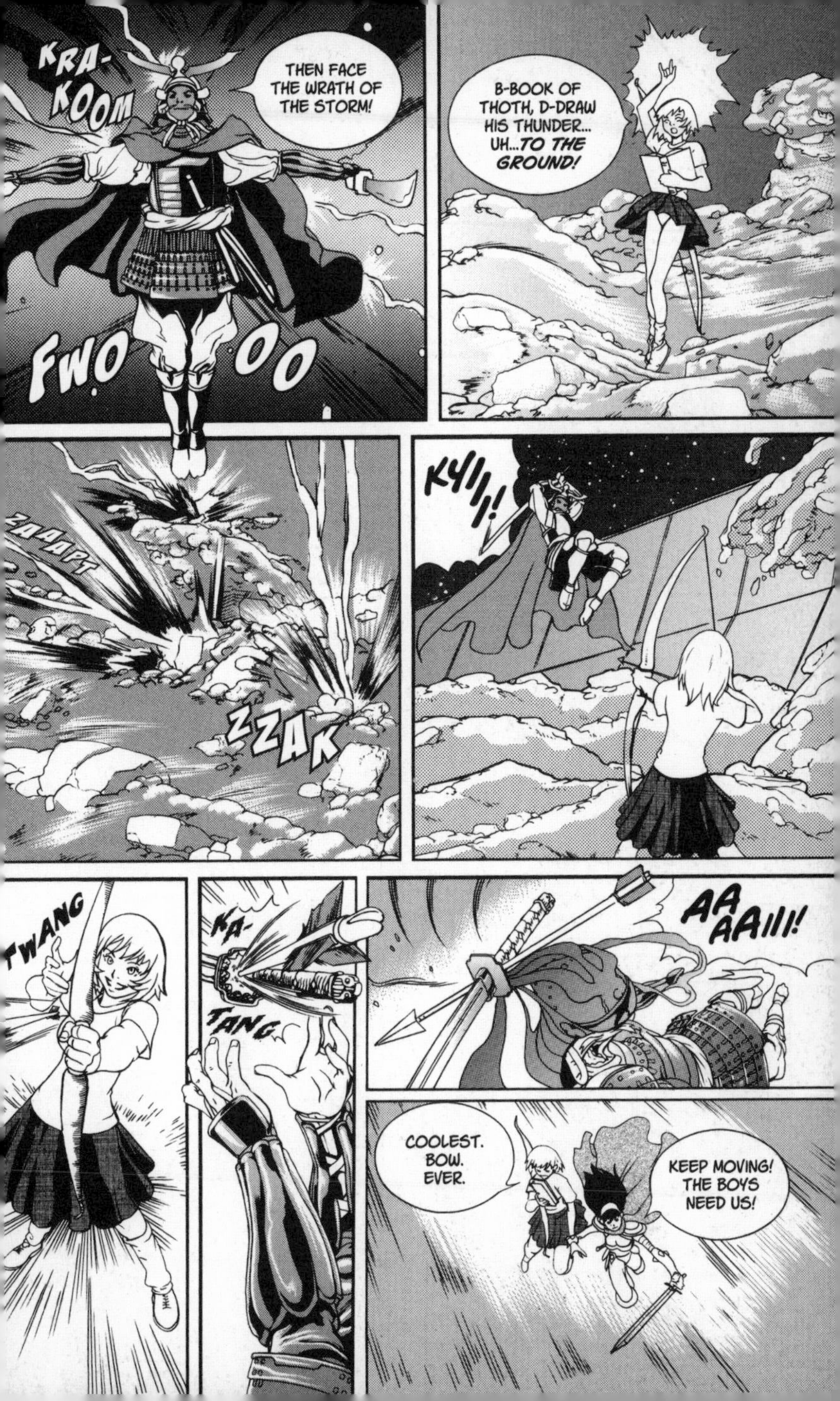
KRA-KOOM
THEN FACE THE WRATH OF THE STORM!
FWOOOO
B-BOOK OF THOTH, D-DRAW HIS THUNDER... UH...TO THE GROUND!
ZAAAPT
ZZAK
KYIIII!
TWANG
KA-TANG
AAAAIII!
COOLEST. BOW. EVER.
KEEP MOVING! THE BOYS NEED US!

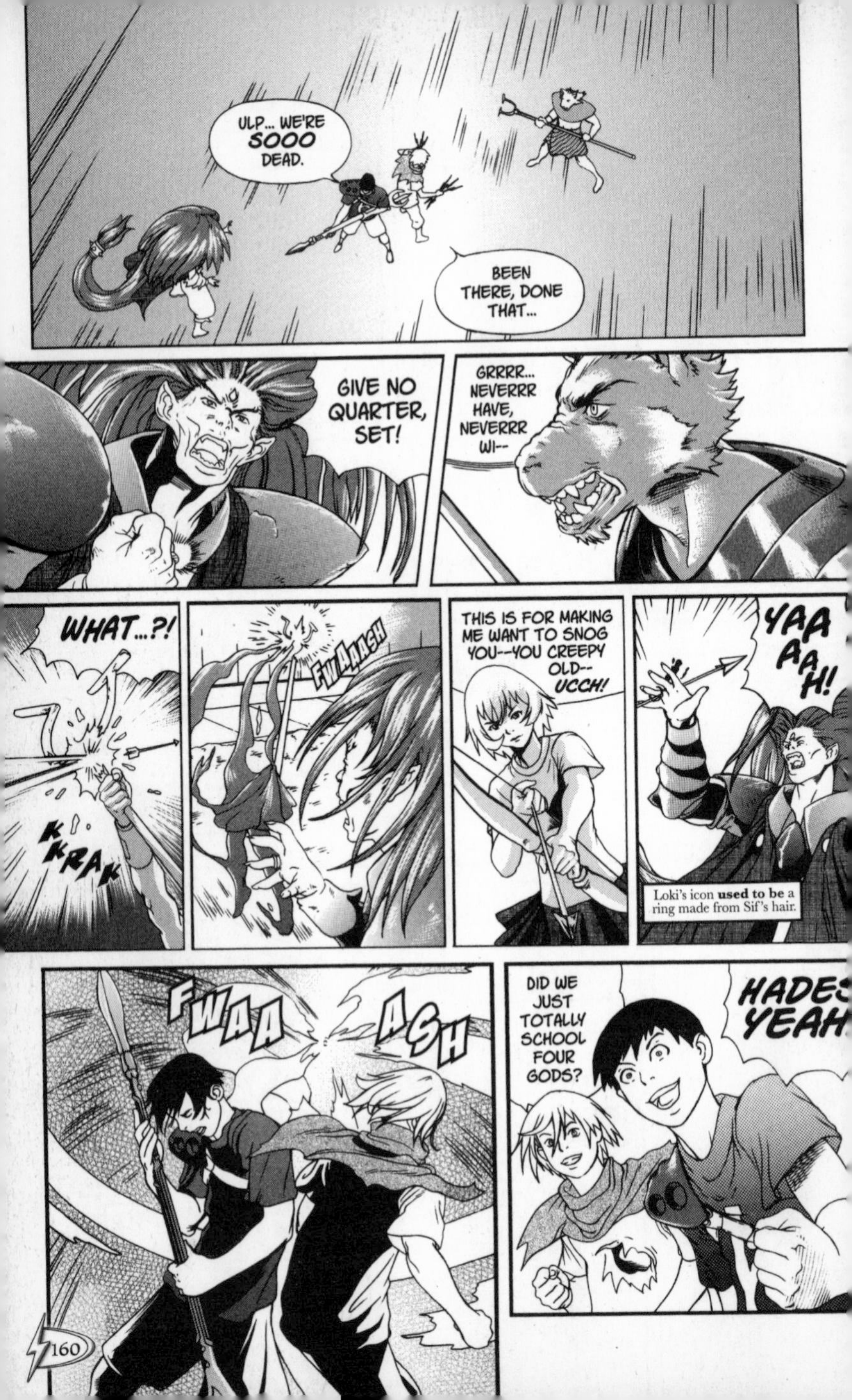
ULP... WE'RE SOOO DEAD.
BEEN THERE, DONE THAT...
GIVE NO QUARTER, SET!
GRRRR... NEVERRR HAVE, NEVERRR WI--
WHAT...?!
KKRAK
FWAAASH
THIS IS FOR MAKING ME WANT TO SNOG YOU--YOU CREEPY OLD-- UCCH!
YAAAAH!
Loki's icon **used to be** a ring made from Sif's hair.
FWAAASH
DID WE JUST TOTALLY SCHOOL FOUR GODS?
HADES YEAH

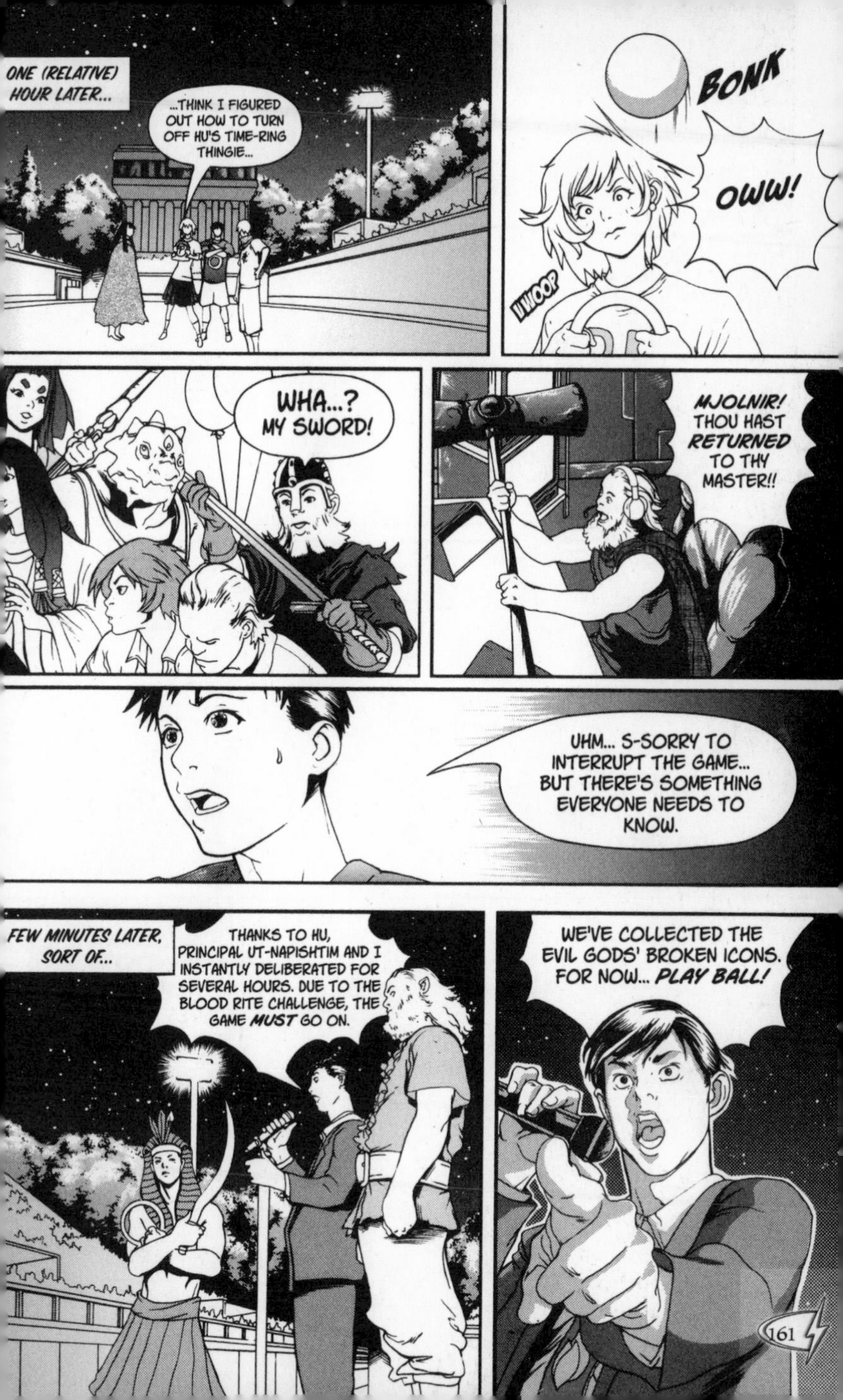
ONE (RELATIVE) HOUR LATER...
...THINK I FIGURED OUT HOW TO TURN OFF HU'S TIME-RING THINGIE...
BONK
OWW!
WWOOP
WHA...? MY SWORD!
MJOLNIR! THOU HAST RETURNED TO THY MASTER!!
UHM... S-SORRY TO INTERRUPT THE GAME... BUT THERE'S SOMETHING EVERYONE NEEDS TO KNOW.
FEW MINUTES LATER, SORT OF...
THANKS TO HU, PRINCIPAL UT-NAPISHTIM AND I INSTANTLY DELIBERATED FOR SEVERAL HOURS. DUE TO THE BLOOD RITE CHALLENGE, THE GAME MUST GO ON.
WE'VE COLLECTED THE EVIL GODS' BROKEN ICONS. FOR NOW... PLAY BALL!

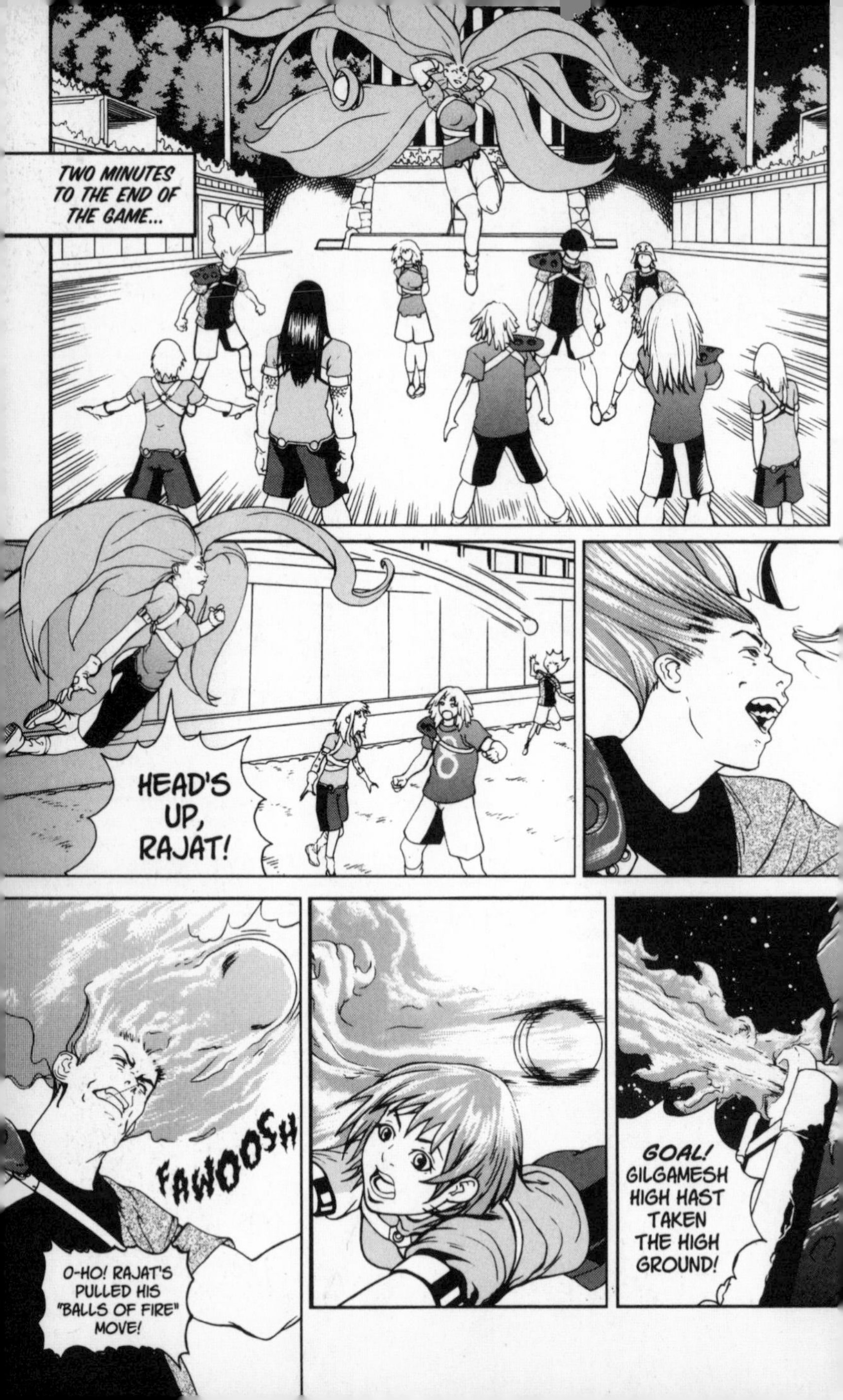
TWO MINUTES TO THE END OF THE GAME...
HEAD'S UP, RAJAT!
FAWOOSH
O-HO! RAJAT'S PULLED HIS "BALLS OF FIRE" MOVE!
GOAL! GILGAMESH HIGH HAST TAKEN THE HIGH GROUND!

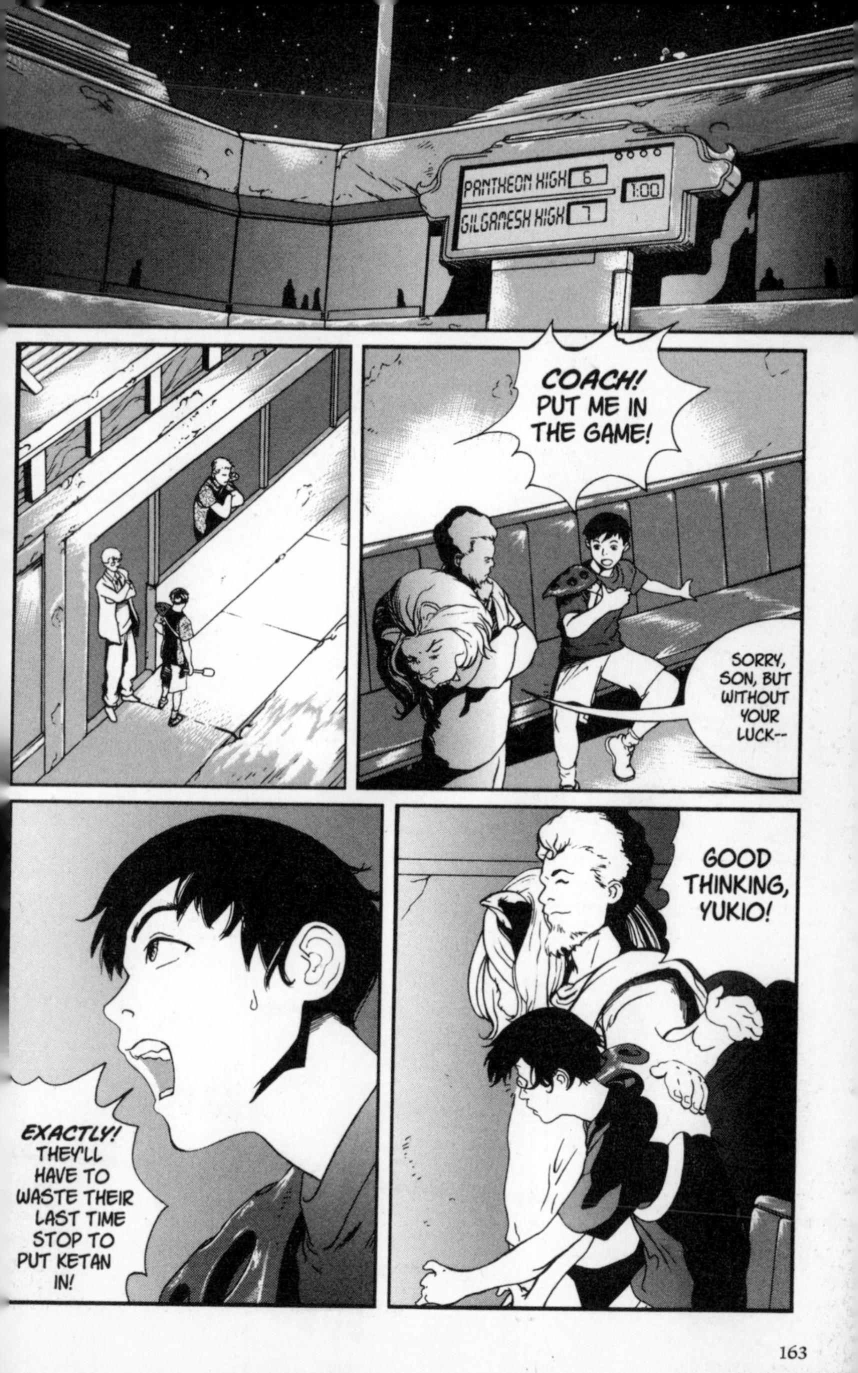
PANTHEON HIGH 6
1:00
GILGAMESH HIGH 7
COACH! PUT ME IN THE GAME!
SORRY, SON, BUT WITHOUT YOUR LUCK--
EXACTLY! THEY'LL HAVE TO WASTE THEIR LAST TIME STOP TO PUT KETAN IN!
GOOD THINKING, YUKIO!

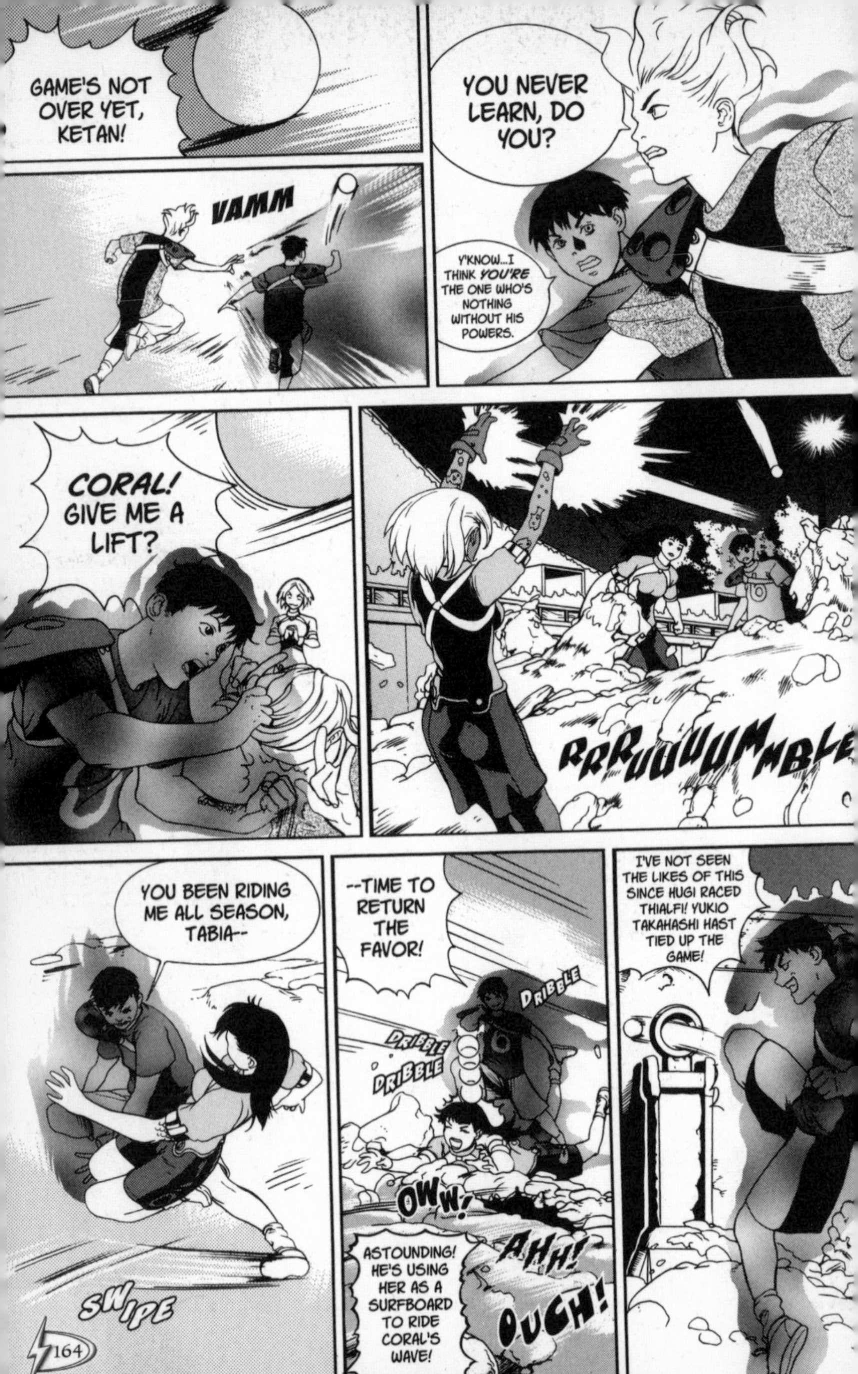
GAME'S NOT OVER YET, KETAN!
YOU NEVER LEARN, DO YOU?
VAMM
Y'KNOW...I THINK *YOU'RE* THE ONE WHO'S NOTHING WITHOUT HIS POWERS.
CORAL! GIVE ME A LIFT?
RRRUUUUMMBLE
YOU BEEN RIDING ME ALL SEASON, TABIA--
SWIPE
--TIME TO RETURN THE FAVOR!
DRIBBLE
DRIBBLE
DRIBBLE
OWW!
AHH!
OUCH!
ASTOUNDING! HE'S USING HER AS A SURFBOARD TO RIDE CORAL'S WAVE!
I'VE NOT SEEN THE LIKES OF THIS SINCE HUGI RACED THIALFI! YUKIO TAKAHASHI HAST TIED UP THE GAME!

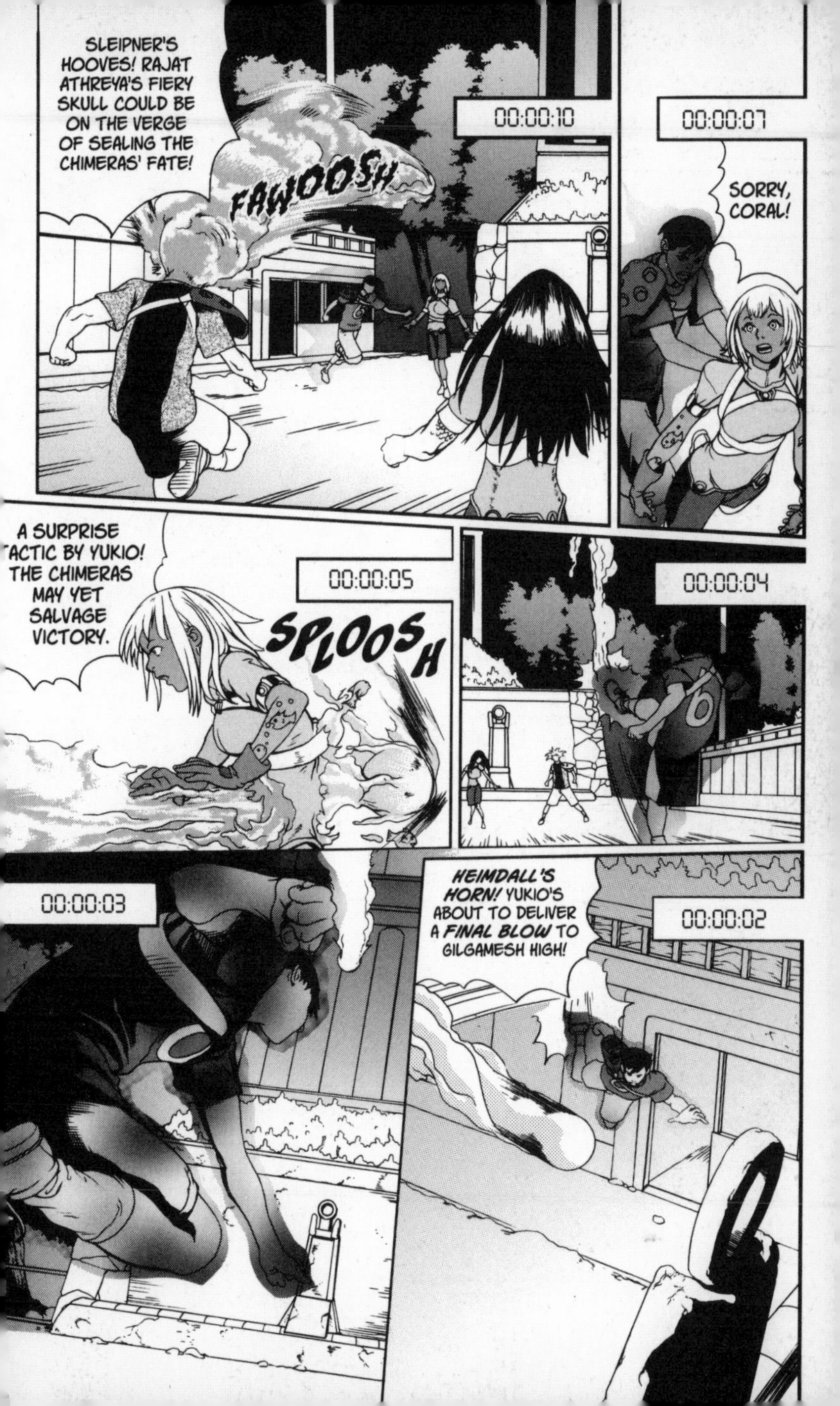
SLEIPNER'S HOOVES! RAJAT ATHREYA'S FIERY SKULL COULD BE ON THE VERGE OF SEALING THE CHIMERAS' FATE!
FAWOOSH
00:00:10
00:00:07
SORRY, CORAL!
A SURPRISE TACTIC BY YUKIO! THE CHIMERAS MAY YET SALVAGE VICTORY.
00:00:05
SPLOOSH
00:00:04
00:00:03
HEIMDALL'S HORN! YUKIO'S ABOUT TO DELIVER A FINAL BLOW TO GILGAMESH HIGH!
00:00:02

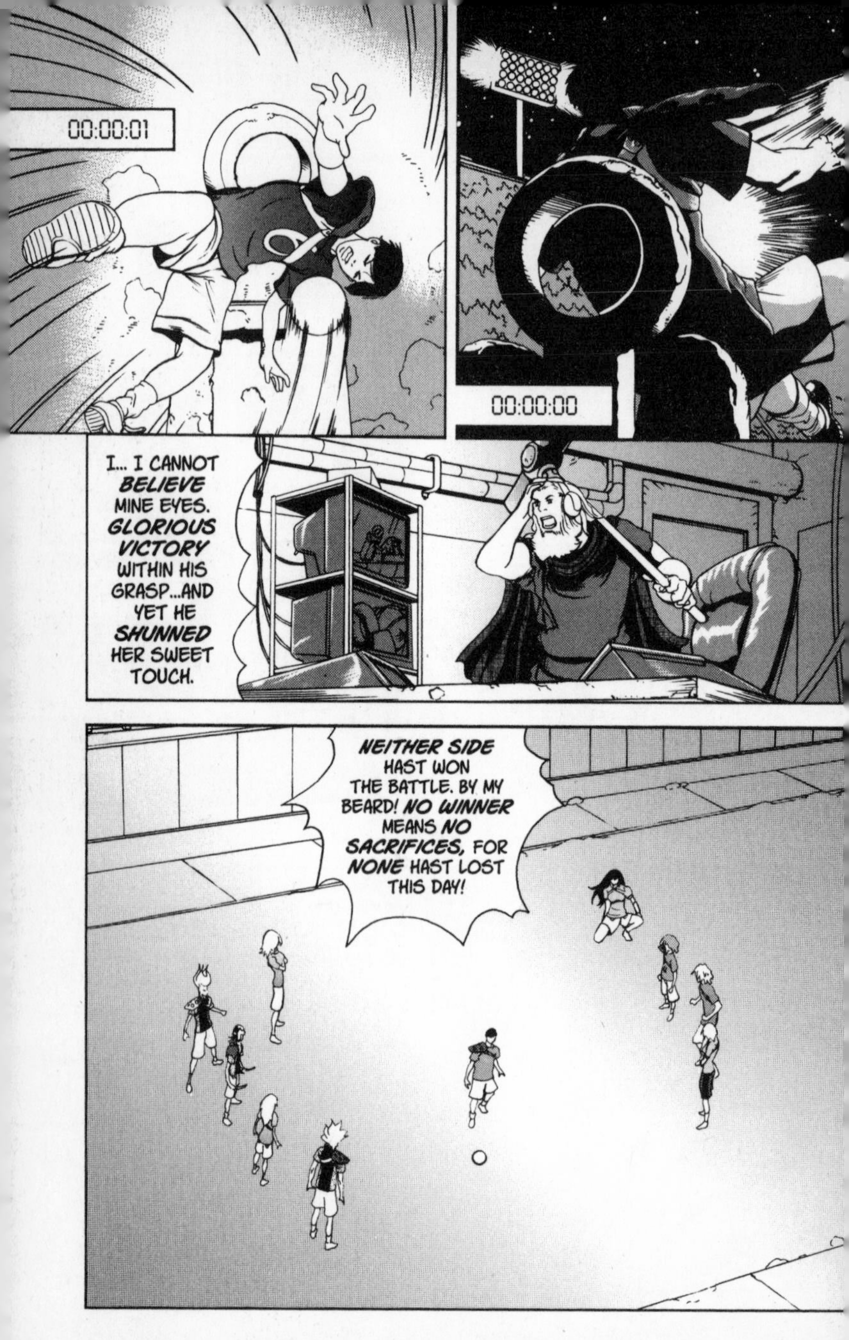
00:00:01
00:00:00
I... I CANNOT BELIEVE MINE EYES. GLORIOUS VICTORY WITHIN HIS GRASP...AND YET HE SHUNNED HER SWEET TOUCH.
NEITHER SIDE HAST WON THE BATTLE. BY MY BEARD! NO WINNER MEANS NO SACRIFICES, FOR NONE HAST LOST THIS DAY!

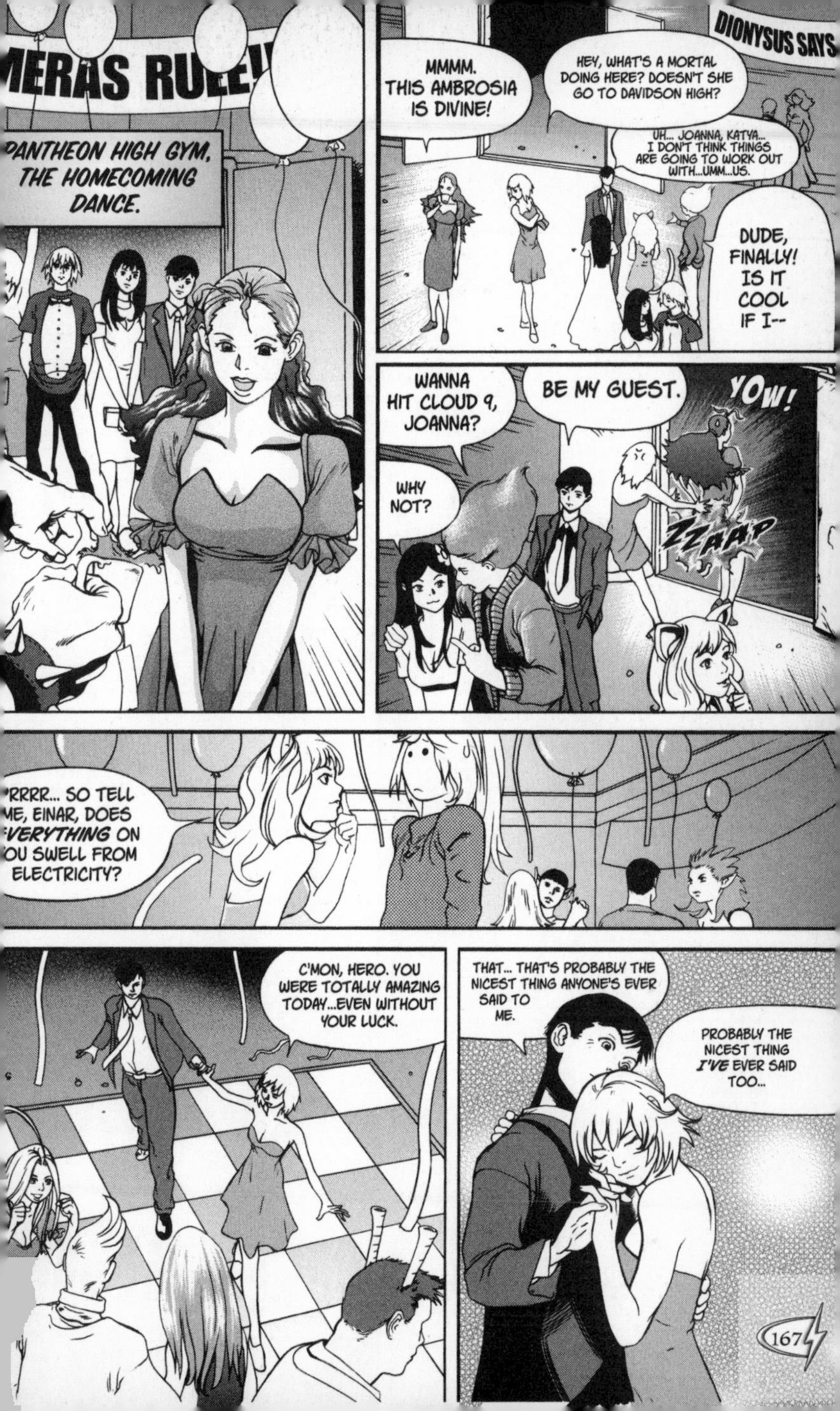
MERAS RULE!!
PANTHEON HIGH GYM, THE HOMECOMING DANCE.
DIONYSUS SAYS
MMMM. THIS AMBROSIA IS DIVINE!
HEY, WHAT'S A MORTAL DOING HERE? DOESN'T SHE GO TO DAVIDSON HIGH?
UH... JOANNA, KATYA... I DON'T THINK THINGS ARE GOING TO WORK OUT WITH...UMM...US.
DUDE, FINALLY! IS IT COOL IF I--
WANNA HIT CLOUD 9, JOANNA?
WHY NOT?
BE MY GUEST.
YOW!
ZZAAP
PRRRR... SO TELL ME, EINAR, DOES *EVERYTHING* ON YOU SWELL FROM ELECTRICITY?
C'MON, HERO. YOU WERE TOTALLY AMAZING TODAY...EVEN WITHOUT YOUR LUCK.
THAT... THAT'S PROBABLY THE NICEST THING ANYONE'S EVER SAID TO ME.
PROBABLY THE NICEST THING *I'VE* EVER SAID TOO...

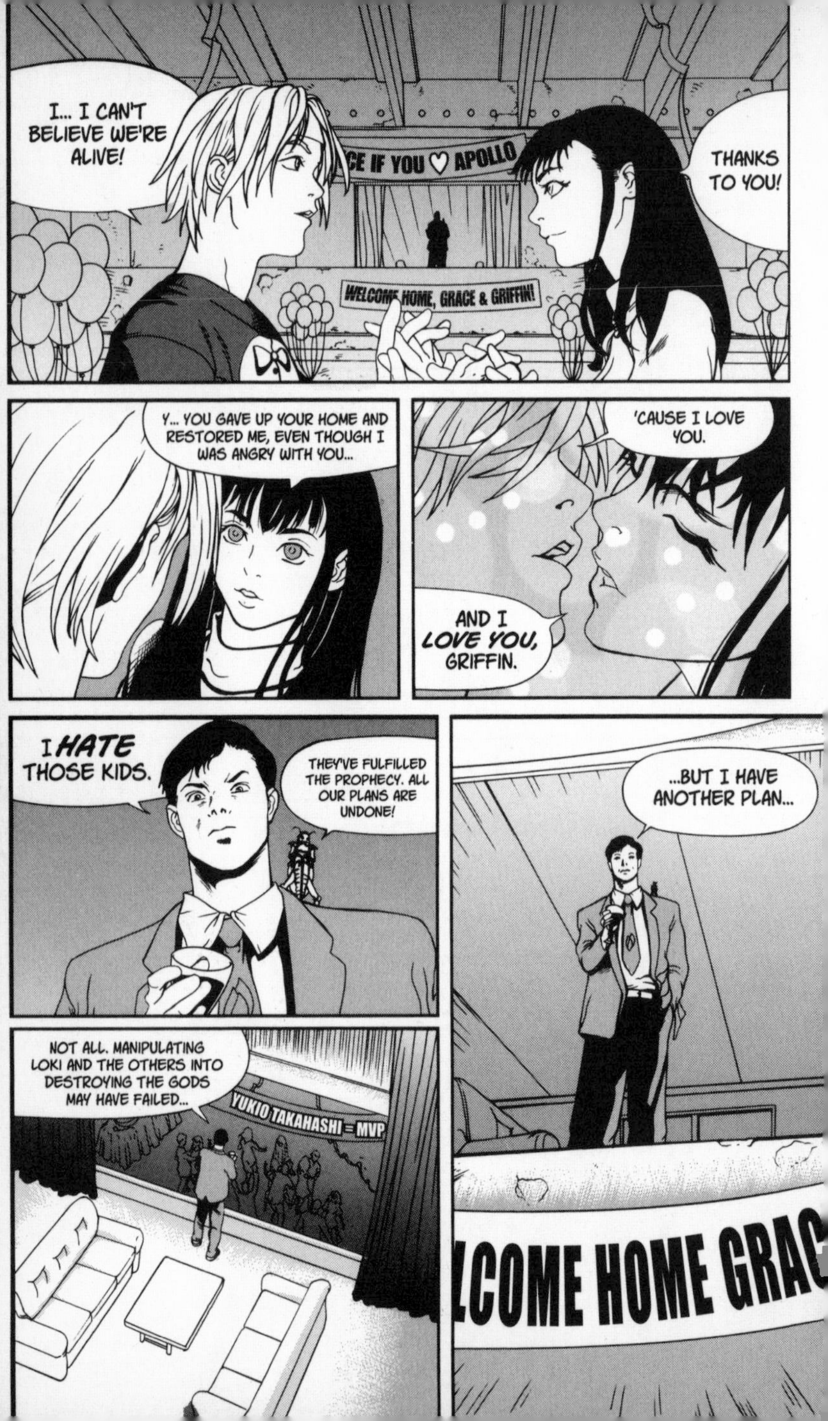
I... I CAN'T BELIEVE WE'RE ALIVE!
CE IF YOU ♡ APOLLO
WELCOME HOME, GRACE & GRIFFIN!
THANKS TO YOU!
Y... YOU GAVE UP YOUR HOME AND RESTORED ME, EVEN THOUGH I WAS ANGRY WITH YOU...
'CAUSE I LOVE YOU.
AND I *LOVE YOU,* GRIFFIN.
I *HATE* THOSE KIDS.
THEY'VE FULFILLED THE PROPHECY. ALL OUR PLANS ARE UNDONE!
NOT ALL. MANIPULATING LOKI AND THE OTHERS INTO DESTROYING THE GODS MAY HAVE FAILED...
YUKIO TAKAHASHI = MVP
...BUT I HAVE ANOTHER PLAN...
LCOME HOME GRAC

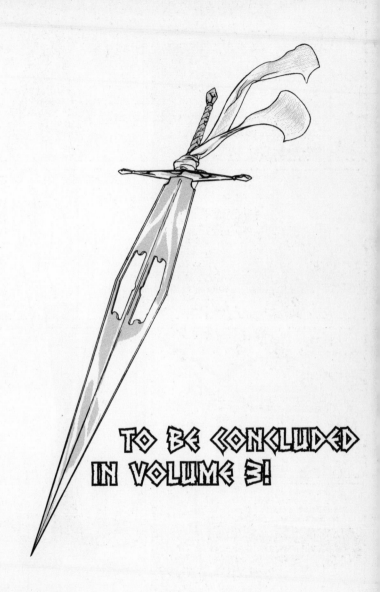

TO BE CONCLUDED
IN VOLUME 3!

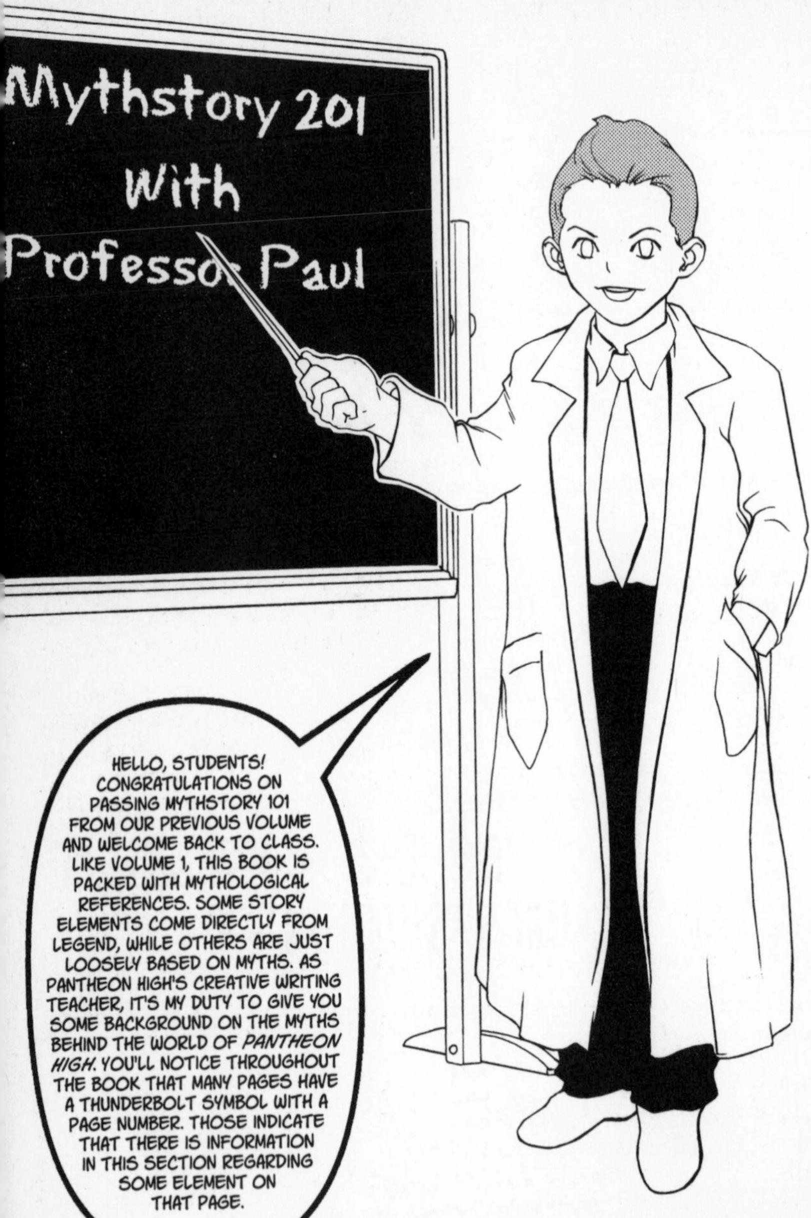
Mythstory 201
With
Professor Paul
HELLO, STUDENTS! CONGRATULATIONS ON PASSING MYTHSTORY 101 FROM OUR PREVIOUS VOLUME AND WELCOME BACK TO CLASS. LIKE VOLUME 1, THIS BOOK IS PACKED WITH MYTHOLOGICAL REFERENCES. SOME STORY ELEMENTS COME DIRECTLY FROM LEGEND, WHILE OTHERS ARE JUST LOOSELY BASED ON MYTHS. AS PANTHEON HIGH'S CREATIVE WRITING TEACHER, IT'S MY DUTY TO GIVE YOU SOME BACKGROUND ON THE MYTHS BEHIND THE WORLD OF *PANTHEON HIGH*. YOU'LL NOTICE THROUGHOUT THE BOOK THAT MANY PAGES HAVE A THUNDERBOLT SYMBOL WITH A PAGE NUMBER. THOSE INDICATE THAT THERE IS INFORMATION IN THIS SECTION REGARDING SOME ELEMENT ON THAT PAGE.

PAGE 10: Daikoku, the Japanese god of wealth, is also a symbol of the household, the kitchen in particular. That's why Daikoku is often portrayed with mice nearby. Though most people today would call the exterminator if they found mice in the pantry, in ancient Japan mice signified that a family had plentiful food in its storerooms.

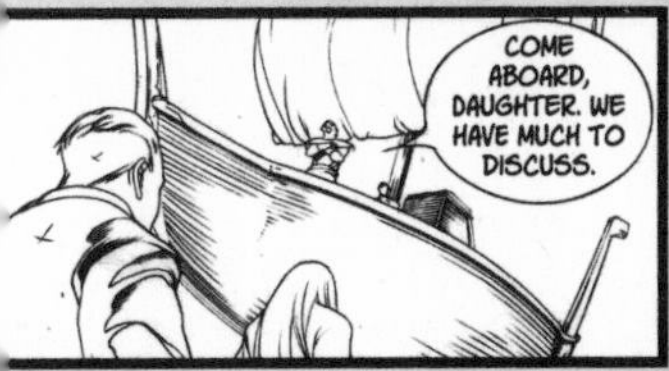
COME ABOARD, DAUGHTER. WE HAVE MUCH TO DISCUSS.

PAGE 11: Aziza's father, Ra, is the Egyptian god of the sun. Ra drives the sun across the sky every day in his solar barge. During the height of the cult of Ra's influence in ancient Egypt, Ra was viewed as the king of all the gods. Some even believed that the other gods were merely manifestations of Ra. Though the Ra of mythology was eventually subsumed into the falcon-headed deity Horus, Aziza will be happy to point out that in the world of Pantheon High, her father, Ra, remains ruler of the gods.

PAGE 12: The gods trust Imhotep to lead the effort to cure their children because he's among the smartest of deities. Imhotep was a brilliant (and possibly the first) architect and physician in ancient Egypt. He was also chancellor to the pharaoh and high priest of Ra. The real-life Imhotep was so influential, he was believed to have ascended to godhood after his death, becoming the deity of medicine and science.

PAGE 14: If you don't know who Jormungandr is, you weren't paying attention in class. Please read the Pantheon High Volume 1 textbook so that you can prepare for next week's exam. That said, there's still plenty of material to cover when it comes to these three Gilgamesh High students.

Kahoku gets his volcanic temper from his mother, Pele. She is Hawaii's famous goddess who spread volcanoes as she fled from island to island to escape her angry sister, the sea goddess Namaka. Legend has it that she met her demise near Hana on the island of Maui, where her bones formed the hill Ka-iwi-o-Pele.

Samudra is the son of Varuna, the Vedic/Indian god of the sea and keeper of the souls of the drowned. Varuna is attended by the snake-like nagas, hence Samudra's rather unusual lower torso. Those water spirits hanging with Samudra are spirits of drowned sailors, sent to serve him by his father.

Zahir is the son of Enlil: Mesopotamian god of winds, storm and rain. Though he only later became a god of the wind (hence Zahir's whirlwind powers), Enlil started his career as a rain god who sent a flood to destroy all life on Earth. Sound familiar? There's a flood myth in just about every culture's mythology, from Greek to Hindu to the Hebrew Bible's tale of Noah's ark.

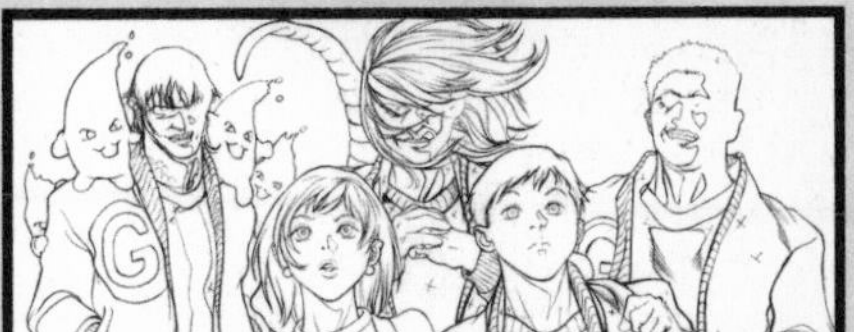
G
PHS

PAGE 19: The exact history of Tlachtli is lost in the mists of the past. What we do know is that the sport was played for thousands of years by many Mesoamerican cultures, including the Aztecs. The game was played with a solid rubber ball, and though the rules seem to have varied from culture to culture, it is believed that some played according to the same rules practiced by Gilgamesh High.

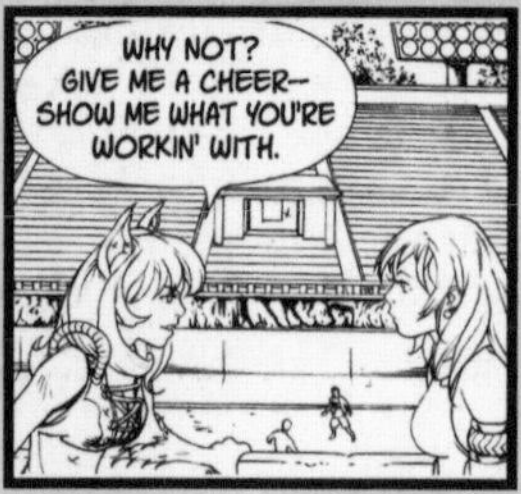
WHY NOT? GIVE ME A CHEER-- SHOW ME WHAT YOU'RE WORKIN' WITH.

PAGE 23: In Norse myth, the Valkyries were Odin's warrior maidens and "choosers of the slain" who came to the battlefields to collect the souls of fallen warriors.

PAGE 24: Idun's apples of immortality keep the Norse gods young and healthy. For more on the side effects of this divine medication, see Volume 1.

PAGE 25: Let's see...the River Mnemosyne... I can't remember-- Oh yeah, it's the river in Hades that reverses the effects of the memory-wiping River Lethe. The river shares a name with the Titaness called Mnemosyne, whose memory was as long as her beautiful hair.

PAGE 28: Though Valkyries are often depicted riding winged horses, the earliest myths portray them using wolves as their mounts. This myth most likely came about because packs of wild wolves would often feast upon the bodies of those slain in battle. The Valkyries mention the "Bellerophon estate" because it was Bellerophon who rode Pegasus in the tales of ancient Greece.

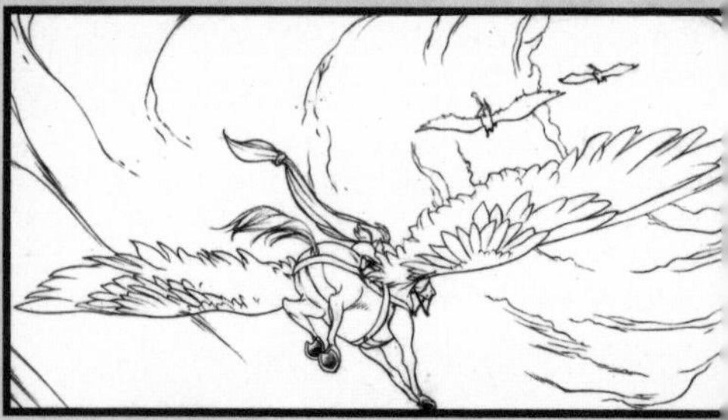

PAGE 29: Odin's mead hall, Valhalla, is enormous, with five hundred and forty doors and a roof shingled with shields and held up by row upon row of warriors' spears. After the Valkyries escort their charges to Valhalla, the warriors (known as the Einheriar) train daily for future battle. One day they must be prepared to face the forces of evil in the apocalyptic battle of Ragnarok.

PAGE 30: Hugin and Munin are Odin's ravens who travel the world to seek out information for their master. Hugin is "thought" and Munin is "memory." Odin is often portrayed with a raven on each shoulder as Hugin and Munin whisper their secrets into his ears.

THE WARRIORSH CLASSH DAILY IN PREPARASHUUN FOR RAGNAROK.

PAGE 32: Odin's eight-legged horse, Sleipner, is swifter than the winds of a storm and can ride upon the air itself. Strangely enough, Loki actually birthed the eight-legged colt destined to bear the king of the Norse gods! How? Well, that's a very interesting story worthy of your further research!

PAGE 35: Odin's famous spear, Gugnir, is a powerful weapon in the hands of the Allfather. Whenever warriors clashed, Odin would ride out to witness the battle. He would decide which army was the strongest, then throw Gugnir over the heads of the side he had chosen to lose.

PAGE 37: Mimir was the wisest of giants living in Jotunheim and keeper of the Well of Wisdom. In exchange for a chance to drink from the well and thus gain incredible knowledge, Odin plucked out one of his own eyes and gave it to Mimir, thus providing the wise jotun with Odin's all-seeing vision. From then on, Mimir was one of Odin's closest advisers. When Odin's Aesir gods met the Vanir gods for the first time, he gave them Mimir as part of a truce agreement. After a perceived insult, the Vanir cut off Mimir's head and sent it back to Asgard. Once the Aesir and Vanir made peace, Odin breathed life back into Mimir's head so that he might retain the brilliant jotun's invaluable council.

PAGE 43: You can tell from the bike messenger's gear that he worships Hermes, the god of messengers in ancient Greece. As herald of the gods, Hermes' wore a pair of winged sandals with which he could fly at great speeds from the heights of Mount Olympus to the lands of the mortal world.

PAGE 46: Nemesis is the sister of the three Fates in Greek myth. In early tales, it was her job to see that both evil and good deeds were repaid in kind. However, her name eventually became more synonymous with divine retribution.

Forseti, on the other hand, was known in the Norse pantheon as a true and just god who was always calm and fair in his judgments. That's why he got tapped as the Norse god of justice.

And if anyone knows the dangers of divine judgment, it's Prometheus. He stole fire from the Greek gods and gave it to mortals, for which he was chained to the top of Mount Caucasus. There, an eagle flew down and ate his liver every day. Prometheus' liver grew back by morning, and every day the eagle returned for a snack until Hercules freed Prometheus as one of his famous Twelve Labors.

PAGE 54: That enormous ash tree is Yggdrasill, the World Tree. It connects the nine realms of the Norse cosmology, from Asgard down to Hel, the land of the dead. The beast gnawing on the roots of Yggdrasill is Nithog, the dragon of destruction. The Norse believed that Nithog would continue to undermine the World Tree until the great battle of Ragnarok, when the tree would shudder and lose all its leaves and the monster would rise to the surface to celebrate the end of the universe.

PAGE 56: If you don't recognize that oath breaker and his famous catchphrase, ask your parents who he might be...

PAGE 57: Modgud is the giantess who watches over the bridge into Hel. Though the dead pass freely across the bridge into the land of the dead, the feet of the living make a clangorous din.

PAGE 59: Knowing how much trouble Loki could cause, Odin was quite concerned when the god of mischief fathered three children with the giantess Angerboda: the serpent Jormungandr, Fenris Wolf, and a girl as pale as death on one side and dark as night on the other. Odin cast the girl down into the underworld to rule over the dead not slain in battle. She was called Hel and her realm was named for her. Hel's hound, Garm, was set to watch the gates of her home to keep the souls of the dead from fleeing.

PAGE 61: The ceiling of Hel's great hall, Eliudnir, is a mass of writhing snakes. Their burning venom drips down upon the dead souls within her hall.

PAGE 66: In the myths of China, Yu Huang Shang-ti is known as the Jade Emperor. He is the ruler of the Chinese gods and patron of the Chinese emperors. In some tales, he is even the creator of humankind.

PAGE 67: When Hercules was sent on his famous Twelve Labors, Herc's second task was to slay the nine-headed Hydra. Hercules traveled to the swamps of Lerna to hunt the beast. Though Hercules was able to knock off one head after the other with his mighty club, the Hydra's heads grew back before the hero could destroy them all. Finally, Hercules seared the wounds with fire after dashing off each head, preventing them from growing back so that he could slay the creature once and for all.

PAGE 70: Though the rules of Tlachtli varied from culture to culture, it is clear that the game was closely associated with human sacrifice. In some cultures, it may have even been tradition for the skull of a former player to form the core of a new rubber ball.

PAGE 75: Jake Smith's old man is Hephaestus, the Greek god of the forge, who supplies Zeus with a steady inventory of thunderbolts.

PAGE 78: At different times in history, both Osiris and his son, Anubis, were worshipped as the god of the dead. The most famous story of Osiris is also a tale of his brother Set's greatest evil. Set killed Osiris out of jealousy, then dismembered him and spread Osiris' body parts to locations all over Egypt. Isis tracked down Osiris' various parts and used her magic to restore him to life. After a bloody struggle among the gods, Set was disgraced for all eternity, while Osiris became the king of the Egyptian underworld, Duat.

PAGE 79: Ammit was one of the most fearsome beasts in Egyptian mythology. Part lion, part crocodile and part hippopotamus, Ammit devoured the hearts of those who failed to prove their innocence in the soul weighing.

PAGE 85: Grace wants to meet the great Greek mathematician Pythagoras, who has likely been a resident of Hades for thousands of years. If you haven't taken geometry yet, you'll learn about him and his Pythagorean theorem soon enough.

PAGE 88: In Norse myths, the dwarves created fantastic objects and weapons for the Asgardian gods. Among the items crafted was a boat called Skidbladnir. The boat was given to Frey, god of sunlight. Frey's ship could be folded up and placed in his pocket. Clearly Mr. Freyrson's enchanted SUV can do the same.

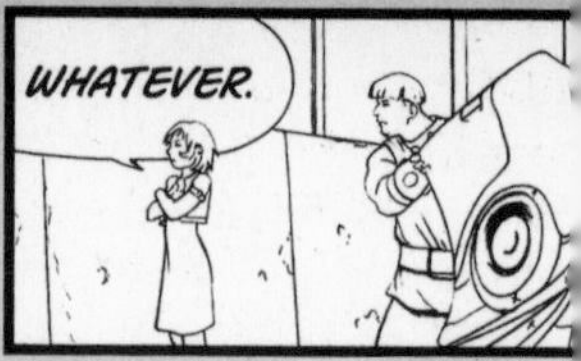
WHATEVER.

PAGE 90: Cerebrus is the three-headed dog that guards the entrance to th
Greek underworld to prevent the dead from leaving. He's a mean and viciou
beast.

PAGE 93: Tabia el Sobek's father is Sobek, crocodile god of the Nile. Crocodile
were a dangerous fact of life in ancient Egypt and Sobek was often feared a
a representative of the beasts.

Einar Thorson's father is Thor, the most legendary of the Norse gods.
Gretchen Shiina is the daughter of Raiden, Japanese god of thunder an
lightning. Raiden was often seen as a red-skinned demon with long, shar
claws.

Coral Kale is the daughter of the Grecian sea god, Poseidon. Her father is
moody and violent god who could easily destroy ships and claim them fo
the sea.

Tobias El Ptah's father is the Egyptian god of creation and craftsmen. He i
sometimes represented as a dwarf of small stature, but Ptah's power is might
for he brought the entire universe into being.

Rikard Ullrson is the child of the great Asgardian archer and skier, Ullr, wh
shredded the slopes as swiftly as his arrows left his bow.

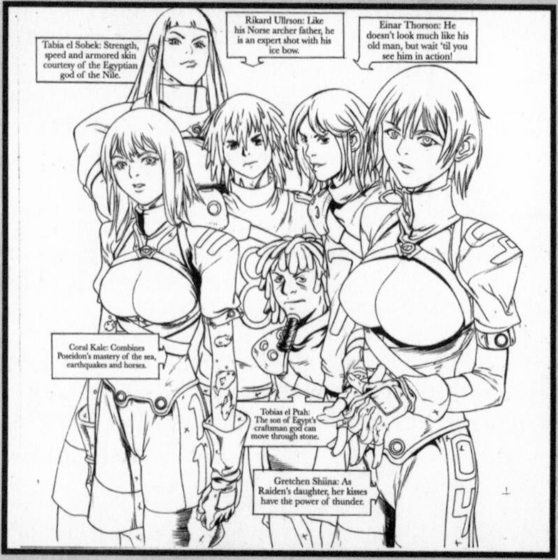
Tabia el Sobek: Strength, speed and armored skin courtesy of the Egyptian god of the Nile.
Rikard Ullrson: Like his Norse archer father, he is an expert shot with his ice bow.
Einar Thorson: He doesn't look much like his old man, but wait 'til you see him in action!
Coral Kale: Combines Poseidon's mastery of the sea, earthquakes and horses.
Tobias el Ptah: The son of Egypt's craftsman god can move through stone.
Gretchen Shiina: As Raiden's daughter, her kisses have the power of thunder.

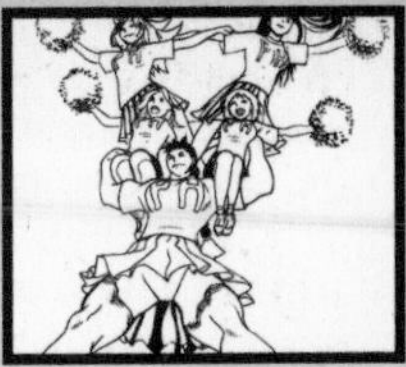

PAGE 95: Ayn is the cheerleader-lifting daughter of Atlas, the Titan who holds the sky on his shoulders. As punishment for siding with the Titans in the war against Zeus and his siblings, Atlas was forced to hold up the vault of the sky for all eternity.

PAGE 99: Izanagi and her brother, Izanami, used the Heavenly Jeweled Spear to stir the ocean and create the islands of Japan. Later, the two siblings married (I know... ewww...) and had many children. However, Izanagi died giving birth to the god of fire and went down to the Japanese underworld, Yomi. Izanami braved the land of the dead to rescue his wife, but she had already eaten the food in Yomi and was thus tied to the underworld. She planned to petition the gods of Yomi for release, requesting only that her husband not look upon her. But Izanami lit a torch and saw that his wife had become hideous and putrefied, her body possessed by the eight thunder-snakes.

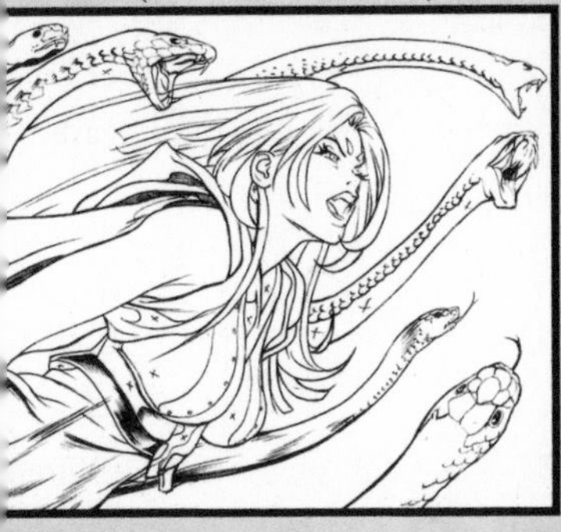

PAGE 101: Ashamed and enraged that her husband had looked upon her hideous form, Izanagi attempted to attack her husband, pursuing him to the edge of Yomi. There, Izanami blocked the entrance to Yomi with a boulder so that he might escape his late wife's righteous anger.

PAGE 106: Zeus fathered children with many women, both human and divine. He appeared not only in his own form, but also as an eagle, a snow-white bull, a cuckoo, a swan, a golden rain shower and more. His children include: Ares, Persephone, Athena, Hephaestus, Apollo, Artemis, Hermes, the nine Muses, the three Fates, Castor and Pollux, Minos, Tantalus, Perseus, Hercules and many, many others.

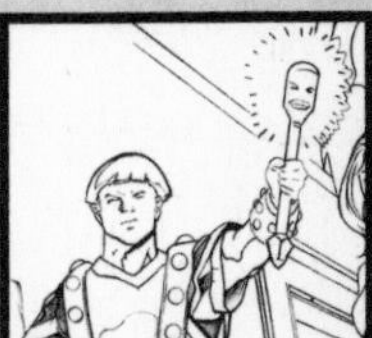

PAGE 108: Bahir's father, Ninurta, is said to carry a magical, talking mace called Car-ur. Hence Bahir's cheeky mace, Aesir.

PAGE 112: In Mesopotamian myths, Tiamat is a primordial goddess of chaos, sometimes depicted in the form of a dragon.

PAGE 116: The giant, one-eyed Cyclopes are the children of Gaea and Uranus. Because of their hideous faces, their father cast them down into the underworld prison of Tartarus. Zeus later freed the Cyclopes, in exchange for their aid in the war against the Titans. The Cyclopes helped forge Zeus' first thunderbolts, Hades' helm of invisibility and Poseidon's trident to aid in the battle.

PAGE 120: Gaea was so angry with Uranus for the way he treated their children, she asked them to take a sickle she had made and use it to slay their own father. Only Kronus was brave enough to take up the weapon. Kronus used the sickle to defeat Uranus, taking his place as lord of the universe. Knowing that his own children might treat him in the same way, Kronus ate each child born by his wife Rhea so that none would depose him. But Rhea hid her sixth child, Zeus, from Kronus. When Zeus was old enough, his first wife, Metis, took Kronus an herb she claimed would make him unconquerable. Kronus ate the herb and immediately got sick, vomiting up Zeus' siblings: Hades, Poseidon, Hestia, Demeter and Hera. The six gods rose up against Kronus and overthrew the tyrannical Titan.

PAGE 123: Zeus granted Tithonus immortality, but not eternal youth. Over time, he finally grew so old and shriveled, he became a grasshopper. His personal knowledge of the ages makes him an excellent mythstory teacher. That's why the kids know that Loki often appeared to the other Norse gods as an old crone, tricking and deceiving them for his own gain.

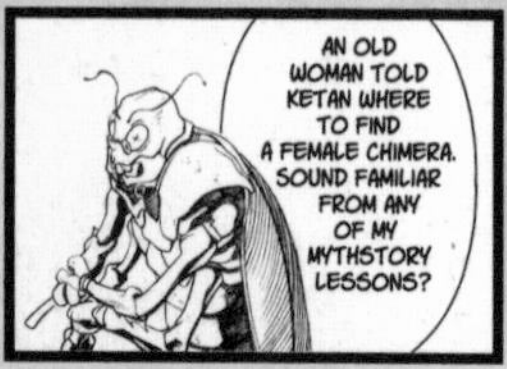
AN OLD WOMAN TOLD KETAN WHERE TO FIND A FEMALE CHIMERA. SOUND FAMILIAR FROM ANY OF MY MYTHSTORY LESSONS?

PAGE 126: One of the main sources of Mesopotamian myths is the Epic of Gilgamesh. One of the tales is the story of Humbaba, a fearsome, lion-headed monster set to guard a cedar forest by Enlil, the Mesopotamian god of winds, storm and rain. Gilgamesh and his friend Enkidu slew Humbaba so that they could cut down the trees in the forest for lumber.

PAGE 131: Hu, sometimes called Huh, was the Egyptian god of eternity. In Egyptian hieroglyphs, his shen ring represents the never-ending cycle of time.

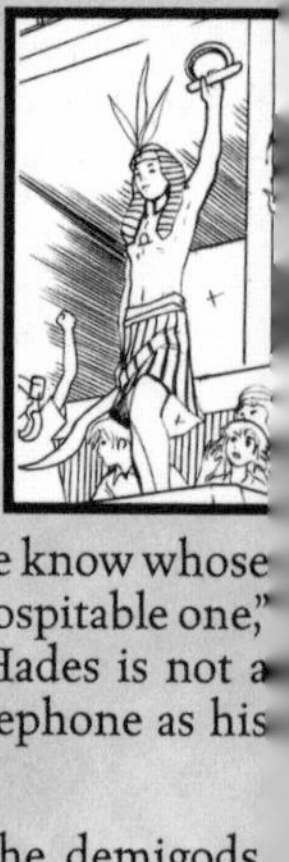

PAGE 137: That cloaked figure with beautiful bone-structure is Charon, the ferryman who takes Greek souls across the River Styx to Hades. However, he did very little boating on the River Lethe, from which the dead were encouraged to drink so that they would forget both the joys and tribulations of their past lives.

PAGE 141: Hades was a dark and quiet god of few words--I guess we know whose side of the family Griffin gets it from... Hades was known as "the hospitable one," because he always had room for one more dead soul. Though Hades is not a ladies' man like his brother, Zeus, the story of how he took Persephone as his wife is a famous one, worthy of your extracurricular reading.

PAGE 142: Zeus' children are among the most famous of all the demigods Hercules was known for his incredible strength and his Twelve Labors. Minos was the son of Zeus and Europea and grew up to become the king of the island of Crete. Perseus was a hero through and through. He went on a great quest and slew the gorgon called Medusa. Eventually, Perseus became a king.

PAGE 151: Frey's sword was one of the most powerful Asgardian weapons, for it fought of its own volition. When Frey fell in love with the giantess Gerd, his loyal servant Skirnir journeyed to Jotunheim to woo her for his master. Frey's magic sword kept Skirnir safe in his dangerous travels.

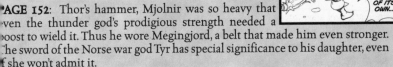

CARE-FUL! FREY'S SWORD HAS A MIND OF ITS OWN...

PAGE 152: Thor's hammer, Mjolnir was so heavy that even the thunder god's prodigious strength needed a boost to wield it. Thus he wore Megingjord, a belt that made him even stronger. The sword of the Norse war god Tyr has special significance to his daughter, even if she won't admit it.

Hades' helm of invisibility and Hermes' winged sandals were both used by Perseus when he went to slay Medusa. However, Perseus never got a chance to throw Zeus' thunderbolts.

Thoth was the scribe of the Egyptian gods and therefore would have been the keeper of many powerful spells and formulae. Neith was the Egyptian goddess of the hunt and was often depicted holding a bow and arrows. Her bow never misses its target.

The heavenly spear of Izanagi was used to create the islands of Japan. The mirror of Amaterasu became famous when a prank by her evil brother Susano caused the solar goddess to hide in a cave. The mirror was used to coax her back outside, thus returning sunlight to the world.

PAGE 160: One of the best-known tales of Loki is the story of how he snuck int the home of Thor and Sif one evening and cut off all of Sif's beautiful, golde hair, which was said to gleam brighter than the lightning from her husband's hammer. To make up for his foul prank, Loki tricked the dwarves into spinning Sif a new head of hair, this time from real gold. Knowing that the gods might still be angry, Loki went an extra step and had the dwarves create Odin's great spear, Gugnir, and Frey's folding ship, Skidbladnir. I must admit, though: Loki's ring made from Sif's hair is purely a creation for Pantheon High. As far as the Norse myths go, he never wore such an item.

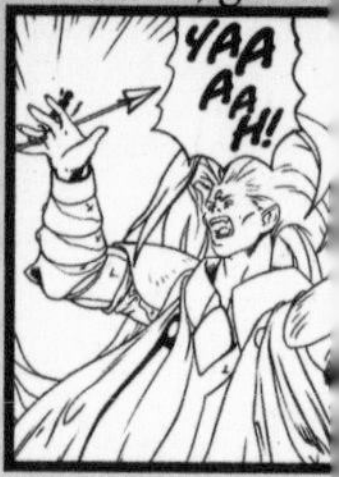
YAA AAH!

PAGE 161: Principal Ut-napishtim of Gilgamesh High is the Mesopotamia equivalent of Noah. When the gods decided to flood the earth, the god Ea tol Ut-napishtim about the gods' plan so that he could build a ship to save himsel Ut-napishtim built the boat according to the precise measurements provided b the god, then loaded his family and many wild animals aboard. After this ordea Ut-napishtim and his wife were rewarded with eternal life.

PAGE 164: When Thor visited the hall of the giant called Utgard-Loki (n relation to the god called Loki), Thor, his servant Thialfi, and Loki the trickste god agreed to participate in a series of contests. Thialfi was swift, so he was to ru a race against a young man named Hugi. But though Thialfi ran like the wind, h could not beat Hugi. In the end, Utgard-Loki revealed that he had tricked Tho and his companions with illusions during each of their contests. For exampl Hugi was no young man at all, but a personification of Thought. And who coul run faster than Thought itself?

PAGE 167: While Steven and Megumi were still illustrating Pantheon Hig volume 2, TOKYOPOP ran a contest to find out whose high school mos resembled Pantheon High. The winner was Roxii of Davidson High Schoo in Davidson, Michigan. Thus Roxii was bestowed with immortality by th TOKYOPOP gods as Steven and Megumi set her likeness forever upon th final pages of Pantheon High volume 2. There she visits the divine school homecoming dance, much to the chagrin of the god-snob, Aziza.

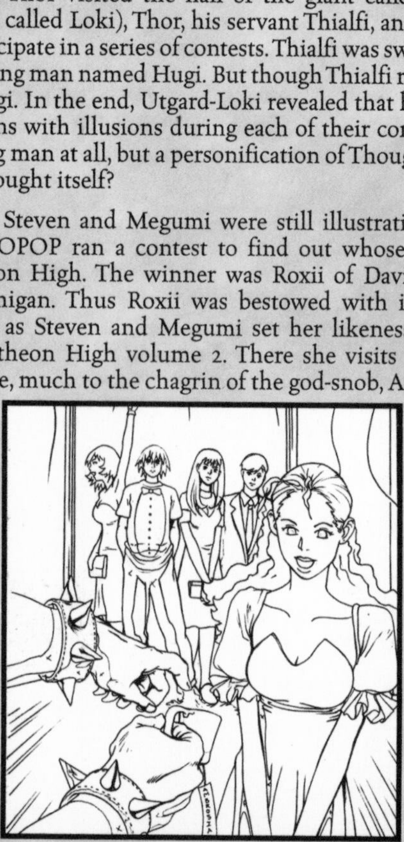

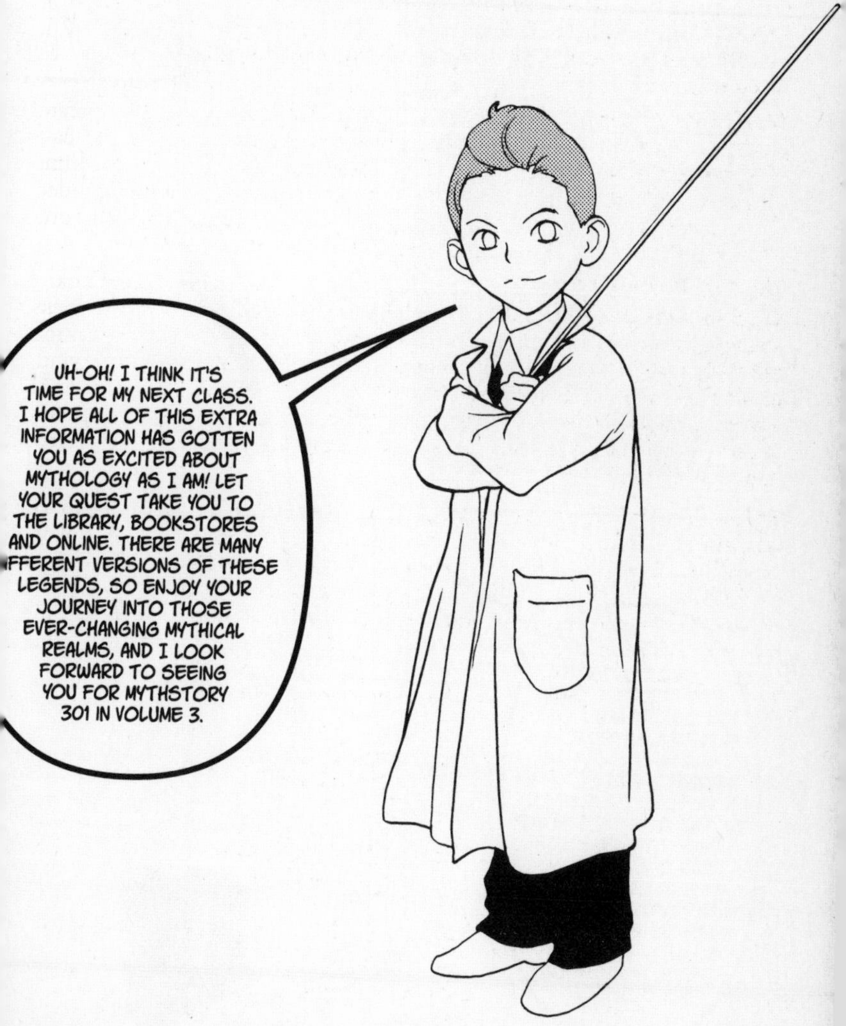
UH-OH! I THINK IT'S TIME FOR MY NEXT CLASS. I HOPE ALL OF THIS EXTRA INFORMATION HAS GOTTEN YOU AS EXCITED ABOUT MYTHOLOGY AS I AM! LET YOUR QUEST TAKE YOU TO THE LIBRARY, BOOKSTORES AND ONLINE. THERE ARE MANY FFERENT VERSIONS OF THESE LEGENDS, SO ENJOY YOUR JOURNEY INTO THOSE EVER-CHANGING MYTHICAL REALMS, AND I LOOK FORWARD TO SEEING YOU FOR MYTHSTORY 301 IN VOLUME 3.

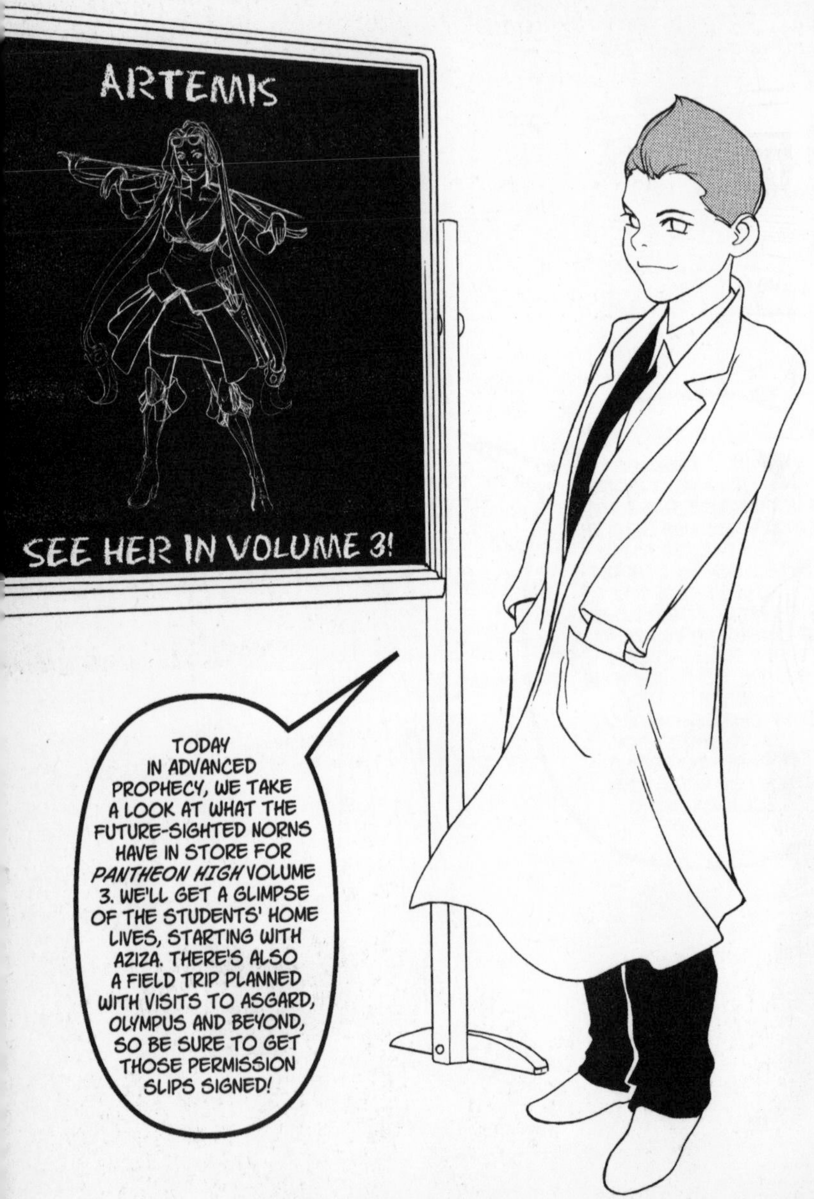
ARTEMIS
SEE HER IN VOLUME 3!
TODAY IN ADVANCED PROPHECY, WE TAKE A LOOK AT WHAT THE FUTURE-SIGHTED NORNS HAVE IN STORE FOR *PANTHEON HIGH* VOLUME 3. WE'LL GET A GLIMPSE OF THE STUDENTS' HOME LIVES, STARTING WITH AZIZA. THERE'S ALSO A FIELD TRIP PLANNED WITH VISITS TO ASGARD, OLYMPUS AND BEYOND, SO BE SURE TO GET THOSE PERMISSION SLIPS SIGNED!

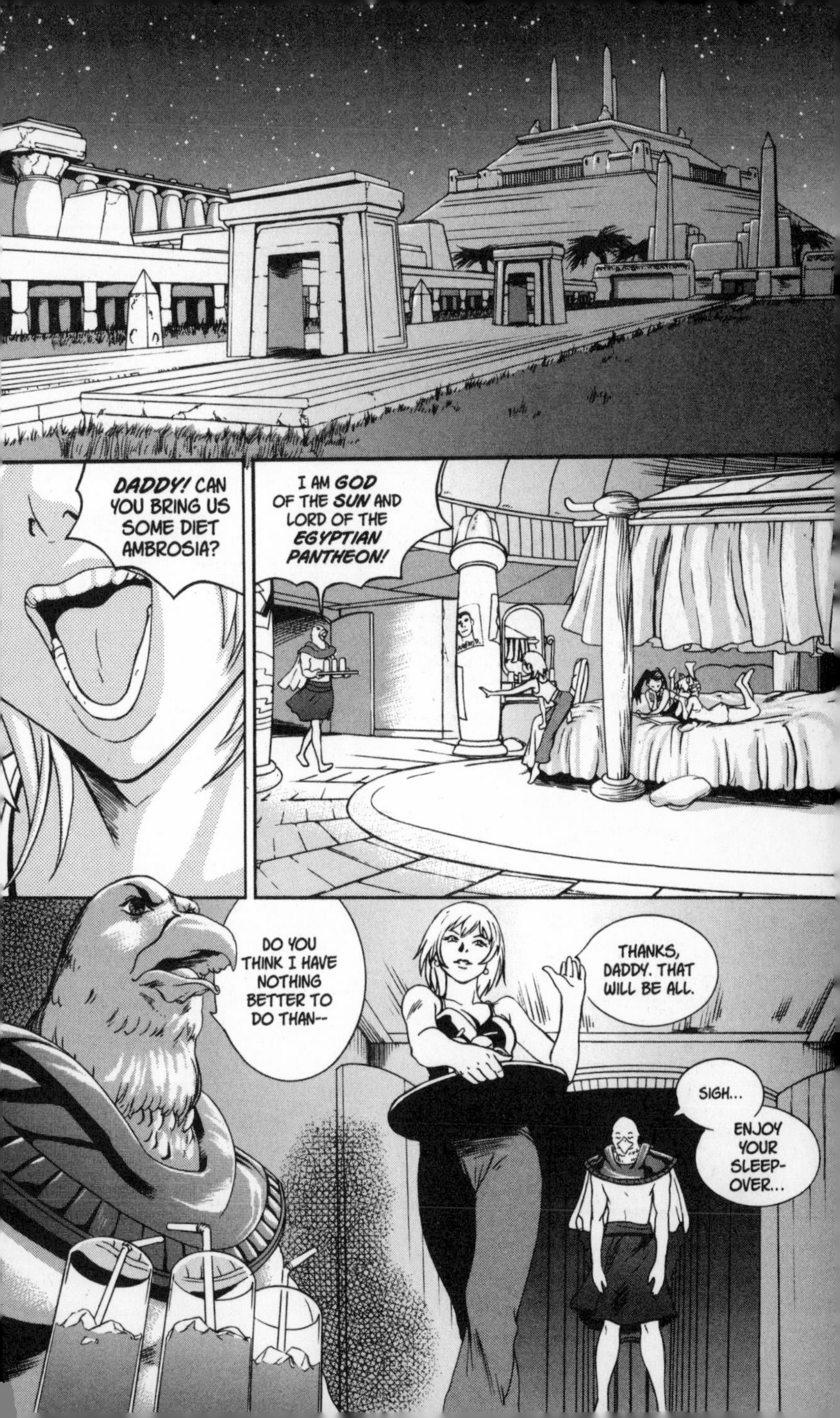
DADDY! CAN YOU BRING US SOME DIET AMBROSIA?
I AM GOD OF THE SUN AND LORD OF THE EGYPTIAN PANTHEON!
DO YOU THINK I HAVE NOTHING BETTER TO DO THAN--
THANKS, DADDY. THAT WILL BE ALL.
SIGH...
ENJOY YOUR SLEEP-OVER...

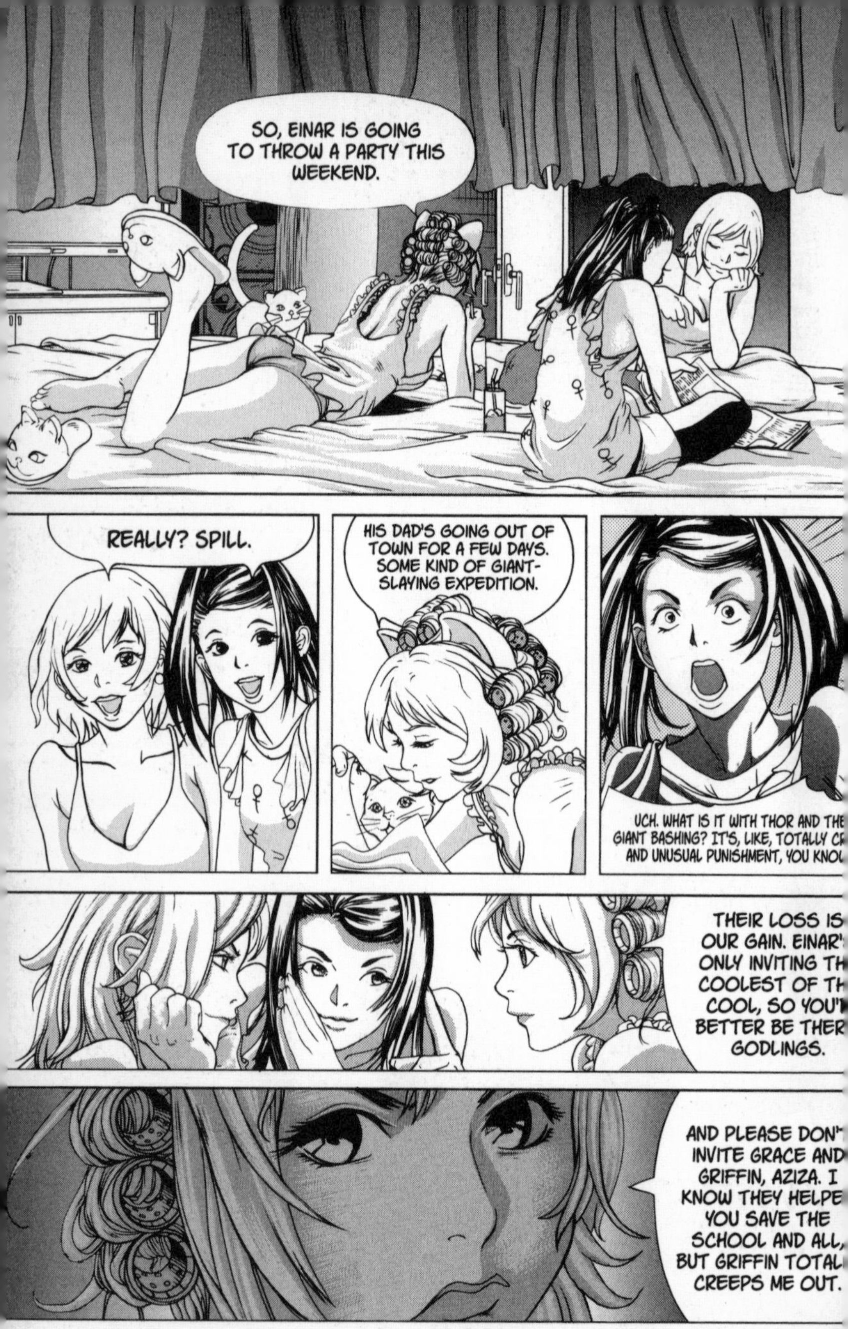
SO, EINAR IS GOING TO THROW A PARTY THIS WEEKEND.
REALLY? SPILL.
HIS DAD'S GOING OUT OF TOWN FOR A FEW DAYS. SOME KIND OF GIANT-SLAYING EXPEDITION.
UCH. WHAT IS IT WITH THOR AND THE GIANT BASHING? IT'S, LIKE, TOTALLY C AND UNUSUAL PUNISHMENT, YOU KNO
THEIR LOSS IS OUR GAIN. EINAR' ONLY INVITING TH COOLEST OF TH COOL, SO YOU' BETTER BE THER GODLINGS.
AND PLEASE DON' INVITE GRACE AND GRIFFIN, AZIZA. I KNOW THEY HELPE YOU SAVE THE SCHOOL AND ALL, BUT GRIFFIN TOTAL CREEPS ME OUT.

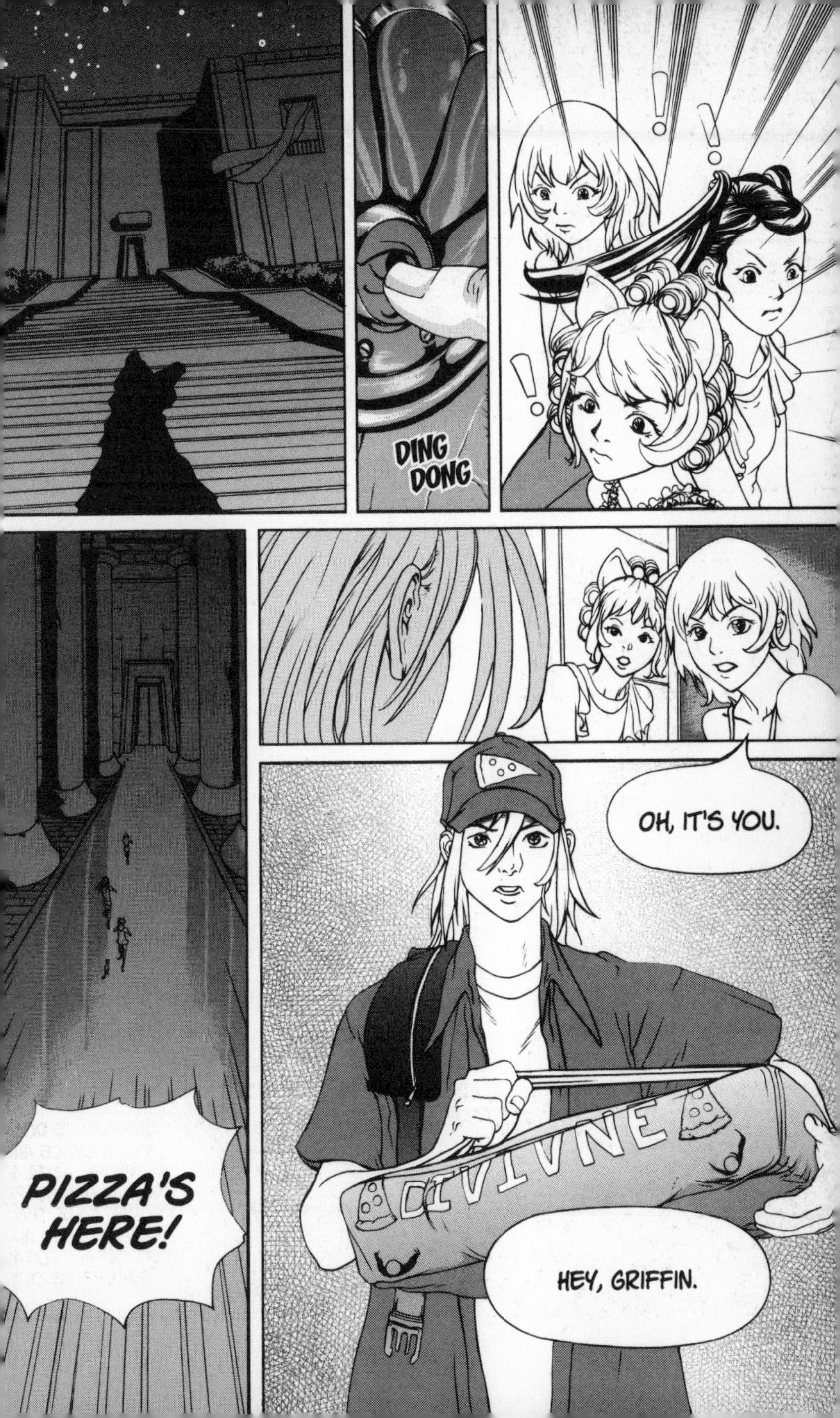
DING DONG
PIZZA'S HERE!
OH, IT'S YOU.
DIVINE
HEY, GRIFFIN.

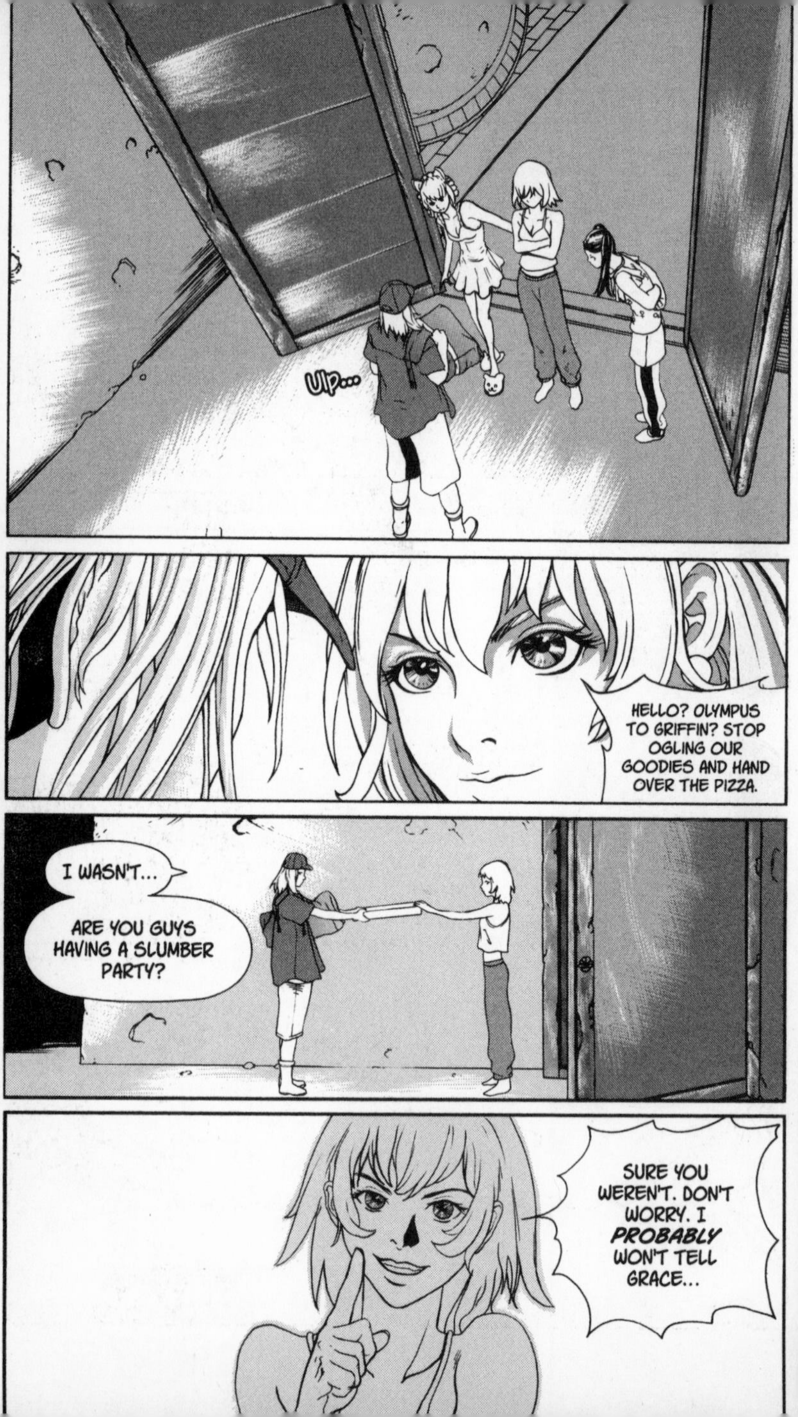
ULP...
HELLO? OLYMPUS TO GRIFFIN? STOP OGLING OUR GOODIES AND HAND OVER THE PIZZA.
I WASN'T...
ARE YOU GUYS HAVING A SLUMBER PARTY?
SURE YOU WEREN'T. DON'T WORRY. I *PROBABLY* WON'T TELL GRACE...

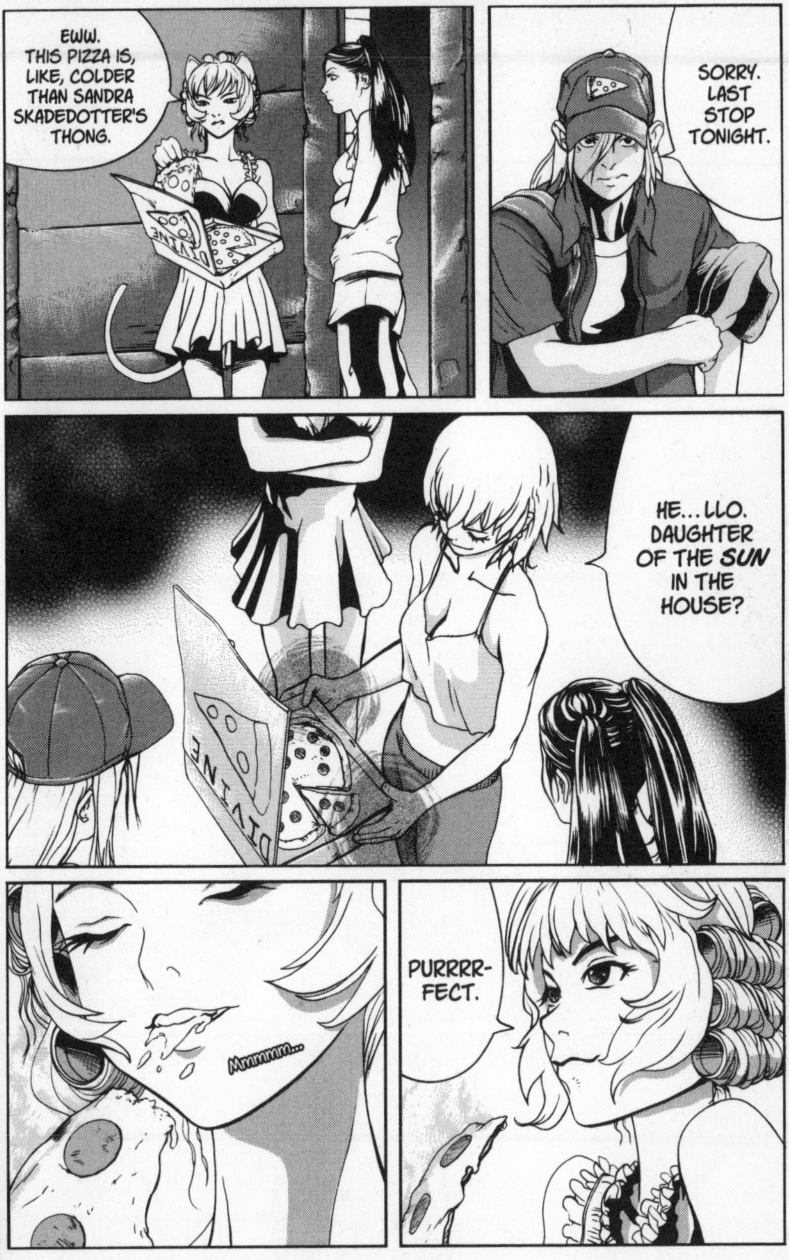
EWW. THIS PIZZA IS, LIKE, COLDER THAN SANDRA SKADEDOTTER'S THONG.
DIVINE
SORRY. LAST STOP TONIGHT.
HE...LLO. DAUGHTER OF THE *SUN* IN THE HOUSE?
DIVINE
Mmmmmm...
PURRRR-FECT.

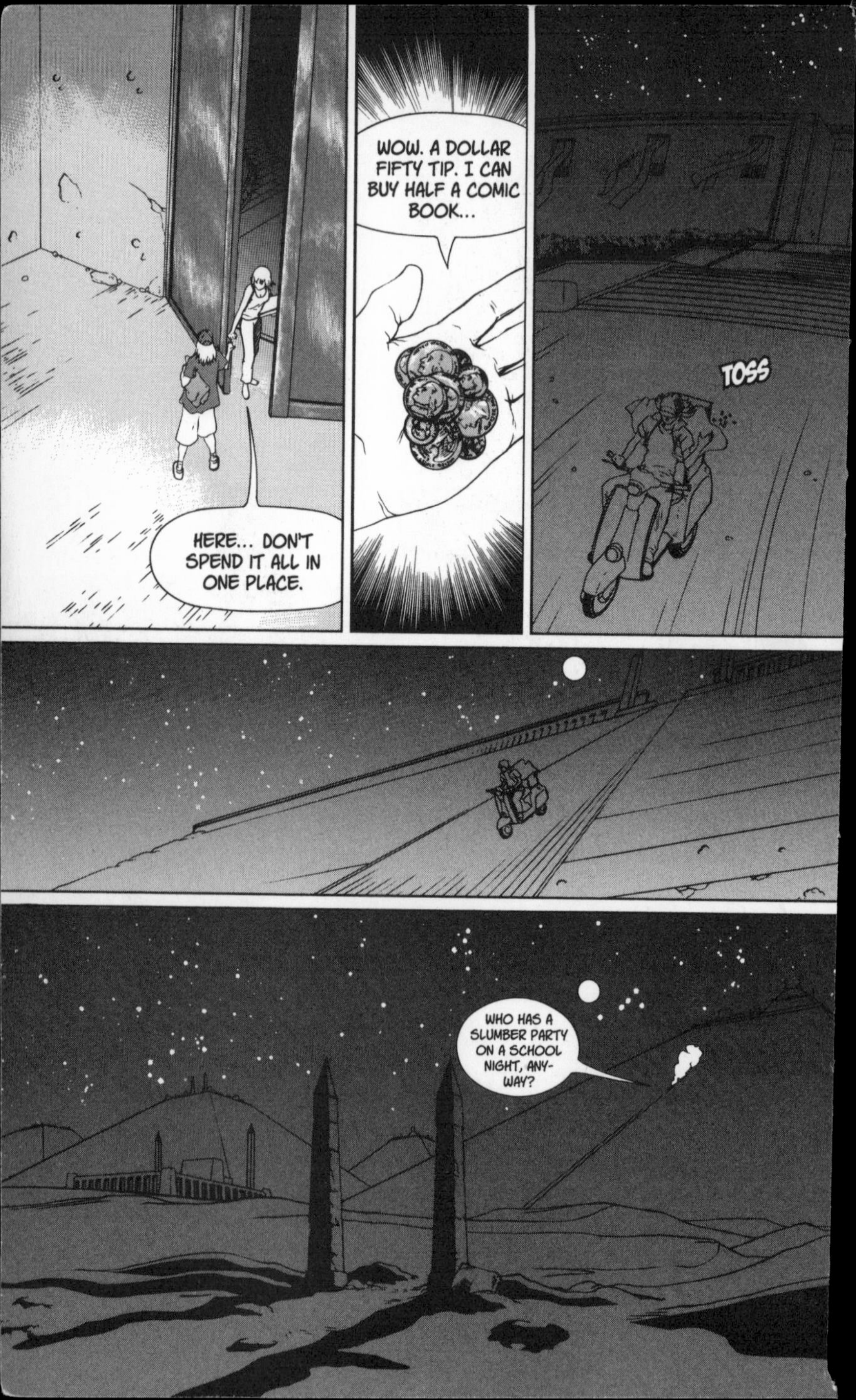
HERE... DON'T SPEND IT ALL IN ONE PLACE.
WOW. A DOLLAR FIFTY TIP. I CAN BUY HALF A COMIC BOOK...
TOSS
WHO HAS A SLUMBER PARTY ON A SCHOOL NIGHT, ANY-WAY?

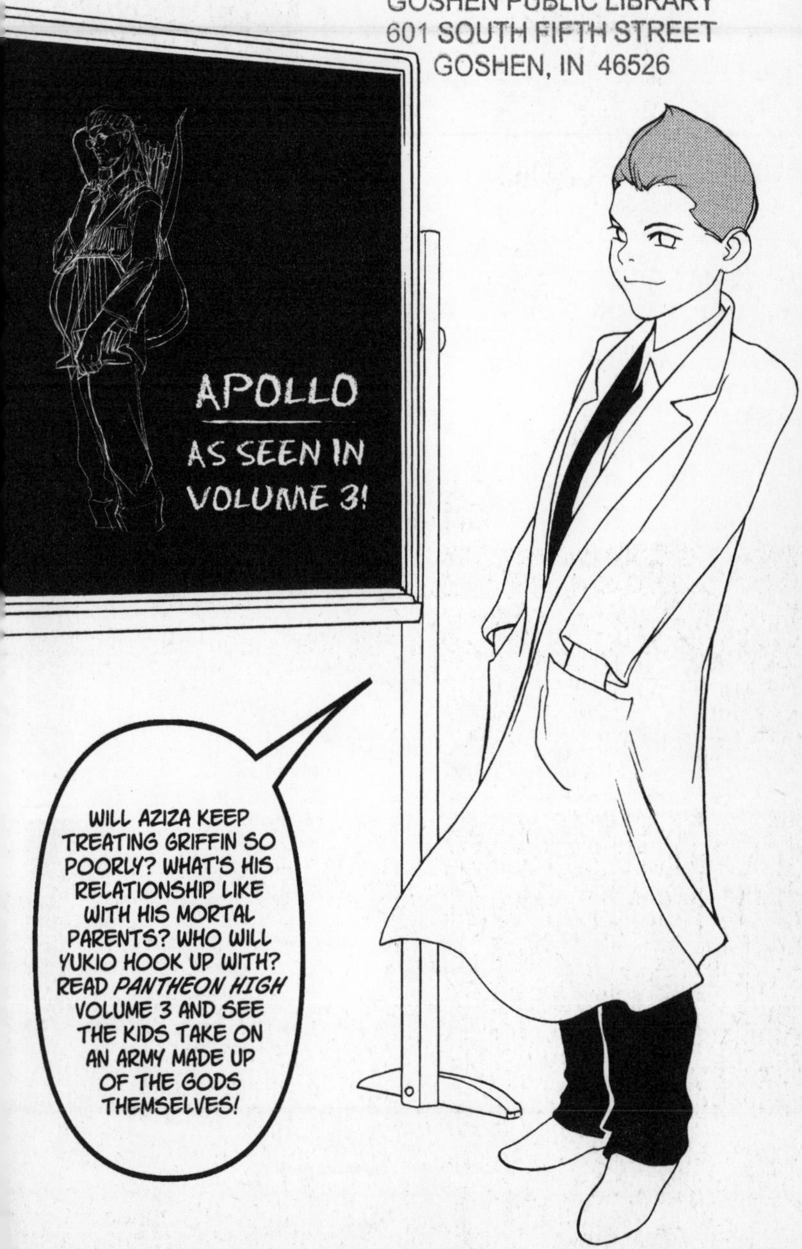
APOLLO
AS SEEN IN VOLUME 3!
WILL AZIZA KEEP TREATING GRIFFIN SO POORLY? WHAT'S HIS RELATIONSHIP LIKE WITH HIS MORTAL PARENTS? WHO WILL YUKIO HOOK UP WITH? READ *PANTHEON HIGH* VOLUME 3 AND SEE THE KIDS TAKE ON AN ARMY MADE UP OF THE GODS THEMSELVES!

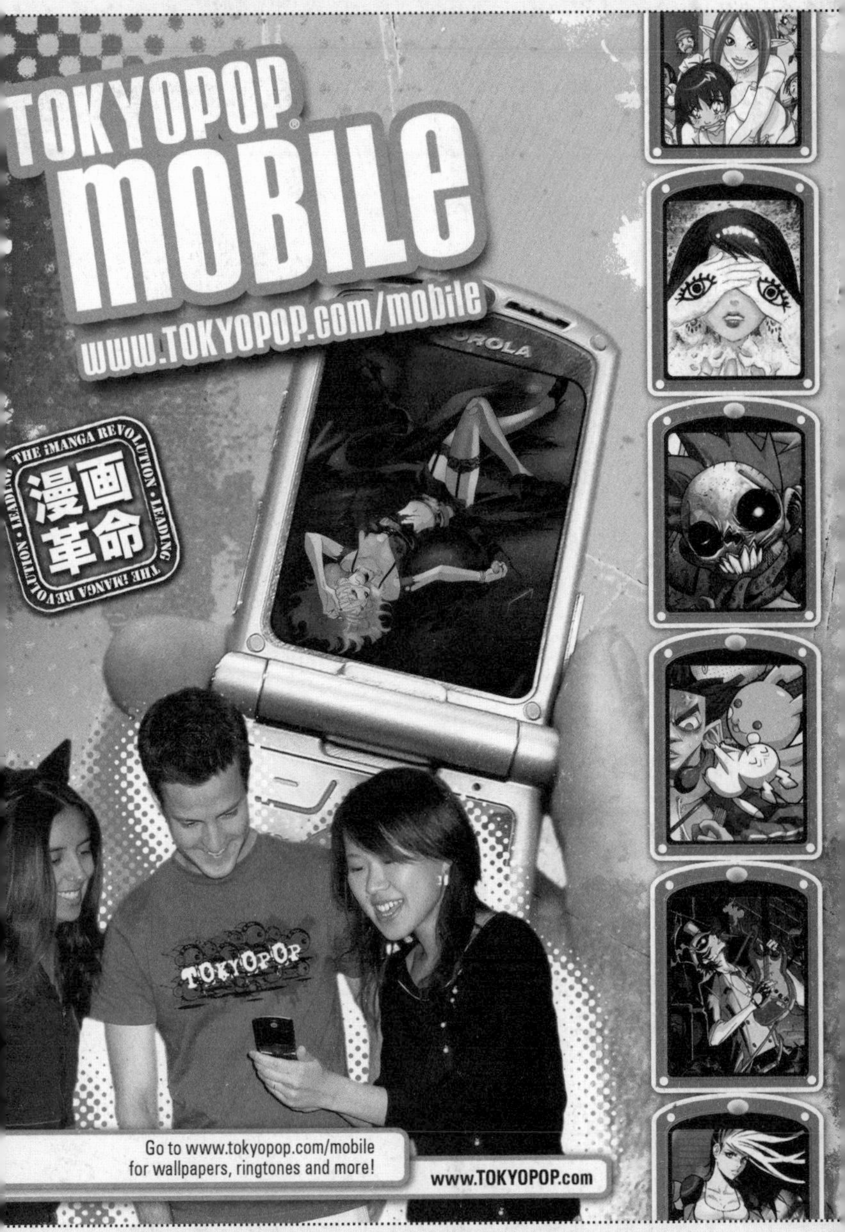
TOKYOPOP® MOBILE
www.TOKYOPOP.com/mobile
LEADING THE iMANGA REVOLUTION
漫画革命
Go to www.tokyopop.com/mobile
for wallpapers, ringtones and more!
www.TOKYOPOP.com

FOR MORE INFORMATION VISIT: WWW.TOKYOPOP.COM

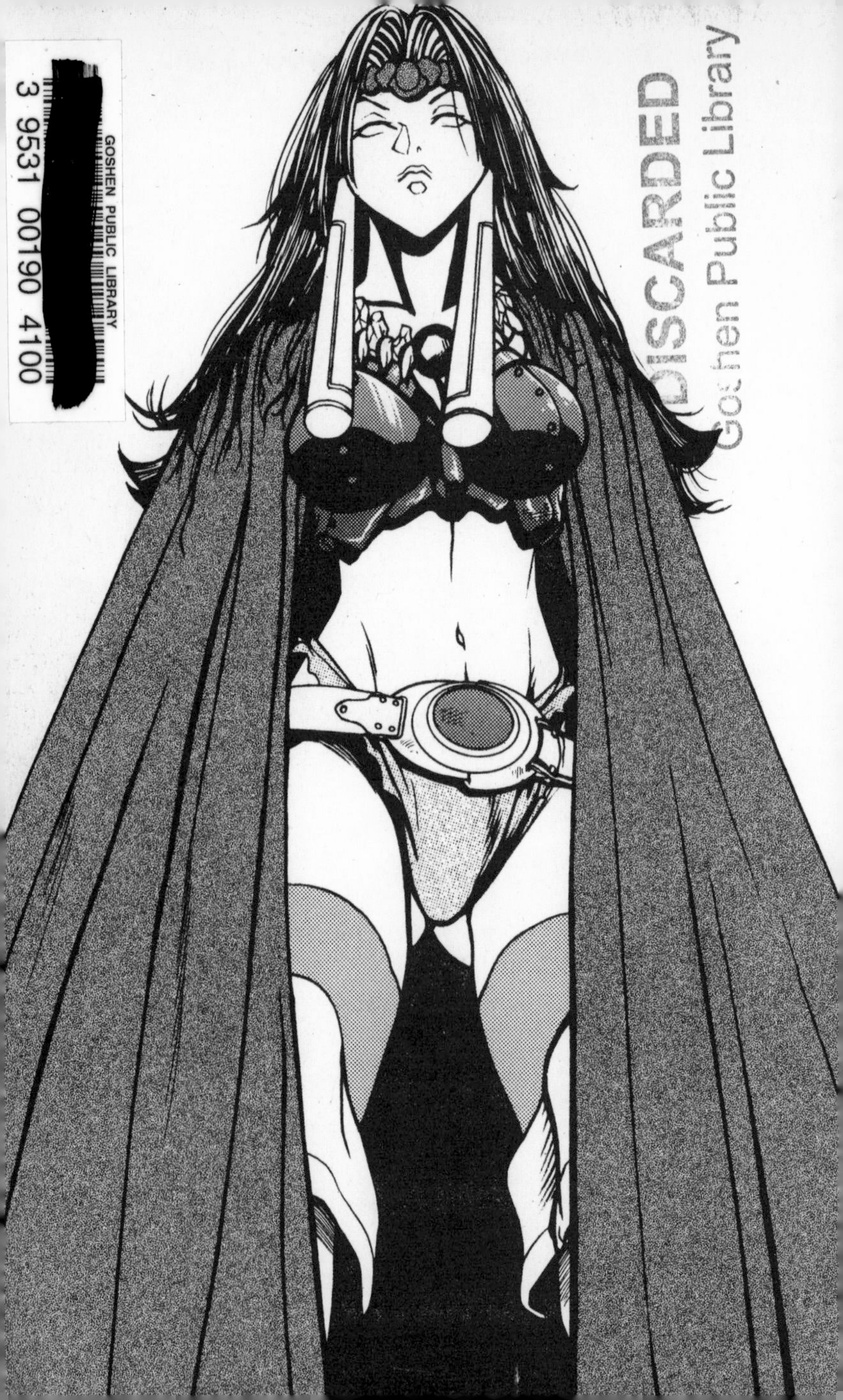